TEEN DAYS

MYTH AND RITUAL IN THE ANCIENT NEAR EAST

By the same Author

MYTH AND RITUAL IN THE ANCIENT NEAR EAST

An Archeological and Documentary Study

by

E. O. JAMES

D.Litt., Ph.D., F.S.A., Hon.D.D. St. Andrews

*Professor Emeritus of the History of Religion in the
University of London. Fellow of University College
and Fellow of King's College, London*

FREDERICK A. PRAEGER
New York

CONTENTS

5

PREFACE

THE wealth of new material recovered from the Ancient Near East through recent archaeological excavation and investigation and the discovery, decipherment and translation of a number of texts hitherto unknown have made possible a clearer knowledge and understanding of myth and ritual in this crucial region from prehistoric times to the end of the Bronze Age. In the last quarter of the century attention has been concentrated very largely on a welldefined complex of beliefs and practices, which appear to have become established in and before the second millennium B.C., centred in the Annual Festival and the sacral kingship, particularly by a group of eminent Scandinavian scholars. In pursuing this inquiry too much emphasis unquestionably has been laid on a rigid "pattern" in the development of the theme and too little account taken of the dissimilarities between, for instance, the Mesopotamian and the Egyptian outlooks and approaches to this type of myth and ritual. Here, as Professor Frankfort rightly contended, it is important that the differences as well as the similarities should be given their full value and significance, whether or not they be interpreted in terms of a common body of beliefs and practices. Moreover, it has to be recognized that however closely myth and ritual may have been allied, the myth has been by no means always or merely the spoken part of a rite; and when the two have occurred together as an entity an aetiological element often can be detected. Though on the whole it would seem that the ritual aspect is the earlier and the more fundamental, a considerable corpus of myths has occurred in a noncultic context.

In view of the many problems that have arisen around this

vital theme in the history of religion and the development of civilization, particularly in the Ancient Middle East and the Eastern Mediterranean, and of the importance now attached to the place and function of myth in the higher Faiths of mankind (of which the current "demythologizing" controversy in theo-logical circles is an example), a re-examination of the position in relation to the archaeological and textual material now avail-able seems to be required. The purpose throughout this inquiry has been to concentrate upon the evidence in the first-hand sources of information irrespective of any particular hypothesis, such as that to which reference has been made, in the hope that thereby the situation may be more accurately determined and some of the obscure and controversial issues resolved.

Egypt, Mesopotamia, Asia Minor and Syria were so inter-related as the cultural centres of the Ancient Near East, often with antecedents going back well into Palaeolithic times, that they have been treated as a composite whole; though in the peripheral regions outside the Nile and Euphrates valleys the myth and ritual, like the rest of the culture, were derivative to some extent in the formative period. In the Eastern Mediter-ranean this was often more apparent, but, here again, the contacts with Asia Minor and the Fertile Crescent in general were such that they cannot be ignored in an investigation of this character. Thus, so far as the basic cultus is concerned, the entire region from the Persian Gulf and beyond the Caspian Sea to the Aegean, Crete and North Africa may be regarded as a single area having common elements diffused throughout its extensive boundaries, with outposts in the Indus valley and Northern Europe. Nowhere is this more clearly shown than in the distribution of the Asiatic worship of the Great Goddess and its mythology in intimate association with the vegetation cycle and the figure of the youthful male god as her son or consort. From Asia Minor to the Minoan-Mycenaean civiliza-tion the cult recurred with the same fundamental theme in the agricultural calendrical myth and ritual giving it an organic unity in spite of fundamental local differentiations. However, if the problem of similarity is to be solved the inquiry must be pursued throughout the region in which the available data occur.

Moreover, it was in this vital area—the cradle of civilization which once again is in process of becoming the dynamic centre of world affairs—that the higher living monotheisms, Judaism, Christianity and Islam, emerged. Since in each and all of these religions myth has now raised a number of very acute problems both for theology and for faith, an objective investigation of its antecedents in their respective cradlelands seems to be required if the resultant products are to be correctly assessed and evaluated.

Oxford   E. O. JAMES

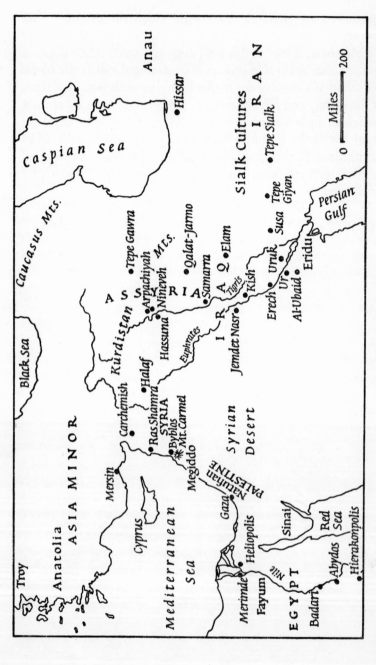

Map of the Ancient Near East

CHAPTER I

The Emergence of Ritual and Myth

THEORIES OF MYTHOPOEIC THOUGHT

It is now widely recognized that the characteristic feature of religious thought is essentially mythological. In the higher religions it is true the cruder types of myth and ritual have been eliminated or transformed into symbolism, but the myth has never been wholly excluded or distinguished very clearly from symbol. Throughout the ages religious belief has been formulated in the terms of this manner of thought, language and experience, though it is only in recent years that the function and significance of mythology, and of the sacred actions with which it has been so closely associated, have become apparent as a result of the scientific study of the phenomena.

The Philological Hypothesis

In the last century when attempts were first made to discover the origins of religion by etymological analyses of the names of the gods, attention was concentrated especially on the mythology of the Veda, the Avesta, Homer and the Edda. From the character of human speech it was thought the origin of the mythological personifications of natural objects, notably the sun and the constellations, could be deduced. Indeed, according to Max Müller, myth was a "disease of language", a pathological condition of the human mind arising out of an inability to express abstract ideas except by metaphor. While it "breaks out more fiercely during the early period of this history of human thought, it never disappears altogether". It is, in fact, "the dark shadow which language throws upon thought, and which never disappears till language becomes entirely commensurate with thought, which it never will".[1] But, as Ernst Cassirer says, "to regard a fundamental human activity as a mere monstrosity, as a sort of mental disease, can scarcely pass muster as an adequate interpretation of it".[2] And it only required the production of anthropological evidence from peoples in a primitive state of culture to show how inadequate were the foundations on which this philological hypothesis rested.

The Anthropological Approach

Thus, in the second half of the century E. B. Tylor, following Comte, declared that "the history of culture began with the appearance on earth of a semi-civilized race of men, and from that state of culture has proceeded in two ways, backward to produce savages, and forward to produce civilized men".[3] Everywhere and at all times the human mind was said to operate according to fixed laws of thought and action rather than as a result of cultural contacts. Therefore, the beliefs and customs of primitive peoples were interpreted in terms of "survivals", likened to rudimentary organs in animals and man, in an effort to reconstruct the hypothetical history of religious and social organization. Recurrent practices, ideas and systems were attributed to "the like working of men's minds under like conditions", the modern savage being the contemporary representative of Early Man at corresponding levels of evolutionary advance or decline. The Australian aborigines and the Greeks had similar myths, according to Andrew Lang, because "the ancestors of the Greeks passed through the savage intellectual condition in which we find the Australians".[4]

By comparison with the philological hypothesis this anthropological approach at least made a serious attempt to investigate the phenomenon critically, comparatively and empirically. Where it failed was in drawing general conclusions from disparate phenomena brought together on the principle of superficial resemblance regardless of diversities, comparability and provenance, based on the assumption of the unity of mental processes working according to fixed laws of progress. Stratified stages of advance from savagery to civilization were assumed, successive in time and progressive in development,[5] scant attention being paid to the purpose for which they existed and the function they exercised in the structure of society and the life of the individual and that of the community. For example, Frazer's neat and tidy threefold scheme of transition from an "age of magic" through an "age of religion" to an "age of science", determined by the operation of immutable laws working dialectically in Hegelian fashion,[6] fitted admirably into this hypothetical framework. So regarded, myths became "the reflections or shadows of men cast upon the clouds" in which real human beings were conceived euhemeristically, or, conversely, regarded as the personifications of natural objects and processes,[7] unless they were represented as dramatizations of figurative language in magical rites.[8]

The Functional Attitude

Myth, however, is not typically aetiological in its aims, and cannot be reduced to certain fixed static elements, be they centred in outstanding personalities or in natural phenomena, elaborately woven into a tale. As Malinowski says, "myth as it exists in a savage community, that is, in its living primitive form, is not merely a tale told but a reality lived. It is not in the nature of fiction such as we read today in a novel but it is a living reality, believed to have once happened in primeval times, and continuing ever since to influence the world and human destinies. This myth is to the savage what to a fully believing Christian is the Biblical story of Creation, of the Fall of Man, and of Redemption by Christ's sacrifice on the Cross." It is "not an explanation in satisfaction of a scientific interest, but a narrative resurrection of a primeval reality, told in satisfaction of deep religious wants, moral cravings, social submissions, assertions, even practical requirements". It "expresses, enhances and codifies belief" and vouches for the efficacy of the ritual in which it lives on, just as it provides a supernatural sanction for faith and ethical conduct.[9] In the words of Marett, "myth is not aetiological but fidejussive. Its business is not to satisfy curiosity but to confirm the faith. It is there to cater, not for the speculative man with his 'Why?' but for the practical man with his 'How if not thus?'"[10]

Looked at from this functional standpoint, which now holds

the field in social anthropology in this country, Tylorian and Frazerian theories of origins are given no more credence than were the theological revelational interpretations by the previous generation. Both are dismissed as lying outside the sphere of verifiable knowledge. Now it cannot be denied that a funda-mental defect in the earlier theoretical reconstructions of the origin and development of myth and ritual, and of other religious and social beliefs and institutions, was that the evi-dence on which they relied was often unverifiable, and that the conclusions were based mainly on conjectural situations and hypothetical laws of progress "from the simple to the complex, and from the homogeneous to the heterogeneous", as Herbert Spencer affirmed. Therefore, they were regarded, like the geological and biological evolutionary sequence, "as stratified as the earth on which man lived".[11] Furthermore, the material was collected very largely among peoples with no documentary history and very little, if any, archaeological data behind them, so that what lay in the background could be only conjectural.

In recent years, therefore, attention has been concentrated upon the functional value and significance of customs, beliefs and institutions in relation to the system as a whole, whatever may have been their history. It has, indeed, been maintained that the existing social and religious organization and structure can be understood and evaluated without reference to their antecedents, or any attempt to unravel their origins and develop-ment. But, as Professor Evans-Pritchard has pointed out, "the fact that nineteenth-century anthropologists were uncritical in their reconstructions ought not to lead to the conclusion that all effort expended in this direction is waste of time. The claim that one can understand the functioning of institutions at a certain point of time without knowing how they have come to be what they are, or what they were later to become, as well as a person who, in addition to having studied their constitution at that time, has also studied their past and future, is to me an absurdity."[12]

This is manifestly true in the case of myth and ritual. Even the native tribes of Australia, though they have no recorded history, have traditions which presuppose a very definite conti/nuity with the past when inexorable laws, customs and organizations were given to their tribal ancestors in the Alcheringa, or Dream/time of long ago, when the culture heroes lived on the earth and determined the existing structure of society. Therefore, for them the past furnished the pattern of the present established order, and the present has yielded the perspective from which to view and understand the past. Thus, history, in the sense of the course of significant events, is an integral part of the tribal tradition in terms of the myth and ritual which preserve the network of social relations and the state of tribal equilibrium and stability. To dismiss it as irrelevant in the study of these vital aspects of culture "prevents the functionalist anthropologist not only from studying dia/chronic problems but also from testing the very functional constructions to which he attaches most importance, for it is precisely history which provides him with an experimental situation".[13]

In the case of mythology the historical background of the story certainly cannot be regarded as of no consequence, as Malinowski contended, since, as he himself has shown in the quotation cited, the part it has played as an integrating factor in society has been that of "a living reality believed to have once happened in primeval times and ever since continuing to influence the world and human destinies".[14] Moreover, as we have seen, he equated it in its primitive guise with the rôle it has exercised in Christian faith and practice, where its validity depends very largely upon the historical events on which it rests; namely, the life, death and resurrection of Christ.

Now it is true that myth and ritual can and often do perform their functions as the expression of the ways in which members of a community have adjusted themselves to society and to their own total experience quite apart from the truth or falsity of the beliefs they enshrine, but only so long as they carry conviction to those who adhere to them. Once the presuppositions on which they rest are undermined by doubts about their veracity, they begin to lose their functional value and significance as a consolidating dynamic. When they cease to be "a narrative resurrection of a primeval reality" having absolute supernatural authority, they no longer fulfil their religious, social, moral and practical requirements.

If the experience is felt to be a valuable one, the belief may be retained after its symbolical character has been recognized as a temporary expedient, usually through a process of sublima⁄ tion or of psychic archetypal transformation. Recently attempts have been made by Bultmann and Berdyaev to interpret the whole body of the Christian faith in this symbolical sense. But it is difficult to understand how such a position can be sustained since the archetype is essentially an historical figure upon whose historicity and claims, and all that is therein involved and implied, authentic Christianity as an historical phenomenon depends in the last analysis for its validity. It is in its sacred history that the redemptive events of its myth and ritual are rooted and grounded. Therefore, neither a purely functional nor a wholly symbolical and existential approach suffices, because so much of fundamental importance in the evaluation of myth and ritual depends on what lies behind and beyond the existing religious and social structure, and its relationships.

The Archaeological Evidence

Thus, in the Near Eastern religions, which constitute the background of most of the living religions today (e.g. Judaism, Christianity, Zoroastrianism, Hinduism and Islam), a con⁄ siderable corpus of documentary data is available concerning the mythology and ritual organization having a long history going back well into prehistoric times. Indeed, the significance of much that is said and done in the myths and their rites can only be understood in the light of the cultus out of which they have emerged, and of which they are the expression. Therefore, it is to the archaeological evidence that recourse has to be made to discover the circumstances under which this myth and ritual arose and the functions they fulfilled in their original environ⁄ ment before they were incorporated in the texts. But the deeper the roots of mythopoeic thought and practice are laid in a pre-literary subsoil, the more difficult it is to determine their nature and content. Generally they are brought to the surface by the spade of the archaeologist in bits and pieces, and it is only those aspects which have become embodied in concrete form associated with sanctuaries, cult objects and ritual tech-niques that have survived the ravages of time to afford some indication of what took place before they were preserved in documentary records, after the introduction of the cylinder seal and of scripts in and after the fourth millennium B.C.

RITUAL TECHNIQUES AND INSTITUTIONS

The antecedents of writing perhaps may be detected in pictorial representations which first occur in the Upper Palaeo-lithic, both in the decorated caves and in the parietal art, while the markings on the painted pebbles from Mas d'Azil in Ariège seem to bear some resemblance to linear signs. It can hardly be maintained, as Petrie suggested, that these signs arose when drawing was at its rudest and crude marks sufficed to symbolize the intended meaning,[15] since the cave art had reached an advanced stage of technical skill long before geo-metrical conventionalized designs appeared on the Mesolithic Azilian pebbles and on Neolithic pottery in Egypt. Therefore, the underlying realistic pictures must be of earlier date, and these unquestionably arose out of the need of exercising ritual control over the food-supply.

The Ritual Control of the Chase

Under Palaeolithic conditions the deepest emotions and most heart-felt wants, hopes and fears hardly can fail to have been centred in nutrition and propagation since, living under the precarious circumstances in which Early Man found himself, his subsistence depended upon the vagaries of the chase and of such roots, fruits and berries as he might be able to collect, except when he could supplement this diet by fishing. Judging from the numerous bones found in his habitations and the fact that four-fifths of the representations in his parietal art are zoomorphic designs, animals appear to have constituted his chief means of subsistence. Moreover, the position and manner of execution of the paintings and engravings make it abun-dantly clear that the decorated caves in fact were sanctuaries in which magico-religious rites were performed to make the species depicted increase and multiply, to control the fortunes of the chase by casting spells upon them, and to establish a beneficial relationship with the supernatural source of the food-supply.

Thus, in the great caverns in the departments of the Dor-dogne, Ariège, Corrèze, Haute Garonne, Gard and Ardèche in France, and in the provinces of Cantabria and Asturias in Northern Spain, the paintings invariably are situated in the most inaccessible and obscure recesses, sometimes, as, for instance, at Niaux near Tarascon sur Ariège, as much as half a mile from the entrance. To gain access to the cave of Pasiega on the Cantabrian limestone hills above Puente Viesgo, south of Santander, a descent has to be made by a narrow, very long passage 6 feet long, and then a veritable labyrinth of very small corridors has to be negotiated in order to reach the designs placed in the remotest clefts and crannies. In one of the larger chambers, which was almost certainly used for ritual purposes, there is a throne-like structure hewn out of the rock, on which a stone implement was found.[16]

About half a mile across the valley, nearer to the village, is a second cave—that known as Castillo—accessible only after a steep scramble up the high carboniferous limestone hill. In it are a galaxy of paintings and engravings of bison, horses, hinds, an elephant (possibly *antiquus*), stags, ibex and chamois, and a frieze of stencilled human hands, together with tectiform designs (interpreted as either houses or traps) on a ceiling of a very obscure alcove. Unlike most decorated caves, the mouth of Castillo appears to have been inhabited, but Palaeolithic Man never lived in the depths of any cavern as the inner recesses were too damp and dark for human habitation. The majority of those containing paintings were used, in fact, exclusively as sanctuaries, entered for the most part, in all probability, only by ritual experts and their attendants for the performance of the rites upon which the maintenance of the food-supply was thought to depend.

Thus, the cave of Lascaux, discovered in 1940 near Montignac in the Dordogne, must have been frequented by generation after generation of cult practitioners, as every phase of the sacred art of Périgord is represented in the vast array of paintings in it, ranging from hunting and fertility ritual designs to commemorative symbolism depicting the hazards of the chase in a "problem picture", situated in the most difficult and dangerous "crypt". There the stylized figure of a man with a bird-shaped head is represented as having been killed by a bison with its flank transfixed by a spear exposing its entrails. In a different style a woolly rhinoceros is shown slowly moving away after perhaps having ripped up the bison. In front of the man is a bird-sign on a pole resembling an Egyptian ceremonial stave. This may have been a votive painting to a deceased hunter buried in the cave as the Abbé Breuil has suggested,[17] or it may have had a more sinister motive to bring destruction on the hunter by black magic, although this does not seem to be very probable as his death is shown to have been avenged by the rhinoceros. In any case, the scene was delineated in this perilous and inaccessible spot for good or ill to control the chase and the fortunes of the hunters. In the main hall or "nave", near the entrance is a masked figure of a sorcerer in a spotted skin of some *bovida* impersonating a mythical or sacred animal, or possibly an ancestral spirit responsible for fertility and successful hunting. Large oval spots on the flank of this strange creature could be interpreted as wound marks. On its forehead are two long horns, and in another group at the end of the axial passage a horse is depicted falling over a precipice or into a pit, doubtless to bring about its destruction. On some of the paintings tectiform or other magical signs have been superimposed, perhaps to indicate traps or tribal marks.[18]

Taking the evidence collectively it is clear that Lascaux was a tribal sanctuary from the Aurignacian culture phase at the beginning of the Upper Palaeolithic, some 20,000 years ago, until the end of the Old Stone Age. There in the seclusion of the sacred precints masked ritual experts executed their gestures, dances, incantations and enchantments to control the luck of the men going forth to the hunt. Thus, at Niaux in Ariège, it is only in the heart of the mountain beyond a lake, originally 6 feet in depth, artificially deepened, that decoration occurs. There three small cup-like hollows were cleverly utilized to represent wounds by drawing round them the outline of a bison and marking the cups with arrows in red ochre. Similarly, in front of an outline figure of an expiring bison are club-shaped designs depicting missiles.[19] In Haute Garonne over twenty models of wounded animals were found in the gallery of a cave at Montespan amid numerous mural engravings. On the floor the figure of a horse showed thrusts in the neck, and marks made by spears were visible on the neck and chest of a bear, and on the breast of a lioness. In another gallery a small horse covered with stalagmites is represented falling backwards, and at the end of the passage a scene is depicted in which the Count Bégouen identifies a corral surrounded with palisades into which wild horses are being driven by darts and stones.[20]

In these sanctuaries the rites appear to have been concentrated on casting spells on the animals in the chase. Most of the figures are those of species suitable for food and the frequent occurrence of superimpositions, as, for example, at Marsoulas near Salies du Salat in Haute Garonne, suggests that certain spots in the caves were thought to have been peculiarly efficacious for this purpose. Judging from the fact that at Montespan the headless bear and some of the felines were covered with spear-marks, it would seem that the same model had been used time after time, and at Marsoulas a series of polychromes with spear-marks had been painted one above the other as if constantly renewed. At Les Trois Frères in Ariège the head of a lioness engraved on stalactite had been redrawn three times in different positions, and from the number of arrows on it, it must have been in constant use as a magical effigy. The Abbé Lemozi has made the interesting conjecture that the absence of eyes and ears on representations of mammoths and cattle at La Grotte-Temple du Peche-Merle at Cabrerets in Corrèze was in order to render their counterparts in the chase an easy prey by depriving them of sight and hearing.[21] But in this cavern there are also headless female figures, and it is a common practice to depict only parts of animals (e.g. the horns) as magical symbols.

Frequently, however, the designs were executed with con-summate artistic skill, as at Altamira near the Cantabrian village of Santillana del Mar in the neighbourhood of San-tander, where cave art was first accidentally detected in 1879 by the small daughter of a Spanish nobleman. There the famous bison in polychrome, together with paintings and engravings of other Pleistocene animals in all kinds of positions of rest and movement, stencilled hands and tectiforms, consti-tute what has been aptly described by the Abbé Breuil as "the Palaeolithic Sistine Chapel" with Lascaux as "the Versailles of Palaeolithic art". In all these cult-centres the symbolism was displayed with very great skill in technique. Thus, at Font de Gaume, 23 kilometres from Lascaux in the valley of the Beune just outside Les Eyzies on the Sarlat road, there is a fine painting of a woolly rhinoceros and of a lion in a very narrow crevice high up on the left-hand wall, drawn perhaps by the artist standing on the shoulders of an assistant. But excellent as is the craftsmanship in these designs, it cannot have been "art for art's sake" that caused them to be executed in such a position where they can be seen only with the greatest difficulty even with the aid of a modern elaborate installation of electric light. In Font de Gaume the sacred enclosure begins at a stalactite barrier about 65 metres from the entrance. From this "Rubi-con" onwards the paintings abound on both walls until at the end of the cave the narrow crevice containing the rhinoceros separates the "holy of holies" from the rest of the sanctuary; now marked off by a small gate to prevent damage to these precious paintings.

Increase Rites

It was to these remote and carefully secluded inner recesses of their caverns that the ritual experts resorted doubtless before a party set out on a hunting expedition to manipulate their magic by drawing or marking designs, or piercing the images with a spear, as they uttered their spells destined to produce the reciprocal effect on the prey in the chase. But killing the animals required for food was not the only aspect of the cave ritual. The supply had to be maintained as well as procured. Therefore, recourse was made to the sanctuaries to render prolific the species on which Palaeolithic Man depended for his subsistence. This has been revealed in the Tuc d'Audoubert near Saint/Girons in Ariège, first entered since the end of the Palaeolithic by the Count Bégouen and his sons when in 1912 they rowed up a small subterranean stream, the Volp, hacked their way through stalactites in a very long narrow ascending passage, and finally, 700 metres from the entrance, reached a chamber containing the clay models of a female bison followed by a male, placed against a projecting rock. Here a fertility motif is apparent. In a recess near by were pieces of clay in the form of a phallus, and on the soft clay floor of the gallery were impressions of human feet and an incomplete bison 13 centi/metres long. To the right were fifty small/sized youthful heel/marks thought to have been made by a dancer or dancers engaged in a fertility dance round the small hillock in the centre in the presence of the clay bison.²²

Not far from the Tuc on the Count Bégouen's estate, Montesquieu Avantes, where the river Volp descends at Enlène in its subterranean passage for the distance of 2 kilo/metres, emerging at the entrance (actually the back door) of Tuc d'Audoubert, his three adventurous sons—"les trois frères"—during their military leave in 1918 completed the exploration of the cave of Enlène which they had begun before the war. After having made their way through a very narrow passage at the end of the gallery into a second complex of corridors and chambers, decorated with splendid paintings and engravings, they reached a stalagmite alcove on the right/hand side containing a rock shaped like an altar on which a lioness and her cub were painted and engraved, apparently guarding the sanctuary. Beyond this lay a small chamber covered with engravings of a great number of animals, and at the end of a winding corridor opening into a kind of window about 4 metres above the ground was the extraordinary figure known as "the Sorcerer" engraved in black on the rock wall, 75 centimetres high and 50 centimetres wide. The head is full face with round eyes like an owl, and between them is a nose ending in a small arch. The ears are those of a wolf and the two antlers above the forehead are those of a stag. The claws are of a lion and the tail is of a horse or a wolf. The forearms are raised and joined horizontally, ending in two hands. The feet and toes are carefully made and show a movement suggestive of dancing.

Whether or not, as was first supposed, this remarkable figure was the representation of the arch-sorcerer, or shaman, embodying the attributes and functions of the animals it portrayed, [23] or, as Bégouen and Breuil now think, [24] the Spirit controlling the multiplication of game and hunting expeditions, a cult is indicated in which human beings and animals were brought together in a joint effort to conserve and promote the food supply. The emphasis clearly was on fecundity to secure abundance of the species on which man depended for his means of subsistence. The numerous representations of men wearing animal masks or heads, such as the three figures masquerading in the skin of a chamois at Abri Mège, Dordogne, those with animal heads at Marsoulas, Hornos de la Peña, Altamira and Lourdes, confirm the evidence from Les Trois Frères and Tuc d'Audoubert respecting kinship with the animal creation and the mimetic dance in the Upper Palaeolithic.

The Mimetic Sacred Dance

When a ritual expert arrayed himself in the skin and antlers of a stag, or in the feathers of a bird, and imitated the behaviour of the species he personified, he did so in the belief that for the time being, and for the prescribed purpose, he was what he represented himself to be. In that capacity he did not imitate but actually did what he set out to do. He caught and killed his prey; he made the copulation of male and female effective in the reproduction of offspring; he established a sacramental relationship between man and the supernatural source of his food-supply. That this involved the practice of totemism, as has often been suggested, is not very probable since the representations of so many different varieties of animals are found in the same cave, even though, as Breuil has pointed out, the bones of the animals depicted are absent from the midden-heaps at the entrance.[25]

But while it is scarcely likely that such a complex social and religious organization as is involved in totemism had been devised in the Palaeolithic, nevertheless it seems that a sense of kinship with the animal creation was a characteristic feature of the ritual and belief, and from this in due course totemism arose and developed as a socio-religious institution among peoples in primitive states of culture. This is most apparent in the sacred dances and their mimetic representations when those who took part in the rites, with the aid of masks, antlers, skins of animals and feathers of birds, and appropriate realistic gestures, identified themselves with the species they believed themselves to have become through a process of "participation". The sacred ally, however, was not just "the clan itself personified and represented by the imagination under the visible form of the animal or vegetable which served as the totem", as Durkheim contended.[26] Behind and above "the collective representations" which united in "a unified system of beliefs and practices relative to sacred things" those who adhered to them, apparently there has always been the conception of a transcendental order manifesting itself in the universe and controlling its processes and human affairs, whether collective or individual.

It has been with this supra-mundane sacredness external to man and society and the phenomenal world that a ritual technique has been devised to establish efficacious relations with the ultimate source of life and well-being, stability and equilibrium. Thus, by means of dances, rites and symbols the tension consequent upon the perpetual struggle for survival and the ever-present strain of unpredictable and uncontrollable occurrences was relieved and sublimated, and human energies were directed into new activities, thereby affording mental and emotional relief, and supplying hope and confidence and an integrative dynamic in society.

Under Palaeolithic conditions the discharge of emotion and longing was centred in the food-supply, in the mystery of birth and propagation, and in the final transition through death to the after-life at the dissolution of the existing organism. It was, therefore, in relation to these critical, arresting and disturbing necessities and occasions that the ritual cultus functioned and gave expression to the most urgent needs of an intense situation fraught with far-reaching consequences for all who were inti-mately concerned in them. In respect of the food-supply the position was complicated by the sense of kinship felt to exist between man and the sacrosanct animals on which he was so dependent, but which he was compelled to hunt, and whose killing he was forced to condone. It was largely out of this contradictory situation and its emotional tension that the cave ritual emerged. The symbol in which both the human group and the sacred species participated was regarded and treated in the same way as the spiritual entity it symbolized, by virtue of the supernatural quality it had acquired. Hence the efficacy of the mimetic dances in which the ritual expert arrayed himself in animal disguises and imitated the behaviour of the sacred species, or conversely that of his companions in the chase, in order to procure the desired ends by the actions performed.

The "Venus" Cult

While the Magdalenians concentrated upon the maintenance and control of the chase, their predecessors in the Upper Aurignacian, now called Gravettians (i.e. the successors of the Châtelperronian culture who made their way into Central Europe and thence to Germany, France, Italy and the north-west from the South Russian plain and Western Asia), were primarily interested it would seem in the maternal aspect of the mystery of birth. Thus, it was they who introduced into Europe the female figurines commonly called "Venuses" fashioned in bone, ivory, stone and bas-relief, with the generative organs grossly exaggerated. In the rock-shelter at Laussel on the Beune near Les Eyzies, the nude figure of a woman, probably pregnant, was carved in relief on a block of stone about 18 inches high, holding in her right hand what seems to be the horn of a bison. The body had been coloured with red pigment widely employed in Palaeolithic ritual as a life-giving agent, the surrogate of blood.

Among four other reliefs on stone from this site two fragments represent women, and a third design has been interpreted as either an accouchement or a copulation.[27] Near by on the same side of the valley of the Beune in the direction of Les Eyzies, just over a mile from Font de Gaume, in the long subterranean tunnel-like cave at Combarelles, female dancers clothed in skins and wearing tails[28] have been thought to have served an erotic purpose, but from the author's own observations of this scene and that of the so-called "copulation" from Laussel, which he inspected some years ago at the house of Madame Lalanne at Bordeaux, while an erotic tradition may have been inherent in the Venus cult, it seems to be by no means clear that this is the correct interpretation of these two scenes. The main purpose of the symbolism, as is shown in its long history in the Near East, was the promotion and conservation of life mediated through the outward signs and symbols of maternal fecundity.

Like the rest of the Gravettian culture, it came into Europe from the Russian steppes and the valley of the Don, where numerous examples of these female statuettes occur at Gagarino, Kostienki, and at Malta near Lake Baikal in Siberia. Thence it passed to the Danube, recurring at Willendorf in Austria, and at Vistonice and Unter Wisternitz to the north-east in Moravia. In Southern France the figurines have been discovered at Brassempouy in the Landes and at Sireuil in the Dordogne in purely Aurignacian rather than a Gravettian context, and finally they reappear in the Grimaldi caves on the Franco-Italian frontier, and in Emilia at Savignano sul Panàro. Since a conventionalized Venus engraved on ivory has been found at Prědmost in Moravia, assigned to a late Aurignacian date, the cult in Central Europe must have survived until the coming of the Solutreans. Another highly conventionalized late Aurig/ nacian figure in ivory comes from the Grotte des Rideaux at Lespugne in Haute Garonne, with very low and exaggerated pendulous breasts and the legs brought together to a point, the sex organ having been concealed by a loin/cloth.[29]

That their cradleland was in Western Asia is indicated by their being most numerous at Malta, in Siberia and compara/ tively common in Eastern and Central Europe, becoming relatively scarce in the west, and sometimes, as in the Lespugne, Prědmost and Dolni Wisternitz specimens, more naturalistic than stylized. But the chief purpose of the artist, whose skill in execution often was considerable, appears to have been to represent pregnancy and the attributes of childbirth in order to stimulate fecundity. Thus, in addition to the production of these squat Venuses, cowrie shells were used for ornaments and amulets by the Gravettians and the Aurignacians.[30] These symbols of the portal of birth may have made their way into Europe from the East in association with the statuettes, and were widely used, together with red ochre, as life/giving agents in the cult of the dead.

Funerary Ritual

Long before the arrival of *Homo sapiens* on the human scene, the mysterious and disturbing phenomenon of death had arrested the attention of Early Man and led to attempts to employ a ritual technique to deal with the perplexing situation. This becomes apparent in the care taken to inter the body in a carefully prepared and protected grave, and to provide the deceased with implements and offerings of food, ornaments and amulets, and a steadily increasing equipment of funerary furni/ ture. The head seems to have been regarded as the seat of potency, and so it was preserved for ritual purposes, the brain sometimes being extracted and eaten to imbibe its life and magico/religious qualities. As the earliest indications of this practice are to be found in the Chinese caves at Dragon/bone

Hill near the village of Choukoutien, 37 miles from Peking, in Middle or Lower Pleistocene strata, from which the skull of *Sinanthropus* was extracted in 1929, on Dr Zeuner's dating it may go back to "the neighbourhood of 500,000 years ago",[31] as all the remains of Peking Man recovered from these deposits are thought to be the debris of cannibal feasts of this nature.[32]

The numerous skulls and headless bodies that have been found in Palaeolithic and Neolithic sites suggest that the custom was widespread and persistent.[33] Thus, for example, a Neanderthal skull discovered in 1939 in Goat's Cave in Monte Circeo on the Pomptine Marshes in Italy afforded evidence of cannibalism and ritual treatment in the last Glaciation, from 70,000 to 100,000 years ago, as it showed signs of death from violence, followed by the extraction of the brain through the foramen magnum. This had been enlarged for this purpose, as in the crania from the Solo river in Eastern Java in what corresponded in Indonesia to the Riss-Würm Interglacial in Europe. It was then placed in a ritual position in an inner chamber of the cave within a circle of stones as a trophy or object of worship with the fractured metacarpal bones of an ox and a deer beneath it. Surrounding it and piled up around the walls were the bones of deer, hyena, elephant and lion,[34] very much as in a spur of the Jura known as Ofnet a nest of twenty-seven decapitated skulls had been deposited in a cave in the Mesolithic period at the end of the Old Stone Age. Here again after death the heads had been deliberately cut off from the trunk with flint knives and ceremonially preserved. Then they had been dried and immersed in red ochre, and placed in the ossuary in a westerly direction, sometimes crushing those that were already there.[35]

In addition to the cult of skulls ceremonial interment was practised continuously from the Middle Palaeolithic, as is shown by the disposal of the skeleton of a Neanderthal youth in the cave at Le Moustier near Peyzac in the Dordogne in a position of rest with the head on a pillow of flint flakes and a fine Acheulean hand-axe and a scraper near the left arm. In the grave were the bones of the wild ox (*urus*) charred and split, suggesting the remains of a funeral feast.[36] At La Chapelle-aux-Saints in Corrèze a similar interment occurred in a pit dug in the floor of a low-roofed cave and surrounded with flint implements, the foot of an ox, the leg of a bison and the vertebral column of a reindeer near by. The earth above the body also contained bones of Pleistocene fauna, some of the long bones having been split by the Mousterian implements found in the same deposit, presumably to extract the marrow consumed at the feast, or feasts, held in the cave.[37] Near Le Bogue, Dordogne, the skeletons of a man and woman were buried in a grave at La Ferrassie, here the male skeleton was found to have been protected with stones over the head and shoulders, the right leg and left forearm, and covered with bone flakes. In the adjacent trenches were the remains of two children, and those of a third child in a grave in the floor covered by a stone with artificial cup-markings on it; while a baby was found under a tiny mound. All the members of the family, as they appear to have been, were orientated from east to west, and associated with a quantity of implements and animal bones (which included those of the woolly rhinoceros, bison and ibex) in what may have been a funerary deposit.[38]

The care bestowed on the disposal of these bodies leaves little room for doubt that a funerary ritual was established in the Middle Palaeolithic in districts like the Dordogne and Corrèze where cave burial was possible and the interments have survived the ravages of time and of wild beasts. The equipment suggests some conception of human survival in and beyond the grave under conditions requiring food and tools, prompted probably by a combination of respect, regard and fear. In the Upper Palaeolithic, after the arrival of the Crô-Magnons and their contemporaries, the cult of the dead became more elaborate. Thus, at the rock-shelter at Les Eyzies, from which the Crô-Magnon type of *Homo sapiens* takes its name, three hundred pierced marine shells (chiefly *littorina*) were discovered with the burials, apparently originally strung together as necklaces. As in so many graves of this period (e.g. those at Grimaldi,

Paviland, on the Gower coast in Glamorgan, Chancelade near Périgueux, Brno, Hoteaux and Obercassel), the skeletons were stained with red ochreous powder, the colour of blood, as the life-giving agent *par excellence*. This was doubtless an attempt to make the deceased live again in his revivified body.

In the first of the series of caves on the Italian frontier at Grimaldi, between Menton and Ventimiglia, that known as Grotte des Enfants derives its name from the two children clad in a shroud of nearly a thousand *Nassa* perforated shells who had been buried in it. Below this interment was another with a crown of shells round the head and a quantity above the thorax, while at the bottom were the tightly flexed bodies of a youth and a woman ornamented and surrounded with shells and stained by peroxide of iron, the heads protected by a flat stone.[39] The adjoining Grotte du Cavillon, the fourth of the series, contained no less than 7,868 marine shells of which 875 were pierced. Of these, 200 were placed about the head of a Crô-Magnon man buried in the contracted position. On the cranium was a fillet of sea-shells, near the frontal bones were twenty-two perforated canine teeth of deer, across the forehead lay a bone implement, two flakes against the occiput, and the entire skeleton was covered with powdered haematite, staining it scarlet.[40] Similarly, at Barma Grande, the fifth cave, in a grave lined with red ochre a male and a female skeleton were adorned with perforated *Nassa* shells, deer teeth, fish vertebrae, ivory pendants, a necklace and two large cowrie shells as a garter. At the back of the cave were two other bodies similarly ornamented.[41] At Laugerie Basse, near Les Eyzies, cowries were arranged in pairs upon the forehead, the arms and feet, and four near the thighs and knees,[42] in a manner highly suggestive of a ritual purpose, probably connected with giving life to the deceased rather than for ornamentation.

That the flexing of the body symbolized the foetal position of the embryo adopted to secure rebirth beyond the grave, as has been suggested, is most improbable since it is very doubtful whether the ante-natal position was known in Palaeolithic times. It is much more likely that tight flexing before *rigor mortis* had set in was to prevent the ghost from "walking" to molest the living. Contracted burial merely with the legs drawn up, on the other hand, probably was suggested by the normal sleeping posture except when it was a question of economy of space. The care taken, however, in the disposal of the dead, the protection and treatment of the body, its adornment with life-giving amulets and substances like ochre and shells, the provision of food, fires and grave-goods generally, accompanied sometimes by re-burial and the preservation and ritual treat-ment of the skull, taken collectively are indicative of a respect and regard for the departed going beyond fear of their return to harm the survivors, though this element in the funerary ritual cannot be ignored. But for the sake of everybody concerned, the living and the dead, it was important that those who left the world should be effectively installed in the mysterious after-life as otherwise they were always liable to avenge any neglect in the due performance of the mortuary rites. Trussing may have been a precautionary measure but the best safeguard was the observance of the prescribed ceremonial to bring about the desired result and enable them to rest in peace. The preservation of trophies and brain-extraction, on the other hand, appear to have been adopted as a means of obtaining communion with the dead and of imbibing their virtue and strength.

As in the case of food, birth and fertility, the sacredness of death rendered it a tabu condition to be approached and treated with the utmost caution and respect as a transitional state with its own *rites de passage*, both as a protection for the mourners and kinsfolk against the death contagion and the malign influences always rampant on such occasions, and for the well-being of the deceased. When the precarious life of the chase gave place to the cultivation of the soil and the keeping of flocks and herds in the Neolithic and Chalcolithic periods in the Near East in and after the fifth millennium B.C., the sequence of the seasons and its ritual had its counterpart in the cult of the dead and in the vegetation death and resurrection drama. Thus the Venus figurines began to find a place in the prehistoric graves at Badari in the Nile valley on the spur of the desert, in Mesopotamia at Tell Arpachiyah near Nineveh, and west of Iran in the Chalcolithic Halaf levels associated with the painted pottery culture. They were of common occur-rence in the deposits in the great funerary mound at Tepe Gawra near Nineveh, which cannot be later than 5000 B.C., often highly stylized in a conventionalized "fiddle" type, showing only the torso, prominent breasts and exaggerated abdomen. At Tell Hassuna near Mosul they conform to those at Arpachiyah, and west of Iran the Goddess cult became the predominant influence, until at length she herself appeared in funerary architecture and its symbolism in her life-giving capacity to the dead, especially in the megalithic civilization in the Mediterranean and Western Europe.[43]

The Neolithic Vegetation Cultus

The establishment of husbandry and domestication, however, gave a new emphasis to the function of the male in generation, and when the maternal principle was personified as the Mother-goddess she soon acquired a spouse to exercise the rôle of the begetter, though in Mesopotamia he was her son as the king was her servant. In the Nile valley, on the other hand, when "the two lands" of Upper and Lower Egypt were united as a single nation under one ruler, the Pharaoh attained divine status as the incarnation of the Falcon Sky-god Horus, and subsequently by the Fifth Dynasty (*c.* 2500 B.C.) he had acquired a filial relationship with the Sun-god Re through the influence of the Heliopolitan priesthood. It then only remained for the solar Horus to be identified with Horus the son of Osiris for the king to reign as the living Horus, and at death to become Osiris, the god of the dead and the lord of vegetation.[44]

Now it was out of the new political and religious situation that arose in the Ancient Near East when food-gathering gave place to food-production that a ritual drama with a vegetation theme began to take shape, as will be considered in the next chapter. But behind this myth and ritual lay the Palaeolithic cults out of which they emerged, designed originally for the

purpose of obtaining and maintaining the food-supply, promot-
ing birth and fertility and giving life to the dead. That at first it
was in a ritual technique rather than in a mythology that the
hopes, fears and needs of struggling humanity living precari-
ously under adverse and strenuous conditions found expression
is suggested by the available evidence. The desire to act dis-
charged itself on the symbol so that ritual was at once a visual
language and a vent of pent-up emotions and longings. As the
artist externalizes a feeling or mood, an inner quality of life, an
emotional impulse and interpretation of reality as he conceives
it, so the ritualist gives visual and dramatic expression to
fundamental requirements, realities and values; to the will to
live, to the vital urge and rhythmic relations to life, in response
to concrete situations. It is not surprising, therefore, that ritual,
art and drama should have been conjoined in their earliest
manifestations, and that out of this triad myth should have
emerged.

Under Neolithic conditions the most vital needs of mankind,
which hitherto had centred very largely in the chase and
fecundity in the animal creation, were transferred in agricultural communities to the emotional reactions concerning the
sequence of the seasons. Thus, the annual course of nature was
given mythological form in relation to the vegetation cultus,
and with the invention of writing, the stories which grew up
around the calendrical rites were recorded in documents, many
of which have survived as a valuable source of information
concerning their nature and content.

LITERARY SOURCES
The Egyptian Pyramid Texts
These literary records for the most part are very composite in
character, recovered by archaeological research from a variety
of sources, written in scripts some of which are still in the process
of decipherment. The Egyptian Pyramid texts, for example,
represent a vast collection of incised hieroglyphs on limestone
inscribed on the walls of five pyramids at Sakkara from the
Fifth and Sixth Dynasties (*c.* 2580–2250 B.C.) for the purpose

of bestowing immortality on the Pharaoh. This oldest extant body of considerable written material in the world, which now fills two quarto volumes with no less than 1,051 texts,[45] contains fragments of funeral and other rituals, astronomical lore, magical charms and hymns, as well as myths and legends, some of which go back to predynastic times. The material is arranged in a haphazard manner, each headed "utterances". Being a series of spells to enable the dead king to enter the celestial realms of Re, the Sungod, their order and disorder were of little consequence. Therefore, the priestly editors were content to copy anything and everything available that was considered to be magically efficacious for this purpose. Some of the material was drawn from earlier sources to which references are made, prior to the union of Upper and Lower Egypt as a single nation about 3000 B.C. Some of the texts may have existed in oral form before the art of writing had been accomplished. They were then written on papyrus and potsherds and finally collected and incised on the walls of the pyramids at Sakkara.

The Osiris Myth

While the solar theology predominates, very ancient myths of Osiris have been incorporated in the texts, and it is from them that our earliest knowledge of the Osirian cult comes, long before the story was told in a connected form by Plutarch in the first century B.C.,[46] going back, in fact, to the predynastic period in some cases. But as the worship of Osiris became established as the popular cult and was then incorporated in the solar mythology, the redactors introduced the name of the culture hero into the Heliopolitan collections, and, conversely, the name of the Pharaoh into the original Osirian texts. Therefore, they cannot be expected to present a coherent whole, and the piecing together of the composite myth and ritual is a hazardous undertaking, expecially as the rôles of Osiris and Re were confused. Moreover, the king reigned both as the son of the Sungod and the living Horus, the son of Osiris, and at death, like everybody else, he became Osiris, though he dwelt with his Ka in the celestial realms of his heavenly father Re, where Osiris also was "lord of the sky" as well as the ruler of the underworld. In fact, by the Middle Kingdom (*c.* 2000–1780 B.C.), when the texts were written on the inner surfaces of coffins, Re had been as completely fused with Osiris as had the Pharaoh in his dual capacity. It was then that the great dramas of the death and resurrection of Osiris were held annually at Abydos.

In the New Kingdom (*c.* 1546–1085 B.C.) the Coffin texts were succeeded by the so-called Theban Book of the Dead when the magical spells, taken largely from the Pyramid texts, were inscribed on papyrus and deposited with the body of the deceased in the tomb. By this time the Osirian eschatology had acquired an ethical significance as it no longer sufficed merely to have the prescribed magical equipment and knowledge, as in the Pyramid Age. Now at death every man had to appear before Osiris as the judge of the dead and to be declared "true of heart and voice"—i.e. to have lived a virtuous life on earth like Osiris himself—when his heart was weighed against the feather of truth by Anubis, the jackal-headed funerary physician, and Thoth the scribe of the gods and the traditional inventor of the hieroglyphic script. By the side of the scales "the devourer of the dead" waited to destroy the deceased should the test fail to justify his admission to the kingdom of Osiris.

In the Pyramid texts the judgment of Osiris by the divine Ennead is recorded as an established element in the myth. It would seem, therefore, that long before the Eighteenth Dynasty of the New Kingdom this conception of the hereafter was inherent in the cult of the dead in Ancient Egypt and intimately associated with the death and resurrection Osirian myth and ritual. To this subject a whole section of the Pyramid texts is devoted (1976–82), as well as references to it in other redactions (e.g. 572, 617, 634, 1299, 2092, 2201 f.). The manner of his death is variously described, but usually his brother Seth is represented as the instigator of the assassination, and his restoration to life to have been effected either through the agency of Re,[47] to correlate it with the solar theology, or as a magical

operation.[48] The event was re-enacted annually in a mystery
play at Abydos, where it was alleged to have occurred, and at
first identification with the risen Osiris was a royal prerogative,
until eventually, after the Sixth Dynasty, it was extended to
every man.

Whether or not Osiris originally was a civilizing king, as has
been suggested,[49] who became the centre of a death and resurrection cultus before he developed into a composite figure as
the lord of the dead, the god of vegetation and the personification of the fructifying waters of the Nile, and his sister-spouse,
Isis, was personified as his throne, his cult was established at
an early date in the Eastern Delta at Busiris (Per-Usire or
Djedu), the capital of the ninth nome. It is possible he may
have been a prehistoric nomadic chief or leader who introduced
agriculture among the indigenous people in the Eastern Delta
and eventually came to blows with their ruler Seth when the
intruders penetrated up the Nile as far south as Abydos. If
Osiris was killed in this campaign his son Horus may have
rectified the position, and the episode eventually was immortalized in tradition in terms of a death and resurrection myth
and ritual in which the culture hero (Osiris) played the leading
rôle.

But such an historical background for the story requires a
considerable amount of subsequent mythological elaboration
to explain the myth in its literary forms, some of which undoubtedly were supplied under the influence of the Heliopolitan
priesthood when the Osirian cult was solarized and the hero
acquired a place in their Ennead as the son of Nut, the Sky-
goddess, and Geb the Earth-god, the descendants of Atum-Re.
It was from this source again that the victorious kings of Upper
Egypt identified the Falcon-god Horus with Re in the composite
deity Herakhite, "Horus of the Horizon", and were themselves
given a Horus-name in and after the Second Dynasty, until at
length they were equated with Horus the son of Osiris after the
solar cult had been Osirianized.

If the original home of Osiris was in Western Asia (i.e. Syria)
before he and his followers reached the fertile Delta of the Nile,

his connexion with vegetation[50] could be explained by his having brought nomads from arid plains into a fertile oasis, like Adonis of Byblos, where they learnt to practise agriculture under his guidance. So in Egyptian literature he became the Corn-god from whose body the grain sprouted.[51] In a mystery play of the Twelfth Dynasty, about 1900 B.C., but containing much earlier material,[52] he was identified with the barley and the emmer that nourished the gods in heaven and man on earth, having made the corn from "the liquid that is in him".[53] Like so many other prehistoric ideas and practices, this tradition lingered on until the Ptolemaic period and found expression in the very ancient custom of watering figures of Osiris (i.e. the "gardens of Osiris") made of earth and corn to make the grain appear to sprout from his body as a symbol of his resurrection, as in the temple of Isis at Philae.[54] Effigies of him in the form of a mummy, moulded of bruised corn and earth, were buried in the fields to ensure a plentiful crop.[55]

Similarly, he was identified with the life-giving waters of the inundation responsible for the annual rebirth of vegetation with a precision that never failed. Such a rhythmic sequence doubt-less acquired a divine significance at a very early period, and in the Pyramid texts Osiris primarily was equated with the fertilizing waters of the Nile.[56] In them, according to one version of the myth, he was alleged to have been drowned,[57] and in another his corpse was said to have been cut in pieces, thrown into the river and subsequently found by Horus his son, "youthful in thy name of 'Fresh Water'".[58] When the dead king Unis was identified with Osiris it was said of him, "Unis makes the verdure to flourish in the two regions of the horizon", and "it is Unis who inundates the land".[59]

Thus Osiris is represented as the life-giving waters and the soil of Egypt, which is fertilized by the Nile flood. When the inundation receded the land ceased to bring forth because he had died. On the reappearance of the waters nature revived on the assumption that the god had come to life again. Therefore, since vegetation and the Nile were so intimately associated, Osiris was at once the god of the inundation and of fecundity, and in this dual capacity he came to be the lord of the dead and the bestower of immortality, identified at the end of the Old Kingdom with the dead king, and ultimately with every, body, when commoners as well as the Pharaoh and the aristocracy became Osiris at death and placed their hopes in him for a blissful resurrection.

The Mesopotamian Texts

In Mesopotamia, on the other hand, the unpredictable be, haviour of the Tigris and the Euphrates in contrast to that of the Nile, and the variability of the climatic conditions, gave rise to a myth and ritual which, though having many common features with those contained in the Egyptian texts, differed from them in certain important respects. In the first place, unlike the hieroglyphic records which centred around the magico, religious control of the food-supply, the solar theology and the cult of the dead, and their principal theological figures, Osiris, Isis, Seth, Horus and Re, and their Enneads, the Sumerian cuneiform tablets were largely concerned with the organization and administration of the city-states, contracts, accounts, legal procedure, excerpts from political events and business memoranda, rather than specifically with myth and ritual. Nevertheless, they were connected with the temples and included lists of kings, royal inscriptions, incantations, infor, mation about divination, astrology and spells, together with ritual texts and legends, from which it is possible to obtain a fairly accurate knowledge of belief and practice in Mesopotamia from about 3000 B.C. when the art of writing in a wedge-shaped script on clay tablets arose out of the very early pictographic archetype represented by the tablet from Kish in the Ashmolean Museum in Oxford and its successors from Jemdet Nasr, Fara and Uruk.[60]

Thus, it is from these literary sources that our knowledge of Babylonian myth and ritual very largely is derived. Earlier stories, traditions, ritual, lamentations, hymns and omen-texts were not only copied but commented upon and edited; some, times transliterated in liturgical versions, Semitic and Sumerian, thereby disclosing almost all the contemporary material. For example, among the famous collection of texts in the royal library at Nineveh, founded by Asurbanipal during the last days of the Assyrian Empire (668–626 B.C.), almost every branch of Sumerian and Babylonian learning and knowledge is to be found, going back to a very early period, since the priests and scribes were commissioned by their royal patron to collect, revise and catalogue the extant texts, and to make a thorough search of the oldest temple archives throughout the country. The bulk of the material was of a religious character, the product of the temple schools, and among the most important tablets recovered were the fragments of the Gilgamesh heroic epic—one of the finest literary products of Babylonia, the earliest Akkadian version of which belongs to about 2000 B.C. with still earlier material on the tablets.

The Gilgamesh Epic

This story of the legendary founder of the city of Erech and the temple of Ea Anna is a composite narrative of not less than 3,000 lines of text on twelve tablets containing elements originating at different times, unified in and around the hero as a national epic. Within it the Tammuz theme, the Deluge myth and the adventures of Utnapishtim (Ziusudra), and the quest of immortality in what seems to have been a *rite de passage* through the waters of death, are intermingled with nature myths, necromancy and the cult of the dead, skilfully combined to produce a heroic tale of profound human interest, and of very considerable significance for the student of myth and ritual. The final form is the product of a long and complicated literary process, from various originally unrelated sources, put together as a harmonious whole to give a meaning and purpose to the establishment of the cultus in relation to the proper burial of the dead and the celebration of the Annual Festival to ensure a prosperous New Year.[61]

Throughout the story the frustration which characterizes Mesopotamian myth and ritual is apparent, and reaches its climax in the fruitless attempt of Gilgamesh to find everlasting life, cheated by a serpent of the magic rejuvenating plant he had secured to renew his youth.[62] The same mood of despair and defeat found expression in the Babylonian lamentations for Tammuz or Marduk imprisoned in the "mountain" which symbolized the nether regions. Even though, as will be considered later,[63] his liberation was celebrated at the New Year Festival with rejoicings when death in nature appeared to have been vanquished at the return of the rains, it was only life on earth that was renewed. For man, although the grave was not the absolute end of existence, unlike the Egyptian hope of sharing in the kingdom of Osiris after death, it led to the dreaded abode of Irkalla which none could leave once it was entered. The gods alone, and a very few privileged heroes like Utnapishtim, his wife and daughter, could be revived and live for ever. This is confirmed in the myth of Adapa, where again mankind is represented as having lost immortality by a trick of the gods.[64] Therefore, the decline and revival in nature is as near as the Babylonians ever got to the renewal of life emerging from death, though as the obsequies in connexion with the royal tombs at Ur reveal, at the beginning of the dynastic period kings appear to have expected to require in the after-life a full complement of retainers, and a galaxy of wealth.[65]

The Tammuz-Ishtar Myth

In the Tammuz-Ishtar myth, embodied in the Tammuz liturgy from the Third Dynasty of Ur at the end of the third millennium B.C., the Mesopotamian suffering and resurrected god is represented as the archetype of the recuperative powers of the Euphrates when it was flooded by the revitalizing waters of the two rivers in the late winter, transforming the parched desert into a fertile oasis. But the incalculable behaviour of this inundation and the vagaries of an uncertain rainfall prevented the dwellers in Mesopotamia from having the same confidence in the cyclic sequence of the seasons that prevailed in the Nile valley.[66] This uneasiness and lack of stability found expression in the myth and ritual in the primeval struggle between two opposed forces of Tiamat and Enlil or Marduk, and in the complex figures of the suffering god Tammuz or Dumuzi and his mother-spouse Inanna or Ishtar in their respective rôles of the creative powers of spring and the fertility of nature. In the primeval and perennial struggle between the two opposed forces in its elaborate mythological setting the Goddess always was supreme because she was the source of life, her male partner being primarily her son and only secondarily her husband. In short, the creative powers were at a discount and dependent upon forces over which man had but a limited measure of control. All life was born unto death, and even the Great Mother was a tragic figure pursuing her search for her lover-son amid lamentation and wailing and woe. But behind this pessimistic view of the world and the natural order lay the earlier conception of the magico-religious control of the cosmic forces which always endeavoured to find expression in the later ritual and myth, if with little success.

Canaanite Myths and Rituals

From the clay tablets discovered since 1929 at Ras Shamra, the ancient city of Ugarit on the coast of Syria near the modern town of Latakia, dating from about the middle of the second millennium B.C., it seems that a fertility cult was established in Palestine at the time of the Hebrew settlement in the country in which a renewal ritual was held periodically (perhaps every seven years). At present the texts are too fragmentary and the decipherment of the cuneiform signs in which the Canaanite dialect akin to Hebrew and Phoenician was written is too incomplete to arrive at any very definite conclusions about the precise nature of their contents. But it is beginning to appear that early Canaanite myth and ritual conformed in outline and basic structure to that of Mesopotamia and the rest of the Near East despite local variations as elsewhere. Like the Babylonian tablets they appear to be part of the archives of the local temple, prior to the fourteenth century B.C., and variant examples of the same Semitic alphabetic script have been found at Beth Shemesh and Mount Tabor. This Canaanite-Hurrian dialectal adaptation of cuneiform being suitable only for use on clay tablets, which were not the normal Palestinian medium of writing, it was of short duration. Nevertheless, the very considerable number of cultic texts produced show that while it lasted it was an active and prolific literary enterprise, largely concerned with the myth of Aleyan-Baal and Mot, the marriage of Nikkal and the Moon, and the legends of Danel and Keret.[67]

Documents in Mycenaean Greek

In Crete some 4,000 documents inscribed on clay were brought to light by Sir Arthur Evans in the Minoan palace of Knossos dating from the latter part of the Bronze Age (*c.* 1900–1400 B.C.). These inscriptions, inventories and accounts were written in a script which recurs on engraved seal-stones on the Aegean mainland at Orchomenos, Thebes, Mycenae, Eleusis and Tiryns. Evans worked out three stages in Cretan writing: (1) a hieroglyphic pictographic writing; (2) a cursive script known as Linear A; and (3) a later revision, Linear B, which was in use when Knossos was destroyed in 1400 B.C., and which continued on the mainland until the Dorian invasion of Greece about 1100 B.C.[68] In 1952 further tablets were published from Knossos while more than 600 pieces of clay tablets, which had been extracted in 1939 by Professor C. W. Blegen from a Mycenaean palace near Pylos in Greece of a rather later date (*c.* 1200 B.C.), also were identical in script with the Linear B documents.[69] It remained, however, for Dr Ventris, in conjunction with Mr J. Chadwick, to show in 1952 that the language was in fact not a *lingua franca*, as had been suggested, but a very archaic form of Greek written in a syllabic script which had survived in Arcadia, and probably had been taken over by the Achaeans and adapted from the earlier Minoan Linear A.[70]

The difficulties of decipherment have been and are very considerable. Not only is the writing very clumsy and apparently an adaptation for Greek of a system devised for another idiom (i.e. Linear A), but although the spelling is consistent each syllable may be used in a number of different ways. Moreover, the Mycenaean vocabulary does not derive very much help from that of classical Greek, notwithstanding resemblances to Homeric forms, and the proportion of non-Greek words may have been higher than in Attic, or even in Homeric Greek. It is possible that more than one language was in use in Mycenaean Greece, but all the larger tablets produce evidence of having been written in Greek in spite of differences in respect of Attic-Ionic. The affinities definitely are with East Greek (i.e. with the Arcado-Cyprian dialect group), and the Cypriote syllabary appears to have been based on a Mycenaean prototype in which some elements of the Linear B script were incorporated. Thus, a clay tablet inscribed with what is believed to be a Cypro-Minoan script in association with painted pottery in the Mycenaean IIIc style of the end of the thirteenth century B.C. was discovered in a Mycenaean settlement at Enkomi near Famagusta in Cyprus.[71]

While many problems of decipherment await solution, the remarkable achievement of Dr Ventris in 1952 has revealed pre-Homeric Greek literary sources going back to the Late Bronze Age in the fifteenth century B.C.[72] At present the clay tablets with the Linear B script are all inventories interlarded with abbreviations. But although no documents of a literary character have been found comparable to those in the Near East, doubtless they existed in the Aegean inscribed on less durable material than clay. Such an elaborate script could hardly have been invented and employed exclusively for recording inventories and supplying receipts for goods, even though, as Ventris and Chadwick say, these are a necessary precaution against theft, whereas "poetry, liturgies and laws can be preserved orally".[73] In fact, the recurrence of the names of the Olympian gods (e.g. Zeus, Dionysos, Hera, Hermes, Artemis, Poseidon, Athena, Enyalios (? Ares), *Hephaistios* which could be Hephaestus, and *da-ma-te* which might be interpreted as Demeter[74]), shows that the cultus was well established as the deities are mentioned in the lists as the recipients of various offerings, usually of grain, flour, oil, wine, figs and honey,

together with an ox and two rams to Poseidon. This is suggestive of the scene on the Late Minoan sarcophagus at Hagia
Triada[75] which may represent the cult of the Goddess in a
funerary setting with her priestesses as the officiants in a sacrificial oblation on behalf of the deceased. At Pylos a priest called
We-te-re-u is given prominence on a land-tenure document,
and a priestess of the winds at Knossos. The Goddess also
appears as the principal deity, doubtless in the guise of the
Minoan Mother, but no information is forthcoming concerning
the religious status of the king.

The dividing of a tablet from Pylos by cross-lines into five
sections of varying length is thought to represent a calendar of
the ceremonies prescribed for the days of a month in which the
name of the Goddess recurs as the Mistress (*Potniai*) in association with her priestesses.[76] Similarly, in the Knossos series
discovered by Evans in 1900, eleven tablets have now been
recognized to begin with month-names as part of a ritual
calendar recording offerings sent to certain shrines, priests and
divinities.[77] This also applies to fragments of tablets from the
palace on which consignments of oil are recorded as sent to
different places in particular months. Thus it would seem that
a calendrical ritual was practised which included offerings of
unguents to tutelary gods and goddesses at specific shrines at
specified months. But unless and until texts containing liturgies,
myths or rites are produced, what was said and done during the
observances cannot be ascertained. All we know at present is
that such a seasonal cult appears to have existed, and that the
earliest Hellenic epics in all probability were written in the
Linear B script of Mycenaean Greece.

CHAPTER II

The Seasonal Cult Drama

FROM this general survey of the emergence of ritual and myth under prehistoric conditions from the Palaeolithic to the Bronze Age it has become apparent that in the first instance it was very largely in relation to the food-supply and the mysteries of birth and death, as phenomena of daily occurrence and anxiety, that beliefs and practices arose which at the dawn of civilization in the Near East had acquired a variety of modes of expression. While the cultus and its mythology everywhere had their independent characteristics, nevertheless there was a common dramatic presentation and underlying theme. This is not surprising since they gave expression to the same pressing problems and the recurrent hopes and fears of mankind living under similar circumstances. But although the general attitude to the environment was the same, the surroundings themselves often were very different, as, for example, in the Nile valley and Mesopotamia.[1] Consequently, the myth and ritual assumed their own particular forms in response to the milieu in which they occurred. Their occasions, however, followed the same sequence of seasonal events.

THE SEASONAL FESTIVALS IN EGYPT

In the Palaeolithic the importance of the breeding seasons in all probability were recognized, as they were, for instance, among the native tribes of Australia,[2] but it was not until husbandry and herding began to supplant hunting and collecting food that definite evidence occurs of a cult drama celebrated annually, either in the spring or in the autumn. In Egypt, since so much depended upon the rise and fall of the Nile, the agricultural calendrical observances were based on its inundations brought into conjunction with the Osirian ritual, notwithstanding the fact that the civil calendar bore little or no relation to the seasons. In theory the year began on the 19th July, coinciding with the rise of the river at "The Season of Inundation" (Thoth) in the peasants' year. Four months later "The Season of Coming Forth" (Tybi) was observed when the waters were at their height, and in February or March "The Season of Deficiency" marked their decline after the grain sown in November had disappeared and the summer was approach-ing (March to June). Since Osiris as the personification of the Nile was the principal figure in this sequence of events, his death and resurrection were celebrated on the last five days of the month of Khoiak at "The Season of Coming Forth".

The Feast of Khoiak

This autumnal festival, held when the Nile had reached its height, opened with an effigy of the dead Osiris being cast in a mould of gold in the form of a mummy, filled with a mixture of barley and sand wrapped in rushes and laid in a shallow basin. From the 12th to the 21st of Khoiak it was watered daily, and then on the ninth day it was exposed to the sun just before sunset and sent on a voyage until the 24th, when it was buried in a coffin and laid in a grave from which the image of the previous year was thereupon removed. On the last day of the festival (30th), which coincided with the subsidence of the inundation and the sowing of the grain, the interment of Osiris was enacted, and the *Djed*-column was raised by the king and the priests as a symbol of his resurrection.[3]

Thus, on the tomb of Kheryaf at Thebes the Pharaoh, the queen and their sixteen daughters holding rattles and sistra, assisted by a priest, are represented as raising the column with ropes while a sham fight is in progress between the inhabitants of Buto, the predynastic capital of Lower Egypt, and the king and his subjects with herds of cattle and asses are depicted in procession round the walls of Memphis.[4] In the Hall of the Osirian Mysteries at Abydos, the reputed home of the body of Osiris, Seti I and Isis are shown setting up the pillar between them, and the *Djed* swathed in a cloth.[5] If Sethe is correct in thinking that the Memphite Festival of Sokaris commemorated the accession of Menes, the traditional founder of Memphis and of the centralized Egyptian State, the suggestion of Gardiner that the Feast of Khoiak was considered the proper occasion for any Pharaoh to ascend the throne,[6] gives a reason for the association of the king and the queen with the erection of the pillar, regarded as it was as the embodiment of Osiris, at the beginning of spring on the first day of the year.[7] It was this ceremonial action on New Year's Eve that was thought to secure the rebirth of Osiris in the celestial realms, but as he was entombed as a mummy while the rite was being enacted, it would seem that its primary purpose was that of enabling the living Horus (i.e. the king) to exercise his beneficent functions at "The Season of Coming Forth" when the fertilizing waters of the inundation were due to begin their fructification of the land, and the grain was ready to sprout as it were from the body of Osiris.

If the recession of the Nile flood showed the diminution of the power of the author and giver of life, Osiris, it was but the prelude to a fresh display of his vigour in the grain that was about to spring forth with renewed energy in the sprouting fields. Thus, in the Ptolemaic temple of Isis at Philae, this was symbolized by the stalks of wheat growing from the mummy of the dead god watered by a priest from a pitcher. Before the bier the *crux ansata* is figured as the symbol of life and the inscription records that "this is the form of him who may not be named, Osiris of the Mysteries who springs from the return-ing waters".[8] In the Eighteenth-Dynasty tombs Osirian figures made of earth and seeds were placed on a bier and watered for a week until they germinated to give life to the dead.[9]

This association of Osiris with the sprouting grain, taken in conjunction with the rites at the festival in the month of Khoiak, shows how very intimately the annual renewal in nature was related to his resurrection interpreted in terms of the rise and fall of the Nile with which the ritual and its symbolism coincided. Though he was not strictly a vegetation deity, or the personification of the earth like the Earth-mother, he was, nevertheless, immanent in the annual germination of vegetation in the soil. In the Memphite Mystery play performed at the accession of Senusert I in the Twelfth Dynasty (*c.* 1900 B.C.), the text of which contains much earlier material ante-dating the Middle Kingdom,[10] he is identified with the barley and the emmer that nourished the gods in heaven and man on earth, just as in the Ptolemaic temple at Denderah he was said to have made the corn from the liquid that was in him.[11] That this belief lingered on from prehistoric times until the Ptolemaic period is an indication of the significance attached to the resurrection of Osiris in its several aspects and implications alike in the myth and ritual of the official cult and in popular belief and practice in the Nile valley.

The Feast of Min

In the official calendar, however, the Harvest Festival was dedicated to Min of Koptos, who from the dawn of Egyptian civilization had personified the generative force in nature as the bestower of procreative power. He was also a rain god "open-ing the clouds", and so gave life to vegetation.[12] Therefore, he was regarded as the power immanent in the grain, and at the beginning of the dynastic period a Pharaoh was represented hoeing the ground, and perhaps attending to the irrigation dykes in the presence of Min,[13] with an attendant who may be scattering seeds on the ground at the end of the inundation.[14]

It is not surprising, therefore, that the several "comings forth" of this oldest god of fertility and sexual reproduction, whose colossal statues at Koptos belong to the prehistoric Gerzean Age,[15] were celebrated in the calendrical ritual especially at the beginning of the harvest. It was then that his ithyphallic statue was carried on poles on the shoulders of priests, hidden except for their heads and feet beneath hangings decorated with the names of the Pharaoh, preceded by a white bull, the god's sacred animal. Behind it bundles of lettuces (his plant) were carried, and in front of the statue the king walked. The god was then installed on a throne under a canopy, and offerings were made to him. A sheaf of spelt was cut by the Pharaoh, and it may have been offered to the bull to strengthen him as

the embodiment of fertility and to avert sterility.[16] Since, however, in the Middle Kingdom Min was regarded as a form of
Horus, the son of Osiris,[17] Gardiner may be correct in assuming that the king impersonated Horus and in this capacity he
reaped the emmer "for his father", Osiris.[18] In that case Min,
personifying the fertility of the newly sown fields, was brought
into relation with the reigning sovereign as the living Horus,
and the king exercised his functions at the Harvest Festival to
secure a plentiful supply of the crops in the ensuing year.

It is possible that a ritual sexual intercourse between the king
and queen constituted an integral part of the rite as a priest
proclaimed, "Hail to thee, Min, who impregnates his mother!
How mysterious is that which thou hast done to her in the
darkness." Since Min was very intimately connected with the
kingship in ancient times, that an heir to the throne should be
begotten at this festival is in line with the royal accession ritual
in Egypt. Moreover, at the end of the observance four birds
were released to carry to the four cardinal points of the earth
the proclamation: "Horus son of Min and Osiris has assumed
the Great Crown of Upper and Lower Egypt." This connects
the Min Harvest Festival with the coronation ceremony when
after the enthronement a similar release of birds seems to have
heralded the announcement of the accession.[19] But at the Min
feast it was the assumption of the crown by the god through his
union with the Pharaoh, symbolizing the harmonious interlocking of nature and society in the person of the sovereign,
that was duly announced; not the king's actual accession. Thus,
as Frankfort says, "the state celebrated the reaping of the crops
with the worship not of Osiris, but of a deity whose exuberant
fertility was immune against the depredations of the reapers
upon the earth's growth".[20]

THE NEW YEAR FESTIVAL IN MESOPOTAMIA

In Mesopotamia the calendar and the seasonal ritual followed
a different sequence since, as we have seen, the Tigris and
Euphrates were too precarious in their behaviour to be a
reliable index for calculating their rise and fall in relation to

the crops. But New Year festivals always have been movable feasts in ancient agricultural society determined not by the solar year, as in the higher and later systems, but by the periodicity of nature and the recurrent renewal of life, whatever may be the cause and occasion of the events. The mythopoeic concep/ tion of time is qualitative and concrete,[21] and, therefore, the emphasis is on succession and transition requiring the collective effort of the community to effect a safe passage from one phase to another, beset as the critical junctures are by so many and such great dangers. In Egypt the Pharaoh in his divine capacity was charged with the daily responsibility of repeating the coronation rites in the Toilet Ceremonies he performed every morning to ensure the course of the sun across the horizon,[22] as well as taking part in the Harvest Festival. Each sunrise and each New Year's Day was a repetition of the initial creation when the current sequence of events began by divine initiative. Similarly, in Babylonia the king commenced his reign on New Year's Day, and ever after played a significant part in its annual celebration when the story of creation was recited as an integral part of the ritual renewal in the autumn after the devastating heat of summer had spent its force.

In this festival the revival of nature was secured by a dramatic re/enactment of the primeval cosmic battle against Chaos in order to establish and maintain the orderly sequence of the seasons. This was the vital concern of mankind at all times, but especially at the turn of the year when in the hazardous Mesopotamian environment so much was at stake. To control the critical situation it was necessary for the community to identify itself with the great cosmic forces in the universe. For this purpose the king assumed the rôle of the god, Enlil, Marduk or Ashur, who had fought the powers of Chaos at the threshold of creation and vanquished Kingu, the leader of the hosts of Tiamat. In his Tammuz capacity as the generative force in nature he was thought to have been held captive in the land of the dead during the drought of summer, and it was not until the New Year rites had been performed that his release was secured with its reciprocal effects in nature.

Lamentations in the Tammuz Liturgies

In the Tammuz liturgies, and subsequently in the Annual Festival, this theme of the suffering god and the sorrowing goddess was enacted, accompanied by bitter wailing and the singing of dirges over the effigy of the dead god when the scorched earth seemed to threaten a return of the desolation believed to have stricken the earth when Ishtar wandered in barren fields and empty sheepfolds during her search for Tammuz in the underworld.[23] From these sinister regions the cry of the suffering god was echoed in the laments of the priests and people until he was released by the Goddess and restored to the upper world as her "resurrected child". Then sorrow was turned into joy and defeat into victory, celebrated with a royal banquet, and concluding with a doxology addressed to the reunited gods in the bridal chamber.

The Akitu Festival in Babylon

In this recreative ritual Sumerian rulers as the servants of the gods played the part of Tammuz-Dumuzi incarnating the creative forces of spring through union with the goddess Inanna-Ishtar, the source of all life, with whom the king and the priestess became identified for the purpose of engaging in a sacred marriage to restore fecundity in nature.[24] The cult drama was held either in the spring (i.e. Nisan) when the rains had produced the new growth, and/or in the autumn (i.e. Tishri) when the harvest had been gathered. Either of these occasions constituted the beginning of the year, and at Ur and Erech New Year festivals were observed on both occasions.

When Babylon became the capital and Marduk replaced Tammuz as the central male divine figure, the event, known in Akkadian as the *Akitu*, was celebrated only in the spring, during the first eleven days of the month of Nisan. Opening with elaborate purification rites and the recitation of the *Enuma elish*, on the fifth day atonement was made for the king. Escorted by the priests to the shrine of Marduk, he was left there alone. The high-priest then emerged from an inner sanctuary, where the statue of the god stood, and divested the monarch of his regalia, slapped his face, pulled his ears, forced him to his knees before the image and extracted from him a negative confession:

> I have not sinned, O Lord of the lands,
> I have not been negligent regarding thy divinity,
> I have not destroyed Babylon.

To this the priest replied by a kind of absolution and blessing from Marduk, and restoring to him his insignia he re-established him in his royal office for the ensuing year.

In the meantime there had been increasing commotion in the city during the search for Marduk, who was imprisoned in the "mountain" of the underworld, and whose captivity was reflected in the desolate state of the land. Mock battles ensued for the purpose of releasing him. This was accomplished on the sixth or seventh day by his son and avenger Nabu, as is suggested on several of the Akkadian seals of the middle of the third millennium B.C.[25] There the mourning for Tammuz by the Goddess is represented. The fighting groups may refer to the battle which was waged during the festival to free the god, while the goddess scenes would seem to depict Inanna, later called Ishtar, seeking and leading forth Tammuz (i.e. Marduk) from his mountain-grave, expressed, as we have seen, in some of the lamentations and rejoicings in the liturgies and in the rituals.[26] But the designs show the myth rather than the rite, thereby indicating the antiquity of the mythological theme enacted in this cult drama.

After the liberation of Marduk and the reinstatement of the king, the statues of the gods were assembled in the Chamber of Destinies in order of precedence on the 8th of Nisan to confer upon their leader, Marduk, their combined strength for the conquest of the forces of Chaos and death, and to determine the "destinies". In other words, to decide the fate of society during the forthcoming year which still hung in the balance because the course of nature in Mesopotamia was so very indeterminate. The king holding his sceptre in his hand then proceeded to the great hall to receive a fresh outpouring of divine power. "Grasping the hands of the great lord Marduk", he and the other gods went forth in procession along the sacred way to the Festival House (*Bit Akitu*) on the outskirts of the city, like the victorious army of gods in conflict with Tiamat depicted on the copper doors with which Sennacherib adorned the *Bit Akitu* of Ashur (the Assyrian designation of Marduk) with his own figure standing in the god's chariot.[27] This suggests that the king personified Ashur as the "victorious prince" who had conquered the forces of evil (i.e. Tiamat), and it is probable that it was in the Festival House that the primeval battle was re-enacted, or in some way made effica-cious. Thus, at the conclusion of the rites in the *Bit Akitu,* a banquet was held to celebrate the triumph of Marduk, and all that this involved for the well-being of the country.[28] Then, on the 11th of Nisan, after the banquet, a return was made to the *Esagila.* There the sacred marriage was consummated by the king and a priestess, probably of the royal blood,[29] perhaps in a chamber decorated with greenery, called *gigunu,* erected on one of the stages of the ziggurat.[30] By this ritual union the fertility of the fields, the flocks and men was restored because the god and goddess upon whom fecundity in nature depended were united and from their intercourse life sprang forth.

It now only remained for the gods to reassemble on the 12th of Nisan in the Chamber of Destinies to ratify the divine decree concerning the fate of society in the ensuing year to ensure its prosperity. This duplication of the determination of destiny on the eighth and twelfth days of the festival followed the preced-ent in the creation story where such an assembly of the gods is said to have been held after Marduk was elected the head of the pantheon, and again after his victory when it was decided to create the human race to serve them. It was upon the fulfilment of their destiny as the servants of the gods and of the goddess that their fate depended. Therefore, the Annual Festival con-cluded with this final act before the gods returned to their cities and men to the cultivation of the new crops under what they hoped and believed were auspicious circumstances because the hazards at the turn of the year had been safely negotiated.

Throughout the Mesopotamian cult drama there was always an underlying element of doubt which reflected the geographical and climatic conditions of the country. Neither the kings, the administration nor the community at large had an assured and completely secure position rooted and grounded in a transcendent unifying principle standing over the mutable order. Marduk rose to pre-eminence by the transference of political jurisdiction from Nippur to Babylon. His triumph, however, was short-lived, and, like his predecessors, he was at the mercy of the fortunes of his cult-centre. His own destiny was as precarious as that of mankind, for neither his supremacy nor the empire in which he was predominant, so magnificently organized by Hammurabi, survived the death of the founder. Nevertheless, as Marduk reproduced the nature, attributes and function of Tammuz, so he lived on in Ashur, retaining his time-honoured position as the hero of the cult drama, thereby preserving the continuity in the mythological theme and its ritual enactment.

THE CANAANITE CULT DRAMA
The Baal-Anat Cycle
In the Canaanite myths and legends from Ugarit (now Ras Shamra) on the Syrian coast the death and resurrection theme recurs in the Baal-Anat cycle, although in the fragmentary state of the tablets the contents often are conjectural. Nevertheless, it appears to have been after a victorious struggle with a dragon, Yam or Nahar, that Aleyan-Baal was installed in a royal palace, and engaged in a combat with Mot, the lord of the underworld.[31] In the heat of summer Aleyan was killed by his adversary, his descent into the nether regions being symbolized in Tammuz fashion by the withering plants and parched ground during the season of drought. Then follows an account of the search for his body by Anat his consort, the goddess who plays the principal part on the tablet—the Ishtar of the episode—and her encounter with Mot, who feigned ignorance of the whereabouts of Aleyan. Thereupon she seized him, split his body with a ritual sickle (*harpé*), winnowed him, scorched him in the fire, ground him in a mill, scattered his flesh over

the fields like the dismembered body of Osiris, and gave him to the birds to eat. In short, she treated him as the reaped grain. Aleyan, after fighting many battles with a number of gods, eventually was restored as king. Mot, who was also revived after his rough treatment by Anat, was urged by the Sun-goddess to capitulate. El "overturned Mot's throne" and "broke the sceptre of his dominion". Therefore he was forced to surrender and acknowledge the kingship of Baal. The drought ended and fertility was re-established on the earth.[32]

Septennial Celebration

Thus the central theme would seem to be a battle between life and death in nature in the usual vegetation setting, and the measures taken to secure the renewal of the beneficent forces of fertility at their ultimate source, along the general lines of the cult drama in the Ancient Near East. Moreover, as will be considered later, there are indications that the rites may have concluded with a sacred marriage.[33] Be this as it may, the close correspondence of the poems with the vegetation drama in Mesopotamia suggests that they contain the Canaanite version of the Tammuz cult, though it may not have been the annual death and revival of the god of fertility that was celebrated since drought and famine in Canaan were not regular occurrences in the seasonal sequence.[34] Thus Professor Gordon maintains that the rites were associated with a seven-year cycle of alternating drought and fertility.[35] But even so, Baal represented the rainy and most fertile part of the year and his death was connected with the languishing of the earth.[36]

If the septennial celebration is correct, the reason for this modification in the normal vegetation theme and its ritual enactment may have been that famine in Palestine not being an annual occurrence when it did occur it produced an emotional tension which found expression in this myth and ritual. Bad years were exceptional and might be prolonged. Therefore, in the myth Danel cursed the ground where his son was murdered with seven years of drought through the withholding of Baal's life-giving waters,[37] like the seven years of famine in the Joseph story in the Old Testament.[38] Therefore, if the Ras Shamra rituals were a Canaanite version of the Tammuz-Adonis cult, which unquestionably was very firmly established in Syria, it would seem to have undergone some modification in the manner and time of its observance. More-over, Baal was not the only god on whom fertility depended.

Although great advances have been made in the interpreta-tion of these difficult and fragmentary texts since their discovery by Professor Schaeffer in 1928 and their subsequent transcribing and translation by Professor Virolleaud, and more recently by Professor C. H. Gordon and Professor G. R. Driver, much is still very obscure concerning their significance for and relation to the myth and ritual of the Fertile Crescent. It would be premature to attempt to arrive at definite conclusions in the present state of the available data. Nevertheless, in broad outline the Baal-Anat cycle appears to conform to the general pattern of fertility rituals centred in the vegetation theme, notwithstand-ing the marked and important divergencies in the mythology contained in the poems which differentiates it from that embodied in Mesopotamian and Egyptian texts. Therefore, while a common element can be detected in this type of ritual myth, care has to be taken to avoid hasty generalizations based on similarities without giving full weight to the fundamental differences and peculiarities which recur in the ritual and myth of the cult drama in the Ancient Near East.

THE CULTUS IN ANCIENT ISRAEL
Yahwistic Syncretism and the Vegetation Cult

This caution is even more necessary in the case of the Hebrew festivals and their cultus. That the desert tribes when they eventually established themselves in Palestine after their succes-sive invasions in the fourteenth century B.C. came under the influence of the Canaanite ritual observances and their mytho-logy is clear from the Old Testament narratives. There the conflict between the mono-Yahwists and the rest of the nation who practised the indigenous vegetation religion is a constantly recurrent phenomenon. If the graphic description of the contest on Mount Carmel is popular tradition rather than sober history,[39] nevertheless, it illustrates the perennial prophetic struggle between the two opposed groups which continued throughout the period of the monarchy, as is shown by the repeated denunciations of the cultus and its syncretisms by the canonical prophets in the eighth and seventh centuries B.C.

In such a highly composite nation as was Israel after the settlement in Palestine, the fusion of its various religious traditions was inevitable, notwithstanding the later fiction of a common lineage and a single national monotheistic faith based on the Abrahamic covenant. In fact, when the Yahweh cult was introduced the nature and attributes of the Canaanite Baals were transferred to the God of Israel, and in the sanctuaries devoted primarily to his worship the cultus was indistinguishable from that of the earlier occupants. The story of the golden calf, which probably is later than the revolt of Jeroboam, reflects the cultus practised in the northern kingdom. It was only by later writers influenced by the reforms of Josiah in 621 that the institution of the bull cult and a non-Levitical priesthood at Bethel and Dan were represented as innovations after the separation from the southern kingdom of Judah.

It is possible that at the accession of David the ark had been established at these shrines in place of the bull image,[40] and, therefore, that Jeroboam subsequently did restore there the earlier cultus and its hierarchy. In any case, image-symbolism was no novelty in the worship of Yahweh as a syncretistic deity,[41] either in the central sanctuary at Jerusalem or in the local shrines. So deeply laid was it that the Josiah reform proved to be only a temporary expedient. The Deuteronomic laws were established officially, but in practice they lapsed during the reigns of the four last kings of Judah and the composite cultus continued as heretofore, together with additions introduced from Babylonia.[42]

The Nature and Position of Yahweh in Ancient Israel

The position of Yahweh in this complex situation is not easy to determine prior to the rise of the prophetic movement with its absolute ethical monotheism and its denunciations of the cultus and its syncretisms.[43] If he is to be equated with the Western Semitic deity whose name occurs on a number of Aramaean, Canaanite, Babylonian and Hebrew inscriptions and documents as *Ya*, *Yami*, or *Yaum-ilum*,[44] it is possible he was known in Canaan as a minor god before the Israelite settlement as the name *Abi-yahu* occurs on a cuneiform tablet at Taanach dated between 2000 and 3000 B.C. But there is no conclusive evidence of the name Yahweh in cuneiform litera-ture before the eighth century B.C.[45] However, he seems to have been primarily a desert deity who probably was wor-shipped among the Kenites before he was first encountered there by Moses, as is suggested in the E document from the northern kingdom in the book of Exodus, and later in the Priestly tradition.[46] On the other hand, in the J narrative current in Judah he is said to have been known to the ancestors of Israel from the time of the mythical Enoch, and indeed of the first parents of the human race in Eden.[47] Why the northern tribes, which *ex hypothesi* were not acquainted with Yahwism until after the time of Moses, should have attributed the origin of the Sinaitic cultus and covenant to him is not explained. Professor Rowley meets this difficulty by suggesting that the tribes that were not with Moses at the time of the Exodus were the ones that did not ascribe the beginning of their Yahwism to him, while those that were with him did.[48] In any case, notwithstanding these obscurities, however and wherever the cult may have arisen, it stood in a different tradition from that of Osiris in Egypt, Tammuz and Marduk in Babylonia and Aleyan-Baal in Canaan.

It was not until Palestine became officially "the land of Yahweh" after the conquest that the Hebrew and the Canaanite traditions were assimilated as a result of the intermingling of the invaders and the indigenous inhabitants in a composite Israelite people. As the settlers learnt from the Canaanites their agricultural and other technical methods, so they adopted their religious observances and sacred places. Moreover, a section of the Israelite community had lived in the relatively advanced agricultural civilization of Palestine without interruption since long before the invasions in the second millennium B.C., from the east under Joshua and from the south by Caleb and Othniel, and already had adapted themselves to the highly developed Canaanite vegetation cultus. Therefore, with the advent of the invading Hebrew tribes they too adopted the indigenous composite myth and ritual with their many common features with the cult drama in the rest of the Fertile Crescent.

The Fertility Cults

Thus, as we have seen, the Ras Shamra texts with their Aleyan-Baal-Mot vegetation theme were contemporary with the period of the Hebrew settlement in Canaan, and reveal innumerable parallels with the Old Testament in sacrificial terminology, poetic style, ritual practices and divine names. Some of these resemblances have been exaggerated, but the great Baal epic bound up with the seasons and agricultural operations can hardly fail to have had a profound influence on the Yahweh cult during the formative period before the monarchy. Indeed, in the northern kingdom of Israel at any rate Yahweh was a fertility Baal as late as the eighth century B.C.[49] and the prophetic polemic against the national religion very largely was based upon the transference of the control of vegetation to Yahweh in the traditional seasonal ritual.[50] The serpent cult continued to be an integral element in Yahwism until drastic steps were taken to eradicate it by Hezekiah,[51] and like the bull at Bethel, it was a prominent feature in the vegetation myth and ritual, both the serpent and the bull being everywhere fertility symbols of the Mother-goddess.

It was not denied that Yahweh by his mighty hand and stretched-out arm had brought the captive tribes out of Egypt and through the wilderness to their promised land, but in Palestine the controlling force were the gods of the land and their prescribed rites, to be neglected at grave peril. It was they who dealt with fertility rather than Yahweh, the desert divine deliverer, the Lord of Hosts, mighty in battle, and jealous of

his rights and privileges among his chosen people. Conse/
quently, it was upon the local fertility Baals that attention
was primarily concentrated lest as masters of the situation in
Palestine they should become hostile and withdraw their fructi/
fying powers from the land if their worship were neglected.

This then was the nature of Canaanite religion when the
Hebrews established themselves in Palestine, and, according
to the Abrahamic tradition, even in their ancestral home in
Mesopotamia they "served other gods".[52] Therefore, although
undoubtedly they had a nomadic Aramaean element in their
history,[53] both in their Mesopotamian and Palestinian back/
grounds they were essentially a product of the agricultural
civilization of the Ancient Middle East in which the seasonal
vegetation myth and ritual occupied such a prominent place.
Baal, in fact, as an inclusive name in the Old Testament for
the gods other than Yahweh, usually had a fertility significance,
frequently in association with goddesses (e.g. Astarte (Ash/
toreth) and Asherah) whose emblems in the form of female
figurines and plaques abounded in Palestinian sites.[54] Indeed,
until it was ousted by Yahwism in the time of David, Baalism
was virtually the official religion in the north, notwithstanding
the Song of Deborah[55] where Yahweh seems to have been
indistinguishable from Baal or Hadad as a storm god who sent
a generous rain over his inheritance when it was exhausted.[56]

The association of Bethel with Jacob in its later cult legend[57]
was an attempt to give a legitimate place and significance in
Hebrew tradition to a famous ancient Canaanite centre of bull/
worship, which became a serious rival to the central Yahwistic
sanctuary at Jerusalem after it had been restored to its original
status by Jeroboam. The feast he instituted on the fifteenth day
of the eighth month (i.e. at full moon)[58] was connected with
the fertility cult at the beginning of the rainy season,[59] in
accordance with established Canaanite custom in the earlier
agricultural religion, to ensure the food/supply in the usual
manner. Yahweh was acknowledged as supreme by right of
conquest after the settlement, but, as Meek says, "his department
was the larger one of the state and not the affairs of ordinary

everyday agricultural and commercial life".[60] Therefore, if he was to secure and retain the allegiance of the masses, it was essential that he should be presented and worshipped in the appropriate manner of a fertility god rather than in that of a desert god. Anathema as this might be to the majority of the canonical prophets before the Exile, Hosea at least recognized its significance. Therefore, he did not hesitate to interpret the doctrine of the Covenant in terms of the sacred marriage in spite of its earlier associations.[61]

The Jerusalem Cultus

After the disruption of the monarchy at the death of Solomon, as Jeroboam had attempted to consolidate the northern section of the community in the sanctuary at Bethel, so in the southern kingdom of Judah the temple at Jerusalem and its cultus became the unifying centre. That the south was less syncretistic and more firmly established in the Yahwistic tradition is shown beyond dispute. For four centuries the Davidic dynasty persisted without interruption, surviving the dissolution of Israel at the fall of Samaria in 586. The relationship between David and his successors and Yahweh unquestionably was an important factor in the stabilization of the social structure and the cultus. It is true the king in the Hebrew monarchy was never the dynamic centre of the nation like Pharaoh in Egypt any more than he was in Mesopotamia. The emphasis in Judah was on the Covenant, first with Abraham, then with Moses, and finally with the house of David. The theocratic relationship, however, was essentially with Yahweh who was represented as Israel's king, the reigning monarch being his anointed deputy installed in the royal office to maintain the Covenant (*bĕrith*, i.e. the cultus). Therefore, it was his duty to superintend the organization of the cultus in all its aspects after David had made Yahwism the official religion.[62]

The northern kingdom repudiated its inheritance in the house of the son of Jesse when his grandson refused to listen to their demands,[63] and reinstated the bull cult at Dan and Bethel.[64] Attempts have been made to interpret these bulls as

images of Yahweh, like the cherubim in the temple at Jerusalem,[65] but clearly the intention was to return to the former
fertility cultus. The festival instituted at Bethel in the eighth
month, which appears to have been a counterpart of that
already established at Jerusalem,[66] was designed to keep the
people from going up to the Davidic capital a month later to
take part in the Zadokite rites.[67] In the pre-exilic community
the annual harvest festival was celebrated in the month of
Ethanim, described after the Exile as the "seventh month"
Tishri (i.e. October–November). It was then that the temple
was dedicated when the usual annual pilgrimage was made to
the shrine at the end of the year, and at the full moon of Tishri
the Feast of Sukkôth (Tabernacles) was held at the turn of the
year.[68] When the Babylonian calendar was adopted after the
Exile the earlier autumnal rites at "the going out of the year"
continued to be observed, although Nisan now became "the
beginning of months"[69] when the Passover was held. Therefore, like the Babylonians, they virtually kept a dual observance
of the New Year, the *Rosh hashshanah* in Tishri at the time of
the Ingathering,[70] and the spring Paschal rites in Nisan.[71]

So far as the autumnal festival is concerned, it occurred at
the end of the harvest season[72] when the rain was urgently
required to water the parched earth that it might bring forth
abundantly in the months ahead. Therefore at this feast the
rites were directed to the beneficent bestowal of rain upon which
the life and well-being of the community depended at "the turn
of the year".[73] Indeed, in the post-exilic book of Zechariah it
is said that "whoso of all the families of the earth goeth not up
to Jerusalem to worship the King, the Lord of Hosts, upon
them the rain shall not come".[74]

In Palestine anxiety about the rainfall sometimes was as acute
as it was in Mesopotamia concerning the condition of the irrigation canals, the vagaries of the two great rivers, and the climatic
hazards, as is illustrated, for instance, by the Carmel episode.[75]
Therefore, at the critical juncture in the seasonal cycle the New
Year rites at the autumnal Festival of Sukkôth, or Tabernacles,
were performed for the purpose of controlling the weather

when the "former rains" were due to commence that the pros/
perity of the country might be assured. As the political situation
deteriorated in the pre/exilic period, the growing anxieties found
ritual expression in the cult drama and the eschatological ideas
associated with the "Day of Yahweh",[76] for the belief in Yah/
weh's lordship in the natural order carried with it his control
of the nation's vicissitudes[77] coupled with a forecast of rain.[78]

Whether or not the Psalms in which the enthronement of
Yahweh is celebrated (i.e. Ps. xciii, xcv–xcix) were an integral
part of the New Year liturgy is still a matter of dispute.[79]
Unfortunately, most of the available evidence comes from post/
exilic sources, and we cannot be sure that the Coronation
Psalms were in fact used at the autumnal festival, especially as
they do not occur in the *Rosh hashshanah* liturgy, or in the syna/
gogue commemoration, where they are used as Sabbath Psalms.
Therefore, if originally they belonged to the New Year Festival,
they must have lost their earlier significance in the later post/
exilic worship before and after the destruction of the Temple
in A.D. 70 when in the second century A.D. the New Year
Festival was associated with the Kingdom of God. But how/
ever they are to be interpreted, unquestionably their theme is
that of the enthronement of Yahweh over the physical universe
manifest in the bestowal of the seasonal rains and the prosperity
of the nation along the lines familiar in the cult drama in the
Near East, notably in Mesopotamia and in the Ugaritic texts.
The appropriate occasion for their recitation would be the
celebration of the triumph of Yahweh as the universal King
at the Annual Festival, when his victory over the forces of
death and destruction was enacted in a triumphal procession
like that when the Ark was installed in the Temple at Jerusa/
lem,[80] to promote the fortunes of the country in the coming
year. Although the majority of the Enthronement Psalms listed
as such by Mowinckel may be post/exilic, there are also some for
which a pre/exilic date can be substantiated (cf. Ps. xlvii, xciii,
xcv–c) and which may have influenced the thought of the
Deutero/Isaiah at the end of the Exile.[81] Therefore, it can
hardly be maintained that this source of evidence has no

bearing upon the earlier New Year observances, especially in the light of the Ras Shamra texts.[82]

That the Feast of the Ingathering, which was later called Tabernacles, was taken over by the Hebrews from the Canaanites when they established themselves in Palestine is reasonably certain, apart from whether or not it contained an Enthronement rite. It was held at the turn of the year in the autumn for much the same purpose as formerly in the seasonal agricultural ritual. Behind it lay the drama of the dying and reviving Yeargod, however much the theme may have been modified under Yahwistic influence and made to conform to the independent status of Yahweh transcending the Kingship as a divine institution. In the Jerusalem cultus the Davidic dynasty exercised its sacerdotal functions in the Temple as the anointed servants of Yahweh before these were taken over specifically by the priesthood after the dissolution of the monarchy, as will be considered later,[83] and eventually acquired a Messianic significance.

But Yahweh was never a dying and rising vegetation god, like either Tammuz or Osiris. The cultus gave stability to the nation because it was the means by which the Covenant was maintained both before and after the Exile. The ritual order and its festivals centred at Jerusalem made the Temple the focalpoint of the theocracy. Only there could the sacerdotal rites be duly performed in the postexilic community so that even the Passover at the vernal full moon was made a temple institution,[84] together with the Feast of Weeks at midsummer and the Feast of Ingathering (Sukkôth) in the autumn. Thus, the Jerusalem cultus was the most powerful factor in the cohesion of Jewry after the disturbance of the Exile.

THE MYSTERY DRAMA IN GREECE AND ROME

In Greece the principal seasonal events in the agricultural year —those of sowing, ploughing and reaping—were the occasion of a cult drama in spring and autumn in which the greater part of the community engaged to control the processes of vegetation at the critical junctures in the annual sequence. When these rustic rites became public cults in the citystates in the classical period they rapidly acquired a new splendour and magnificence and elaboration, though in their essential nature and function they were little changed. As they developed into the great dramas in the sixth century B.C., tragedy first appeared to give expression in literary form to the death and decay in nature and in human experience, with comedy as the "revel-song" emerging from the rural ritual designed to make the crops grow, and held amid merry-making and the lifting of all restraints in word and action. When the year was divided rather arbitrarily into twelve months, it seldom coincided with the seasons with any degree of exactitude, except that it began approximately at midsummer. How the New Year was celebrated is not known, but as the first month was called Kekatombaion it may be assumed that a hundred cattle were offered at its festival on the seventh day, dedicated to Apollo. On the 12th of Kronia (July) a very ancient harvest festival, wherein masters and slaves rejoiced together, appears to have been observed in honour of Kronos, probably a god of harvest represented in art carrying what may have been a reaping-hook.

The Eleusinia

It is not improbable that the Eleusinian Mysteries arose out of a very ancient agricultural festival celebrating the bringing up of the corn from the silos in which after threshing in June it had been stored away until it was ready to be sown in October. During the four summer months in which it was below ground the fields were barren and desolate until the autumn rains began. Then the ploughing season opened in Attica, the corn was sown and immediately the fields became green again as the crops sprouted in the mild winter months (except in January). The flowers having appeared in early spring (i.e. February–March), by May the grain was ready to be reaped and threshed at the beginning of the dry season (June). The Goddess Demeter was very intimately associated with this vegetation cycle, though it is a matter of debate whether she was the goddess of the earth and of fertility in general, or exclusively the Corn-mother as Nilsson insists,[85] with her daughter Kore, the Corn-maiden, as the embodiment of the new harvest. In either case her cult at Eleusis was essentially an agricultural ritual which no doubt was centred very largely in the cultivation of the grain on the Rarian plain, as one interpretation of her name suggests, if the first syllable *de* is rightly rendered as "spelt". What is beyond dispute is that she was quite unquestionably a Greek goddess, but behind her lay the Minoan Mother-goddess who was primarily concerned with birth and generation in the human, animal and vegetable orders. Therefore, while her Mysteries at Eleusis very likely originated in a corn ritual, they acquired a wider and deeper significance, and she herself fulfilled the rôle of Mother-goddess in her several capacities that extend beyond the cornfields.[86]

Nevertheless, Nilsson may be right in thinking that her cultus and its legend were suggested by the stowing away of the corn in the subterranean silos after it had been threshed in June, represented in the myth by the descent of Kore to the realms of Plouton, the god of the wealth of corn in the grain and of other fruits of the soil. Her return was celebrated four months later when the silos were opened and the seed corn was brought up for the autumnal sowing; an event which coincided with the Greater Eleusinian Mysteries,[87] just as the Lesser Mysteries at Agrai, a suburb of Athens, were held when the crops were ripening in the spring and the Anthesteria, the Feast of Flowers and commemoration of the dead, was observed.

This association of the seasonal cycle in the growth of the grain and of vegetation in general with that of death and resurrection beyond the grave in the sequence of human life here and hereafter was very prominent in the Greek mind. Therefore, it was not difficult to bring together the two parallel processes and their mythological representation in the Eleusinian cult drama. Thus, Kore later became identified with Persephone, the queen of Hades and abducted wife of Pluto, whose name easily could be confused with Plouton. When this was accomplished the way was opened for the legend to describe the abduction of the daughter of Demeter as she was gathering flowers in the meadows with the daughters of Okeanos on the rich Rarian plain. Appearing suddenly in his golden chariot, the amorous Pluto bore away the lamenting Persephone to the underworld. Thereupon her sorrowing mother wandered far and wide in search of her, carrying a torch to light up the deep recesses where she might have been concealed. Such was her grief that she withheld her fructifying gifts from the earth till universal famine was threatened.

Disguising herself as an old woman, Demeter went through-out the land until eventually she came to Eleusis. There she sat down near the wayside well, called the Fountain of Maiden-hood, and was encountered by the daughters of the wise lord of Eleusis, Keleos, to whom she told a fictitious story about her escape from pirates. Having won their confidence, she was taken to the palace and became nurse to Domophoon, the infant son of the queen, Metaneira. To make him immortal she secretly anointed him with ambrosia, the food of the gods, and breathed upon him by day, and at night hid him in the fire to consume his mortality, unknown to his parents. As a result of this treatment the child grew like an immortal being. Disturbed, however, in these fiery operations one night by his mother, Metaneira, who screamed with terror at seeing her son in the fire, Demeter revealed her identity. Although in her wrath at this spoiling of her plans she refused to complete the immor-talizing process of Domophoon, or to continue her stay in the royal household, before she left the palace she commanded the people of Eleusis to build a sanctuary in her honour on the hill above the fountain where she had first met the daughters of Keleos, and there the rites she would teach her votaries should be performed for the purpose of bestowing immortality on all who henceforth would be initiated into her Mysteries. After another terrible year of drought and famine, which even deprived the gods on Olympus of their gifts and sacrifices, Zeus intervened on behalf of Kore. Sending a messenger in the person of Hermes to the underworld, it was arranged that she should be released provided that she had not eaten the food of the dead. Pluto, however, had forestalled this by giving her surrepti-tiously some pomegranate seeds. This bound her to him for the third part of the year, marked by the decline in vegetation, but for the remaining eight months she lived with her mother and the gods, returning when the new life began to appear after the fructifying rains.[88]

In the form in which the cult legend is told in the so-called Homeric Hymn, assigned to the seventh century B.C., there is a good deal of confusion and intermingling of myths. That both the story and the ritual are pre-Hellenic in origin is suggested by the Mycenaean foundations of the sanctuary at Eleusis and the primitive agrarian character of the rites with their affinity to the very ancient Thesmophoria, celebrated by women at the autumn sowing. Indeed, Demeter was herself called *thesmophoros*, and she and Kore were the two *thesmophoroi*. As in Crete, the rites seem first to have been held in the open air as a fertility festival to promote the growth of the crops before they were given a more personal application as an esoteric mystery cult to secure a blissful immortality for those who underwent the elaborate process of initiation, after Eleusis was incorporated with Athens, probably between 625 and 600 B.C. The Mysteries were placed under the direction of the Archon of the ancient Eleusinian clans, assisted by the priestly families, the Kerykes or the Eumolpidae, who were in charge of the rites which were open to everybody who could speak or understand Greek, regardless of sex or social status, bond or free.

Precisely what form the ceremonies and revelations took when the cult was first established in its later guise is very difficult to determine, as the available information comes mainly from relatively late sources. The *mystae* underwent a course of instruction in the secret knowledge to be imparted to them, together with purifications and asceticisms of various kinds, before they were led forth in procession along the Sacred Way from Athens to Eleusis, pausing at the shrines, temples and baths *en route* to perform the appropriate rites at each. On arrival at Eleusis they bathed in the sea and roamed about the shore with lighted torches in imitation of Demeter's search for Kore recorded in the myth. On the 22nd day of the month of Boedromion, coinciding with the autumnal sowing, after a nocturnal vigil the neophytes repaired to the *telesterion* for the final rites. There, veiled in darkness and in complete silence, probably they underwent a profound emotional experi- ence as they sat on their stools covered with sheepskins and beheld sacred sights which never could be revealed. These may have included some kind of dramatic performance depicting episodes in the life of the sorrowing Mother-goddess, and, according to the post-Christian writer Hippolytus, an ear of corn was reaped in a blaze of light before their wondering eyes, and the birth of a divine child, Brimos (or Iacchos, a variant of Bacchos), was solemnly announced. Whether or not this had reference to a sacred marriage between Zeus and Demeter, symbolized by the union of the hierophant and the chief priestess in their respective rôles, only can be conjectured.

Hippolytus seems to have confused the Phrygian Attis rites with those of Demeter,[89] but if a corn-token was one of the sacred objects revealed to the initiates, as is not improbable, such a ritual marriage would be in accordance with the vegetation setting of the mystery at this season of the year. The germinating ear would be at once the symbol of the harvest of the grain, and that of the immortality of the human soul.[90] And it was from the association of Demeter with the fertility of the land that her Mysteries became the means whereby a joyful resurrection in the delectable meadows of Persephone could be secured.

During the excavation of the sacred precinct reliefs were discovered, as will be considered later,[91] which demonstrate the vegetation background of the cult, together with its chthonian and mortuary character. Moreover, a corn-token symbolism would be in keeping with a harvest festival as a sign of rebirth alike in nature and in the initiate. This is confirmed by a passage in Proclus, the Neoplatonist writer of the fifth century A.D., emended by Lobeck, in which the worshippers are alleged to have gazed up to the sky and cried aloud, "Rain (O Sky), Conceive (O Earth). Be fruitful."[92] This formula, as Farnell pointed out, "savours of a very primi- tive liturgy that closely resembles the famous Dodenaean invoca- tion to Zeus, the Sky-god, and Mother-earth; and it belongs to that part of the Eleusinian ritual 'quod ad frumentum attinet'". Late though it is, it has every indication, as he says, of being "the genuine ore of an old religious stratum sparkling all the more for being found in a waste deposit of Neoplatonic metaphysic".[93] Therefore, it is highly probable that the seasonal cult drama theme recurred at Eleusis, vested as a hereditary possession in ancient priestly families, before it was transformed into a death and resurrection ritual to bestow a blessed hereafter on its initiates, though in the Greek mind the two aspects of fertility always were very closely related.

The Dionysiac

A foreign version of this cultus in a very much less restrained form made its way into Greece in the seventh and sixth centuries B.C. from Phrygia and Thrace when the orgiastic worship of Dionysos was introduced. In his Thraco-Phrygian cradleland his votaries were chiefly women, known as *maenads*, who may have been largely responsible for developing the wilder characteristics of the Dionysiac when they assembled on mountains in remote places to engage in frenzies in order to break down the barrier between the human and divine. With the aid of thrilling music, phallic symbols, the free use of wine and giddy dances in the light of torches, during their emotional orgies they surrendered themselves body and soul to the object of their devotion. Devouring the raw flesh of bulls and calves in a savage sacramental *omophagia*, in which Dionysos under the name of Zagreus was believed to be present, they felt themselves to be so united with him that they proclaimed themselves to be Bacchoi (i.e. mystically united with Dionysos, or Bacchos as he was also called). Originally, however, although Dionysos was a composite deity, including both Thracian and Phrygian elements, he was a god of vegetation who had absorbed several of the characteristic features of the religion of Asia Minor with its deeply laid fertility cults. To these were added ecstasy and immortality as he gathered round him divinities of the countryside and the wilds as well as those of the underworld, until, under the influence of another movement centred in a Thracian hero, Orpheus, the Dionysiac gradually became sobered after it had penetrated to Greece and became established there in the sixth century. But even at Delphi, the seat of the oracle of Apollo, where the cult was firmly entrenched, wild revels at night were held on Mount Parnassus to attain mystical union with Dionysos, who had now gained a place in the Olympian divine family.

The Orphic Teletae

Thus, as the composite myth took shape in Greek tradition he was represented as the son of Zeus by Semele (a Phrygian Earth-goddess), the Hellenic counterparts of the original parents of Zagreus (Dionysos), the Phrygian Dios and Zemele, probably Sky and Earth. In the Orphic literature Demeter was identified with Rhea as the mother of Zeus by whom she conceived Kore, who in her turn bore Dionysos to Zeus; the Cretan Rhea thereby displacing the Thraco-Phrygian goddess Zemele or Semele. But behind this mythological confusion, in the pre-Hellenic background the union of heaven and earth, sym-bolized by the sacred marriage of the Sky-father and the Earth-mother, seems to have been deeply laid in the *teletae*, or initiation rites, which became associated with the names of Dionysos and Orpheus. As Dr Guthrie says, the tales of Dionysos must have been "the central point of the Orphic story for the worshipper even though the legendary Thracian musician was not a Bacchic figure".[94] Similarly, the descent of Dionysos from Demeter, and his fertility functions under the title of Bacchos (i.e. Iacchos), the young god of the Mysteries, gave him a place at Eleusis where in reply to the cry of the torch-bearer (Daduchos), "invoke the god", he was loudly proclaimed "the Son of Semele, Wealth-giver". In other words, the bestower of the fruits of the earth by virtue of his being the offspring of the Earth-goddess.

Once the connexion between Dionysos and Orpheus was established the crude cult-myth of the killing and devouring of Zagreus by the Titans under the direction of Hera, the official wife of Zeus, and his rebirth as Dionysos became allegorized and made the basis of the Orphic doctrine of reincarnation.[95] It then became the purpose of the cult to eradicate the Titanic element in human nature, introduced by Zeus having made mankind from the ashes of the Titans when he destroyed them with his thunderbolt.[96] By participation in the Orphic *teletae* and the adoption of the Orphic way of life, the Dionysian element could be cultivated until at length, after a number of births, the divine soul incarcerated in a mortal body could be liberated and attain virtual deification and eternal bliss.[97]

Thus, when the Thraco-Phrygian ecstatic Dionysos-Bacchos secured a place in the Olympian divine family, and by identification with Iacchos (also in the Eleusinian worship) under the restraining influence of Delphi, his cult acquired a mystical significance. Here, again, a myth and ritual that was closely associated with the death and resurrection seasonal drama was transformed into an allegorized eschatology and hope of immortality—a way of salvation and communion with the spiritual world leading at last to the Elysian Fields, when the "boisterous" Maenads (or "Thyiads" as they were called in Athens and Delphi) turned their flight to the mountains in spring and autumn to more serious account in the Orphic quest of divine unity.

The Maenad tradition, however, continued with its Thyiad tumultuous dancing at the Dionysian festivals at stations such as Panopeus on the road from Athens to Parnassus,[98] when the Dionysiac was brought into relation with the Eleusinian Mysteries. This paved the way for the welter of oriental cults in the Graeco-Roman world after the conquests of Alexander in the fourth century B.C. The wild Bacchanalia, when frenzied Bacchants rushed to the Tiber with blazing torches, was suppressed by the Roman Senate in 185 B.C.,[99] but the strange spectacle of the Phrygian goddess Cybele, the Magna Mater, being conducted through the streets of Rome followed by her mutilated priests (*galli*) gashing themselves and leaping and dancing amid the strains of outlandish music of the Phrygian pipe and the cymbal,[100] remained after her worship had been officially established in the capital in 204 B.C., under pressure of the Hannibalic war. No Roman citizen, however, was allowed to become a *gallus*, or to take part in the procession, until in the time of Claudius (A.D. 41–54) it became naturalized and the celebration of the death and resurrection of the Goddess during the *Hilaria* (March 15th–27th) was presided over by a Roman *archigallus*.[101]

The Attis Cult

This crude Easter drama was essentially a spring festival celebrating the rebirth of nature at the vernal equinox in the setting of the Attis-Cybele cult. After a preliminary fast extending over a week, on the first day of the festival (15th) the finding of the youthful Attis by the Goddess in the reeds of the Phrygian river Sangarius was commemorated by a ceremony known as "the entrance of the reeds". This was enacted in a procession of "reed-bearers" (*cannophori*), and the sacrifice of a six-year-old steer by the *archigallus*. On the 22nd a pine-tree was carried by the *dendrophori* ("tree-bearers") from the wood of Cybele outside Rome to her temple on the Palatine Hill, representing the tree under which Attis was said in the myth to have killed himself by castration, though behind this rite may lie an earlier Phrygian symbolism of Attis in a vegetation capacity as a sacred tree.[102] In any case, the tree was treated as the dead Attis, adorned with violets, and a figure of the god was bandaged like a mummy.[103] After a day of fasting, mourning and lamentation, on the 24th, the *Dies sanguis*, the funeral rites were performed. It was then that the neophytes originally castrated themselves while the *galli* cut their own flesh in a frenzy of flagellation. As a substitute for these wild mutilations to ensure the fruitfulness of the Magna Mater and the renewal of the crops, the *archigallus* cut his own arm amid loud wailing of the Phrygian pipe. After a vigil during which the initiates were united with the Goddess in the relationship of a new Attis, sorrow was turned into joy with the announcement, presumably about dawn, of the resurrection of the god. The next day, the 25th, the *Hilaria* was celebrated with feasting and merriment, until on the 27th the cult drama concluded with the bathing (*lavatio*) of the statue of Cybele in the river Almo.[104]

Cybele and the May Queen

Anything less Roman than these celebrations hardly could be imagined. Their occurrence in the spring leaves little room for doubt that they were a survival of the agrarian seasonal ceremonies of the Phrygian peasantry, and that from them many of the folk customs associated with May Day have been derived. Thus, in the Julian calendar the spring rites observed at the *Hilaria* in March were transferred to 1st May,[105] very much as when the Magna Mater was replaced in Christian tradition by the Virgin Mother, and 25th March became Lady Day in commemoration of the Annunciation of the Incarnation to Mary the Madonna; the month of May was also dedicated to her. The earlier pagan rites, however, still persisted in the folk festival on 1st May when the rôle of Cybele was assumed by the May Queen and that of Attis by the Green Man and his symbol the Maypole decorated with greenery. As the sacred pine-tree representing the emasculated god was taken to the Palatine temple in Rome by the *dendrophori*, so in many parts of peasant Europe youths repaired to the woods after midnight on the dawn of May morning with music and the blowing of horns. There they cut down branches of the trees and decorated them with flowers. At sunrise they returned in procession to the village, fastened the branches over the doors and windows of their houses, and erected the Maypole on the village green. Sometimes a doll was placed in the middle of a garland, or carried by young girls in a basket or cradle from house to house,[106] just as an image of Attis was inserted in the middle of a tree in the Cybele rites.

The decorated Maypole often stood more than sixty feet high, and like Cybele in her car drawn by a yoke of lions, it was conveyed by twenty to forty oxen, each adorned with garlands on the horns, followed by several hundred men, women and children "with great devotion", as Stubbes affirms. They then danced round it.[107] Sometimes, however, only lovers were allowed to dance, presumably because they were the potential founders of families. Not infrequently it was the May Queen herself who rode in a decorated cart drawn by youths or maids of honour, and headed by the Maypole. On her arrival at the green she was crowned and the revels that followed were performed before her throne rather than round the Maypole.[108] Similarly, the May King might be repre-sented by a man clad in a framework covered with leaves—the Jack-in-the-Green—who was taken to the village green on a sledge, or on horseback with the pyramid over him, surrounded by a cavalcade of young men.[109]

As Cybele was the Earth-mother responsible for the flower-ing of the fields, the budding of the trees and the fruitfulness of all living things, so the May Queen often sat in an arbour wreathed with flowers like her prototype in her car, and was treated with similar royal honours, as was her spouse the Green Man in the rôle of Attis. It would seem, therefore, that May Day observances in the folk cultures of Europe with their ingrained vegetation theme represent a survival of the Attis cult in Ancient Rome, and of all that lies behind it in the death and resurrection drama in the Ancient Middle East and the Aegean.

CHAPTER III

The Sacral Kingship

KINGSHIP IN THE NILE VALLEY

THAT the king or his surrogate was a central figure in the seasonal drama and played an essential rôle in its myth and ritual is not open to question. What often may be more debatable are his precise status and function, and the extent, if at all, they have conformed to a common pattern in a given region, such as the Ancient Near East. This problem, indeed, has been one of the storm-centres in the investigation of myth and ritual in recent years,[1] and it cannot be denied that there has been a good deal of conjecture in this field which has not been substantiated by fuller inquiry. For example, Frazer's contention that the king was lineally descended from the medicine-man through the sacred chief[2] is a generalization in the manner typical of the speculations of the school of evolutionary social anthropologists at the turn of the century. Nevertheless, it is true that both in primitive and ancient society chieftainship invariably is and was a sacred office. Moreover, the paramount chief not infrequently has vested his claims on descent from a mythical ancestor or divinity which has given him a firmly established unique position in the community, sometimes carrying with it divine status.

Whatever may have been the hereditary succession and its causes lying behind a ruler in specific cases, which hardly can be reduced to a single principle, the occupant of the throne, or of the "sacred stool", has tended to be in the nature of a ritual expert engaged in the exercise of sacral functions, particularly in connexion with the vegetation cycle and the supernatural control of the weather. So intimate, in fact, has been his relation to fecundity in nature and to the well-being of society that in the words of Dr Seligman "he has not been allowed to become ill or senile lest, with his diminishing vigour, the cattle should sicken and fail to bear their increase, the crops should wither in the fields, and men, stricken with disease, should die in ever increasing numbers".[3]

The Shilluk Kingship

The classical example of this practice is that recorded among the Shilluk of the Nilotic Sudan which seemed to confirm Frazer's theory of "the dying god".[4] The evidence, however, has now been questioned by Professor Evans-Pritchard, who regards the tradition as a fiction that has arisen from the dual personality of the king who was thought to be both himself and the embodiment of the dead ancestral ruler Nyikang, the culture hero of the Shilluk. In this capacity he reigned as Nyikang, and then disappeared like his prototype. That Shilluk kings usually met a violent death is not disputed, but, it is suggested, this generally was the result of their leading a rebellion.[5] But the killing of kings has been a firmly established practice in Africa[6] and usually it has been connected with the renewal of vegetation and rain-making. Thus, the Shilluk *reth* (king) invokes his ancestor at the sacrifices for rain held at the shrine of Nyikang by virtue of the position he occupies in the ritual order as the royal high-priest.[7] Being the official representative of the creator of the nation (i.e. Nyikang), he becomes responsible for the maintenance of its food-supply, the right ordering and consolidation of society, and the control of the weather on which the harvests depend. Therefore, the throne must always have a virile and healthy occupant because the Kingship is its dynamic and unifying centre. To dispose of the king when his natural forces show signs of waning and of so becoming a less potent bond between the human and the divine orders is a logical result of this conception of the office.

The Pharaoh in Egypt

Although there is no adequate evidence that this custom was adopted in Ancient Egypt, the Egyptians, nevertheless, regarded the kingship in much the same way as the Shilluk and other modern East African tribes deeply rooted in the subsoil out of which the higher civilization of the Nile valley grew in the fourth millennium B.C. That customs have survived throughout the ages in this region without much significant change is shown by peculiar arm-rings still worn by the Masai which are identical with two found in an Egyptian grave of between 3000 and 2700 B.C. containing the body of a foreigner from Punt or Somaliland; a people with whom contacts were maintained in the Old Kingdom.[8]

Before the unification of Upper and Lower Egypt and the establishment of the Pharaonic dynasty, traditionally attributed to Menes about 3200 B.C., each nome was believed to have been ruled by its local god as its king, much in the same way as the Shilluk regarded Nyikang as the original ancestor of the reigning *reth*, and to have bestowed his supernatural powers and gifts upon him at his enthronement on the sacred stool when he became incarnate in its new occupant. In Egypt the ancient god-kings were succeeded by the dynastic human rulers, who, however, were also regarded as incarnations of the gods, as the heirs and successors of their divine predecessors. Thus, the predynastic king Scorpion, who probably preceded Menes, was regarded as an incarnation of the Sky-god Horus. When his worshippers in the north conquered Upper Egypt their rulers reigned as incarnations of Horus and made Edfu (Behdet) their cult-centre. Therefore, Horus the Behdetite became the predominant figure in the kingship, represented as the last of the god-kings in visible form and henceforth embodied in the Pharaohs upon whom he bestowed his Horus-name.

Osiris, however, was also thought to have lived on earth as a culture hero like Nyikang, and with him, as we have seen,[9] the kings were identified at death after having reigned as Horus during their lifetime. Here, again, the nature and function of the royal office were centred in the life-giving powers of the gods whom it represented in their several capacities. The same conception reappears in the solar theology where the Pharaoh is considered by some Egyptologists to have been the son and successor of the first king Re.[10] As deities became more and more merged with one another he became identified with

Atum, the god of Heliopolis, who was regarded in the Heliopolitan theology as another aspect of Re, having emerged from Nun, the primeval waters of Chaos, at the creation, appearing in the form of a phoenix on the top of the primordial "sandhill" which became the centre of the earth.[11] On this sacred spot "the House of the Obelisk" was erected as the solar temple *par excellence*.

Memphis, however, also claimed to stand upon land that had arisen from the primeval ocean, and after the union of Upper and Lower Egypt Menes established the capital there. Its chief god was Ptah, who was proclaimed the sole creator of the universe with all the other gods as his attributes, mani⁄ festations, or conceptions of his mind. Thus, Atum was repre⁄ sented as his tongue and heart because he created the Helio⁄ politan Ennead, and these were said to be the organs of creation when an attempt was made between the Third and Fifth Dynasties to reconcile the Memphite and Heliopolitan theogonies. Ptah, nevertheless, remained supreme as the "Great One who begot the gods" and called all things into being by the thought of his "heart" (mind). He settled the nomes, made the cities, installed the gods in their temples and their embodi⁄ ments, the Pharaohs, in the throne. Therefore, for more than three thousand years the coronation was held at Memphis in a dual rite under the auspices of Ptah in which was re⁄enacted apparently the original ceremonies performed when the "two lands" were unified in a single dynasty.

Finally, in the New Kingdom, when the capital was perma⁄ nently established at Thebes in the middle of the second millennium B.C. and its god Amon⁄Re became the head of the pantheon, combining in his personality the local Theban god Amon with the old Heliopolitan Sun⁄god Re, he was represented as embodying himself in the king and, in this form, visiting the queen in order to beget a successor to the throne.[12] It was in this way that Queen Hatshepsut, the daughter of Thutmose I, was alleged to have been conceived in the Eighteenth Dynasty, and the unique situation of a woman occupying the throne was justified by the fiction of a divine visitation of Amon-Re to the queen-mother for the express purpose of "placing in her body" his daughter who was thereby divinely ordained to "exercise the beneficent kingship in this entire land".[13] This placed her in the same position as the first three kings of the Fifth Dynasty, who were similarly accredited with divine paternity. Indeed, all Pharaohs were regarded as having been born of a union between a god and the queen.[14] Therefore, whether it be in the capacity of Horus or of an incarnation of Re, Ptah, Atum or Amon-Re, they reigned with a divine status embodying the Creator-god and inherited from him his nature and beneficent functions.

After the incorporation of the Osiris myth in the solar cultus in the Sixth Dynasty their position was further enhanced by every Pharaoh being at once the son of Re in his various manifestations and syncretisms, the embodiment of all the deities of the "two lands", and the successor and son of Osiris reigning as the living Horus who had been established in the throne by divine decree when Osiris was vindicated by the heavenly tribunal. From birth onwards the divine qualities in the future occupant of the throne were carefully nurtured, and when he came of age he underwent a ceremonial purification before he was crowned at the Dual Shrines of Upper and Lower Egypt respectively.

The Coronation Rite in the Pyramid Texts

Precisely what took place at the Coronation can only be determined from information that can be gleaned from the Pyramid texts, the temple reliefs of the New Kingdom and the Mystery play that was performed at the accession of Senusert I, the script of which occurs on a papyrus roll dated at about 2000 B.C. In the Pyramid texts there are references to the crowning of the kings of Buto in Lower Egypt.[15] In the Dual Shrines the two crowns appear to have been placed on the head of the Pharaoh in order to bestow upon him the supernatural power inherent in them,[16] but in the Pyramid texts only the predynastic red crown of Lower Egypt is mentioned.[17] The doors of the shrine containing it were opened and the crown itself in which the Goddess Neith of Sais was immanent was addressed as the "Fiery One", the "Great One", the "Magician" and the "Eye of Horus".[18]

The king declared that he had come forth from the Goddess, yet because as "Horus he had fought to protect his Eye" she seems also to have come forth from him and to have been reborn by his coronation—"how beautiful is thy face when thou art new and young". The Horus Eye, being the means by which Osiris was revivified in the myth, was the symbol and seat of royal power and beneficence. Therefore, the crown as its embodiment was regarded as the efficacious sacramental sign of its virtue, addressed as the goddess. Consequently, it was a mythological concept of great complexity with so many life-giving connotations reacting one on the other that the Eye of Horus stood at once for royal potency in all its many and various forms and manifestations in relation to both the living and the dead, derived from the Sky-god Horus brought into relation with the son of Osiris. It was also the personification of the protective goddess, and the "daughter of the Sun-god". In all these several aspects it was essentially the source of life and power, and so was immanent in the crown which gave the new king the plenitude of divine potency by virtue of his relationship with his celestial father, the Sun-god and the creator of Atum—"the Great One has borne thee; the Exalted One has adorned thee". This enabled him to reign as the living Horus—"for thou art Horus who has fought for the protection of thine Eye". Finally, he was made "to stand over the land which has come forth from Atum", and so to be seen by Re, his father.[19]

The Temple Reliefs

In the birth scenes in the temple of Hatshepsut at Deir el Bahari the presentation of the infant to the protecting goddesses is shown, and the presiding Goddess Meskhent declares, "I surround thee with protection like Re. Life and good fortune are given to thee more than to all mortals; I have destined thee for life, luck, health, excellence, affluence, joy, sustenance, food, victuals, and all other good things. Thou wilt appear as King of Upper and Lower Egypt for many *Sed*-festivals, while thou art living, remaining fortunate—while thy heart is in joy with thy Ka in these thy Two Lands on the throne of Horus for ever."[20] Then follows the presentation to Amon, her heavenly father, who addresses her as "daughter of my loins, whom I love, royal image, thou who wilt make real thy risings on the throne of the Horus of the living, for ever". Finally she is shown, acknowledged and worshipped by the other gods, and the divine promises made to her are inscribed upon the celestial books.[21]

The birth and divine recognition of the anomalous queen duly accomplished, she is next represented visiting the temples "beautiful to look upon" and "like unto a god". On her arrival at Heliopolis she was crowned by the king, Thutmose I, and set upon his throne before Amon-Re in the presence of the nobles and state officials, who did homage to her. Entering the sanctuary, she is depicted having the white crown of Lower Egypt placed on her head by the priests in the guise of Horus and Seth, and then the red crown of Upper Egypt. Wearing the double crown, she appears seated on a throne between the two gods of the south and the north (i.e. Horus and Seth), who tie together under her feet lotus flowers and branches of papyrus, the emblems of Lower and Upper Egypt, to symbolize the union of the "two lands". Finally, arrayed in her crown and mantle and holding in her hands the scourge and flail of Osiris, her procession round the walls of the sanctuary is shown to indicate her taking possession of the domains of Horus and Seth which henceforth she will protect. The scenes conclude with her being led to the shrine of Amon to be embraced by her celestial father as his daughter, duly installed by him in the throne of Horus.[22]

These reliefs depict the principal episodes in the coronation ceremony in Ancient Egypt from proto-historic times to the days of the New Kingdom. Thus, after various preliminary purifications by priests impersonating Horus and Seth (or Horus and Thoth), the Pharaoh visited the Dual Shrines of

Upper and Lower Egypt before being crowned with the two diadems by Horus and Seth, embraced by the god of the temple, and led in procession round the walls. An enthrone⁄ment ceremony seems to have followed in which the new king was again purified and presented first to the gods and then to the people. His official names were proclaimed, the crowns were presented and sacrifice was offered.

The Mystery Play of the Accession

From the Mystery play of the Accession of Senusert,[23] the second king of the Twelfth Dynasty, it appears that the Pharaoh visited a number of cities on the royal barge imme⁄diately before his coronation, and at each town, supported by the princes, officials, courtiers and others, he played the part of Horus in the enactment of the installation myth and ritual. By so doing he was identified with Horus and established an efficacious relationship between the throne and the land over which he was called to reign in his divine capacity, and on which its prosperity depended. Thus, the victory of Horus over Seth in the myth was among the scenes, described as Horus taking possession of the Eye (i.e. of his royal power located in the crown), and the treading of barley by oxen on the threshing⁄floor, symbolizing the dismemberment of Osiris by Seth and his fellow conspirators in a vegetation setting. This was avenged by Horus (i.e. the king), who ultimately revivified his father (Osiris). The coronation of the Pharaoh was then enacted in a series of scenes which included his investiture with the royal insignia, censings, the distribution of half⁄loaves of bread as the symbol of life, to those who made homage to him, and crowning with the predynastic two feathers, thereby show⁄ing the great antiquity and northern origin of the drama in the Delta. Next followed dirges in honour of the dead Osiris by two women in the guise of Isis and Nephthys as a prologue to the burial rites when the corpse had been "found" by the priests called "spirit⁄seekers" impersonating Thoth. The "Opening of the Mouth" ceremonies were indicated by the articles offered to them, and the play concluded with a scene portraying the ascent of Osiris to heaven, and a banquet. Thus, the myth integral to the kingship was ritually enacted to establish in the throne of Horus its new occupant with all that this was believed to involve for the well-being of the nation, of mankind and of the natural order.

The Toilet Ceremonies

It was not, however, only at the time of the accession that he was solemnly installed in his divine office and status, and publicly acknowledged by the god as his son after he had been purified with "the water of life which is in the sky" in order to unite him with the Sun-god. These rites in essence had to be performed every morning in the daily royal renewal ritual. In early childhood the heir apparent was sprinkled with water by the priests in the guise of Atum and Thoth, or Re-Harakhte and Amon, and he was then regarded as having received official filial recognition by the god.[24] After his accession the lustrations were repeated in the Toilet Ceremonies each day in the House of the Morning as a re-enactment of the coronation rites, just as the coronation purification was a renewal of that undergone in infancy. As at the coronation, the new sovereign was endowed with the divine qualities of his sacred office by a priest impersonating the god Yahes (*I'ho*) with the words "I purify thee with the water of all life and good fortune, all stability, all health and happiness"[25]—symbolized in the scenes depicting these ablutions by water issuing from vessels as streams of the *crux ansata*[26]—so in the daily Toilet Ceremonies he was continually revivified. After the asperges he was censed to unite him with Horus and he was then given balls of natron to chew to complete his rebirth. Finally, he ascended the stairs of the great window to behold his celestial father and symbolize his rising like the morning sun from the waters before being vested and crowned. Therefore, as the Sun was purified and reborn every morning in the House beneath the Horizon, so his earthly incarnation had to undergo the same daily ritual process in the House of the Morning to identify himself with the lord and giver of life.

These rites had their counterparts in the temple liturgy. Every morning at dawn the cult-image in the Heliopolitan solar temple was asperged, censed, anointed, vested and crowned with the royal diadem of Upper and Lower Egypt, and presented with the flail and the crook and the sceptre.[27] What had been done to the Sun-god and his incarnation on the throne had to be done to the image, their visible local embodiment. All three ritually were one and the same and so had to receive identical treatment. When, however, the solar theology was Osirianized, under the influence of the Osiris myth the ritual to some extent was transformed. The god in the shrine now became regarded as the dead Osiris requiring revivification every morning. Therefore, the Pharaoh in his Horus manifestation took the dead god in his arms and restored him to life. Then he performed the Toilet of the image, made offerings to it and replaced it in the shrine. In most of the reliefs the king himself is represented as the sole celebrant in the temple Toilet liturgy, the object of the official worship being to obtain the continual favour of the divinities concerned with the well-being of the Pharaoh. But in fact he only performed the rites in person on comparatively rare occasions, his place being taken by a deputy and his assistants who had to undergo the same purifications as the king, since they were impersonating him, and when the cult had been Osirianized they fulfilled the rôle of Horus.

The Sed-festival

In addition to these daily renewal rites a special ritual observance was held—the *Sed*-festival—at specific intervals to rejuvenate the throne and its occupant. Sometimes it appears to have been celebrated thirty years after the accession and then repeated every three years, but it might be performed at shorter intervals.[28] It is probably the oldest feast of which any trace remains, going back before the time of Menes.[29] Its date usually coincided with that of the coronation, namely, the first day of "The Season of Coming Forth" after the raising of the *Djed*-column at the Khoiak festival when the inundation was subsiding. Therefore, it was intimately associated with the mysteries of Osiris, though he did not play any part in the *Sed*-festival, which was essen-tially a rejuvenescence and re-investiture of the reigning king already established on the throne to confirm his beneficent rule over Upper and Lower Egypt, first accomplished by Menes.

Unless a new temple was created for the purpose, a Festival Hall containing the great throne was constructed within an existing sanctuary equipped with obelisks and a robing chamber (the "Palace") of the House of the Morning (*per duat*). To it the gods from other shrines came, personified in their statues, and were accommodated in the court, having been met and visited by the king and his court upon their arrival. Offerings of the royal bounty were made to them in return for which they gave "life and prosperity" to the king.[30] For the next few days processions followed in which the Pharaoh, the statues of the gods and their priesthoods, the standard of the Royal Placenta, fan-bearers and attendants took part. Seated on his throne the king received pledges of loyalty and had his feet washed by two courtiers before he entered the "palace" to re-vest.

From the reliefs it would seem that more loyal addresses and exchange of gifts followed, and then he went to the double throne preceded by the ensign of the god Upuaut of Siut, and sat alternately on each of the thrones to symbolize his rule over Upper and Lower Egypt. To assert his power over the land he ceremonially crossed the area marked out in the temple court known as the "field" (i.e. the whole of Egypt), thereby fulfilling one of the chief purposes of the festivals.[31] Finally, he was carried on a litter to the chapel of Horus of Libya, where wrapped in a cloak he held the sceptre, flail and crook as the symbols of his royal office and its powers, and sat on the throne to receive the blessing of the gods and the allegiance of his subjects after having been proclaimed four times. In return he made appropriate offerings to the gods, took off his cloak and, clad only in a kilt having the tail of an animal, with the crown of Upper Egypt on his head and carrying a short sceptre and whisk, he ran four ritual courses offering to Upuaut his insignia. The proceedings concluded with a visit to the chapels of Horus of Edfu and Seth of Ombos, where the priests of each gave the Pharaoh a bow and arrows to shoot an arrow to each of the four points of the compass, just as he was enthroned four times facing in one of the four cardinal directions.[32]

Since the purpose of the festival appears to have been the renewal of the occupant of the throne in his kingship rather than the establishment of the succession as in the coronation rite,[33] it was his dominion over the forces which he controlled, and the maintenance of beneficial relations between heaven and earth, that had to be secured by the ritual. Apparently the Osiris myth was not re-enacted as in the mysteries which preceded it, and it seems improbable that the king impersonated Osiris and assumed his insignia, as has been supposed.[34] Nevertheless, as it was performed to renew and strengthen his life and to re-establish him in his divine office, the Osirian theme was inherent in it. This is shown in the declaration, "thou beginnest thy renewal, beginneth to flourish again like the infant god of the Moon, thou art young again year by year, like Nun at the beginning of the ages, thou art reborn by renewing thy festival of *Sed*".[35]

THE KINGSHIP IN MESOPOTAMIA

Although the kingship in Mesopotamia never occupied the same consolidating position as it did in the Nile valley, being organized on a local rather than a national basis in a conglomeration of city-states so that no Sumerian ruler (*patesi*) was a cohesive force, albeit it was regarded as a divine institution. Indeed, in the traditional king-lists it is said to have "descended from heaven", presumably as a gift of the gods, before and after the Flood in the third millennium B.C. The royal insignia originally rested "before the throne of Anu"[36] and as the assembly of the gods conferred kingship on Marduk, giving him the sceptre, the throne and the "royal robe" (?),[37] so the same divine power immanent in the insignia was bestowed upon human beings destined by the gods to occupy the throne on earth. Thus, Hammurabi did not hesitate to declare that he had been called to the kingship by Anu and Enlil "to cause justice to prevail in the land" when he established his rule over Southern Mesopotamia and made Babylon the capital.[38]

The Sumerian Kings

Before the Flood royalty was conferred only on a very few Sumerian kings who were said to have reigned by divine prerogative and selection, and to have lived to fabulous ages like Methuselah in Hebrew tradition. With the exception of Dumuzi or Tammuz, they were all mortals detailed to become "shepherds of the people".[39] Only a remnant of the population survived the Deluge and the Kingship had to be started afresh by a second descent from heaven. Dumuzi alone continued the antediluvian régime in the legendary Second Dynasty of Erech, between Lugal-banda and Gilgamesh.[40] The "Shepherd" *par excellence*, however, was the historical Sumerian ruler of Umma, Lugal-zaggisi, who at the end of the Early Dynastic period, after he had attacked and subdued Lagash, introduced the new title, "King of the Land", under the sanction of Enlil. As the "son born of Nisa-ba, fed by the holy milk of Ninhursaga, he assumed dominion over the entire country and prayed that he might fulfil his destiny and always be "the shepherd at the head of the flock".[41]

Although in fact the rulers of Ur, Kish and Lagash had all exercised a similar jurisdiction on the authority of Enlil, who himself was the national god having universal sovereignty over Mesopotamia as a whole, Lugal-zaggisi went beyond his predecessors in claiming ascendancy over all countries from east to west, from the Persian Gulf ("the Lower Sea") to the Mediterranean ("the Upper Sea").[42] Consequently, when in due course he was defeated by Sargon of Akkad his conqueror called himself "the ruler of the Four Quarters", while the son of Sargon, Naram-Sin, assumed the title "King of the Four Quarters", thereby adopting the designation of the gods Enlil, Anu and Shamash.[43] Although no attempt was made to equate the king with these supreme deities, the new title did carry the implication of universal rule on earth comparable with that of the heavenly counterparts of the king. In the Third Dynasty of Ur, as the practice was continued, to it was added "King of Sumer and Akkad", and in a Tammuz liturgy the title was appended to eleven kings of Ur and Isin,[44] where it was not uncommon for royal descent to be claimed from a god and suckling by a goddess.[45]

No Sumerian king, however, was a cohesive force in the country as a whole, because the city-state was the unit of the political organization ruled over by the *patesi*, the "tenant-farmer" of the principal local god, renewed annually in his office at the New Year Festival. In this capacity, as well as being the chief priest of the temple representing the god on earth, he stood at the head of the civic administration as law-giver, judge and commander. To exercise his functions as the tenant-in-chief of the god he required a staff of officials among whom the *sangu mah* administered the temple revenues and its organization as a kind of high-priest while the *ensi* acted as the governor of the city-state to manage the god's estate in its temporal aspects and maintain law and order, resorting often to divination to ascertain the will of the god. The two offices, however, frequently were combined and held by the same person.

In times of crisis members of a ruling house might claim the title of king (i.e. *lugal* or "chief man") instead of *patesi* or *ensi*, though in fact only a few of the early dynastic rulers adopted this designation.[46] The first of these, Ur-Nina of Lagash (*c.* 2900 B.C.), seems to have been engaged mainly in building temples, digging irrigation canals and fortifications, but his grandson Eannatum waged war on the city of Umma to the north, and claimed to have conquered Ur, Erech, Kish, Mari, and even Elam, thereby becoming virtually lord of Sumer and Akkad. All this he attributed to his having been established in his office by Enlil, endowed with strength by Ningirsu, the city-god of Lagash, and suckled by Ninhursaga, the Goddess of the Earth, often regarded as the Great Mother.[47]

In Mesopotamia, therefore, the Sumerian city-state was under a threefold control with the governor occupying a permanent status in the civic government, and the chief priest a corre‚ sponding position in the sacred organization, while the king only held office for a limited period when crises arose. As these, however, were so frequent as to be almost perennial, the King‚ ship seems to have become a permanent institution in some cities. Moreover, when the governor or king was himself a priest he established his claim to rule as the *lugal* by assuming priestly functions in a temple, like Lugal‚zaggisi, the priest of Anu, who when he conquered Sumer became the priest of Enlil and ruled in his name. Gilgamesh is represented as the human despotic king of Erech (Uruk) in Southern Babylonia, but he was two‚thirds a divine being, and Gudea, the *ensi* of Lagash (*c.* 2400 B.C.), was the steward of the god Ningirsu whose temple he was commissioned to build.

The Babylonian Monarchy

When the city‚state gained the leadership it gave its name to the dynasty in the king‚lists—Ur, Kish, Erech, Isin and Larsa —thereby preparing the way for a national state as an extension of the political and religious organization which was to find expression in the myths based on the cosmic state ruled by the gods. It was not, however, until Anu and Enlil chose Marduk to be exalted over all the gods of the earth and to exercise the administrative functions of Enlil, when his city Babylon became the capital, that Marduk's human steward, Hammurabi, at‚ tained a status at all comparable to that of the Pharaoh in Egypt. Then he was raised up, he declared, to be "the exalted prince, the worshipper of the gods, to cause justice to prevail in the land".[48] But even so, Marduk never occupied the position in Mesopotamia that Osiris held in the Nile valley. He was not the god of the dead, nor did Hammurabi, or any Babylonian or Assyrian king, reign in the capacity of Nabu, the son of Marduk, like the Pharaoh as Horus.

Furthermore, when Hammurabi unified the state into an Empire with Babylon as the capital and Marduk as the head of the pantheon, it was only a temporary stability that was attained. The earlier triad of great gods, Anu, Enlil and Ea

(Enki), with their respective priesthoods, were only partially eclipsed, each continuing to rule over one of the three divisions of the universe allotted to him, heaven, earth and the waters. Therefore, Marduk was never regarded as the creator and source of all the other gods like Re or Ptah. Rather he was a syncretistic figure with whom the functions of the other gods were identified. Thus, it was in his Tammuz rôle that he was an Osirian figure, "creator of the grain and plants, causing the grass to spring up",[49] and giving to the kingship its sacred character and significance.

But although divine election remained the foundation of the institution until the end of the Assyrian Empire, as the favour of the gods always could be withdrawn on any pretext, the monarchy lacked the secure unique position it held in Egypt throughout its long unbroken history. Indeed, there were times in Mesopotamia when the gods appointed no human kings on earth at all, and the change in supremacy of both a city-god and his steward as the agents of Enlil of Nippur was a recurrent phenomenon, as, for example, when the city of Isin and its goddess Nininsina gave place to Babylon and Marduk and Babylon to Ashur, the Assyrian Marduk and Enlil. Behind all these vicissitudes the national deity, Enlil, remained as the executive divine authority, but, nevertheless, the Babylonian kings were never equated with him as the Pharaohs were with Amon-Re and Osiris, or with Hathor and Isis.

The Accession Rites

Thus, in Mesopotamia there was neither a strictly observed hereditary succession to the throne through the eldest son, nor a mythological qualification of royal descent. However the choice of the gods may have been determined, about which information is lacking, in Assyria when a successor had been selected he repaired to the "Palace of the Crown Prince", or "House of Succession", in the month of Nisan to be inducted before the gods Ashur, Sin, Shamash, Nabu and Marduk, who confirmed his "primacy".[50] He then received the insignia in the temple of the city-god in accordance with the Sumerian precedents at Erech, where in the temple of Inanna (Ishtar) the ruler approached the throne of "the Lady of the Crown", Nin-men-na, having taken the sceptre in his hand and placed the crown on his head. He then received a new name from "the Lady of the Sceptre", Nin-pa.[51]

In Assyrian times the king was carried on a throne to the temple of Ashur in the ancient city of the god from whom it takes its name (the Assyrian Marduk). On his arrival he dismounted, kissed the ground, made an oblation of incense and deposited his gifts before the statue of Ashur. These included a gold bowl containing oil with which he may have been anointed. He was then crowned by the priest with the words, "may Ashur and Ninhil (his spouse), the lords of thy diadem, put it upon thee for a hundred years". Delivering to him the sceptre, he said, "with thy straight sceptre make thy land wide. May Ashur grant thee quick satisfaction, justice and peace."[52] The procession re-formed and when the duly installed king reached his palace the nobles and officials did homage, placed their insignia before him, and took them again at his request. Rejoicings may have greeted the new reign, but if they did they are not recorded. The coronation observances, in fact, were singularly restrained and devoid of any public acclamation.

The Status and Function of Kings

The sovereign had been chosen by the gods and sealed by the prescribed ritual but he was never accorded the complete divine status of the Pharaoh in Egypt, even though he might have been thought originally to have been begotten of Anu or Enlil and born of the Goddess. Nevertheless, he officiated as high-priest and exercised his royal functions in that capacity as a ritual expert occupying a central position in the cultus, concerned particularly with the interpretation of the will of the gods and maintaining right relations with them for the well-being of the nation by the due performance of the daily cult for which he was responsible. He was an executive officer of the gods, but he was never the dynamic centre of the cosmic order.

Whether or not the deification of kings in Mesopotamia was confined to those who became the bridegroom of the Goddess, as Frankfort suggests,[53] while unquestionably they not in-frequently claimed to be the son of various gods and to have been nourished with the milk of goddesses,[54] their human parentage also was recognized and in practice their status often was that of a servant rather than a son.[55] Even Dumuzi (Tammuz), the "faithful son of the waters which came from the earth", was dependent upon his divine mother-spouse Ishtar for his release from the underworld; the vegetation background of the myth reflecting the Mesopotamian sense of insecurity and uncertainty in a world in which neither the throne nor the seasons nor the geographical conditions could provide stability and permanence. Human destinies were in the hands of the gods and their ways were past finding out. Kings might boast of divine ancestry or nurture, but they had to humble them-selves annually before the statue of their patron and his priest, relinquish their regalia and submit to re-installation at his hands. Similarly, their people were in a state of turmoil in the city until the fate of society during the coming year was deter-mined by the gods who throughout held the initiative.[56] Therefore, in Mesopotamian myth and ritual the kingship, like everything else, was in a state of flux.

THE KINGSHIP IN PALESTINE

The King in the Ras Shamra Texts

In the Ras Shamra texts the seasonal motif recurs in the Aleyan-Baal cycle with Baal in the Tammuz rôle, and Danel and Krt as divine kings exercising control over the crops.[57] Thus, Baal was essentially a rain and fertility god whose descent into the nether regions caused the languishing of the earth, whatever may have been its duration, a matter upon which the texts are by no means clear. Nowhere is it said to be an annual occur-rence, but the death of the god certainly seems to have been equated with the drought in the hot summer,[58] and he is said to "appoint the due seasons of his rains".[59] Moreover, he engaged in a victorious struggle first with Yam, the god of the seas and rivers, to become the viceroy of the supreme god El, and then with Athtar, god of the springs and wells, his rival claimant.[60] Having established himself as king, he next deter-mined to destroy Mot, the god of aridity and death, and with this end in view he descended to the underworld in search of him. It was during his absence that rain and vegetation ceased on the earth until he was revived with the help of his sister Anat, who destroyed Athtar and defeated Mot. It only remained for Baal to marry the goddess Anat and ascend the throne unchallenged under the suzerainty of El to exercise his life-giving functions as the god of rain and fertility.[61]

Although the texts are silent about the relation of Baal to the Ugaritic king, apart from a passing reference to the king offering sacrifices to Baal,[62] if, as seems probable, they represent a cult drama, they must have had the same significance as had the corresponding rituals elsewhere in the Near East respecting the renewal of the vitality in nature and the well-being of society. Therefore, as Baal in the cult myth was seated on his throne by the gods after his victorious struggle with the forces of death and sterility, so his earthly counterpart it would seem must have played the customary rôle of the central figure in the drama. Therefore, it would be very surprising if the Ugaritic king did not perform the same functions in the cultus as his opposite numbers in the rest of the Fertile Crescent.

The Hebrew Cult of Kingship

Although the Israelites were not typical nomads and readily accommodated themselves to agricultural conditions during the period of their settlement in Palestine from the middle of the thirteenth century until about 1100 B.C., in Hebrew tradi-tion Yahweh, unlike the Canaanite deities in Ugaritic mytho-logy, was not in origin a vegetation god. His immediate background is represented as that of the desert,[63] as was later stressed by the prophets,[64] and under the influence of the mono-Yahwists the conflict between him and the Canaanite pantheon and its cultus was more pronounced. As early as the eleventh century this became apparent when Gideon, having been elevated to hereditary kingship in Manasseh, deposited a gold-plated statue of Yahweh in a sanctuary at Ophrah and made this royal shrine so popular a cult centre that eventually "all Israel went awhoring after it", as the Deuteronomic editor lamented, viewing the situation from the standpoint of the subsequent Jerusalem cultus.[65] The success of Gideon's sanctuary, however, shows that Yahweh was becoming recognized as the god of Canaan with an increasing popular following which in the days of the Davidic monarchy became consolidated in the worship of the Temple on Mount Zion when the Jebusite fortress was made the capital. Nevertheless, side by side with this growth in Yahwism, the syncretistic movement persisted as Yahweh himself came to be regarded as a particular national divinity exercising much the same functions as the Canaanite gods and their cults.

Therefore, after the covenant with the house of David had been ratified, in the sanctuary in Jerusalem, David and his successors performed the customary rites like other sacred kings in the Near East, except that they did so as intermediaries rather than as earthly embodiments of Yahweh.[66] David, in fact, was later described as the anointed servant and son of Yahweh in a Messianic capacity,[67] and during his lifetime he wore an ephod when he danced ecstatically before the Ark of the Covenant which was the chief cult object embodying the divine presence.[68] When it was installed in the shrine erected for it on Mount Zion, which henceforth was to be the abode of the national deity, Yahweh was besought to be gracious to the reigning sovereign for the sake of his servant David.[69] His son and successor Solomon three times a year is said to have offered burnt offerings and peace offerings on the altar he had erected there to Yahweh, and to have burnt incense upon it in his priestly vocation.[70]

But although the king was a sacred person and the cult leader, the monarchy came to be regarded with the gravest suspicion by the prophetic movement in the period immediately preceding the Exile, doubtless because of its approximation to the traditional Kingship cult.[71] Thus, it was represented in the book of Samuel as an affront to Yahweh[72] as he was conceived by the ethical monotheists who by the eighth century had become a powerful anti-monarchical element in the nation. Their reaction doubtless prepared the way for the survival of the theocracy when the monarchy came to an end in spite of Nathan's decree that the Davidic dynasty should endure for ever.[73] The traditional Abrahamic covenant ratified at Sinai remained the consolidating centre in the post-exilic community independent of the kingship and its cultus. Then the royal office was re-interpreted in terms of the Messiahship and acquired an eschatological significance. The covenant with the house of David became the Messianic reign of Yahweh's adopted son as "a priest for ever after the order of Melchizedek", enthroned eternally on Mount Zion as Yahweh's vicegerent on earth, "having neither beginning nor end of life".[74]

The equation, however, of the Davidic covenant with the traditional Canaanite royal priesthood of Melchizedek shows how very deeply laid was the ancient kingship theme in pre-exilic Israel and its conception of the Davidic dynasty. When he captured the Jebusite stronghold (Jerusalem) David took over the priesthood (which may have been that of the god Zedek)[75] and placed himself at the head of the hierarchy. In adapting its myth and ritual to Yahwism he could hardly fail to have transmitted to the Jerusalem cultus some of the established elements in the Jebusite worship, however much they may have been modified.[76] There is no reason to suppose that he himself, or any Hebrew king, ever assumed the rôle of the incarnate god like Pharaoh in Egypt, but as Mr Snaith says, "it is clear that the well-being of the nation was regarded as being intimately bound up with the well-being of the king".[77] This found cultic expression in a myth and ritual which had their antecedents in the sacral kingship so firmly established in the religion of the Near East.[78]

Even after the fall of the monarchy the kingship tradition survived when the high-priest combined the cultic prerogatives formerly exercised by the king with those of the priesthoods.[79] Zerubbabel on becoming a governor of Jerusalem in 520 B.C.

as a descendant of David was hailed as the deputy of Yahweh, and occupied a position in the cultus comparable to that assigned to "the prince" by Ezekiel.[80] He ruled, however, in conjunction with the high-priest who was the guardian of the temple and its worship.[81] When his mission came to an end the high-priest alone remained as the consolidating centre of the nation, and around him as the alleged descendant of Eleazer, the eldest son of Aaron, the hierarchic organization and the cultus developed when the Temple was rebuilt and the sacrificial system restored. Then, reverting to type, the civic and ecclesiastical functions of the ruler were combined in one and the same sacred office as the focal-point of the theocratic nation until its final disruption in A.D. 70.

THE KINGSHIP IN THE AEGEAN

Passing from the Fertile Crescent to the Aegean, in which transition the Canaanite theogony and its mythology occupied an intermediate position, Enlil or Marduk, or Hadad and Baal, had their counterparts in the west in Zeus, just as Innana-Ishtar, Astarte, Asherah and Anat corresponded to Aphrodite, Athena, Hera and other Aegean goddesses. The Ugaritic mythology, however, lies midway between that of Mesopotamia and the Aegean. In its later Phoenician form it is closer to the Anatolian and Greek pantheons than to those of Babylonia. Zeus, for instance, was "the father of gods and men", like the Canaanite El, and both were very closely associated with the bull as a fertility symbol in the spring rites in which the king-god played the leading rôle in conjunction with the Goddess as his consort.

The Palace Cult at Knossos

At Knossos the Minoan priest-kings appear to have performed their chief functions in the "Room of the Throne" in which an elaborately carved throne stood with frescoes of griffins behind it and guarding the entrance to the inner shrine. On either side of the throne and in front of the shrine are stone benches, while opposite to it is a tank probably used for lustrations. To the

left an overturned oil-jar was found, perhaps employed for
anointing, as Evans suggests, when the king was enthroned
there "as the adopted Son on earth of the Great Mother of its
island mysteries". One of these priest-kings, he thinks, may
have been depicted in the palace in a relief of a figure wearing
a plumed lily crown and leading, as he supposes, a sacred
griffin.[82] Be this as it may, the Knossian palace with its
elaborate equipment of shrines, sacred objects and furnishings,
unquestionably was a sanctuary in which the ritual associated
with the kingship throughout the Near East and the Eastern
Mediterranean was duly performed by the Minoan rulers and
their deputies in the customary manner, and centred in the cult
of the Mother-goddess.

The Mycenaean Kingship

On the mainland a similar situation seems to have recurred.
The close association of the worship of the Goddess and that
of the Mycenaean kingship is shown by the temples of Hera
or Athena having been built on the ruins of the royal palace
at Mycenae, Athens, and probably at Tiryns.[83] Similarly, it
was the Archon of Athens (having the title of βασιλεύς) who
was in charge of the Eleusinian Mysteries, and the hierophant
and his principal assistants were members of the two ancient
priestly Eleusinian families, the Eumolpidae and the Kerykes,
who were probably of royal descent. Moreover, in the icono-
graphy on reliefs in the sanctuary at Eleusis, which is of
Mycenaean origin, one of the princes is depicted with the culture
hero Triptolemus going about the earth in a chariot teaching
men how to till the soil under instruction from the Goddess,
as in the Osiris-Isis myth. In his right hand he holds the ears
of corn, and looks intently at Demeter in an attitude suggestive
of listening to her instructions. In his raised left hand he holds
the sceptre and is shown seated on a magnificently carved throne
drawn by winged dragons. He is also represented on a plaque
dedicated to the gods of Eleusis similarly enthroned in a chariot
holding out his left hand to receive the corn from Demeter,
who sits in front of him. At the back is the figure of a young

man carrying a torch who is probably Eubuleus, one of the youthful Eleusinian king-gods to whom the relief is dedicated.[84]

After the arrival of the Indo-European Greeks from about 2400 to 1300 B.C.—with their Sky- and Weather-god Zeus and his subsequent union with the Goddess (Hera) on his reaching Argos, who is represented by Hesiod as his sister,[85] together with other consorts (e.g. Demeter)—the kings exercised sacred functions[86] in the Greek city-states and were honoured as embodiments of Zeus. Some of the early traditional rulers, in fact, bore the title of the Sky-god (e.g. Agamemnon, Amphiaraos, Asklepios).[87] Agamemnon, for instance, is represented as appearing in the assembly with the sceptre which Zeus gave his ancestor Pelops and by him was handed down in the royal line of descent until it was bestowed upon Agamemnon by Thyestes as a symbol of his sovereignty over Argos.[88]

The great beehive tholoi at Mycenae and Dendra in which the kings were buried show that, like the Egyptian Pharaohs, they were given imposing "everlasting habitations" befitting their exalted rank in this life. This is further indicated by the wealth of the grave furniture in the chamber-tombs and in the earlier shaft-graves,[89] comparable to that in the temple-tombs of the priest-kings of Knossos, where there were all the signs of a royal mortuary cultus indistinguishable from that practised in Egypt in predynastic times.[90] In the royal tomb of Isopata north of the palace of Knossos a magnificent Middle Minoan porphyry bowl, for example, is similar in design to the vessels in hard stones in the royal graves of the early dynasties in Egypt,[91] and in its general plan and contents it reveals a remarkable conformity to the rock-cut tombs of the Twelfth Dynasty in the Middle Kingdom (i.e. Middle Minoan III in Crete). The size and position of this tomb, indeed, led Evans to equate it with the legendary resting-place of Idomeneus, the grandson of Minos and leader of the eighty Cretan ships against Troy, while that of his half-brother, Meriones, he located at the rock-cut chamber-tomb near by.[92] At Mycenae the so-called "Treasury of Atreus" and the "Tomb of Clytemnestra" afford examples of the same imposing mode of sepulture on the

mainland, traditionally associated with the heroic age and inspired, it would seem, from the residential centre of the Minoan
priest-kings at Knossos.[93]

Mycenae, however, was the meeting-point of the Eastern and
Western cultures in the Bronze Age at which two contemporary dynasties coexisted, the one burying their rulers in
shaft-graves, the other in tholoi. Both had affinities with the
Minoan priest-kings, though they were not themselves clean-
shaven Cretan rulers as the death-masks reveal. Rather were
they Helladic lords of the indigenous inhabitants of the mainland settled in Greece before the Minoan civilization penetrated
the Peloponnese about 1600 B.C. Occupying an important
strategic position on the trade-route leading from Corinth to
the north and west, they had a status and an influence in the
Late Bronze Age quite independent of Crete, however much
the Knossian priest-kings may have been predominant when
Minos ruled the waves.

In the light of the recent archaeological evidence it now
seems that Minoan influence on the Aegean mainland in the
later part of the second millennium B.C. was far less than was
formerly supposed,[94] and that the Mycenaean princes were
politically independent of Crete, as is reflected in the shaft-
graves by the indigenous character of much of the mortuary
equipment,[95] and the fundamental difference between the two
cultures in their respective attitudes, for example, towards war.
While the Minoans were relatively pacific, the Mycenaean
rulers were warriors and builders of massive fortifications.
When they engaged in successful campaigns they received the
lion's share of the booty, including the cities and lands they
conquered, and at their death they were buried in their imposing beehive tombs in keeping with the royal splendour of their
palaces and of their status as sacred functionaries.

As at Knossos, a room of the throne has been excavated at
the palace on the acropolis of Mycenae with a floor of painted
stucco and below it a few fragments of fresco. An oblong
space against the north wall originally was sunk about 0·015
metres below the level of the rest of the floor, containing in all

probability a throne,[96] as in a larger megaron at Tiryns.[97] It would seem, however, to have been an audience chamber rather than, as at Knossos, a sanctuary. Nevertheless, in a room called the Shrine on the north side of the North Corridor in the palace at Mycenae two movable stucco altars of Minoan type have been discovered, partly covered by the terrace of the temple, in a Late Helladic III deposit.[98]

If the remarkable ivory carving of two squatting women with a youth standing before them, found among a variety of objects in two small Mycenaean rooms at the base of the great north terrace wall on which the temple foundations rest at the north end, came originally from the shrine of the palace, they may represent the divinities to whom the temple was dedicated. The mention of Athena on an inscription of the sixth century B.C. found on the summit of the citadel[99] suggests that she may have been the patroness, though the three figures more easily could be regarded as representing the Eleusinian trio, Demeter, Persephone and Iacchos. In support of this latter conclusion might be urged the Mycenaean foundation of the Eleusinian Mysteries and their myth and ritual, and the fact, recalled by Dr Wace, that a sanctuary of Demeter existed in Argos and another between Argos and Mycenae.[100] In any case, here, as at Knossos, the principal object of worship apparently was the Goddess of many names of whom both Athena and Demeter were examples, as was the Cretan Rhea from whom they were alleged to have been descended, directly or indirectly, with a youthful goddess and the young god as a subsidiary figure. This is shown by the frequent recurrence of her emblems—the double axe, snakes, oxen and figurines, mostly of women—in the palace and at Mycenaean shrines everywhere. Therefore, the Mycenaean and Minoan royal cultus in the palace sanctuaries was identical in its general setting, and the status and sacral functions of the king remained little changed, until at length in the Greek city-states the palace was replaced by the temples in which the ancient myth and ritual and their symbolism persisted in the cults of the gods and goddesses for whose worship they were established.

THE KINGSHIP IN INDIA AND IRAN

The Indus Priest-kings

As in Greece the myth and ritual of the Aegean centred in the Mother-goddess was overlaid by the Indo-European Olympian tradition, with Mycenae as the meeting-point of East and West, so in India after the Aryans had made their way into the Punjab from their cradleland east of the Caspian Sea in the middle of the second millennium B.C., and later moved east-wards, a similar situation arose. From about 2500 to 1500 B.C. a homogeneous urban civilization flourished in Sind and the Punjab with a social and religious structure which seems to have been theocratic in its administration. Thus, the ancient cities of Harappa, Mohenjo-daro and Chanhu-daro, excavated since 1922, appear to have been linked together by river com-munications and religious sanctions exercised by an autocratic hierarchy of priest-kings constituting the civic and ecclesiastical focus, not unlike that which obtained in Sumer.[101]

At Mohenjo-daro the citadel is based upon an artificial mound on the top of which now stands a Buddhist *stupa* and monastery erected in the second century A.D., thereby preserving possibly the tradition of its ancient sacred significance. Although a temple has not yet been discovered below the Buddhist mud-brick reliquary and its court, the general character of the citadel area with its adjacent great bath and priests' cells, which may represent the central sanctuary for ritual bathing[102] (a wide-spread and ancient practice in Hinduism), suggests its having been the seat of the theocratic government. The uniformity of the ground-plan and the equipment of the cities, together with the temple-citadel as the civic and religious focus, are indicative of an ordered administration under divine sanction exercising a unified sovereignty over the southern kingdom, along the lines followed by the priest-kings in Mesopotamia. This also applies to Harappa, which doubtless fulfilled the same rôle in the north.

It was in these Indus cities where life continued little changed from about 2500 B.C. until they were invaded and left in ruins rather more than a thousand years later, that the foundations of

Hindu myth and ritual appear to have been laid. There the sacral kingship, as will be considered in the next chapter, was intimately connected with the worship of the Mother-goddess, as is shown by the female statuettes akin to those in Western Asia and Baluchistan, which have been found in large numbers in the sites of the Harappa culture.[103] Figures of male gods also were prevalent, though they seldom occurred in association with those of the goddesses. Nevertheless, the presence of phallic symbols, prototypes of the Hindu *linga* sometimes in conjunction with the *yoni*, or vulva, shows that a pre-Aryan fertility cultus existed in line with that which prevailed throughout the region from the Aegean to the Indus valley.

About 1500 B.C. a very different religious tradition was introduced when the people of Indo-European stock and language poured over the passes of the Hindu Kush into North-west India and settled in small village groups with their flocks and herds and cultivating grain, each ruled by a chieftain, or rajah, whose office was hereditary. By contrast with the dark-skinned earlier inhabitants, whom they designated *dasa* as a term of reproach (i.e. "slave" in Sanskrit), they declared themselves to be of noble birth and descent (i.e. *Aryas*). Yet it was apparently from the fusion of this "Iranian" or "Aryan" culture and language with the earlier indigenous populations, and what remained of the urban Harappan fortified citadels of the Indus civilization, that the composite Hindu religious and social organization eventually emerged as a single unified structure, until by the fifth century B.C. a rigidly devised caste system became prevalent.

The Vedic Conception of Kingship

For several centuries before this the Aryans in the Ganges valley had been established as the upper level of the population in a number of districts ruled by hereditary rajahs with non-Aryans as a depressed class. In the meantime, with the advance of the Indo-Europeans in every direction, the Brahmins had replaced the earlier priest-kings as the dominant caste, represented in the Vedas and the Puranas as the Kshatriyas or warriors and nobles. Thus, in the Brahmanic texts, compiled between 800 and 500 B.C., the creation ritual is closely asso‐ ciated with the king as a member of the Kshatriya caste called into being as a military necessity to enable the gods to defeat the demons who beset them, just as Indra had been installed by the gods as their king because he was the most vigorous and valiant deity.[104] In the Rig‐veda in a hymn attributed to Trasadasyu, the Puru king claims to be Indra and Varuna and the recipient of the energies characteristic of the Asuras.[105] In the later Brahmanas the king is identified with Prajapati, the Lord of Production, at once Creator and creation, through his sacrificial functions, whereby "being one he rules over many".[106]

In the Code of Manu, variously dated from 300 B.C. to A.D. 150, the king is represented as "a great deity" in human form whom Brahman created from the particles of the gods for the protection of the world. "He showers benefits upon his realm as Indra sends rain upon the earth; he must be as omni‐ potent as the wind; he must control all his subjects as does Yama; he must draw revenues from his kingdom as the sun draws water from the earth."[107] In short, he was assigned the status of a priest‐king just as in the Rig‐veda he was identified with the gods associated with the maintenance of the cosmic order (*Rta*), upholding the moral law and controlling the forces on which nature and man depended for their sustenance and well‐being (Mitra, Agni, Indra and Varuna).[108]

In the very ancient coronation (*abhishaka*) and inauguration (*rajasuya*) ceremonial he was given his place and function in the ritual order in the traditional manner, which included the customary lustrations, unctions, investitures, drinking the sacred beverage (*soma*), circumambulations and contests.[109] Dressed in his royal robes, he was anointed by the priests. He then set his foot on a tiger's skin, symbolic of his having become as powerful as the tiger. He next undertook a mimic cattle‐raid, and with bow and arrow in hand he stepped in the direction of each of the cardinal points. Finally, he played a game of dice and by winning the last throw he became victorious over his supernatural enemies and was qualified to perform the most sacred horse-sacrifice by having undergone successfully this *Rajasuya* installation rite.

In the Vedic period the Brahmanic priesthood usurped the position previously occupied by the kingship in the supreme control of the fortunes of heaven and earth, of the gods and of men, and of the state and the forces of nature, though not infrequently priests worked in the service of princes and associated with them in battle. It may be that the Upanishadic reaction against sacerdotal supremacy was due in some measure to a deeply laid antagonism between the Brahmin and Kshatriya castes, representing a perennial struggle between the Aryan priesthood and the royal princes of Ancient India, since the Upanishads ascribed their characteristic doctrines to royal personages, some of whom are known to have been patrons of Brahmins. But the *Brahmanvidya* (the quest of knowledge of Brahman) was never the carefully guarded preserve of the Kshatriay caste as the sacrificial offering became of that of the Brahmins. Its members, therefore, ceased to occupy the key position in the control of the universe and of human affairs and destinies. Nevertheless, with the establishment of the Mauryan dynasty about 322 B.C. an urban civilization arose which conformed to the Harappa pattern. Its bureaucratic civic administration was under the supreme authority of an autocratic ruler and his viceroys (who usually were members of the royal family), assisted by officials with a Brahmanic background, reminiscent of the Harappa urban civilization rather than of the nomadic pastoral Aryan culture.[110] Therefore, as the Minoan-Mycenaean strain in combination with the subsequent Indo-European element was a determining factor in the Greek myth and ritual and life and thought, so the influence of the pre-Vedic Indus civilization, with its cultural interrelations with the Fertile Crescent, was felt long after the Aryanization of the Punjab and the Ganges basin, not least in the increasing domination of the priestly tradition as the Brahmins usurped more and more the prerogatives of the ancient priest-kings and gained pre-eminence over the Kshatriyas.

Indo-Iranian Kingship

A similar sequence of events occurred on the western section of the great plateau, stretching from the Indus valley to that of Tigris and Euphrates, where at the end of the Neolithic in the fifth millennium B.C. a sedentary population settled in large agricultural village communities, the oldest of which is the settlement at Sialk near Kashan in Western Iran, south of Teheran.[111] This was an outpost of the prehistoric civilization of Susa to the west on the plains of Elam in the lowest levels of which (Susa A) naked female figurines were modelled in clay,[112] indicative of the Goddess cult as elsewhere in this region. In the second millennium B.C. the nomadic pastoral Indo-European tribes began to enter the plateau in a succession of waves. Some of them pressed on in an easterly direction into the Indus valley; others went into Western Asia, while a third group later in the millennium settled permanently in Iran, which then became known as *Ariana*, "the Empire (or land) of the Aryans".[113] Although they brought with them their pantheon of nature gods whose names and attributes are preserved in the Indian polytheistic Vedic tradition, in Iran they transformed the beneficent *devas* ("shining ones") into evil spirits (*daevas*), and made the demons (*asuras*) the "lords" and "masters" (*ahura*); in other words, the true Iranian deities. Among the few Vedic gods who retained their status, Mitra became Mithra, the god of light and of war, Soma, the Vedic king-god, survived as Haoma in the form of an intoxicating sacramental beverage, and eventually Ahura Mazda, proclaimed by Zarathushtra as the Wise Lord and only God, inherited the attributes and function of Varuna, the all-knowing and all-encompassing sky.

The Iranian kingship in its political and sacral aspects reflects these two strains in the civilization of the plateau. In the north-west the Aryan tribe known as Amadai, or Medes, became firmly established early in the first millennium B.C., and in the south the Parsua, or Persians, occupied the territory near the Persian Gulf. Both dynasties were predominantly Indo-European in origin, and, therefore, they retained this tradition of the kingship against its ancient Caspian background with all the power and prestige the royal office enjoyed. Thus, the king was sacred in his own person, having a fraternal relationship with either the Sun or the Moon, and being the recipient of a firenature from Mithra, symbolized by the aureola.[114]

Important rulers were assigned the title "King of Kings", which has persisted until modern times in the designation of the Shahs, though in the Parthian period, and sometimes in Sasanian times, the king was in fact *primus inter pares* among the rulers of the dominant clans. Nevertheless, he was accorded royal honours befitting his sacred status in the court ceremonial, and officiated in a priestly capacity at the horsesacrifice, and later in the firetemples. At the New Year Festival, like Marduk in Babylon, he engaged in a ritual combat with the dragon, Azi Dahaka, to renew the vital forces in nature. Thus, Cyrus the Great (558–530 B.C.), who claimed divine descent, did not hesitate to continue the ritual of the Chaldaean kings in "taking the hand of Bel" at the *Akitu* to legalize the new royal line in Babylonia. Thus, he declared that "Marduk had visited all lands in search of a just prince, a king after his own heart, whom he took by the hand. He pronounced his name, 'Cyrus of Anshan', and he signified his name for kingship over all."[115]

In the two texts of the NabunaidCyrus Chronicle and the Cylinder Inscription he as the chosen of Marduk is said to have restored the statues of Marduk and Nabu to their original homes, while by the DeuteroIsaiah he is addressed as "the shepherd of Yahweh", his anointed, before whom all nations should be subdued; and as the one whom Yahweh had called and in whom he delighted.[116] Only on the assumption that he modelled his kingship on Mesopotamian prototypes and acted in accordance with the divine quality with which he was endowed, are such utterances explicable. In the *Cyropedia* of Xenophon he is represented as offering sacrifices with the assistance of the magi to a number of gods under Greek names,[117] doubtless the counterparts of Iranian deities of the Younger Avesta, who included Ahura Mazda, Mithra and

Anahita, the goddess of fertility. In so doing he continued the royal sacerdotal tradition wherein the Iranian kings as ritual experts functioned as priests, especially in the offering of the sacred fire (*atara*) in the fire-temples.

The Achaemenid dynasty (558–330 B.C.) reached its height in the reign of Darius I (522–486 B.C.), who declared himself in his own inscriptions as "King of Kings, King of the Lands, son of Hystaspes, the Achaemenid". Moreover, he claimed that "this Kingship which I hold from Sardis which is beyond Sochdiana to Kush, from India to Sardis, Ahura Mazda gave me who is the greatest of the gods".[118] It was "by the will of Ahura Mazda" that he reigned and subdued the other nations, and had been invested with sovereign power, though for him Ahura Mazda was only "the greatest of gods", or "the god of the Aryans", occupying a position in Persia not so very different from that of Yahweh in pre-exilic Israel.[119] Nevertheless, there can be no doubt that for Darius and his successors Ahura Mazda was the deity *par excellence* upon whose grace and favour they depended for all their achievements.[120]

Thus, like his father Darius, Xerxes (486–465 B.C.) declared that he had been made "sole king of many, sole commander of many" by the will of Ahura Mazda through whom he had accomplished all that he had done. His successors, however, Artaxerxes I, Artaxerxes II and Artaxerxes III, in acknowledging their indebtedness to Ahura Mazda, mentioned along with him other gods (e.g. Anahita and Mithra).[121] Artaxerxes II also erected statues to Anahita in the chief towns of the empire, showing that under increasing Magian influence the ancient Iranian nature religion was regaining its strength and the kingship assuming more and more its traditional place and status in the cultus with the recrudescence of pre-Zoroastrian myth and ritual, until a new mythology developed round the person of Alexander the Great after his conquest of Persia in 331 B.C.

CHAPTER IV

The Mother-goddess and the Sacred Marriage

WHETHER or not the Mother-goddess was the first deity the wit of man devised, her symbolism unquestionably is a predo-minant feature in the archaeological record of the ancient world from the Gravettian Venuses and the stylized images of the decorated caves in the Palaeolithic to the emblems and inscrip-tions of the Fertile Crescent, Western Asia, the Indus valley and the Aegean. At first the cult centred in the mystery of birth and, therefore, the emphasis was on the maternal functions of womanhood as the female figurines reveal, in many of which, as we have seen,[1] the sex organs were exaggerated and condi-tions of pregnancy, and occasionally of childbirth, were suggested. Their purpose was to promote life in ever-increasing abundance, alike in the human species, the animal creation and in nature, so that birth and generation were linked with the conservation of the food-supply upon which sustenance depended.

THE MOTHER-GODDESS IN MESOPOTAMIA

With the rise of agriculture and the keeping of flocks and herds as the cult developed, especially in the Ancient Near East, the figure of a goddess personifying maternal functions became more clearly defined. In the first instance it was as the unmarried Goddess that she became the dominant influence from India to the Mediterranean. In Mesopotamia, however, as Langdon pointed out, whereas "the intensity of the worship of other gods depended somewhat upon the political impor-tance of the cities where their chief cult existed, before the orders of the gods of nature arose, before the complex theology of emanations supplied the religion with a vast pantheon, in which the masculine element predominated, the productive powers of earth had supplied in prehistoric times a divinity in which the female element predominated".[2] But in Sumer the Mother-goddess did not stand alone. In the earliest texts she was provided with a son who was also her lover representing the birth and death of nature.

Inanna-Ishtar and Dumuzi-Tammuz

It was in this setting that the myth and its ritual enactment were celebrated in the cult festival at Isin in Southern Mesopotamia in the third millennium B.C. centred in the sacred marriage of the Goddess Inanna (the Sumerian counterpart of the Akkadian Ishtar), the incarnation of the fertility of nature, to the Shepherd-god Dumuzi, or Tammuz, the embodiment of the creative powers of spring. The god being the personification of vegetation, the rise and decline of which were reflected in the death and resurrection myth, it did not suffice for him to remain merely the child of the author and giver of all life (i.e. the Goddess). Nothing less than the marriage of the two deities could be efficacious for the maintenance of the seasonal cycle, and this union had to be ritually enacted by the ruler of the city-state and a priestess in the capacity of Dumuzi and Inanna, or Tammuz and Ishtar, to give it its local application. By identifying themselves with their divine archetypes their union had a reciprocal re-creative effect on the natural processes in the spring "increasing the fertility of the land" and filling it with abundance.[3]

Thus, when the cult of the Great Mother was brought into relation with the seasonal cycle and its vegetation ritual it ceased to be conceived primarily or exclusively with the processes of birth. As the Earth-goddess she was the source of generative power in nature as a whole and so became responsible for the periodic renewal of life in the spring after the blight of winter or summer drought. Consequently, she was a many-sided goddess, as in the case of Inanna-Ishtar, both mother and bride, the Magna Mater and the Magna Dolorosa, known by many names and epithets—Ninhursaga, Mah, Ninmah, Nintu or Aruru. Thus, Ninhursaga was Ninsikil-la, "the pure lady", until she was approached by Enki when she became Nin-lu ama Kalamma, "the lady who gives birth, the mother of the land". When she accepted him she was Dam-gal-nun-na, "the great spouse of the prince", and having conceived as the fertile soil and given birth to vegetation she was Nin-hur-sag-ga, "the lady of the mountain", where nature manifested its powers of fecundity in the spring on its lush slopes.[4]

Similarly, Inanna-Ishtar, although as a marriageable girl she was represented as having accepted the divine farmer Enkidu for her husband and rejected the advances of the divine shepherd Dumuzi,[5] nevertheless her nuptials with Dumuzi-Tammuz were celebrated annually at the spring festival at Isin to reawaken the vital forces in nature. Her short-lived marriage, however, was but the prelude to her mourning the loss of her husband, Dumuzi, who incarnated the powers of spring and symbolized the decline in nature in the devastating heat of summer over which she was regarded as exercising supreme control. Because from her all life originated, from her the male god was born as her son, but he was also her husband because only through the union of male and female can the reproductive process be maintained. Consequently, since the intercourse of the god and the goddess had its reciprocal effect in the revivi-fication of nature, the annual sacred marriage was an essential ritual observance in the seasonal cycle. Indeed, all the principal deities in Mesopotamia are represented in the texts as celebrating their nuptials,[6] which on earth were re-enacted in the temples by the king as the divine bridegroom and the queen (or a priestess) as the Goddess.

The Union of the Goddess and the King

Thus, in a hymn to Ishtar as the planet Venus, written for the cult of the deified king of Isin-Dagan, third king of the Amorite dynasty (c. 2258-2237 B.C.), he is represented enjoy-ing the embrace of the Mother-goddess on earth at the season when she returned with Tammuz from the underworld (i.e. at the New Year Festival). As a result he became the symbol of life and death in his Tammuz capacity of the dying and reviving god. Addressing her as the "Queen of heaven, garment of the sky" arising in heaven like a shining torch, he dwelt with Innana in the "temple of the King of the lands who is a god". There she rises at the break of day, and

> At the festival of the New Year, the day of decisions,
> For my queen a couch I have laid.
> My queen upon her couch goes to repose,
> Beside it a chair as her seat I set.
> To cause them to recline upon the chair, the seat of happiness.

Then follows a description of the lustration of the "holy pedestal" on which the images of Inanna and Isin-Dagan were placed, and its anointing with cedar oil, leading up to the physical union:

> She embraces her beloved husband.
> Holy Inanna embraces him.
> The throne in the great sanctuary is made glorious
> Like the daylight.
> The king like the Sun-god
> Plenty, happiness and abundance before him prosper.
> A feast of good things they set before him
> The dark-headed people prosper before him.
> Upon the instrument of loud sound (music or lamentation)
>   which roars more than the storm-winds,
> The *algar*, whose voice is sweet—much is its adornment—
>   upon the harp, upon the flute, songs of gladness we
>   recite to them.
> The king with food and drink is fitly provided.
> The divine mother, fearful dragon of heaven, with food
>   and drink is fitly provided.
> The temple gleams, the king rejoices.
> Daily the people are satisfied with abundance
> The divine mother, fearful dragon of heaven, rejoices.[7]

Throughout the Goddess is represented as taking the initiative. It was to her "far-famed temple" that the king went, bringing to her cakes "to set the table for the feast", and it was she who embraced her beloved husband. He was merely her consort subservient to her will and enjoying the favours she was pleased to bestow upon him. Again, it was the Goddess who actually vouchsafed the prosperity for the new year and the bounty which the ritual marriage secured. Her husband the king was only the instrument whom she employed to convey her gifts to mankind. It was Inanna, Queen of Heaven and Earth, who gladdened the heart of the king of Isin, Enlil-bani, by choosing him to be her spouse.[8]

This has led Frankfort to suggest that "only those kings were deified who had been commanded by a goddess to share her couch".[9] In support of this contention is quoted the deification of Lipit-Ishtar after he had been appointed by Anu as king of Isin by being fused with Urash, a fertility-god, as a prelude to his sacred marriage with Ishtar.[10] Whether or not this was a universal rule, it seems that in Mesopotamia the kingship was vitally connected with a nuptial relationship between the local human ruler and the Goddess in which she was the dominant partner. Hence the fundamental importance of the sacred marriage in the New Year celebrations as the culmination of the ritual in the ancient Sumerian agricultural cult drama to secure the revival of nature in spring.[11]

THE GODDESS IN EGYPT

Hathor and Horus

In Egypt, on the other hand, it was the Pharaoh rather than the Goddess who took the initiative because he exercised his life-giving functions in his own right by virtue of his divine origin, begotten by his heavenly father, the Sun-god, and succeeding to the throne as Horus, the son of Osiris, who was also said to have been the son of Hathor in another capacity.[12] Thus, in the third nome in the Delta, Hathor, whose name means the "House of Horus", was worshipped in the form of a cow, and became the mother of Horus the Elder. This Horus is called the son of Atum or Geb, and in the Pyramid texts he is equated with Re.[13] But as the son of Geb he was the brother of Osiris before the enmity between Osiris and Seth arose. When in the Isis myth he was identified with the posthumous son of Osiris, as Hathor was regarded as the mother of Horus the Elder, so Isis often was represented with her cow's horns.

In the New Kingdom Hathor appeared as the mother-wife of Horus when the various traditions were brought together, and all the great goddesses became "forms and attributes of Hathor worshipped under different names".[14] She was, however, predominantly one of the many wives of Horus, and their marriage was celebrated annually at Edfu where he was born as the Falcon-god (Behdetite) and symbolized as the solar disk with the outspread wings of a hawk. But she was not exclusively the husband of Horus, as Junker has contended,[15] and being essentially the goddess of birth originally she seems to have been his mother as Tammuz was the son of Ishtar. It was not until he became identified with the son of Osiris (of whom Hathor never was the spouse) that the nuptial relationship was established. Then she (Hathor) was equated with Isis, who henceforth adopted her horns, and as the "throne woman"[16] was thought to give birth to the prototype of the living king in his Horus capacity and the avenger of the death of Osiris.

Both goddesses, therefore, were closely associated with motherhood and the kingship, and their similarities of function gave rise to the confusion in the subsequent mythology that grew up around them to give expression to their respective attributes and offices. Thus, at Philae Isis-Hathor personified all the goddesses in one. At Sais in the Eighteenth Dynasty, Neith was identified with Isis and Hathor and so became at once the wife of Osiris, the mother of Horus, and the mother of the gods.[17] In short, the rôle of Hathor in Ancient Egypt was that of the Great Mother in her original form who as the cow-goddess *par excellence* exercised her maternal functions, especially in the suckling of kings here and hereafter[18] and conferring upon them their divinity. And so while they reigned as Horus, the son of Osiris, as regards their divine potency they were Horus, the son of Hathor.

The Sacred Marriage of Hathor at Denderah

Moreover, when the Goddess eventually became the wife of the chief god who was formerly her son, on the 18th day of the tenth month (Payni) the image of Hathor was taken by her priests by ship from her temple at Denderah to visit her consort Horus at Edfu. On reaching their destination on the 1st day of the eleventh month (Epiphi), after a sojourn there for a fortnight, Horus and his retinue went in solemn procession to meet the Goddess on her ship on the eve of his festival (commemorating his victory over Seth). They then proceeded with her and her fleet to Edfu. After passing the night near the temple the various gods and their worshippers who had assembled were led to the upper temple on the desert level to perform the prescribed rites. The triumph of Horus in his combat was enacted by the "scribes of the sacred books" to the satisfaction of Isis who rejoiced "because he (i.e. Horus) had undertaken this his charge with a glad heart". When "all that was commanded had been accomplished", the procession broke up and went to the halls of the school to offer a goat and an ox as a burnt offering. After reading "the veneration of Horus, whose inheritance is made sure", and four other books, offerings were made to Re, who was called upon "in all his names". Loaves, jugs of beer, dates, milk, geese and wine were brought to him. Then the priests proclaimed, "Praise to thee, Re; praise to thee, Khepri, in all these thy beautiful names. Thou camest hither strong and mighty and hast ascended beautiful, and hast slain the dragon (Apophis). Incline thy beautiful countenance to the king." Four geese were then liberated to fly to the four winds to tell the gods that "Horus of Edfu, the great god, the lord of heaven, has taken the white crown and has added the red crown thereto". Four arrows were shot to the four quarters of heaven to slay the enemies of the god. An ox was killed and its right leg thrown to a man called Horus, and a number of ceremonies were performed having as their purpose the destruction of the enemies of the god and of the king, before those taking part in the rites celebrated the victory by "drinking before the god", and "spending the night gaily".[19]

Since Hathor is stated in the inscriptions to have sailed from Denderah "to consummate the beauteous embrace with her

Horus",[20] at this festival a ritual marriage must have occurred as a result of which, on the fourth day, the young Horus was conceived to be born on the 28th of the eighth month (Pharmuthi).[21] This is confirmed by a similar procession by river in barges of the image of Amon and his consort Mut and their son Khonsu, escorted by the king and queen, the priests, musicians and nobles, from his temple at Karnak to his *harîm* at Luxor, depicted on the reliefs on the walls of the court of Amenhotep III at Luxor.[22]

The "God's Wife"

Since in the New Kingdom Amon-Re was believed to incorporate himself in the reigning Pharaoh in order to beget the heir to the throne,[23] the queen as the "God's Wife" was regarded as the embodiment of Hathor, while the musician-priestesses in the temple at Luxor were his concubines presided over by the "God's Wife". It was doubtless at the "southern *harîm* of Amon" that union of the god and the queen took place when at the Theban Festival of Opet he visited the sanctuary in all his magnificence for this purpose in the later half of the second month (Paophi).[24] Therefore, the conception and birth of the Pharaoh is depicted on the reliefs in the temple[25] similar to those in the temple of Hatshepsut at Deir el Bahari[26] because in all probability it was here that the sacred marriage was consummated between the king and the queen as the earthly counterparts of the god and the goddess.

In Egypt the essential function of the mother-goddesses was that of the reproduction of life, but they were not, as in Mesopotamia, the actual source of all life. Instead of inviting their male partners to share their nuptial couch, it was the god in his incarnate form as Pharaoh who in the Nile valley went to the queen in his divine majesty and "did all that he desired with her". She willingly and gladly "let him rejoice over her" because she was the "God's Wife", just as the consort of the ancient king of Heliopolis was the wife of the Sun-god's embodiment and so was identified with Hathor, his celestial spouse. She was, therefore, regarded as the earthly consort of

the god, and it was through her that he became the physical
father of the Pharaoh. Consequently, notwithstanding her
nuptial relations with her divine consort, she did not play the
dominant rôle in the union.

The first recorded instance of the wife of a Pharaoh being
assigned the title "God's Wife" is Ahhotep, the mother of
Ahmose I, the founder of the Eighteenth Dynasty, whose
husband was Kemose, the last Pharaoh of the Seventeenth
Dynasty.[27] But since the Heliopolitan queen as the wife of the
high-priest of the Sun-god acted in this capacity, she must have
been identified with Hathor by virtue of her divine embodiments. Therefore, from the Fifth Dynasty the title was in theory
inherent in the status and function of the high-priestess in the
Heliopolitan royal solar cult, and when the god's *harîm* was
established and human concubines were assigned to certain
deities as musicians (i.e. to Amon of Thebes, Khnum of
Hermopolis), the wife of the high-priest as their leader became
the "God's Votary". Since her principal duty seems to have
been that of playing the sistrum before the beautiful face of
Amon, assisted no doubt by her musician-priestesses,[28] her
office and its functions may not have conflicted with those of
the queen who stood in a more essentially nuptial relationship
with the king-god, as the duties of the concubines consisted
apparently only of playing music before the god.[29]

In the Twenty-second Dynasty, however, the "God's Wife"
overshadowed both the throne and the Amonite priesthood.
The divine kingship had now lost its vitality, and it only
remained for Asurbanipal to conquer Thebes in 663 to reduce
Amon-Re to the rank of a local god from which loss of
status he never recovered. With the establishment of the Saitic
line (*c.* 655–525 B.C.) a succession of five "God's Wives"
became the governors of Thebes who were no longer the wives
of the Pharaohs, and beside whom the high-priests were little
more than figure-heads in the state. The decline in religion, as
in other aspects of national life in Egypt, had now definitely
set in, and neither the king nor queen, and the gods or goddesses
they embodied, were able to regain the power and influence

each had hitherto exercised as the dynamic centre of the nation by virtue of their divine relationships and upon whose union its well-being so largely had depended.

THE GODDESS CULT IN WESTERN ASIA
Anat and Asherah in the Ras Shamra Texts

In Syria and Palestine the Goddess cult seems to have been less deeply rooted and firmly established than in Egypt and the rest of Western Asia. Female figurines, amulets and Astarte plaques have been recovered from Stratum B of Tell Beit Mirsim (*c.* 1200–920 B.C.), Shechem and Megiddo,[30] and in the Ugaritic texts there are unmistakable indications of the Goddess cult and of the sacred marriage as an integral element in the vegetation myth and ritual. Thus, Anat was the consort and sister of Baal, who is also called the "Lady of the Mountain",[31] and in the Baal-Anat text she is said to have been invited by Baal to his mountain, Sapan, after battling victoriously against his enemies to assist him in building a palace.[32] Thereupon she promised to go to her father El and seek his consent for the project,[33] but with what result is not clear. El seems to have promised to give priority in house-building to Yam, "Prince of the Sea", whom he had appointed lord of the earth. At this point, however, the texts are very obscure and may have become misplaced.

For our present purpose the incident is significant only in so far as it indicates the prominence of Anat in the Ugaritic mythology where frequently she occupies a predominant position as elsewhere in the Near East and the Aegean. She was the chief patroness of Aleyan-Baal, and when he was killed by Mot, like Ishtar and Isis, she went in search of him, hunting every mountain in the land, lamenting him as bitterly as Adonis grieved for Attis,[34] and desiring him as does "a cow her calf or a ewe her lamb".[35] Indeed, in this text Anat is mentioned in association with a wild cow, the symbol of the Mother-goddess,[36] and as Aleyan-Baal is said to have mated with a heifer in the desert to produce a child called Mos, so Anat was the lover of Aleyan-Baal, thereby, it would seem, identifying her with the cow symbolism of the Great Mother in Egypt and in Western Asia.[37]

On a statue at Tanis she is represented as a draped figure, showing her breasts and wearing the crown of Upper Egypt with horns and two plumes.[38] On an obelisk Rameses II is described as the "suckling of Anat", and on another double statue Anat and Rameses II are depicted with inscriptions describing Anat as the mother of the Pharaoh "loved of Amon" and of the "Lady of the Sky" (Anat).[39] Thus, it would seem that from the Nineteenth Dynasty Anat and her Phoenician counterpart Ashtart, whose names frequently occur together on Egyptian papyri of this period,[40] had acquired a recognized status in the Hathor tradition in the Nile valley. Anat, in fact, is mentioned as one of the names of Hathor in a Graeco-Roman inscription on the temple wall at Denderah,[41] but from the Eighteenth Dynasty she was known as a goddess of war, as in Syria where her warlike characteristics were pronounced in the Ugaritic texts.

This is apparent in the accounts of her violent and sanguinary conflicts with the enemies of Baal,[42] but although she delighted in war and slaughter and wallowed in blood, she never ceased to be the goddess of love and fertility, even though in this capacity she was overshadowed by Aleyan-Baal, who became the giver of life *par excellence*. Therefore, she was his consort with whom he had passionate marital intercourse, described in the manner of the sacred marriage mythology, in the Annual Festival cultus.[43] If the Ras Shamra texts were cult rituals of this nature recited dramatically, whether or not they were annually performed,[44] the *hieros gamos* would seem to have been a feature of the observance as elsewhere.

For example, in the Gracious Gods texts (52), first published by Virolleaud in 1933,[45] which Dr Gaster maintains were the libretto of a sacred drama addressed to certain "gracious and beautiful gods", described as "princes" and "high ones", and performed at the Canaanite spring festival of first-fruits, there is an erotic scene between the supreme god El and two girls identified as Anat and Asherah.[46] Having accepted the two women as his wives, they both conceive at a sacred marriage and bear the gods Dawn and Sunset, also called Gracious, who suck at "the breasts of our Lady".[47] These Gracious Gods he identifies with Shr (Dawn) and Slm (Sunset), and not, as has been commonly supposed, with a distinct group of lesser deities or demi-gods.[48] But in any case, the episode gives the appearance of representing the climax of the sacred dance in a ritual marriage between the priests of El and the temple priestesses resulting symbolically in the birth of certain gods and the promotion of fertility, whatever may have been its precise occasion and setting.

That the virgin Anat became the wife of Baal is abundantly evident.[49] Sometimes their union is represented as that of a bull and a cow in accordance with the established symbolism of male virility and female fecundity,[50] so that when Baal is said to love a heifer[51] this is merely the mythological mode of expressing his union with Anat. The situation is complicated, however, by El also having had sexual relations with Anat and with another goddess, probably Asherah. As we have seen, it was he (El) as an aged man, not Baal, who had an affair with the two women which resulted in the birth of the Gracious Gods, and in all probability they were Anat and Asherah. Moreover, Asherah generally has been considered to be the consort of El, though in the Old Testament she is connected with Baal, who in Hebrew tradition, however, was equated with El. In the Ras Shamra texts both the goddesses also are called El's daughters.[52] It is, in fact, by no means improbable, as Kapelrud has suggested, that originally Anat was his wife when El was head of the pantheon before Baal became the dominant figure and most potent force in heaven and on earth, replacing El as Marduk succeeded Enlil when Babylon was made the capital of Hammurabi's empire in Babylonia. But once Baal triumphed Anat assumed the status of his wife and sister while El became her father, as in the A.B. Texts.[53] Therefore, when he was established as the source and controller of fertility, although she took her natural place by his side as the goddess of birth, in a measure she too receded into the background, notwithstanding her prominence in the texts. In the Ugaritic tradition Baal was the supreme figure, dwarfing all the other gods and goddesses. But probably in the beginning it was not so. Then El and the Mother-goddess dominated the scene.

Although Asherah was one of the wives of El originally, she was also his daughter and the rival and enemy of Anat and Aleyan-Baal, when he was represented as the mother of Mot. But this was a passing phase as she became actively engaged in the scheme for the building of Baal's temple as one of his allies.[54] In addition to being "Creatress of the gods", she was "Lady of the Sea",[55] like Aphrodite in Greece and Mary "Star of the Sea" in Christian tradition; titles which place her in the same position as Anat, both of them having a status and fulfilling the functions of the Great Goddess, perennially fruitful without losing their virginity, and concerned principally with love, fertility and war. In this capacity they would readily become at once the consort and daughter, or spouse and sister, of the chief god, be he El or Aleyan-Baal, for this, as we have seen, is a recurrent phenomenon in the cult of the Goddess. In Canaan the emphasis especially was on the warlike and erotic aspects of these patronesses of sexual life and the forces of reproduction in their various manifestations who strove one against the other to become the consort of the leader of the pantheon, and to dominate the natural processes on which the well-being of mankind depended. But in this struggle neither seems to have been victorious, since both Anat and Asherah remained in joint possession of one and the same office without ever merging completely into the "Goddess of many names".

The Goddess Cult in Israel

In Hebrew tradition Asherah appears to have been equated with Astarte, or Ashtaroth, very much as in Egypt Anat and Astarte were fused into one figure, Antart. Thus, in the Old Testament Asherah is associated with Baal,[56] though usually it is Ashtaroth who is represented as his partner.[57] But the word "asherah" is frequently applied to a cult object made of wood set up in sanctuaries beside altars and *mazzebôth* (menhirs), and sometimes in sacred groves where vegetation rites were performed.[58] No doubt when the Biblical narratives were drawn up Asherah and Ashtaroth had become confused and anything connected with the Goddess cult was described under the composite term "Asherah", just as all vegetation gods and their cultus were called "Baal". That Mount Carmel was a sanctuary of the Canaanite Aleyan-Baal is very probable,[59] and the Elijah episode may represent a struggle between Yahwism and the Tyrian Baal-Asherah cult at this important centre of the cultus in Northern Palestine, apparently served by some four hundred and fifty priests of Baal and four hundred priestesses of Asherah.[60] That Asherah was the chief goddess of Tyre is indicated in the Ugaritic Keret text,[61] where the hero, Keret, is said to have reached "the shrine of Asherah of Tyre" and "Elath (the goddess) of Sidon" to have vowed to her on his way to obtain the daughter of King Pabel for his bride.[62] Therefore, as one of his votaries the Tyrian wife of Ahab, Jezebel, doubtless regarded Carmel as a vantage-point in the struggle between the rival cults, and it may well have been there that the ritual battle between Baal-Asherah and Yahweh took place.

If on this occasion Yahwism triumphed, however decisive may have been the victory of Yahweh, who henceforth became the dominant deity in Israel, it by no means marked the end of Baalism. On the contrary, the success of the campaign appears to have been followed by a violent reaction, since in the bitter lamentation of Elijah at Horeb he is represented as declaring that the altars of Yahweh had been thrown down, the Yahwistic prophets slain, and he alone, as he imagined, remained and went in terror of his own life.[63] Indeed, so deeply ingrained was the Canaanite cult that in the days of Jeremiah just before the Exile in the sixth century B.C., the prophet testified that in the cities of Judah and in the streets of Jerusalem the children gathered wood, and the fathers kindled the fire, and the women kneaded dough to make sacrificial cakes for the queen of heaven.[64] When he remonstrated with them they declared that they most certainly would continue to burn incense and pour out drink offerings to the Goddess as their kings and chiefs had always done in Judah and Jerusalem because then there was food in abundance and the nation prospered. Since the ritual had been discontinued under his (Jeremiah's) influence the sword and famine, they maintained, had befallen the country and its people. All he could reply was that the present plight was in fact the result of their former lapse from Yahwism, and he heaped curses on them for their back-sliding. But he could not deny that the cult had been firmly established and widely practised in Israel to secure "plenty of victuals" and general well-being as in the neighbouring countries.[65]

The temples of Asherah and Yahweh, erected side by side on the wall at Mizpah in the ninth century, survived, in fact, until the city was destroyed, while in the Jewish Elephantine community in Egypt the queen of heaven was still worshipped and female consorts assigned to Yahweh in the fifth century B.C. under the names of Canaanite goddesses, Anat-Yahu (or Anat-Bethel), Ashim-Bethel and Haram-Bethel.[66] The widespread practice of male and female prostitution suggests that the sacred marriage was a prominent aspect of the cult. Thus, priestesses appear to have been attached to the temple in Shiloh with whom the sons of Eli had intercourse,[67] and Amos inveighed against those who profaned the name of Yahweh by having congress with the *zonah* at a sacrificial meal and drinking "the wine of the raped".[68] Similarly, Jeremiah chided the people of Jerusalem for assembling themselves by troops in the shrines of the sacred prostitutes (*zonah*) whose blandishments he described.[69] As the Goddess invited the king to her couch in Babylon, so these shrines were equipped with "beds of love" for the priestesses and their lovers"[70] who assumed the same rôle as the king and queen in the dramatiza-tion of the sacred marriage,[71] if, as seems probable, ritual prostitution was a form of this rite.

It may have been, although the episode is very obscure, that the prophet Isaiah resorted to one of these shrines to engage in a sacred union with a professional prophetess to obtain a second child by her as a symbolical action[72] since the attempts to make her his wife are by no means convincing.[73] Be this as it may, ritual prostitutes of both sexes were prevalent in Israel, and however much their cultus was opposed or allegorized by the prophets, it continued to flourish in the pre-exilic community. If Asa drove the Sodomites (*qedeshim*) out of the land[74] it was only a temporary measure, for Hosea (750–735 B.C.) makes it abundantly clear that their female counterparts, the priestesses, exercised their functions with undiminished vigour in his day.[75] In the next century the Deuteronomic law endeavoured to suppress both male and female hierodouloi,[76] but despite the drastic reforms of Josiah, which included destroying the houses of the Sodomites and those of the sacred women who wove hangings for Asherah and practised her rites in the temple at Jerusalem, the cult, as we have seen, persisted during the period of the Exile.

In the metaphorical description of the popular fertility cultic rites in the book of Hosea and in the Canticles traces of the Canaanite lyrical and liturgical elements connected with the sacred marriage adapted to the Yahweh religion are apparent. In the shrines with their couches the union of the god and the goddess was dramatized by the sacred prostitutes, and the sons of the *zonah* were regarded apparently as divine offspring.[77] To modify these cultic implications, in Hosea the children are attributed to Gomer, the faithless wife of the prophet who herself probably originally was a sacred prostitute,[78] though it is still maintained that Yahweh was himself the first husband of the *zonah*, the "lovers" being distinguished from him.[79] The fertility symbolism, however, was retained and interpreted in terms of the marriage of Yahweh with his people.[80]

The Hittite Goddess

In closer association with Palestine and Syria the "Land of Hatti" in the north-east of the Anatolian plateau of Asia Minor, within the circuit of the Halys river (Kizil Irmak), formed the homeland of the Hittite Empire which flourished as a great power in the second millennium B.C., created by kings who, like the pre-Hittite Anatolian princes before them in the Middle Bronze Age, established a stable civilization in this mountain stronghold. Thus, recent excavations (1954-6) at Beycesultan and Kültepe have transformed the semi-mythical figure of King Anittas into an historical character by the discovery of an inscription on a bronze spear-head reading "Place of Anittas, the King", who probably controlled the greater part of the plateau by the end of his reign. It is possible that the royal Hittite line was descended from him, though there is no actual evidence of such a claim. It was from Labarnas, who is said to have subdued the land and to have governed its great cities, that the later Hittite kings traced their lineage,[81] and by 1400 B.C. the kingdom had been established by Suppiluliumas, the Great Prince of Hatti, who conquered and incorporated in his empire the Mesopotamian kingdoms of Mitanni and the Hussilands, and sent armies into Syria and Palestine.

The central city-states were welded as a group under the rule of the "Great King", who, in addition to being the head of the army and the supreme judge, was also the chief priest of the gods, while the queen-mother, the *tavananna*, was the priestess of the Mother-goddess and could act as the regent during the king's absence. Although he was never deified in his lifetime, he was called the son of the gods, and so was brought into the same relation with the goddess through the *tavananna*. Thus, at the great rock-sanctuary of Yasilikaya, about two miles from the capital, Boghazköy, the chief goddess of the pantheon bearing the Hurrian name Hepatu is depicted mounted on a panther, with the Storm- and Weather-god, probably Teshub, wearing a horned mitre, clad in a kilt and carrying a mace or club and a sword. The Goddess, in a full-sleeved robe and crowned with a tiara, stands on a lioness with her right hand raised and her left hand stretched out to greet her visitor.[82] Behind her, also mounted on a panther, is a smaller figure, doubt-less representing Sharma (Sharruma) as her son. Following him are two goddesses vested like Hepatu and making the same gestures, with the wings of an eagle beneath them. They may represent Mezzulla, the daughter of the Sun-goddess of Arinna, and her granddaughter Zintuhi. Processions of lesser divinities in two groups are depicted on the walls of the sanctuary. On the left side are males led by the Storm-god, and females on the right led by the Sun-goddess of Arinna; both moving towards the god and goddess followed by priests and priestesses.

At the west of the entrance are twelve kilted men running in formation and more goddesses followed by their priestesses, all carrying staves with a large figure eight feet high, vested as a priest-king with outstretched arms and a winged disk repre-senting the heavens surmounted by the sun.[83] In a small inner chamber devoted to the young god, leading off the main sanctuary, is another relief of twelve running men carrying what would seem to be sickles[84] like those at the entrance. On a rock-carving of the king, who is designated in hiero-glyphic signs as Tudhaliyas IV, he is shown in the embrace of the young god with his right arm outstretched and his left round a smaller figure with the insignia of a priest-king, presumably also Tudhaliyas, resolved into a sword of which the hilt was in the form of four crouching lions.

Now it is very probable that these reliefs were executed and erected at the sanctuary at Yazilikaya because it was thither that the king and queen repaired, probably at the Spring Festival when the crops were cut, to perform the renewal rites which were almost universal in Western Asia. If this were so, it would seem that the sacred marriage between the Sun-goddess of Arinna and the Storm-god of Hatti, in the presence of their son Sharma, the young god, was enacted in the main hall. Garstang, in fact, has suggested further that it may have been the scene of the union of Teshub with the Hurrian goddess Hebat (or Hapit) of Kizzuwatna (the Cataonia of the Roman period), each with his and her retinue, on the occasion of the marriage of Hattusilis III to the priestess Puduhepa.[85] There is nothing in the texts to confirm this interesting conjecture, but in the Egyptian version of the treaty between Hattusilis and Rameses II, the Hittite queen Puduhepa appears on the royal seal embracing the Sun-goddess of Arinna.[86] The converging processions suggest the perambulations in the New Year Festival ritual closely connected with the sacred marriage, and since the bull is the emblem of the fertility-god everywhere, the presence of the bull-men in them doubtless had a similar significance.

As Arinna was the principal religious centre, so the Sun-goddess located there was the chief Hittite deity whose consort, the Storm-god, was subordinate to her. In the state religion she was "the Queen of the Land of Hatti, Heaven and Earth; mistress of the kings and queens of the Land of Hatti, directing the government of the King and Queen of Hatti". As the inscriptions reveal, in this capacity she, as "Hepat", was the Hittite counterpart of the Earth-mother in the guise of Ishtar, with whom she was sometimes associated, and in her cultus she may have engaged in a second marriage with the Weather-god of Hatti, though she was the dominant partner in the union, as in Mesopotamia.[87]

At Comana of Cappadociae (Kummanni) eventually she became known as Ma, and like Ishtar at Nineveh and Anat at Ras Shamra, developed martial characteristics so that she was identified by the Romans with Ma-Bellona, thereby following the familiar transformation of the Fertility-goddess into a War-goddess. Her consort at first being the Hurrian Storm- and Weather-god, this alliance persisted, recurring at Kummanni, Aleppo, Samuha (Malatya?), Huma and Apzisna. At Yasilikaya, however, as the young Storm-god he was her son and lover, like Tammuz in relation to Ishtar, before he was exalted as "Lord of Heaven", and identified with the Sun-god, who originally does not seem to have been conspicuous at Arinna, despite the fact that the chief deity was the Sun-goddess. It may be that he was not indigenous in the Hittite pantheon, and that it was only after he had been introduced into Anatolia that he acquired a definite status *vis-à-vis* the Sun-goddess.[88] But once he was celestialized as the ruler of the skies he could hardly fail to be identified sooner or later with the sun, even though he contracted his union with the Goddess in the first place as the Weather-god of Hatti. It was this rôle that may have been enacted by the king and queen, probably at the New Year Festival in the winter, after the Sun-gods had absorbed the functions of the Earth-mother and the god of vegetation,[89] when they celebrated their ritual marriage personifying the nuptials of the Goddess of Arinna and her spouse in the manner familiar in the religions of the Near East, and for the same purposes.

The Indo-Iranian Goddess Cult

In the welter of peoples and religions that characterized Western Asia in the second millennium B.C., the penetration of the Indo-Europeans emerging from Transcaspia and making their way through Iran in a south-easterly direction was a determining factor in the development of a composite myth and ritual.[90] This was apparent in the Goddess cult and its ramifi-cations so firmly established in the peripheral regions in ancient Iran. Thus, in the prehistoric civilization on the plains of Elam female figurines modelled in clay were abundant in the proto-Elamite and the first Elamite period (*c.* 2800 B.C.), often adorned with necklaces, bracelets and pendants.[91] At Susa she was worshipped under the Elamite name of Kiririsha, and even after the Elamite power had come to an end in 640 B.C. she continued at Nanaia down to the Parthian period (*c.* 250 B.C.–A.D. 299). It is possible she may also be detected in the Zoroastrian goddess of fertility and water, Anahita, who appears in the Yashts with Mitra along with Ahura Mazda[92] personifying the mystical life-giving river "in the shape of a maid, fair of body, most strong, tall-formed, high-girded, pure, nobly born of a glorious race". As the goddess of springs and streams and of all fertility she was endowed with the form of Ishtar, depicted with prominent breasts, a golden crown of stars and golden raiment. As such she was worshipped as the goddess of generation and all sexual life,[93] with a retinue of priestesses engaged in sacred prostitution.[94] Associated with her was Mithras as the young god and victorious hero who sacrificed the primeval bull to become the source of life for mankind.

No less conspicuous was the cult in Baluchistan and in the Harappa culture where female figurines akin to those in Elam, Anatolia, Mesopotamia, Egypt and the Aegean have been found in very considerable numbers, and clearly served the same purpose as in the rest of their distribution in Western Asia in connexion with the worship of the Mother-goddess. In the Kulli culture of Southern Baluchistan established in Makran before 3000 B.C. in the clay statuettes of women which have been discovered finishing at the waist in a splayed pedestal, although the breasts are not unduly exaggerated usually they are shown, and in one case two infants are represented held in the arms of the figure. The faces are grotesque but the orna-ments which adorn the head include oval pendants resembling cowrie shells. Similar examples recur in the Zhob valley in the north with necklaces and more exaggerated breasts sugges-tive of embodiments of the Goddess. They are, in fact, so uniform in style and features that they appear to have been intended to represent a fertility deity who was also the guardian of the dead "concerned alike with the corpse and the seed-corn buried beneath the earth", as Professor Piggott suggests.[95] That they had a fertility significance is shown by a phallus carved in stone at the mound of Mogul Ghundai near the left bank of the river Khob south-west of fort Sandemann, and at Periano Ghundai on the right bank, by a vulva prominently depicted.[96]

In the Indus valley the terra-cotta female figurines mentioned in the last chapter[97] occurred at Mohenjo-daro at every level, frequently in a mutilated condition, in the streets and in the dwellings, painted over with a red slip of wash, doubtless to enhance their life-giving potency as in Egypt, Mesopotamia and Malta.[98] The majority are nude except for a small shirt round the loins, and they have a large fan-shaped head-dress and side pannier-like projections. Many are adorned with bead necklaces and pendants, ornamental collars, armlets, bracelets and anklets. Some in the high levels were seated with hands

clasped round the knees, roughly modelled and with no orna-
ments. Others (e.g. figures on a faience plaque) were in
postures which suggest that they were engaged in a sacred
dance.[99] That, like their counterparts elsewhere in the region,
they represent a goddess with attributes similar to those of the
Mother-goddess in Mesopotamia, Elam, Egypt and the Eastern
Mediterranean, is very probable.[100] Moreover, as Dr Mackay
suggests,[101] they seem to have been household deities kept in
a niche in the wall in almost every house in the Indus cities,
just as today the Mother-goddess is the guardian of the
house and the village presiding over childbirth and the daily
needs.

Figures of male gods, frequently horned, are prevalent in the
Harappa culture,[102] but they are seldom shown in conjunction
with those of the goddesses. If, as has been suggested, the well-
known three-faced deity seated on a throne in the *yoga* posture
with arms outstretched and what may have been a phallus
exposed,[103] roughly carved on a seal from Mohenjo-daro, is
a prototype of the Hindu god Shiva, his fertility aspects as
Lord of the Beasts (Pasupati) must be pre-Aryan. This is
further indicated by the realistic *lingas*, symbolizing the male
generative organ, and the *yoni* or vulva, which are of frequent
occurrence in the Harappa culture, sometimes in association
with the horned-god and the sacred pipal-tree and the cult of
animals.[104] Among the Saivites the *linga* remains the most
popular object of veneration as a life-giving amulet.

It may be concluded, therefore, that that aspect of Hinduism
which finds expression in the cult of Shiva and the Mother-
goddess has been derived from this very ancient Harappa
civilization, the cradleland of which in all probability was in
the Iranian highlands where its founders shared a common
origin with the Sumerians before they made their way into
North-west India through Baluchistan. Whether it was from
this source that the cult of the cow came is much more doubtful. Although it was and is such a prominent feature in
Brahmanic Hinduism, it was not introduced into India by the
Aryan invasion in the middle of the second millennium B.C.

Thus, it was foreign to the Rig-veda, and in all the earlier Vedas the sacrifice of cattle to Indra, Varuna and other deities was enjoined notwithstanding the fact that it was abhorrent to public opinion. This suggests that they were regarded as sacred by the non-Aryan population, as in Western Asia and the Fertile Crescent where the bull and the cow were so prominent in the Goddess cult. The first Vedic prohibition of cow-killing occurs in the relatively late Atharva-veda which contains indications of non-Aryan influences.

But while the bull sacred to the non-Vedic god Shiva was widely represented as a cult animal in the Harappa civilization, as in Minoan Crete, the cow was conspicuously absent.[105] Nevertheless, the sanctity of the cow was deeply laid in the antecedents of the Indo-Iranian Goddess cult where the Great Mother was herself the cow giving her milk as the life-bestowing agent *par excellence* in the process of suckling.[106] All the available evidence suggests that in India it arose among the indigenous Dravidian population with the development of agriculture, and it may have been a survival of the Indo-Iranian tradition, even though apparently it did not occur in plastic representation at Harappa or Mohenjo-daro. From this source it may have culminated in the deification of the cow in later times, and all that this has involved in Hindu faith and practice.

THE GODDESS CULT IN THE MEDITERRANEAN

In the Eastern Mediterranean where the Great Mother was the principal object of worship, her emblems abound, especially in Crete and Cyprus. There the snake, the dove, the double axe, horns of consecration, obese female figurines and the Goddess standing on mountains or in association with sacred trees and pillars, are characteristic features of the cultus everywhere. While her functions were primarily maternal she was also the goddess of vegetation and fertility, and in this capacity she often was associated with a youthful partner as her son or consort, sometimes holding a bow and wearing the same tiara to mark his divinity.

The Minoan-Mycenaean Mother-goddess

For example, on a gold ring in the Ashmolean Museum, Oxford, said to have come from the Vapheio tomb at Mycenae, a kneeling woman is shown leaning over a large jar in what may be the attitude of mourning. Above her are the human eye and ear symbols, and to the left in the background is a small rigid male figure holding with one hand what seems to be a bow and with the other a disk-like object. This may represent a boy-god as a youthful archer brandishing his bow in response to the gesticulations of a female who in all probability is the Mother-goddess.[107] Since the jar resembles the vessels used in pithos burial it may be a mortuary scene, and in that case the leafless branches of a tree behind an elliptically rounded stone could symbolize the dying vegetation of winter over which lamentation was being made.[108]

This interpretation is supported by a similar mourning scene on a Late Minoan gold signet from Mycenae showing the Goddess in a flounced skirt bowed with grief over a kind of miniature temenos. Within the sacred enclosure stands a baetyl with a very small Minoan shield hanging beside it. Above the Goddess is a branch of a tree in leaf, and to the right of her is a similar female figure, presumably the Goddess repeated, in an upright position about to receive the fruit of the tree extended to her by a male attendant. Here, as Sir Arthur Evans recognizes, there can be little doubt that the scene is a Minoan equivalent of the Attis, Adonis, Tammuz cult in which the young god is depicted as a youthful warrior equated with the Cretan Zeus[109] whose tomb was said to be in Crete.

If the enclosure is a tomb containing a phallic stone, as is probable, the scene is brought into line with the grave of Attis in Phrygia and of Zeus at Knossos.[110] The mourning, therefore, may represent the Minoan version of the suffering Goddess theme in Western Asia and in the vegetation myth and ritual, the budding leaves and the ripening fruits symbolizing the approach of spring. Thus, on a gold ring in the museum of Candia the stem of a tree with scanty foliage is portrayed grasped with both hands by a woman. To the left is an identical female figure in a flounced skirt with the upper part of her body naked, showing prominent breasts, standing with her back to a tree and her arms extended towards a third woman of exactly the same type.[111] Here, again, the epiphany of the Goddess at the approach of spring is suggested.

The Shrines at Knossos and Gournia

As in Asia Minor she was also represented on seals as the Mountain-mother standing on a peak between her guardian lions, holding a lance or sceptre in her hand with a sacred pillar taking the place of the tree, over which sometimes libations were poured by genii.[112] In the Central Palace Sanctuary at Knossos, for instance, facing the central court, there is a rectangular recess, opposite to the base of the central altar, in which a series of seal impressions were found in 1901 showing the Minoan Goddess standing on a mountain guarded by two lions. Immediately behind this shrine is a small chamber in the Late Minoan floor of which were two superficial cists, or open stone vats, in the pavement used probably for the storage of oil. Two larger cists discovered later contained a quantity of relics among which in the eastern cist were two female faience figurines of the Snake-goddess adorned with a tiara and clad in a richly embroidered high-waisted bodice, the breasts exposed.[113]

In a basement to the north of the east-west corridor of the palace full of weights and pottery, are fragments of altars, models of a shrine mounted on horns of consecration and of a portable seat, together with columns of seated doves coloured in polychrome, thought to have come from a sanctuary of the Minoan cult of the Dove-goddess,[114] though no traces of such a shrine have been found.

In many Cretan palaces and villas remains occur of the bases of monolithic pillars of no utility value with pits sunk in the ground round them. In the royal villa at Knossos, excavated by Evans in 1903, double axes were incised upon the pillars and a channel to the east and west on either side containing an oblong receptacle analogous in form and position to the vats in the Central Palace Sanctuary.[115] Similarly, in the house excavated by Dr Hogarth on the opposite hill nearly two hundred small libation cups were arranged bottom upwards in orderly rows on the floor covering little heaps of carbonized vegetable material in an elaborately constructed room containing a central pillar standing up from a paving block of gypsum.[116] Here again the pillars do not appear to have had any structural use.

Almost certainly they were part of the equipment of a domestic shrine of the Mother-goddess and the young god, as symbolized by the double axes, corresponding to the small enclosures, such as the Late Minoan example (*c.* 1500 B.C.) found at Gournia on the northern coast of Crete to the east of Knossos on a hill-top containing a female figure in terra-cotta twined with snakes, and fragments of similar statuettes, two snakes' heads, four doves and a piece of a clay pithos decorated with a double axe, horns of consecration and three terra-cotta cultus vases, assembled around a low plastered earthern table with three legs. These sacred objects are characteristic of the Minoan Goddess cult almost everywhere in the region, though when it was discovered in 1901 it was the first actual example of a domestic shrine sacred to her.[117] In the light of the Minoan III palace shrine at Knossos with its vessels of offering, votive figures and other cult objects still in position as they were left when the site was finally deserted,[118] there could be no doubt about the reconstruction of the Gournia enclosure.

At Knossos it was divided into three parts. The vases stood in the "nave" with its clay floor in the centre of which was a plaster tripod with a slightly hollowed upper surface, evidently used as a table of offerings. On either side were cups and smaller jugs, while behind the dais and table a raised base of clay and rubble about 60 centimetres high ran from wall to wall. On a ledge were two horns in white stucco with painted terra-cotta votive female figures on either side of a very primitive type with arms clasped over the breasts and the body rising from a clay cylinder in baetylic fashion. On one a plant design was painted on the back reminiscent of the tree cult, and another, clad in a kind of bodice, was adorned with necklaces and armlets, a disk on the wrists and a dove on the head. On the opposite side of the base was a male figure holding out a dove to the Goddess, but the central object was the stucco horns of consecration with a socket for the shaft of a double axe rising from between them, and a small votive steatite double axe resting against the left pair of horns. That the horns and the double axes were associated with the Goddess cult is indicated by the presence of the female figures. In the light of this Knossian shrine the construction and contents of that at Gournia fall into place, and their significance in the worship of the Goddess becomes apparent.

The Goddess Cult and the Cult of the Dead

In the scenes depicted on the sarcophagus from Hagia Triada most of the symbols of the Goddess cult occur in what appears to be a funerary setting, including an altar with horns of consecration, an olivetree with spreading branches, a shaft with a double axe and a bird, a priestess with a vessel of offerings, a libation jar, the bull as the sacrificial victim whose blood was collected in what may have been a bottomless vessel to enable it to flow down into the ground as an offering to Motherearth to secure her good offices in the rebirth of the deceased beyond the grave, and the journey of the soul to its final abode.[119] Miss Harrison, on the other hand, interprets the scene as the passing of winter and the coming of spring in the vegetation calendrical drama with its death and resurrection theme.[120]

The cult of the dead has so much in common with the cult of fertility that they frequently coalesce in their myth and ritual and symbolism. In this case, however, the fact that the scenes occur on a sarcophagus suggests primarily a funerary interpretation in relation to the afterlife rather than of the death and revival in nature, though admittedly both are often almost inseparable in the office and function of the Goddess. Therefore, since the imagery is of a composite character the two cults may have been fused, though, as Nilsson points out, no evidence exists for such a union on Minoan monuments.[121] Nevertheless, Crete and the Aegean developed their own distinctive sepulchral traditions, and it is now no longer possible to place the original home of the Goddess cult in this region, since it is known to have been well established at Arpachiyah in Assyria in the Tell Halaf culture a thousand years before it appeared in the Minoan-Mycenaean civilization.

In the Chalcolithic period, probably in the fifth millennium B.C., the double axe, formerly supposed to have been of Cretan origin, was a cult object among the Arpachiyahians and else-where in the Ancient Middle East, together with the dove, as a symbol of the Mother-goddess. There the tholos or "beehive" tomb was at first a circular dwelling which was transformed into a stone temple before it was used for sepulchral purposes. In its diffusion in the Eastern Mediterranean it became essen-tially a stone-built collective grave with a corbelled vault or with the roof thatched and covered with a capstone. In this form it became the characteristic mode of burial in Crete and the Aegean in the Early Minoan II (*c.* 2400 B.C.) as the home of the dead in the womb of Mother-earth when the predomi-nant Goddess cult acquired a more specifically mortuary significance and its emblems found a place in the tholoi and the funerary ritual.

It was then that Crete became such an important centre of the worship in its various forms and aspects that it came to be regarded as the cradleland of the Phrygian mystery of the Great Mother.[122] Worshipped in her own right as the Mistress of Trees and Mountains, and the Lady of the Wild Beasts, in association with her youthful male partner she represented the life-giving principle in nature and in man, until eventually on the Greek mainland her functions and attributes were assumed by a number of goddesses. Thus, Athena, once an earth-divinity, acquired her snake and bird emblems; Artemis her wild creatures, together with forests and streams; and Aphrodite took over her doves.

Maltese Temples and their Cultus

In Malta, however, the West Asiatic tradition persisted.[123] Thus, the great apsidal temples of Mnaidra, Hagiar Kim and

Hal Tarxien, with the Gigantea on the neighbouring island of Gozo and the Hal Saflieni Hypogeum to the north-west of the village of Tarxien, were sanctuaries before at a later stage in their history they became ossuaries or tombs, as at Arpachiyah. When they were erected in the third millennium B.C. they were essentially temples of the Asiatic Mother-goddess, often built in pairs with a double shrine, suggestive of the worship of a male and female divinity, as in the case of Isis and Osiris, Ishtar and Tammuz, Aphrodite and Adonis, or Attis and Cybele.[124] Obese female figurines with Western Asiatic affinities were very prevalent.[125] At Tarxien a very corpulent headless statuette in a sitting posture has the hands resting on the thighs towards the genital organ.[126] In a fragment of a clay female figure found among the Neolithic debris the sexual triangle is shown by a deep incision,[127] while at Mnaidra a female torso with protruding breasts gives the appearance of pregnancy.[128]

A clay model of a woman lying asleep on a couch at the Hypogeum led Zammit to conclude that the temple originally was used for incubation in the consultation of oracles by priests in the service of the Goddess.[129] At Hal Tarxien the colossal figure of the Goddess stood more than 7 feet in height clad in a fluted skirt. In attendance were her priests in long skirts and short wigs resembling Chaldaean officials, offering burnt sacrifice before the statue on an altar near by and passing the blood into a stone vessel with a hollow base, while incense burnt in the cup-shaped tops of cylindrical pillars. In the last of the three temples the Goddess may have given her oracle through a slit in a wall, a priest acting as her voice.[130]

THE GODDESS CULT IN WESTERN EUROPE

Statue-menhirs in Brittany and S.O.M.

From its western centre at Malta the Goddess cult was diffused to the Iberian Peninsula, where in Almeria from about 2700 B.C. it found expression in the hundreds of stylized female figurines and plaques in the huts and megalithic tombs at Los Millares in such profusion that, as at Mohenjo-daro, they

appear to have been part of the domestic equipment in every
household.[131] Some are fiddle-shaped like those in the Eastern
Mediterranean, and often conventionalized almost beyond
recognition with "owl eyes" or bovine phalanges.[132] In
Brittany, the Channel Islands and the Paris Basin (Seine-
Oise-Marne area) the symbolism recurred in the megalithic
civilization in the form of menhir-statues with breasts and
U-shaped necklaces.[133] The centre of the cult in this region
was the Seine and Oise valleys, where it was a characteristic
feature of the S.O.M. culture, introduced probably from the
south of France, Sardinia and the Balearic Isles, spreading up
the Rhône valley to the Paris basin, and the chalk downs of
Champagne. Having acquired a definitely funerary significance,
thence it reached the Amorican peninsula as the great pilgrimage centre, with its Iberian contacts and extensions, to the
Channel Islands and the mouth of the Loire.

The British Isles

Proceeding northwards the megalithic mariners made their
way across the English Channel to Britain, settling on the
chalk downs and uplands from Wessex to Devon in small
agricultural communities. That they brought with them their
Goddess cult is not improbable, as a few isolated female
figurines and phalli in chalk and bone have been recovered
from a number of sites, such as a headless conventionalized
torso at Maiden Castle in Dorset with two holes at the base
for the insertion of legs. At Windmill Hill near Avebury a
female statuette, together with phalli, carved in chalk were
found,[134] while at Trundle above the Goodwood racecourse
a carefully carved bone object could be a phallus.[135] A more
convincing and well-carved example has come from a long
barrow on Thickthorn Down, Cranborne Chase, Dorset, in
association with the Windmill Hill culture,[136] and other
similar finds have been recorded at Whitehawk Camp on the
Brighton racecourse with its causewayed camp typical of the
Windmill Hill period, and in the flint-mines at Blackpatch
on the Sussex Downs.

Although less definitely associated with this culture, an interesting example of the cult has been discovered in pit 15 of the flint-mines at Grime's Graves in Norfolk, where an obese figure of a pregnant woman carved in chalk occurred on a ledge with a phallus below her. Near it was a sort of "altar" composed of blocks of flint in the form of a triangle with a chalk cup at the base opposite the goddess. Upon this structure seven deer antler picks had been laid apparently as an offering.[137] Here, it may be conjectured, was a shrine of the fertility cult placed in an unsterile shaft to restore its productivity, or to make the mine as a whole a rich flint-bed; thereby extending the idea of the earth's abundance to its mineral content. The affinity of this statuette, however, is with the Palaeolithic Venuses rather than with the Iberian technique, and there are no indications that in Britain and Northern France the Goddess tradition culminating in a sacred marriage ever occupied the position it attained in the myth and ritual of the Ancient Middle East.

CHAPTER V

The Myth and Ritual of Creation

TURNING now to the myth of creation we are faced with a rather more complicated situation. Unlike where the mystery of birth and generation, and the ever-present perplexing pheno- mena of fertility and the seasonal sequence with all their hazards were concerned, Early Man was only interested in speculations about cosmic origins in so far as they were vitally related to present realities. But since the present never can be cut off entirely from the past, what lay behind the existing order in human society and its environment could not fail to be of considerable importance. Things are as they are, it was main- tained, because they have been so ordained and determined by the powers-that-be in the beginning when they were first called into being, however this process may have been conceived. But in the absence of speculative thought as an intellectual disci- pline, such as has dominated the problem of creation since in the sixth century B.C. the Ionian thinkers turned their attention to the philosophic study of origins (ἀρχή) in terms of a "first cause" and of a permanent ground of existence, in the ancient world the situation was given a mythological content. This took the form of a story usually enacted in a ritual to enable the events alleged to have occurred in the past to be operative in the present as a living reality. Hence the recitation of the Creation epic as an essential element in the Annual Festival.

The Egyptian Conception of Creation

Thus, the Egyptians, approaching creation from the standpoint of human experience, interpreted the initial event as a series of births in the realms of the gods beginning with a primeval pair who proceeded from an existing state of watery chaos. This is hardly surprising as in the Nile valley the annual inundation was the most significant fact in the environment upon which vegetation depended and all that this involved in the life and economy of the nation. If from it new life emerged in the seasonal sequel, and when it subsided the dry land appeared, so must it have been in the beginning. First came the primordial ocean deified as Nun, from which a cosmic order was established out of a primeval state of chaos, as evidenced by the regularity in the behaviour of the Nile. The rich fertile soil annually renewed by the inundation brought forth abundantly so that the desert blossomed as the rose. And what happened on earth (i.e. in the Nile valley) had its counterpart in the divine order when the creative process began and the gods emerged, including those responsible for the subsequent creations, Atum or Re in Heliopolis, Thoth in Hermopolis, Khnum in Elephantine, and even in some measure the selfcreated Ptah in Memphis.

The many forms which the creatorgods assumed in Egyptian mythology was doubtless the result of an earlier cult of an allembracing Skygod as the Supreme Being brought into conjunction with the very ancient solar worship in its several manifestations. Everywhere the transcendental source of universal creative activity has been centred in the sky, summing up in himself the various attributes and aspects of nature and responsible for the control of the weather. The same linguistic root, for example, connects the heavens, the clouds and the rain with their principal personifications in the heavenly Creator and his manifestations in nature: the storm and the thunder. As Zeus, or Dyaus Pitar, among the IndoEuropeans, like the chief god of the Hittites, Teshub, was primarily the god of the sky, the storm and the weather, known under a number of names before he assumed the functions of the various gods whom he assimilated, so in Egypt the Falcongod Horus, the "Lofty One", was regarded as a celestial deity with a creative capacity before he acquired a solar significance. But in view of the place occupied by the sun in the Nile valley, both as a lifegiving and as a destructive force, it was not surprising that it became the dominant creative symbol, even though the Memphite Ptah retained his position as the sole Creator of the universe and of the gods, who were objectified conceptions of his mind.[1] Since he was the Earth-god identified with the "Risen Land" (i.e. the Primordial Hill) which he created out of the waters of Nun to become the centre of the earth, he was not given a solar significance until very much later. Originally, according to one myth, he was anterior to the Sun-god Atum because the eight gods who brought forth the sun from the primeval waters were his creation, as were the eight primeval elements of chaos with which he was identified as Ptah-Ta-Tjenen, "Ptah of the Risen Land". Therefore, all that exists came from him and functioned through him as the ground of all creation.

This was as near as the Ancient Egyptians came to creation *ex nihilo*, but the Memphite theology made little or no impression on popular belief and practice. Like the later solar monotheism of Ikhnaton in the Eighteenth Dynasty, when Amon-Re was replaced by Aton as the universal god and within the framework of the solar mythology made the sole creator and sustainer of all things, it was too abstract and remote to be acceptable to the Egyptians. For them it was the all-enveloping sun which appeared to fly across the horizon like a falcon in his daily course, rising in the east in the morning from the nether regions (*Duat*) to start his journey as Khepera, the self-created sacred scarab beetle rolling the ball of the sun across the sky, and tottering down to the west as an aged man, Atum, in the evening.

In this mythology the earth was represented as encircled by a chain of high mountains on which the sky rested, personified as the Goddess Nut. Below it was the great abyss (*Duat*) from which the Sun-god was born every morning as at the beginning of creation when he became the father of the gods, the first-born of the primeval ocean (Nun). Heaven (Nut) and earth (Geb) at first were not separated, until Shu, the "atmosphere", the father of Nut, lifted her up and supported her on his arms above the earth. In the celestial realms thus formed Atum, the Sun-god, became supreme and exercised creative functions. Thus, at Heliopolis, where his worship had been long established before it became the capital and centre of the solar cult in the Fifth Dynasty (*c.* 2580 B.C.), he was the head of the Ennead. There the "House of the Obelisk" in the solar temple stood on the Sandhill with a stone of conical shape, regarded as the Primeval Hill on which Atum first appeared, and so it was regarded as the centre of the creative forces. Hence the royal tomb was given the form of a pyramid as a reproduction of the Heliopolitan Sandhill to enable the Pharaoh buried in it to be reanimated like the sun rising from the waters of Nun with the aid of the vitalizing power inherent in this potent re-creative sacred place.

The Heliopolitan Ennead

According to the Heliopolitan mythology the Sun-god existed alone in Nun and had sexual union with himself in order to create Shu, the personification of the atmosphere, and Tefnut, the goddess of moisture. These in turn produced Geb, the Earth-god, and Nut the Sky-goddess, from whom sprang Osiris and his sister-spouse Isis, Seth and his sister Nephthys, who was also his consort.

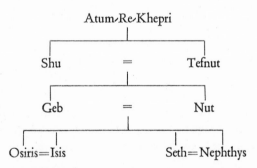

These nine gods together make up the Great Ennead of Heliopolis, and constitute the most important family of gods in the creation story.

When Re became the head of the pantheon after the unifica-tion of Upper and Lower Egypt, he combined all the creative forces in nature and was absolute in his control of the govern-ment of the Nile valley. Around him in the Pyramid Age myths and legends accumulated more than about any other single god in Egypt. He was equated with Atum and so was accredited with begetting the rest of the Heliopolitan Ennead of which in his composite form as Re-Atum he stood at the head. Thus, he became the self-created Creator, the source of life and increase and the father of the gods as well as the personification of the sun in its manifold forms and capacities. [2] Therefore, like the Mother-goddess, he had many names. As "the begetter of the gods" he was addressed as "Creator" and "body" of Atum, Nun, Shu, Geb, Tefnut, Nut, Isis, Nephthys, Horus, Khepri and Re-Harakhte, the youthful god on the eastern horizon, until eventually at Thebes he was worshipped in great magnificence at Karnak and Luxor as "the king of the gods", supreme in heaven and on earth. [3]

These aspects of Deity, together with those of Ptah of Memphis, in due course were blended not in a single mono-theistic Creator but in a pluralism of divine manifestations of independent divinities with the same nature, born at the same time from Nun in which they were immanent from the begin-ning, and so in a sense were self-created or emergent by their own divine powers and attributes. Thus, Atum-Re was a composite figure proceeding from the primeval ocean of chaos as the sun emerged from the darkness of the *Duat* when he arose in the morning to shed his radiance on the earth. Simi-larly, Shu, objectivated as the atmosphere, was "spat out" by Atum on the Primordial Hill and vitalized by the inbreathing of his Ka to endow him (Shu) with his life-giving power [4] as a kind of "paraclete", the strength and stay upholding the heavens with his arms, his feet firmly planted on the earth, after he had united with Tefnut, the goddess of moisture, to pro-create Geb (the earth) and Nut (the sky).

The rest of the Heliopolitan Ennead came into being through normal methods of reproduction. As Geb and Nut were born of Shu and Tefnut, so Isis and Nephthys were their daughters and Osiris and Seth their sons, who respectively became hus-bands and wives, Isis marrying Osiris and Nephthys Seth. Thus, the way was opened for the ancient Sky-god Horus to be Osirianized. As "the seed of Geb"[5] he was transformed into the posthumous son of Osiris born of Isis to avenge the murder of his father by his Uncle Seth.[6] Moreover, in this genealogy the celestial gods and goddesses of the solar cycle were brought into relation with the earth and chthonic divinities of the Osiris tradition and the cult of the dead. But the last four deities—Osiris and Isis, Seth and Nephthys—were in a different category from the first five cosmic gods who collectively exercised the office and functions of the Creator in the creation stories which grew up around them. The four descendants of Nut and Geb, on the other hand, belonged essentially to the royal solar-Osirian mythology in which the creation was explicit but a secondary consideration.

The Memphite Theology

The Heliopolitan Ennead which was formulated before the Pyramid texts were preserved from the Fifth Dynasty, became the pattern followed by other towns and districts in their cosmo-logical schemes, sometimes omitting one of the nine gods of Heliopolis to make room for their own local god, or adding him to the nine. At Memphis, however, Ptah being the Creator who by thinking as the "heart" and commanding as the "tongue" fashioned an egg on his potter's wheel from which the earth was hatched, or carved it as a statue,[7] an entirely different account of creation was in vogue. In it the death of Osiris and the feud between Horus and Seth were incorporated in order to make Geb the awarder of the rule of the whole of Egypt to Horus. Since, as has been pointed out, the Memphite theology conferred upon Memphis and its god superiority over Heliopolis and all other cult centres, the transference of the body of Osiris to the new capital (Memphis) and the assignment of the sovereignty of Egypt to his son Horus, as recorded in the very ancient Mystery play (*c.* 3100 B.C.), justified these claims. Consequently, Ptah in the process of creation became elevated over Atum and the Heliopolitan Ennead as the "Mighty Great" Creator-god from whom the cosmic order emanated virtually *ex nihilo*. It was "in the heart

and on the tongue of Ptah that (something) in the form of
Atum" came into being, and by this creative process of thought
the rest of the Ennead of gods were created and placed in their
temples. This accomplished, "men, animals, all creeping things,
and whatever lives" by Ptah's thought and word were created,
and henceforth the same principles continued to operate
through his power.[8] Thus were the gods born, mankind was
supplied with food, the distinction between right and wrong
established, and all human arts, crafts and activities pursued,
cities built and local gods set in their governing places. Therefore, Ptah's power was greater than that of all the other gods,
but it was not denied that the Heliopolitan Ennead had their
own part, place and function in the cosmic scheme, or, indeed,
any of the other gods of creation.

At Elephantine and Philae, for example, Khnum, the Ram-
god, was regarded as the Creator of gods and men, "the maker
of heaven and earth and the underworld, and of water and of
the mountains", who produced mankind out of clay on a
potter's wheel, as the god *par excellence* of the First Cataract, the
controller of the Nile.[9] Although originally a water-god, his
ram became "the living soul of Re", and he was represented
with the head of a falcon to identify him with Horus, the
Sky-god.[10]

Thoth and the Ogdoad of Hermopolis

Hermopolis being one of the places where the Primordial Hill
was alleged first to have appeared as an island of flames in the
midst of the primeval waters,[11] it too had its own creation story
in which its ancient god Thoth was the head of an Ogdoad
consisting of the eight primeval gods and goddesses who represented the formless chaos before the creation. The first pair was
Nun, the primordial waters, and his consort Nunet, the celestial
expanse above the abyss. The next pair was Huh and Huhet,
the boundless and imperceptible expanses of chaotic formless-
ness. Then came Kuk and Kuket, darkness and obscurity; and,
finally, Amun and Amunet, the intangible and secret aspects of
chaos, like the wind blowing where it listeth without revealing

whence it comes and whither it goes. As in the Hebrew narrative (Gen. i. 1, 2), an attempt was made, therefore, to give mythological expression to a primordial condition in which all things were "without form and void and darkness was upon the face of the deep", prior to the creation of the phenomenal universe. But in the Hermopolitan cosmogony the Creator Thoth emerged in chaos by an act of self-creation and became the heart and tongue of Atum, and also of Ptah. As head of the Ogdoad, however, he stood apart from the eight gods he had created when he laid an egg on the waters of Nun out of which they and all creation emerged.[12] He was regarded, in fact, as the first god, self-begotten, the personification of divine intelligence, omniscient and omnipotent, exercising his creative activity by divine utterance—"the word of his voice".[13]

To him was attributed the invention of hieroglyphic writing —"the words of the gods"—and it was copies of the "Book of Thoth" in the Book of the Dead[14] which the Greeks regarded as the Egyptian "Hermetic Books". He was also, like Moses in Israel, accredited with having been the original Lawgiver who set forth the laws which governed the motions of the heavenly bodies. As the repository of all learning he became the god of wisdom, and eventually virtually the judge of the dead, since it was he who pronounced the verdict when the souls were weighed against the feather of truth at the weighing of the heart before Osiris. Since he was originally in all probability an ancient moon-god of Lower Egypt, his long-established con-nexions with the moon may account for his being regarded as a reckoner of time and of numbers, since all calculations were made by the moon. These later accretions, however, tended to obscure his earlier office and functions as a god of creation.

The Cosmogonic Myth

The creation stories reflect the Egyptian conception of the physical universe. The earth was represented as emerging from the primeval ocean of Nun which remained below it as the waters of the underworld (*Duat*) and surrounded the world, the "Great Circuit" or Okeanos. At its boundaries was a chain of mountains on which the vault of heaven rested, often personified as the Goddess Nut, or as Hathor, the celestial cow whose under-belly was studded with stars and whose four legs constituted the posts on which the sky stood. According to another view, as we have seen, it was Shu, the god of the air, who sustained it with his arms. Or, again, it might be depicted as a woman bending over the earth with the support of Shu after she had given birth to the sun which lay at her feet as a rolling ball (i.e. the solar disk), identified with the scarab beetle, Khepri, the symbol of the sun as the self-created Atum curiously blended with the figure of the Sky-goddess as his mother.[15]

Such contradictions, however, are a characteristic feature of Egyptian cosmology and caused no concern or perplexity because they were regarded merely as complementary approaches to the same general pattern of the universe and its structure.[16] Whether the earth and the sky were supported by a cow, a goddess, mountains, or posts at the four cardinal points of the compass, or the sun was at once the son of the Sky-goddess, the calf of Hathor and the self-begotten Atum-Re-Khepri, depended upon the particular cosmogonic myth that happened to be adopted. This equally applies to the various creation stories in which several gods are held to have been the primary and contemporary source of all existence—Ptah, Khnum, Thoth, Atum-Re, as the case might be at Memphis, Elephantine, Philae, Hermopolis or Heliopolis. Behind them all, notwithstanding the inconsistencies, was divine creative activity manifest in the sun, the wind, the earth and the heavens, making and fashioning all things according to the predetermined designs and purposes, either by thought conception and sacred utterance, or by sexual processes of procreation. The ends and intentions were the same, though the symbolic representations changed according to the manner of approach or method adopted.

In a country like Egypt it was inevitable that the sun, the sky and the life-giving waters of the inundation should predominate in the imagery, while the procreative functions of the bull and the cow hardly could escape notice when cattle played such an important part in the economy. It is not surprising, therefore, that all these familiar and essential objects were personified as divine creative power manifest in cosmic pheno￾mena in the creation stories and the cosmology of which they were an integral aspect. Still less, that among them the sun—the most insistent fact in the phenomenon of nature—came to be regarded as the principal god, the Creator of the universe, the source of all life, whose myth and ritual, centred at Heliopolis, spread over the whole country. As a result every local god was identified with the Sun-god in some way, and the temple cultus everywhere was based on the Heliopolitan liturgy, while its great Ennead and Primordial Hill set the pattern of the cosmic mythology.

Next to the solar cosmology came that of the primeval ocean with its ramifications on, around and below the earth, and ultimately extended to the celestial realm when the goal of the dead became the *Duat* in the Elysian Fields in the northern part of the sky where the circumpolar stars were located. From the *Duat* the Sun-god emerged reborn in the east, having entered it from the west at the end of his daily course across the horizon, to give light and sustenance to its inhabitants. It was in the west that the underworld of Osiris was situated, but he too was celestialized as "he of the horizon from which Re goes forth". In this status he became Orion rising and setting every day, while Isis was the dog star, Sothis, following after him.[17] The waxing and waning moon was also equated with the vicissi￾tudes of Osiris as a god who died and was revived; the waning moon being the injured Eye of his son Horus lost in his fight with Seth.[18] But although it was regarded as a fertilizing influence, the moon does not occupy a prominent position in the extant Egyptian cosmic mythology. It is not improbable, however, that originally it was the twin of the sun, personified possibly as Khonsu who at Thebes became the son of Amon and Mut, and was identified with Thoth as a moon-god in the New Kingdom. But he seems to have been a form of Horus in the beginning,[19] which doubtless explains his royal character as a handsome young prince represented with a lunar disk and crescent on his head, a stiff beard and holding in his hands the whip and shepherd's crook.

The Babylonian Enuma Elish

In Mesopotamia the same general conception of the creation of the universe from a primeval state of chaos was maintained. Nevertheless, while both cosmogonies start from a watery abyss before either the earth or the sky was formed or the gods came into being, instead of the Creator emerging by an act of self-creation, in the *Enuma elish*, the relatively late classic recension of the Babylonian Creation epic, the matrix consisted of "sweet-waters" personified as Apsu, the primeval male, mingled with the salt-water ocean, Tiamat, his female consort. It was from this union that their son Mummu was produced, representing perhaps the mist and clouds arising from the watery chaos. From these three elements as the substratum all life appeared, very much as in the Southern Mesopotamian marshes the waters of the Euphrates and Tigris mingled with those of the sea to produce what must have seemed to be a mysterious power of spontaneous luxuriant growth.[20] This was given mythological expression in the birth of two gods, Lahmu and Lahamu, as brother and sister, followed by a second pair, Anshar and Kishar, who in due course themselves produced the Sky-god Anu. He in turn begot Nudimmud, known as Enki, the Lord of the Land, and Ea, the god of water and wisdom, supreme among his fellow-gods.

The riotous behaviour of these younger divinities, however, became a disturbing influence for their parents and grandparents, who, acting on the advice of Mummu, determined to destroy them root and branch when more conciliatory measures had failed to subdue them. In this course of action, however, Tiamat refused to acquiesce, and when the younger gods became aware of the intention to eliminate them, Ea made a magic circle around Apsu and his allies, rendered him helpless by a spell, slew him, imprisoned Mummu, the vizier, and assumed the leadership. Since Tiamat had not been party to the proposed massacre, she was left unmolested. Ea then took up his abode in a shrine which he called "Apsu", and there his son Marduk was born of Damkina, his wife, and was destined to become "the wisest of the gods", omnipotent in magical power.[21]

In the meantime Tiamat had become disturbed and restless by the course of events, and decided to take action against the gods, stirred up in this intention by Kingu, her second hus‹ band. Therefore, she gave him full authority and invested him with the "Tablets of Destinies", symbolizing the supreme power over the universe. The rebel gods were dismayed and after several fruitless attempts to overcome Tiamat by magical devices, Anshar proposed that Marduk should be sent to vanquish her and her brood. To this proposition the relentless young champion agreed upon the condition that as the price of victory he be made the head of the pantheon and be given "kingship and power over all things". The gods thereupon assembled at a feast and gave their assent to the terms after he had proved his magical powers by causing a garment to disappear and reappear. He was then invested with "irresistible weapons" for the fight, clad in a terrifying coat of mail and equipped with every possible aid to victory, including the arrows of lightning, a rainbow and a net held by four winds.[22]

Setting out to meet his adversary, Kingu and his forces were disordered at the sight of him, and Tiamat alone remained unperturbed, calling down vengeance upon him. He replied by challenging her to single combat. As she opened her mouth to devour him he drove in an evil wind to keep her jaws extended that he might shoot an arrow through them straight into her heart. Like David triumphing over Goliath, he stood upon her corpse, and as her followers fled they were caught in the net. From Kingu he appropriated the Tablet of Destinies and bound him. Returning to Tiamat, he split her body into two parts to create the universe. With one half he formed the sky, with the other he fashioned the earth.[23] In the upper celestial firmament he installed the Triad, Anu, Enlil and Ea, in their respective domains, and set the constellations of the stars and the phases of the moon to determine the year, months and days in the calendar, and the sequence of night and day, to measure time.[24]

After an unfortunate gap in the text on Tablet V the creation of man is described for the purpose of relieving the gods of all menial tasks and enabling them to live in ease and comfort. Kingu having been declared responsible for the revolt of Tiamat, he was killed and from his blood the human race was created, Ea imposing upon it the service of the gods.[25] Marduk then divided the gods of the heavens and earth (the Anunnaki) into two groups, stationing three hundred of them as a guard in the heavens, and three hundred on earth, with their appointed tasks. Thereupon they erected the *Esagila* in Babylon as his temple, and on its completion the gods, having invested Marduk with supreme authority, assembled for a great banquet at which they recited his fifty names to confer upon him their attributes.[26]

The Sumerian Myths of Origin

In this great epic written in Akkadian on seven tablets, now generally assigned to the early part of the second millennium B.C., recited, as we have seen, on the fourth day of the New Year Festival,[27] the creative activities of the earlier Sumerian gods, Ea, Enlil and Anu, were centred in Marduk, his city, Babylon, having become the capital of the empire, just as in Assyria Ashur was the hero of the cosmic struggle renewed annually at the turn of the year. What lies behind it in its Sumerian background is very difficult to determine as such evidence as is available comes from later sources. Nevertheless, as Kramer contends, it is very probable that the cosmological and mythological concepts revealed in the tablets were current in Sumer in the later half of the third millennium B.C. when the culture contacts between Sumerians and Semites in Mesopotamia were considerable.[28] At present, however, no single myth is known which actually describes the creation of the universe, but from the introductory passages to a Sumerian poem entitled "Gilgamesh, Enkidu and the Nether World", and "The Creation of the Pickaxe", it appears that the Goddess Nammu ("the sea"), the primeval ocean, gave birth to the universe; heaven and earth at first being united as a vast cosmic mountain until they were separated by Enlil, the Air-god. Then Anu, the Sky-god, carried off the heaven while Enlil carried off the earth (Ki),[29] which was his mother and later identified with the Goddess Ninhursaga, or Ninmah.

In the heavens where the Sky-gods dwelt, Nanna, the Moon-god begotten of Enlil, begot Utu, the Sun-god, the "shepherd of the land", who lay down at night and arose in the morning. On earth Enlil "caused the good day to come forth" and produced the plant and animal life in conjunction with Enki (Ea), the Water-god, who decreed the fates of Sumer, Ur and Meluhha in Mesopotamia. Together they sent from heaven Lahar, the Cattle-god, and Ashnan, the Grain-god, to make the cattle and grain abundant, having been created to supply the Anunnaki, the children and followers of Anu, with food and clothing.[30] Man was created "for the sake of the welfare of the sheepfolds and good things of the gods", by the joint efforts of Nammu, her son Enki, and the Goddess Ninmah, after Lahar and Ashnan had been fashioned.[31]

To free the gods from labouring for their sustenance Enki was aroused from his slumbers by his mother and counselled to make mankind from the clay of the Apsu to be their servants. When this had been accomplished with the aid of Ninmah, the Earth-goddess, a feast was arranged by Enki to com-memorate the event at which Ninmah fashioned six types of human beings, of whom the last two were sexless. Enki then tried his hand at creating clay men with less success, and he had to seek the help of Ninmah in an attempt to make the feeble creatures speak, eat or stand, but without avail. In disgust she ended by cursing him for producing such lifeless mani-kins. Nevertheless, in this earliest Mesopotamian version of the creation of man, in the third millennium B.C., so far as can be determined from the present readings of these very incom-plete Sumerian texts, it appears that the human race was the product of the combined efforts of Nammu, the primeval ocean, Ninmah, the Earth-goddess, and Enki, the god of water and wisdom, after the heaven and the earth had emerged from the sea and been separated by the air from which the moon was made and became the matrix of the sun. Then plant and animal life appeared on the earth as a result of the union of the air, earth and water, leading on to the more complicated process of the creation of man in which the principal divine personifications of these various elements were involved.

In the Sumero-Babylonian creation stories, however, the gods were not actually creators in the transcendental sense, since they were themselves an integral part of the universe and a product of the inherent creative process, largely dependent upon the creatures they had fashioned out of it and within it for their own subsistence. Conceived in anthropomorphic terms, they were in a constant state of ferment out of which the cosmic structure emerged and the social organization was determined, based on the kingship which is said to have come down from heaven and resided in turn at several of the most ancient Sumerian cities. Against the background of the conflict between the older and the younger groups of gods the cosmic structure was completed, but neither Marduk nor his predecessor Enlil was regarded, like Re or Ptah, as the source of all existence, including the other gods. Creation in Mesopotamia was essentially a political enterprise, and the status of the gods concerned in the process was determined by that of the city over which they presided, rising and falling with its fortunes. It was, moreover, a gradual process of growth emerging out of the struggle between different generations of gods,[32] rather than a series of special creative acts, as in the Priestly story in the book of Genesis in the Old Testament, by one supreme transcendent supreme Creator. As each "age group" succeeded the other something was added to the cosmic order until eventually the whole cosmos was completed and the earth was made relatively secure in its precarious environment, and ready for the appearance of man upon it to render service to the gods in a stabilized social structure.

SYRIA AND PALESTINE

In Anatolia and Syria the situation was different, but in the Hurrian and Hittite texts, as will be considered later,[33] cult myths recur in a very fragmentary condition, having very significant parallels to those of the Mesopotamian cycle with the Weather-god Teshub as the principal figure in a similar vegetation rôle. There, again, gods and men were in very close contact and walked together on earth and in the heavenly places. In the Ugaritic mythology the scene was laid almost entirely on the divine plane, although heroic human beings like Danel and Keret played their part in them as significant characters. But in neither the Anatolian nor the Syrian mythology do genuine creation stories occur corresponding to those we have reviewed from the Egyptian and Mesopotamian texts.

The Ugaritic Epic of Baal

Thus, in the Ras Shamra texts the supreme head of the Canaanite pantheon, El, is represented as a remote shadowy deity living in a cosmic paradise "a thousand fields, ten thousand fields at the sources of the two rivers, in the midst of the fountains of the two deeps",[34] as "the father of years" and of man, the progenitor of the gods. He was also localized at "the Mount of the North" (i.e. Mount Casius, the modern el-Akra) and in various other centres, and was likened to a bull in the midst of a herd of cows and calves. He was espoused, as we have seen, to the Tyrian goddess Asherah, who later was said to be his daughter,[35] but doubtless in the first instance El and the Mother-goddess exercised their creative functions before Aleyan-Baal, the Storm-god, rose to pre-eminence as the principal figure in Ugaritic mythology, full of strength and vigour like Marduk when he replaced Enlil in the Babylonian pantheon. Here no doubt is a recurrence of the older and younger god theme.

Once he was established Baal, personifying the storm, the wind and the clouds, appointed the seasons and controlled the rainfall, ordering a rift to be opened in the clouds and a window within his palace in the heavens,[36] though precisely for what purpose the window was constructed in his house is open to debate. At first he refused to have any windows at all, possibly as a precautionary measure lest one of his adversaries (e.g. Mot or Yam, the Lord of the Sea) should gain access to him through them. But when these misgivings were dispelled he ordered the lattice to be made, presumably to allow the rain to fall on the earth through it when he opened it.[37] Dr Gaster, in fact, suggests that the episode in the text mythologizes a rain-making ceremony during the autumnal festival when windows in the temple at Ras Shamra were opened to symbolize and effect the reciprocal action in the heavenly palace of Baal.[38] Schaeffer has made the ingenious surmise that the rain which was to begin to fall at the decree of Baal was intended to descend through the skylight in the roof on to the face of the god represented on a stele which stood in the sanctuary.[39] However this may have been, Baal was the giver of fertility nourished by the vitalizing rain for which he was held to have been responsible, and in this capacity he exercised his creative functions on earth. He was "lord over the furrows of the field" and "Prince, lord of the Earth",[40] controlling the processes of fertility, so that when he was slain all vegetation languished and fecundity ceased amid universal mourning, lamentation and woe.[41]

Baal, however, was not the only god on whom fertility depended, probably because he had inherited these attributes from his predecessors, being himself originally the young god, the son of El and the son of Dagon, an ancient Mesopotamian vegetation deity who had a temple at Ugarit as well as at Gaza and Ashdod,[42] and who was associated with the Sumerian Anu, the god of heaven. Thus Mot, for instance, who had made rival claims to the kingship,[43] was treated as a grain-god, threshed, winnowed and ground in a mill. Moreover, the various identifications of Baal with the local gods of Western Asia, including Hadad, Yahweh, Aleyan, El, the name being *ba'lu*, a generic word for "lord", and so applicable to different gods, show that he was a composite deity combining a number of creative activities. With such a comprehensive personality his antecedents and functions cover a wide field. In the Ugaritic texts, it is true, he is primarily a storm and vegetation god *par excellence* united in this rôle with his consort and sister Anat, the daughter of El. But his position in the pantheon, unlike that of Marduk in Babylonia, was by no means un╱ challenged. In conflict with his opponents (e.g. Mot, Asherah and Prince Sea) he was destroyed, "falling like an ox" and "collapsing like a bull", until he was released from the under╱ world by Anat to continue his struggle with his enemy Mot, and establish his right to reign over the gods as their king and leader.[44]

Although the Baal epic has points of contact with Meso╱ potamian and Anatolian myth and ritual, it is a theogony in which a creation story is inherent rather than defined. In many respects its hero corresponds to Enlil and Marduk, and the Hurrian Storm╱ and Weather╱god, and the Hittite Teshub. But it lacks a cosmogony comparable to that which occupies such a conspicuous position in Egyptian and Mesopotamian mythology and in the Hebrew literature. No account occurs in the Ugaritic texts of the creation of the universe or of the pantheon, as in the Pyramid texts, the Memphite theology or the *Enuma elish*, where the structural differentiation and ordering of the world of the gods and their emergence from a primordial abyss are described in a series of cosmological myths. In these cosmogonies, however, except in the case of Ptah, and later in that of the Aton, the gods are merged in and emerge from the universe as created beings, and then proceed to organize the cosmos, and ultimately to fashion the human species for their own ends and purposes. When Ptah was elevated above Atum he became virtually the Creator—"the Mighty Great One"—from whom the cosmic order emanated, flowing from his heart and tongue. But the Memphite theology was never able to break away from the conventional mythology in which it arose, so that Ptah was not a genuinely transcendent deity. Even the Aton as the sole creator╱god, like Amon before him, was conceived in terms of the solar polytheistic myth. Thus, he was identified with Re, Harakhte and Shu, and his son Ikhnaton stood in virtually the same relation to him as did any other Pharaoh to Atum-Re or Amon. In Mesopotamia the divine assembly under their leader Anu and his son Enlil, the Storm-god, were essentially powers behind the various phenomena of nature, assigned their respective status, attributes and functions in accordance with the elements in the cosmos and the political order they personified and symbolized. In Anatolia they passed into the Hittite pantheon through a Hurrian medium, but, so far as can be determined from the texts, the leadership was achieved through the defeat of the older "king of heaven", Alalu, who had been ousted by Anu, like El by Baal in the Ras Shamra epic. But in neither case was creation regarded as the outcome of the struggle.

Yahweh as Creator in Israel

In the Hebrew literature in the form in which it took its final shape, Yahweh was represented as the exclusive Creator of all existence in heaven and in the entire universe. Until the end of the period of the Exile it was not denied that the neighbouring nations had their own deities, such as Chemosh of Moab or the Tyrian Baal, and the cults of these foreign gods were widely adopted through intercourse with the Canaanites and sur-rounding Moabites, Ammonites, Assyrians, Hittites and Egyptians. But, notwithstanding the syncretistic worship that obtained in pre-exilic Israel at the local sanctuaries and the hold it had upon the people, there are no indications in Hebrew tradition of any attempt to establish a theogony genealogically relating Yahweh to the neighbouring gods, or to those with whom he shared shrines and feasts. Occasionally, as at Elephantine, he was assigned consorts (e.g. Anat-Bethel and Ashima-Bethel), and he had in his service sacred prostitutes,[45] while angelic beings were described as *benê-El* or *benê ha-'elohîm*, "sons of god" (i.e. lesser divine beings; "the host of heaven"). In the crude myth introduced into the Flood story in Genesis (vi. 1–4), the union of astral gods with mortal women resulting in the birth of heroes or demi-gods (*Nephilim*) is recorded and retained by the later editors of the narrative, presupposing as it did a belief in intercourse between gods and women on earth, prevalent in Babylonian and Greek mythology.

Nevertheless, in spite of all these connexions with the current myth and ritual in the Near East, Yahweh in the later literature was kept free from any compromising family relationships with other members of a pantheon, be it with a spouse comparable to Isis, Ninlil, Ishtar, Hebat, Anat or Asherah, or with sons and daughters, either divine, angelic or mortal. He alone was the one supreme Deity by whose act and word order was brought out of chaos. He stood over and against creation but was never identified with it. He weighed the wind and measured out the waters; he made a decree for the rain and a way for the lightning and the thunder; upholding the earth with its pillars, the heavens with their stars, in true Semitic cosmological fashion; and held dominion over the whole of nature.[46] The heaven was his throne and the earth his footstool, both being the work of his hands, for he transcended the whole creation as its Creator.[47] It was he who stretched out the heavens as a curtain, spreading them as a tent, and like Aleyan-Baal he made the clouds his chariot and the winds his messengers who laid the foundations of the earth.[48] The sky being a dome-shaped structure (the "firmament") resting on the circle of the earth, with its pillars and the bases of the mountains on which it rested deeply laid in the watery abyss below the earth, the representation of Yahweh sitting enthroned above the circle of the earth gave him the key position over all creation. In this exalted state he had only to touch the mountains to make them break into volcanic eruption, to look at the earth and it trembled, and to walk upon the wings of his ministers for the wind to cease and flaming fire to burst forth.[49]

Behind this anthropomorphic imagery lay the Mesopotamian conception of creation interpreted in monotheistic terms. As will be considered in the next chapter,[50] in the background was the ancient conflict with the hostile forces personified as Leviathan and Rahab, while the surrounding waters were regarded as a destructive and sinister element that had to be conquered and tamed before the earth could be made habitable. This was characteristic of the dwellers in the Tigris-Euphrates valley, but not of those who lived in Palestine where water was life-giving and beneficent. Similarly, the structure of the universe was Babylonian, as was the struggle with the malign powers of chaos from which the heavens and the earth merged as an orderly cosmos.

The Yahwistic Story of Creation

In the pre-exilic Yahwist and Elohist creation narrative in Genesis (ii. 4–25), the Mesopotamian background is less apparent. The existence of the world as a barren waste is presupposed after a passing reference to Yahweh-Elohim having made the heavens and the earth and its vegetation. The Creator's activities are centred in the garden which he "planted to the east" after he had caused a mist to descend upon the face of the ground, or possibly to spring up as a vapour or fountain from beneath,[51] to render it fertile and ready for human habitation when man had been fashioned from its dust and vitalized by the inbreathing of the breath of life. No mention is here made of a watery "deep" or *tehôm*, as in the later Priestly story and the Babylonian epic. On the contrary, originally the world was sterile because it was devoid of moisture so that nothing would grow on the parched soil. This suggests a Palestinian setting since unlike Mesopotamia Palestine depended entirely upon its rainfall for its crops. Therefore, before the Creator could begin his operations the ground had to be watered.

This accomplished and the garden duly planted, the human race was brought into being in much the same way as in Egypt Khnum formed mankind on his potter's wheel, or Prometheus moulded the first man out of clay at Panopeus, in Phocis,[52] while Ea, according to Berossus, mixed the blood of Kingu with earth for this purpose.[53] Ninhursaga is also said to have repeated the process before and after the Flood, mixing the flesh and blood of a slain god with clay to this end.[54] Clay was similarly employed in the creation of Enkidu by Aruru, and of certain unusual types, such as eunuchs, in a number of

Sumerian traditions.[55] So in the Yahwistic narrative Adam, a name connected with the word for "ground" (*Adamah*), was moulded in clay by the Creator and the care of the garden was assigned to him. Taking pity on his solitude, Yahweh then resolved to provide him with companions and so created the animals. This, however, proved to be an unsuccessful experiment as they did not meet the requirements of his status in creation. Therefore, a hypnotic sleep was caused to fall upon Adam in order to extract from him one of his ribs from which a human mate was produced, in the person of the first woman Eve, to relieve his loneliness and to be his wife. Then follows the account of the Fall of Man and the expulsion from the garden after the eating of the forbidden fruit at the instigation of the serpent.

In this Yahwistic myth two Palestinian traditions appear to have been combined in a composite narrative; the one recording the fertilizing of the barren world; the other the Paradise story beginning with the planting of the garden and its situation (Gen. ii. 8), to which may have been added the topographical details concerning the rivers that were supposed to flow from it (Gen. ii. 10–14) with their Mesopotamian characteristics. Indeed, the whole of the Eden episode is suggestive of Mesopotamian influences and affinities in contrast to the essentially Palestinian setting of the opening verses (Gen. ii. 2–7). These belong apparently to the very ancient Canaanite creation myth of the waterless wastes inserted in that of the garden paradise and its geography, while the mountain of the gods in which the king of Tyre had his abode in the midst of an array of magical life-giving agents[56] (from which he also was expelled) is another example of the floating tradition.

It would seem then that the Yahwist used a number of myths in the construction of his narrative from a variety of sources, some of which had Mesopotamian contacts superimposed on a Palestinian background. Whether or not the Fall episode belonged originally to the Paradise cycle with its expulsion theme,[57] the current stories of the creation were skilfully woven into a composite narrative by the Yahwist and interpreted in relation to Hebrew faith and practice of the pre-exilic Prophetic period in terms of ethical monotheism. Many of the naïve anthropomorphisms and magical elements in the ancient myths survived. The Deity, for example, fashioned the human race from clay and the bone of a rib. He talked and walked with Adam and Eve in the cool of the evening in the pleasant garden he had planted for them. There too the woman encountered and conversed with the wily serpent to their un-doing, when the irascible Creator discovered their disobedience to his explicit injunction and in consequence drove them forth; the man to labour in the sweat of his brow for the means of subsistence, the woman to be in subjection to her husband and to bear children in sorrow and travail. All because they had infringed a tabu with which a tree with magical properties had been surrounded.

Nevertheless, as told by the Yahwist, the immortal story unquestionably was made to serve the purposes of the infinitely more lofty religious conceptions that had arisen in Israel from the tenth century B.C. and were given expression in the E and J documents of the northern and southern kingdoms respec-tively. Nevertheless, it cannot be denied that the narrative was cast in the form of the original myths from which it was derived, and preserved many of their fundamental ideas and beliefs about the gods and their dealings with the world and its denizens, however much they may have been re-interpreted in monotheistic terms and made the vehicle of a higher theology and theogony.

The Priestly Story

After the return of some of the Jewish exiles from Babylon and their resettlement in and around Jerusalem, about the middle of the fifth century B.C. the account of creation recorded in the opening chapters of the book of Genesis (i–ii. 3) was compiled by the Priestly school of redactors engaged in the consolidation of the restored remnant of the nation in the cultus and the Law (Torah) as the focal-point. That they had before them the Yahwistic narrative is highly probable, since the editor appears to have grafted on to it the new and later story drawn up by the priestly scribes. In this version, however, a much closer approximation occurs to the Babylonian sources, and although it diverges from the *Enuma elish* in conspicuous and important features, it preserves the same sequence of creative activities under similar conditions. Thus, both stories begin with a watery chaos—Apsu or *Tehôm*, the Hebrew "deep"—out of which the heavens and the earth were fashioned. In the Babylonian epic the body of Tiamat was utilized for the pur' pose, whereas in the Hebrew narrative it was accomplished by the spirit of God hovering over "the deep" (i.e. *tehôm*) without any reference to the fight between the two antagonists. This doubtless had been eliminated in the Genesis story by the Jewish priests as unedifying although, as will be considered later,[58] it was a prominent element in the earlier Leviathan' Rahab mythology.

When the firmament had been duly established and the waters were gathered together, in the place of the Marduk' Tiamat conflict the creation of the sun, moon and stars was inserted, followed by that of the birds, fishes, beasts, reptiles, and finally of man, on their respective days, leading up to the Sabbatical rest of the Creator on the seventh day at the close of the momentous week. In the Babylonian prototype after the fight and the fixing of the firmament the stations of the gods were appointed, and the luminaries and the stars were duly set in their positions and made to shine to mark day and night and the divisions of the year. Then followed the fashioning of man, the determining of the destinies and the conferment upon Marduk of his titles.

Therefore, the same order of events virtually was maintained in both stories, beginning with the primeval chaos and ending with the creation of the human species, despite the fact that the Priestly writer had worked over the Babylonian narrative for his own purposes, and in all probability was acquainted with the Yahwistic story. There is little if any fundamental difference in the conception of the Sumero'Babylonian Apsu and the Hebrew *Tehôm* except that in the Genesis narrative the *Tehôm*

was not personified as was the Apsu in the *Enuma elish*. Nevertheless, "the deep" was closely associated in the earlier Hebrew
tradition with the monsters, Rahab, Leviathan, the dragon and
the serpent, who played much the same rôle as Tiamat in the
creation drama and in the many forms she assumed in Babylonian mythology, ranging from the Mother of the gods to a
dragon and an enemy of Ea and Marduk, like the Judaeo-
Christian figure of the Satan as an Elohim transformed into a
fallen angel and the old serpent of apocalyptic speculation.[59]
There can be little doubt, therefore, that a fight with a dragon-
like creature lay in the background of the Hebrew story
of creation, though it was eliminated from the Priestly version
in the book of Genesis. There the earth was represented as
having been created "in the beginning", together with the
heavens by the sole Creator of the universe, though at first it
was without form and void, very much as in the *Enuma elish*
and other Mesopotamian cosmogonic myths, where it was
conceived as having been created from the primeval sea. In the
Sumerian texts, however, different traditions occur concerning
world origins so that no single answer is given to questions
about ultimate beginnings as in the Hebrew Priestly narrative.[60]

Again, in the Babylonian epic there is no account of the
creation of plant and animal life, though Marduk is described
as "the creator of grain and herbs" who caused vegetation to
sprout,[61] while in the Sumerian myth of Lahar and Ashnan
the gods of cattle and grain are said to have been sent down to
earth to bring prosperity to mankind.[62] Similarly, in the
bilingual fragmentary inscription from Nineveh the gods are
stated to have brought forth living creatures, fashioning the
cattle and beasts of the field and the creatures of the city after
they had created the heavens and the earth.[63] Finally, both the
Babylonian and Priestly versions agree in making man the last
creative act, though, as we have seen, they differ in the reason
for his having been called into existence—in the one instance
for the benefit of the gods; in the other to be lord of the earth.

Therefore, it may be concluded that the post-exilic creation
narrative (P) was drawn up under Babylonian influences, but

the redactors assembled the available material, arranged and interpreted in a manner conformable to their monotheistic theology and to meet their ritual requirements. By confining the creative process to a calendar week and bringing it to a dramatic close on the seventh day, they were able to establish a divine sanction for the observance of the Sabbath. As a result it could be and was affirmed that "in six days Yahweh Elohim made heaven and earth, the sea, and all that in them is, and rested the seventh day; wherefore Yahweh Elohim blessed the sabbath day, and hallowed it".[64] Other reasons were given for the command to keep it holy, it is true, such as the need for rest for man and beast,[65] but over and above these practical considerations there was the religious sanction based on the rest of the Creator after he had called all things into being at the beginning of time. Thus, re-enforced in terms of the myth, the observance became binding as no other law, and was hedged round with the strictest tabus.

This, however, was not the only purpose of the Priestly creation story. Just as the *Enuma elish* was recited at the *Akitu* in Babylon during the re-enactment of the creation of the world by Marduk in the cult drama, it seems reasonable to suppose that the Genesis narrative was similarly sung in the temple at Jerusalem when the enthronement of Yahweh as the Creator was celebrated at the Annual Festival.[66] The didactic character of the myth with its repeated refrain is indicative of a liturgy, while the closely associated dragon mythology in Hebrew poetry, references to which recur in the enthronement psalms, is in accord with the triumphal celebration of Marduk's victory over Tiamat, and the vindication of Yahweh's creative work.[67] In an orderly sequence of mighty acts the Creator by his word had called all things into existence from a primeval abyss to the creation of man as a prelude to his subsequent overruling sovereignty set forth in the history of the Patriachs, the Exodus, the Holy Mount, the conquest of Palestine, the establishment of the Monarchy, the Exile and the re-establishment of the post-exilic community in a new covenant with Yahweh. At every stage in this unfolding drama of theocratic history the significant concrete events were given liturgical expression in myth and ritual, revealing their meaning for the complex process as a whole. Therefore, it would be indeed surprising if the opening scene of the great panorama were not commemorated and enacted in the rites, liturgies and festivals that constitute the key to the process in which the meaning of the history of Israel was unfolded, and at each stage made efficacious by a fresh out-pouring of re-creative activity.

GREECE

The Zeus Myth

Throughout, the fundamental theme was that God had made the world and at each step had pronounced his work to be good. Even man, notwithstanding his transgression, as he came fresh from the hands of his Creator, fashioned from the dust of the earth and made into a living soul by an act of divine inflation, was essentially good, notwithstanding the darker side of human nature. Here the Hebrews were in line with the Greek optimistic estimate of man, both being mountain peoples living in secluded valleys. But where the Greeks differed from the Hebrews was that their gods, instead of transcending the world and mankind like Yahweh, shared human weaknesses, passions and intrigues.

Thus, the Olympians were essentially conquering chieftains in their behaviour. They made no claims to have created the universe, or to dispose of human beings summarily as their creatures, as in the religions of the Ancient Near East. Their leader, Zeus, it is true, was originally the Indo-European Sky- and Weather-god of many names who combined the functions of a nature deity with those of the head of an anthropomorphic pantheon centred on Mount Olympus, some 10,000 feet above the plain of Thessaly; the summit of which appeared often to be lost in the clouds of the divine "cloud-gatherer" (Zeus). From his lofty abode he sent down the reinvigorating rain and the devastating tempest, blasting with his thunderbolts gods and men alike when they thwarted his irascible will or frustrated his plans and purposes. In the classical period, from

Homer onwards, he was regarded as dwelling in the sky with which he was equated, a belief which doubtless went back to a time long before he came into Greece with the Aryan invaders between 2000 and 1200 B.C., when "the broad heaven was his portion",[68] as in the case of Varuna, his counterpart in Vedic India.

By another line of mythological tradition the ancient god Kronos was represented as the lord of the universe whose three sons, Zeus, Poseidon and Hades, cast lots for their father's domain. As a result Zeus obtained dominion in heaven, Poseidon in the sea, and Hades in the underworld. The earth became their common property where they lived together on Mount Olympus.[69] This represents the Greek variant of the Anatolian myth of Kumarbi in the Hurrian texts recording a struggle for power between the different generations of gods.[70] The similarity of this crude story to the *Theogony* of Hesiod has been demonstrated by Dr Güterbock.[71] Thus, as Kumarbi became pregnant by swallowing the generative organ of Anu and gave birth to the three terrible gods, so in the Hesiodic theogony Ouranus, the heavens and the first of the gods, mated with the Earth, Ge, and begat the Titans and the Giants, the youngest of whom, Kronos, married his sister Rhea. At the instigation of his mother, Ge, Kronos castrated his father with a sickle, and from the blood the Erinyes (the Furies) and the Melian nymphs were born. Some of the seed fell into the sea, causing a foam from which Aphrodite came forth and landed on the shore at Paphos in Cyprus. Kronos and Rhea then begat the Olympian gods, but Kronos having been forewarned by Fate that he would be dispossessed by one of them, swallowed the children as soon as they were born. At the birth of the sixth child, however, Rhea substituted for it a stone in a blanket, and the offspring, who was Zeus, was reared clandestinely. On growing with great rapidity to manhood, he attacked his father and compelled him to disgorge the children one by one. The first was set up as a stone at Delphi, and another, Hera, after a courtship extending to three hundred years, married Zeus.

The resemblance in the succession of events in the two theo-gonies is indicative of an affinity with the Hittite Kumarbi story, fragmentary as is the Anatolian text. Ouranus, Kronos and Zeus correspond to the Hurrian sequence—Anu, Kumarbi and the Weather-god, with Alalu in the background, who does not appear in the Hesiodic variant. Emasculation is a common feature in both myths, as is the eating of a stone, while the impregnation of the Earth-goddess presents similarities which hardly can have been accidental. Contacts between Asia Minor and the Eastern Mediterranean from about 2000 B.C. were increasingly maintained and groups of Indo-Europeans established themselves on the plateau of Anatolia among the Hittites and the Mitanni of East Syria, while Aryan Kassites conquered Babylonia in the second millennium B.C. Contemporary with these events Greek-speaking Minyans made their way into Hellas, followed by the Achaeans, bring-ing with them in an Aryan and Anatolian setting their Sky-and Weather-god Zeus, the son of Kronos, known to the Indo-European peoples under a variety of names all derived from the same root meaning "to shine", extended to cover "the sky", which sometimes shines brightly and sometimes rains.[72] For the Minyans he was *Dān*, a form of the nominative *Zān* or *Zen*, while his wife *Da* became in all probability the oldest consort of Zeus, Dione, the Earth-goddess.

In the highly complex Zeus myth, therefore, there are many strands derived from a number of different sources. Overlying the original Indo-European Sky- and Weather-god mountain tradition, and that of his associates, came the Western Asiatic Hurrian-Hittite Kumarbi story in the middle of the second millennium B.C., which was subsequently handed on through the Phoenicians and the Cypriotes to the Greeks. It was then developed as a theogony by Hesiod, who had made his way into Boeotia from North-west Asia Minor. In Greece, how-ever, the pre-Hellenic cult of the Mother-goddess, as we have seen,[73] was firmly established, as it was throughout the Aegean. Therefore, it was inevitable that the Indo-European Sky- and Weather-god, with his Western Asiatic accretions, should be united with the Earth-goddess in her various forms as Ge, Rhea and Hera.

In Crete, however, so predominant was the Goddess cult that the Earth-mother, Rhea, was represented as the mother of Zeus, who was born on the island and hidden from Kronos in a cave in the mountain, called by Hesiod Aigaion, but elsewhere said to have been either Mount Ida or Mount Dikte.[74] According to one curious tale, fire issued from this cavern every year when the blood from the birth of Zeus still streamed forth, suggesting perhaps, as Nilsson has argued, that "this child is the Year-god, the spirit of fertility, the new life of spring",[75] as the alleged Cretan parentage of Zeus might indicate. In any case, the Cretan Zeus was a much more primitive figure than the Indo-European Sky-god, embodying the processes of fecundity on earth rather than renewing them by sending the vitalizing rain from the heavens. Nevertheless, the normal relation between the Sky-father and the Earth-mother was that of husband and wife; not of mother and son. Therefore, as the Aryan and Aegean aspects of Greek religion fused, the two traditions found a common centre in "the father of gods and men", and the syncretistic Zeus came to occupy much the same position in the cultus as that of other Sky- and Weather-gods in the Near East. Without essentially changing his character, status and functions, while remaining the head of the pantheon, the rain-giver, the cloud-gatherer, the thunderer and the despotic ruler of high Olympus, Zeus became at once the creator and prototype of mankind, until at length he reached the status of the one primary Being and Life force from whom all existence emanated and to whom it was destined to return. Finally, he was the Eternal God standing outside the world, the principle of supreme might in whom all things lived and moved and had their being, as the Cretan Epimonidas declared about 500 B.C. Thus, Zeus became the ground of all creation, the source and renewer of life, pantheistically conceived by the poets, until in the great Hymn of Cleanthes in the third century B.C. his monotheistic attributes were indistinguishable from those of Yahweh in post-exilic Judaism.[76]

The Hesiodic and Orphic Theogonies

Before he attained this exalted position, however, he had to overthrow the Titans, the sons and daughters of Ouranus and Ge, Heaven and Earth, from whom he was himself descended through his father, Kronos. This may be a reflection of the defeat of the chthonian indigenous cult of the soil by the Olympian Sky-religion, as a result of which many of the earlier fertility elements were incorporated in the later product as the human race was represented in the myth as having imbibed a Titanic strain in its ancestral history in combination with its Dionysian divine nature. This duality is inherent in the Orphic cosmogony, which was based on the same fundamental cosmo-logical conceptions as those of the Homeric and Hesiodic myths. In all of them the structure of the universe was not very different from that which obtained in Western Asia and the Fertile Crescent. Above the flat plain of the earth was the huge dome of the sky touching it at the horizon. Above the horizon on one side the sun and the stars arose, and on the other side they set until they disappeared. The boundary of the terrestrial plain was formed by a great river, Okeanos, flowing in a circle; and in the extreme west, where the sun went down, was the entrance to the nether regions, the abode of Hades, which also might be reached through the various rifts in the rocks on the earth's surface.[77] In attempting to explain the genesis of the universe Hesiod started with Chaos, the Greek counterpart of the Hebrew *Tehôm* and the Babylonian Apsu, as the ultimate source of all things. From it came Earth (Ge) and Tartaros (a dark abode in the depth of the ground) and Eros. How these came into existence is not related. From Chaos Night and Erebus were born, and from Night came Aither (the upper air) and Day, while Ge (or Gaia) herself produced Ouranus (Heaven), and then the mountains and the sea.[78]

In the Orphic cosmology known to us almost exclusively from post-Aristotelian and Neoplatonic sources, more or less the same sequence is maintained except that Night and Erebus were with Chaos the primeval principles. Night laid a world-egg fashioned in Aither by Kronos (Time). From it sprang

Eros (Love), who in the more developed mystical theogonies appears as Phanes, Protogonos or Metis, representing the different aspects of Light and Love (generation), the first-born of the gods and the first Orphic god, the source of all life. Thus, in the late Rhapsodic version of the myth Phanes was Light *par excellence* existing before the sun which was created by him. He was the light of reason, the light of life and the light of love—Light, Life-giver, Wisdom or Counsel, as his three titles indicate, to which a fourth was added, Kapaios, of uncertain interpretation, in the Neoplatonic *Orphica*. As love he was the principle of generation exercising his creative functions in bringing into existence the gods and the world before he was swallowed by Zeus and subsequently reborn from him as Dionysos.

By their ingenious amalgamation of the Orphic and Olympian theogonies, brought into relation with the pre-Hellenic Thraco-Phrygian cult of Zagreus and its mythology, and the Cretan Rhea, Zeus retained his position as the Creator without conflicting with the Orphic doctrine of a dual nature of mankind and its hope of salvation. According to the familiar composite story of the Titans, Zeus had a son Zagreus by his daughter Persephone whom he intended to make ruler of the universe. This incited the jealousy of Hera, the lawful wife of Zeus, and she stirred up the Titans to kill and devour the child, which they did. Thereupon Zeus slew them with his thunder-bolts and from their ashes made mankind, who thus became partly divine, because the Titans had eaten Zagreus, and partly evil owing to their own wickedness. Athena having saved the heart of Zagreus, Zeus swallowed it and then proceeded to beget his son again by an alliance with Semele, the Phrygian Earth-goddess. It was this second Zagreus who became Dionysos,[79] and in this guise was a central figure in the Orphic story.[80] Once the Zagreus myth was referred to Orpheus in a Dionysian rôle, the primary aim of the Orphic way of life was the elimination of the evil Titanic nature in order to attain to divinity, aided by the prescribed *teletae* (i.e. the rites and ordinances) in which the initiates partook to this end.[81] Thus, by the judicious use of an ancient tradition the elusive system which is called Orphism retained its essential *raison d'être* as a mystery cult and ascetic movement with its own myth and ritual brought into conjunction with the Hesiodic theogony and its Olympian background.

Behind its philosophical and mystical approach lay a mythology, the roots of which were very deeply laid not only in Hellenic tradition but with ramifications extending throughout the Near East, particularly in Syria and Asia Minor, in relation to the death and resurrection theme of the oriental cult drama.[82] But as Dr Guthrie says, "the Orphic showed a genius for transforming the significance of his mythological or ritual material, and sometimes saw an opportunity of preaching his religion through the medium of symbols which were in their origin of the crudest and most primitive".[83] For example, while the Hesiodic and Homeric background is little changed, and most of the gods therein continue to play their customary rôles in the cosmic drama with Zeus still assigned pride of place, new features appear, such as the world-egg and the equation of Eros with the Orphic Phanes as the Protogonos and Creator anterior to Zeus. The very ancient Kronos who swallowed his own children, when the first letter of his name was aspirated was transformed into Chronos, the personification of Time, the abstract principle in which all things occur and come to appointed ends.

With the rise of philosophic speculative thought in Greece in the sixth century B.C., with which the Orphic movement coincided, it was inevitable that the problem of the One and the Many should be latent in the growing curiosity about the origins of the universe and the relations of the parts to the whole. This eventually found expression in the words attributed to a pupil of Orpheus, Musaios, "everything comes to be out of One and is resolved into One", but it was Phanes or Zeus who contained within himself the seeds of all being from which the whole phenomenal order of existence emerged.[84] Throughout the Orphic cosmology, in fact, the process of creation is represented as bringing division and order out of the primeval state of confusion to which eventually there will be a return at the end of the era. Moreover, the supreme Ruler of the universe was also its Creator in a sense in which the gods of Homer and Hesiod never were, however much they were retained in name and sometimes in function. But in "swallowing" Phanes the Olympian Zeus was transformed into the Orphic Creator. What was borrowed from the earlier theogonies was transmuted and remoulded and made subservient to the purposes for which the material had been borrowed and utilized in the formation of Orphic myth and ritual.

CHAPTER VI

Good and Evil and the Sacred Combat

As the foregoing analysis of the speculations about creation and the beginnings of the phenomenal order in the ancient world has shown, one of the central features of myths of origins was the conquest of the powers of chaos and darkness embodied in various demonic forms, or in a cosmic struggle between opposed supernatural forces. At first these battles were mainly between the gods and their respective allies, and represented the perennial struggle between life and death, light and darkness, good and evil (as these evaluations were then understood), which appeared to be so fundamental in the universe that its source must lie in some great primordial conflict out of which the present order has emerged, and in which it has continued in nature and in human society. To meet this perpetual challenge in which mankind had become so intimately involved, the primeval situation was re-enacted in a sacred combat as an integral element in the death and resurrection cultic drama as an expulsion ritual summed up in the formula, "out with famine, in with health and wealth". Combined with the ritual marriage to promote and conserve life and vitality, the mimetic contest had for its purpose the triumph of good over evil, of life over death, of summer over winter, by man ranging himself on the side of the victorious powers of beneficence and invigoration, and overcoming not only the blight in nature but the effects of his own rebellions against the gods and his evil deeds.

EGYPT

The Destruction of Mankind

Thus, in Egypt men did not hesitate to murmur and plot against the power and majesty of Re, and so he determined to destroy them. In the text inscribed on the walls of the tombs of Seti I, Rameses II and Rameses III at Thebes from the fourteenth to the twelfth centuries B.C., but following an older original inscription, they are said to have declared that the Sun-god had grown old, that his bones had become silver, his flesh gold and his hair lapis lazuli. Enraged at these insinuations, Re summoned a secret council of the gods who were with him in the abysmal waters of Nun—Shu, Tefnet, Geb and Nut—together with the court of Nun, and sought their help and advice in dealing with the situation. When he had put the case against mankind before them it was decided that his Eye, in the form of the Goddess Hathor, should be sent to slay and utterly destroy his rebels. So fearful, however, was the slaughter that she wrought that the land was drenched in blood, and fearing lest the entire human race should be annihilated Re endeavoured to persuade Hathor to cease the destruction. To this end he had to resort to a ruse. Having caused seven thousand jars of potent beer to be brewed by the gods in which they mixed red ochre to make it resemble blood, they emptied it out over the earth. Therefore, when the goddess went upstream at the break of day to resume her slaughter she found the fields flooded and her face was mirrored beautifully therein. So she drank and became so drunken that she failed to perceive mankind.[1]

Re, Seth and Apophis

This childish tale, unlike the Hebrew Flood story in its present form, is completely devoid of any moral or ethical significance. Behind it may lay a rejuvenation theme, since Hathor appears in the rôle of the avenger of the wrath of Re, the Creator of mankind, who repented that he had made such rebellious creatures, perhaps originally for the purpose of renewing his own vitality when he had become aged. Be this as it may, it was as an old man that the sun was thought to totter down to the west in the evening to be reborn at sunrise as Khepri ("he who becomes") after he had defeated Apophis, the serpent or crocodile monster, at the end of his journey through the underworld. As recorded in "The Book of Knowing the creations of Re and of Overthrowing Apophis", the text of which occurs on the Bremner-Rhind papyrus (No. 10188) in the British Museum,[2] the story of creation is told by the All-Lord Neb-er-der, who assumed the form of Khepri. In this capacity he was identified with Re and Atum in the Heliopolitan cosmology expressed in the more philosophical terms of the Memphite theology in respect of creation by divine utterance.

When heaven and earth had come into being and the Heliopolitan Ennead was established, Seth as a member of the original family of gods, and probably at one time a storm- and weather-god, was on perfectly friendly terms with his brother Osiris and his nephew Horus, until the feud developed between them.[3] It was then after the memorable battle commemorated in perpetuity in the ritual combat in the cult drama, that Seth became the prototype of the leader of the forces of evil and the mythological archetype of all strife in the universe, exemplified in the storm, tempest, eclipse and darkness, with which he had been associated as a weather-god.[4] In his service was Apophis, the snake of the hostile darkness which the sun destroyed daily at dawn in the blackest part of the eastern sky, and who was the personification of the deeds of darkness. But since Seth often was included among the crew of the sun-boat, he was not inherently evil or opposed to Re.[5] On the contrary, he championed his cause against Apophis, and decided the battle in favour of his solar ally in the perennial struggle between light and darkness, which in Egypt was always the fundamental issue in the cosmic conflict. Therefore, it was Apophis, the arch-enemy of Re, who was the devil *par excellence*, represented sometimes as a serpent and sometimes as a crocodile, though in the Twenty-second Dynasty Seth assumed an almost identical rôle when as Typhon he was equated with Apophis, very much as Satan as an Elohim in Hebrew tradition was transformed into "that old serpent the devil".

The Repulsing of the Dragon

In the myth recording the "Overthrowing of Apophis" when the arch-fiend every morning engaged in mortal combat with

Re, how Apophis was repulsed is not disclosed. But whether or not it was with the aid of a spell that he triumphed, he in any case succeeded in binding, piercing and burning him up with his fiery rays. But it was only a temporary victory, as the fight had to be resumed the following night, and so on *ad infinitum*. The text, however, was a liturgy for magical recitation to repulse the dragon and assist Re in his daily contest, and by so doing to expel the forces of evil wherever they might lurk. To these ends a wax figure of the monster, or his associates, was constructed, tied and bound, and his name inscribed upon it. It was then inserted in a papyrus wrapper on which a figure of Apophis had been drawn in green pigment, put in a box, placed on the ground and trampled to pieces by the priest and spat upon. This was done at morning, noon and night, and at certain specified seasons, or when a tempest was raging, heavy rain was falling, or the solar disk was eclipsed. The performance of the rite was calculated to drive away, consume and burn up every enemy of Pharaoh, dead or living, as the son of Re, for Re made Thoth to slay the essence of all evil.

The function of Seth in the overcoming of Apophis is described in another account of "the Repulsing of the Dragon" from the Coffin texts of the Middle Kingdom and the Book of the Dead. When the boat entered the underworld at sunset a serpent over 50 feet long armoured in flint, identified with the Crocodile-god Sebek, a personification of the powers of evil, was encountered on the mountain of the far western boundaries of the earth with a fascinating gaze towards Re in his barque, causing stupefaction among the crew. It was then that Seth ranged himself beside the Sun-god to protect him by the full force of his magic power from the evil eye of the dragon, "so that the journey may progress". Against his supernatural equipment the might of the serpent was of no avail. Therefore, he repelled the beast and enabled Re to make the passage in safety and to be reborn in the morning.[6]

It was these spells that were used to secure the survival and rebirth of the dead in the mortuary ritual like those recorded from the Eighteenth Dynasty in the papyrus of Ani,[7] where the scribe Ani prayed to be delivered from "the great god who snatcheth away the soul, who devoureth hearts, who feedeth upon offal, the gatekeeper in the darkness and the dweller in the boat of Seker". He was reassured by Atum that as Osiris he was destined to live for millions and millions of years. Moreover, Osiris was similarly assured by Atum that he had nothing to fear from Seth who was now constrained to remain in the barque of the sun to fight Apophis, and so Osiris was able to tell Horus that his enemies had been "given into woes, for Selqet (a scorpion goddess) was binding them". Therefore, as at death every man believed that he became Osiris, the text was "a spell for not dying a second time" and for the preserva- tion of the deceased as himself an Osiris.

The Conception of Good and Evil

Although the ancient Egyptians regarded the hereafter as a state of innumerable dangers and conflicts, once they were protected with an adequate magical equipment of spells, charms, amulets and funerary rites to give them "power over the powers that are in them",[8] they adopted an optimistic attitude towards death and its aftermath, and the conquest of the malign forces everywhere. The environment in which they lived gave them confidence in the cosmic order and the rhythm of nature, and made them fundamentally hopeful in their out- look. No attempt, however, was made to work out a teleologi- cal or moral philosophy, or a dualistic theology. Evil as well as everything else was held to have come from the gods, who were themselves subject to the same weaknesses, attacks and influences as mankind. Indeed, so far from being omnipotent, omniscient, all-righteous and infallible, they might sometimes be the champions of good and at other times its opponents, like Seth, who was at once the ally of Re-Atum and the adversary of Osiris and Horus, and all for which these deities stood respectively. Even Horus, in spite of his vindication of the cause of his father, was alleged to have decapitated his mother Isis when she enraged him, and Hathor had as many sides to her character as she had offices and functions.

For the Egyptians, however, the good was not that which in our sense is ethically "right", or the evil that which is morally "wrong". These concepts were conditioned by the environment in which they arose and the associated belief in the divine ordering of the cosmic forces and natural processes on which they depended for their existence and well-being. As these were personified in human form they were subject to human shortcomings and instability in their actions, but the good was what they willed and loved and the evil that which was contrary to their desires and the right ordering of things, and consequently displeasing to them. The most important personi-fication in this connexion was Maat, the right ordering of nature and the nation by divine ordinance, summed up in the goddess of truth and justice, Maat, the daughter of Re, who accompanied him in his nightly passage through the under-world, and stood beside Thoth in the boat when he arose out of Nun. She was "the brightness by which Re lives", and it was she who ushered the soul of Ani into the judgment hall to be weighed by Thoth and Anubis.[9]

But the conception of Maat, although represented concretely as a goddess, was equated with "justice", "truth", "right" and "order", as essential attributes of the universe and of the state. Therefore, it had a cosmic, political and ethical connotation. By it Re lived and ruled and dispelled the darkness when he rose in the east at dawn, just as he had put order (Maat) in the place of chaos when he first called all things into existence. It was equally the duty of his son the Pharaoh on the throne to maintain "justice" (Maat) by ruling the nation with "truth"[10] against anarchy, strife, lawlessness, and to maintain the rhythm of nature. Therefore, to the official name of the king the epithet "living in truth" (Maat) was appended, and during the Ikhnaton movement in one of the hymns the new capital at Amarna was described as "the seat of truth". Similarly, when Tutankhamen restored the worship of Amon-Re he was said to have "driven out disorder from the Two Lands so that order (Maat) was again established in its place as at the first time (creation)".[11]

In the Old Kingdom the relation of the Pharaoh to his subjects was that of a sovereign protector and defender of the right order, for Maat was an enduring principle, "its good and its worth was to be lasting. It has not been disturbed since the day of its creation; whereas he who transgresses its ordinances is punished."[12] Since Maat was this changeless order divinely ordained at the creation, it was of the very essence of existence and right living, fundamentally good and advantageous— something to be striven after and attained by "doing what the king, the beloved of Ptah, desired".[13] Under feudal conditions in the Middle Kingdom when the stress was upon social justice and righteousness, it was declared that "every man had been made like his fellow", and since the social order was part of the cosmic order, social inequality was contrary to the proper equilibrium of society, and no part of the basic divine plan. It was only evil in the heart of man that had upset the balance, but with the break-up of the divinely established dynasty at the end of the Pyramid Age before the inroads of Asiatics, Maat was said to have been "cast out and iniquity to sit in the council chamber. The plans of the gods are destroyed and their ordinances transgressed. The land is in misery, mourning is in every place, towns and villages lament."[14] This was evil *par excel-lence* because it represented the collapse of the established order.

The monarchy, however, by virtue of its divine foundations and functions remained the unifying centre, and when royal power was again able to assert itself as world power, alike cosmic and political in its range, it became the rallying point, as it did also after the collapse of the Aton interlude. Ikhnaton failed because he was unable to transform the royal divine Maat incarnate in him into an effective order of society as a political and administrative force. To be efficacious the Maat of the cosmos had to be transmitted from the gods through the Pharaoh and his priesthood and administrators to society at large, whose business it was to counterbalance good against evil by transforming cosmic-divine Maat into the Maat of a firmly established social order in which sound government, justice, peace and stability were maintained.

MESOPOTAMIA

In the less stable and predictable environment of Mesopotamia with its scorching and suffocating winds, torrential rains, devastating floods and uncertain seasons, the cosmic and political orders could not be interpreted in terms of Maat as in the Nile valley. Under these conditions the human situation and its destinies were as indeterminate as the processes of nature involving a continual struggle for existence and survival. For man death was no less the perennial challenge to the will to live than were the floods that every spring threatened the return of the primeval watery chaos. If to prevent this catastrophe the victory of Marduk over Kingu and Tiamat had to be made secure by a ritual repetition of the original combat in the vegetation death and revival drama, that some attempt should be made to overcome the evil of death with which the human species was confronted and to gain the boon of immortality is hardly surprising.

The Babylonian Myth of Adapa

Here, again, however, the situation in Mesopotamia was very different from that in Egypt. That man in some measure shared the nature of the gods is inherent in early Babylonian myths like those of Adapa and Gilgamesh, where the hero is represented as a semi-divine being. Thus, in the Adapa legend he, as "the seed of mankind", was the son of Ea, begotten by him to be a leader among men and endowed by his father with divine wisdom, though not with immortality. Ebeling equates him with Adam (*A-da-pa*), the first man,[15] but in the story he is said to have been created as the "model" of men, "the most wise among the Anunnaki" to expound the decrees of the land, baking with the bakers of Eridu, the city of Ea, providing bread and water, arranging and clearing the offering table in the temple, and performing its rites daily.

He was also a fisherman, and one day when he was out on the Persian Gulf catching fish for the temple of Ea his boat was overturned by a sudden south wind and he was thrown into the water. Infuriated, he cursed the wind and broke one of its wings. This prevented it from blowing for a week, and when Anu, the lord of heaven, was informed of the cause he summoned Adapa to appear before him. Before he ascended to the sky to give an account of his deed he was instructed by his father Ea how he was to act and what he was to say. Clad in a mourning garment to excite the pity and win the friendship of Rammuz and Gizzida, the gatekeepers of heaven, he was told to explain that the reason for his mourning was their disappearance from the land of the living. Touched by this expression of regret at their demise, it was hoped that they would intercede for him, but Ea warned Adapa not to eat any bread or drink any water offered to him as it would be the food and drink of death. On his arrival so well did the plan work that he was acquitted by Anu and offered the food of life to make him in all respects like the gods, including the endow- ment of immortality. But Adapa, mindful of the counsel of Ea, thinking this was a ruse to destroy him, refused the gift and so he lost the boon of eternal life. Anu thereupon sent him back to earth eventually to die like all other men, very much as Gilgamesh was cheated of immortality by the serpent when he lost the rejuvenating plant.[16]

The remainder of the Adapa story in Fragment IV is so badly damaged that the sequel cannot be determined. Heidel main- tains that by refusing the food and water of life, illness, disease and death were brought upon the human race as a whole.[17] In the text, however, it is merely stated that "what ill he has brought upon mankind and the disease that he brought upon the bodies of men, these Ninkarrak (the goddess of healing) will allay".[18] In any case, whatever its effects, the breaking of the wing, as Heidel agrees, was not the first offence committed by human beings[19] in any sense comparable to the transgression of Adam in the Eden myth. Moreover, contrary to the Genesis story, Adapa lost eternal life through his strict obedience to the dictates of his divine father Ea. Therefore, no moral issue was involved in the episode. Nevertheless, it emphasizes the Baby- lonian belief that death was a misfortune which had befallen mankind, as in the case of Gilgamesh, and could have been averted. It was not inherent in the creation of the human species, the primary purpose of which was to serve the gods in a semi-divine capacity, since it was to enable them to abide in listless leisure that man had been fashioned and given his status in the world.

Flood Myths

Second only to death as the principal calamity, be it in nature or as the evil that has befallen the human race, were the destructive floods of the Tigris and Euphrates, which, unlike the beneficent inundations of the Nile, brought in their wake such a sorry trail of havoc so "grievous to the eyes of man" that it could only be regarded as a divine act of judgment and vengeance.[20] This found mythological expression in the deluge stories which recurred from Sumerian times, as is revealed in the fragment of such a myth found in 1914 on a Sumerian tablet in the Nippur collection in the Museum of the University of California and translated by Dr Poebel.[21] In this text after an account of the creation of man and of the animals and the founding of the five prediluvian cities—Eridu, Badlibira, Larak, Sippar and Shuruppak—the decision of the gods to send a flood to destroy "the seed of mankind" is recorded. There seem, however, to have been some who were by no means in favour of the decree, and the Water-god Enki apparently acquainted Ziusudra, the last of the antediluvian kings and the counterpart of the Biblical Noah, with their intentions and advised him to build a large boat to save himself. In the missing forty lines or so of the column at this point in the text no doubt there were instructions concerning the construction of the ship and who and what it was to contain, but in any case the contents included animals as well as members of his family. In the fifth column the deluge already had been raging in the land for seven days and seven nights with the boat tossing about on the waves. The Sun-god Utu came forth shedding his light on heaven and earth. At this welcome sight Ziusudra opened the window of the craft, and prostrating himself before Utu offered to him the sacrifice of an ox and a sheep, presumably from the cargo. Then follows another long break in the text before the rendering of Ziusudra immortal is described by the bestowal upon him of "life like a god", and "breath eternal", followed by his translation to "the mountain of Dilmun, the place where the sun rises".[22]

In the later version on the Tablet XI of the Babylonian epic of Gilgamesh, the same remarkable resemblance to the Hebrew story is maintained based on the earlier Sumerian myth which had nothing to do with Gilgamesh.[23] According to the Akkadian recension, the flood was decreed by the great Triad, Anu, Enlil and Ea, the Enki of the Sumerians, though exactly why they determined to bring this wholesale destruction on the earth is not made clear. We are merely told that "their heart led the great gods to produce the flood".[24] Eventually when she saw the havoc that was wrought, Ishtar repented of having supported the proposal—"the olden days are alas! turned to clay", she lamented, "because I bespoke evil in the Assembly of the gods".[25] The gods, in fact, "cowered like dogs" as they saw what they had done, and Ea upbraided Enlil for his thoughtlessness in imposing the catastrophe on the human race, threatening the very existence of all sentient life,[26] whatever may have been the unspecified offence of mankind that called for this act of divine vengeance. From the Atrahasis epic[27] it would appear that one of the causes may have been its noisy behaviour which kept the gods awake, as in the similar episode in the *Enuma elish*.[28]

Be this as it may, Utnapishtim, the Akkadian equivalent of the Sumerian Ziusudra and of Atrahasis, who according to Berosus was the tenth antediluvian king in Mesopotamia, was secretly warned in a dream by Ea of the approaching deluge and ordered to build a ship of 120 cubits with seven storeys into which he was to take the seed of all living creatures.[29] This upset the nefarious designs of Enlil since Utnapishtim was thereby able to complete his vessel in a week and laden it with his cargo of "all living beings", human and animal, together with silver and gold, before the floods descended for six days and six nights. Then "the sea grew quiet, the tempest was still, the flood ceased on the seventh day". In the meantime "all mankind had returned to clay" and the landscape was just a vast sheet of water. Utnapishtim opened a hatch and light fell upon his face. No coastline was to be seen, but the vessel came to a halt on Mount Nisir, and there it held fast for a week. On the seventh day a dove was sent out and returned, not finding a resting-place. Then a swallow was set free with the same result. Finally a raven was released and, finding food, cawed and flew away.

Knowing that the waters had abated, Utnapishtim disembarked his motley assembly from the ship and offered sacrifice to the famished gods, who smelt its sweet savour and crowded like flies about the offerer. Ishtar, however, prevented Enlil from foregathering with them since he was the instigator of the deluge. When he arrived at the scene he was admonished by Ea for attempting to annihilate mankind upon whom the gods depended for their nourishment rather than for resorting to more reasonable and less harmful measures to induce them to mend their ways. Realizing his mistake, Enlil went aboard the ship and took Utnapishtim and his wife by the hand, knelt before them and blessed them, raising them to a divine status, and thereby bestowing immortality upon them. Henceforth they were to reside at the mouth of the rivers, which corresponds to Dilmun on the eastern shores of the Persian Gulf in the Sumerian version, though their abode is represented as being far away. This is clear in the Gilgamesh epic, where the journey of the hero of Erech to the place where Utnapishtim dwelt was represented as long and perilous.[30] So far as the human race was concerned, although it was not supposed apparently that it was wholly destroyed, fourteen women, who presumably had survived the deluge, were assembled by Ea, and after he had recited an incantation over the Goddess of Birth, Mama, and requested her to repeat it over a lump of clay from which fourteen human beings were modelled, they were projected into the wombs of the women. As a result seven boys and seven girls were born to replenish the earth.[31]

While the Babylonian flood story and its Sumerian original are by no means explicit about the cause of the catastrophe, it would seem that like the Hebrew derivative it was in some way connected with the sin of man, whatever may have been the occasion and nature of the transgression. If in fact it was only the noisy and hilarious gatherings which disturbed the sleep of the gods, they were prompted more by caprice than by a desire to remove from the earth an essentially perverse and corrupt generation, as in the subsequent re-interpretation of the myth in the Genesis narratives. As in the other Babylonian texts, no moral issue was involved in the episode. Invariably it was the gods who first disturbed the peace and wrought havoc on the earth and mankind by their cosmic struggles, their irascibility, whims and irresponsible actions, which, like the flood, brought considerable trouble and hardship upon themselves, causing them to repent of their own doings.

The Myth of Kur

Moreover, they were beset by malign dragons and a host of malevolent forces in their own realms. Thus, in the Sumerian myth of Kur the slaying of a dragon recurs in three versions of the same story current in the third millennium B.C. In the first, when the Goddess Ereshkigal had been abducted like Kore and carried off to the nether regions, perhaps by Kur, Enki set out in quest of her in a boat. A violent battle with stones followed, and Enki's boat was attacked by the primeval waters of the abyss in which the monster Kur had his abode. What was the outcome of this encounter we are not told, as the passage ends at this point, the rest of the story being devoted to the adventures of Gilgamesh. It is not improbable, however, as Kramer suggests, that it was as a result of his victory over Kur on this occasion that Enki became "lord of the abyss", and his temple was called "the sea-house".[32]

In the second version Ninurta, the Sumerian Warrior-god and son of Enlil, played the rôle of Marduk in the *Enuma elish*, attacking Kur at the instigation of his weapon, personified as Sharur. A fiery encounter ensued in which Ninurta at first was made to "flee like a bird". Urged to continue the fight by Sharur and encouraged in the hope of ultimate victory, Ninurta with all the weapons at his command made a tremendous onslaught upon his adversary and succeeded in utterly destroying him. But as Kur had held in check the primeval waters, when his control of them was removed they rose to the surface and prevented the fresh waters reaching the fields and gardens through the irrigation canals, so that all vegetation ceased. Ninurta then erected a vast heap of stones over the body of Kur to keep back the "mighty waters" of the nether regions, and gathered up those that already were poisoning the land, "guiding and hurling them into the Tigris". Thus, fertility was restored on earth and happiness among the gods in the heavens. "The fields produced much grain, the harvest of palmgrove and vineyard was fruitful. It was heaped up in granaries and hills; the lord (Ninurta) made mourning to disappear from the land, and he made good the liver of the gods." Then he made his mother, Ninhursaga (Nintu or Ki), the queen of the hill of stones he had erected over Kur, and, like the Egyptian primordial hills,[33] it became a creative centre and a kind of paradise, producing all kinds of trees, herbs, cattle, sheep and "fourlegged creatures", wine, honey, gold, silver and bronze. The poem closes with the blessing of his allies and the cursing of those who had joined forces with Kur in the battle.[34]

In the third version it was the Goddess Inanna (i.e. the Sumerian Ishtar) who was determined to destroy Kur unless he acknowledged her power, became subservient to her and glorified her virtues. Addressing An, the god of the heavens, she threatened to hurl a long spear and throwingspear upon him (Kur), set fire to a neighbouring forest, dry up the waters, and remove his dread. An warned her of the powers of her adversary and the terror he had caused among the gods. Nothing daunted, she persisted in her intentions, opened "the house of battle", destroyed Kur and stationed herself on the "mountain Ebih" in Northeast Sumer with which he was equated, proclaiming her own glory and might.[35]

ANATOLIA

The Hittite Myth of Illuyankas

In Anatolia a similar corpus of myths was grouped round the Weather-god as the slayer of the dragon personifying the forces of evil in their various aspects. Some of those recovered from the archives in the ruins of Boghazköy are merely Hittite versions of Babylonian legends. Others are of Hurrian origin. The first described in a very mutilated form the encounter between the Storm- and Weather-god and a dragon Illuyankas, ending in the defeat of the hero of the story (the Storm-god). This led him to appeal to all the gods to come to his aid. In response Inaras, the goddess, prepared a great banquet of wine to which, having solicited the help of one Hupasiyas, she lured the dragon and his children. They ate and drank until they were no longer able to return to their lair. So Hupasiyas came and trussed them up with a rope and the Storm-god slew them. As a reward Inaras built Hupasiyas a house on a cliff in the land of Tarukka, but instructed him not to look out of the window lest he should see his wife and children. After twenty days he pushed it open and saw them. Inaras then returned, but what precisely happened is difficult to decipher, except that a quarrel ensued and apparently she killed the man, and the Storm-god sowed a weed (*sahla*) over the ruins of the house.

According to a later version, the dragon took away with him the heart and eyes of the Weather-god when he vanquished him. To recover them and avenge his defeat, the Weather-god begot a son and eventually married him to the daughter of Illuyankas, instructing him to demand his father's eyes and heart. This he did, and when he restored them to his father the Storm-god recovered his former strength and engaged the dragon in battle, and slew both Illuyankas and, at his request, his own son, who in the rôle of Horus in Egypt had revitalized him.[36]

Although these two dragon stories resemble in certain respects the Babylonian epic of Creation, according to the text they were the cult legend recited at the Purulli Festival, which, as Dr Gaster suggests, may have been held in the spring at the beginning of the dry season when the winter rains had ceased and drought was imminent.[37] Thus, he regards the myth as the libretto of an ancient Hittite ritual drama comparable to that celebrating the victory of Marduk over Tiamat, Horus over Seth, and the Rogation-tide rites in Europe, in all of which the dominant theme was the sacred combat between the forces of good and evil, personified in the victory of the beneficent Weather-god over the dragon of drought or flood. On this hypothesis, Hupasiyas in order to come to the aid of the Storm- and Weather-god had sexual relations with the Goddess Inaras to acquire the necessary strength for the fight with the dragon. It was to protect this supernatural power that he was incar-cerated in the house on the inaccessible cliff, and when he infringed the tabu by looking out of the window at his wife and children, he lost his strength and he and the house had to be destroyed. In the second version the request of the god's son to be slain with the dragon is explained as a result of his having unwittingly betrayed the hospitality of his father-in-law by allowing him to be killed while he was in his house. The concluding portion of the text is a ritual epilogue describing the procession of the gods and their consorts and the installation of the Weather-god in the temple at Nerik at the Purulli Festival, as in the Babylonian *Akitu*.[38]

The Yuzgat and Telipinu Myth of the Vanished God

On a tablet now in the Louvre, which in 1905 was acquired by Sayce at Yuzgat about 30 miles east of Ankara (but probably part of the Boghazköy archive), a similar ritual myth in a very incomplete condition appears to record the disappear-ance of the Sun-god and Telipinu, the vegetation deity, when a drought had brought all life to a standstill. The whole earth was in a state of torpor because it was in the grip of a demon named Hahhimas, so that the waters had dried up, the oxen, the sheep, the dogs and the pigs, and all vegetation were paralysed. In despair the Goddess (Hannahanna) appealed to the Storm- and Weather-god to intervene, but without avail. One god after another was sent to the demon, only to be seized by him, including the powerful Telipinu, until at length the

Goddess herself offered to rescue the Sun-god and return with him to heaven. What happened after this is unfortunately somewhat confused.[39]

In the closely related myth of Telipinu, the god of fertility (Telipinu) himself is represented as having left the land in a rage and taken the grain with him. So the cattle, sheep and mankind no longer bred, and those with young could not bring forth. The vegetation dried up and the trees were unable to produce fresh shoots. Thus, famine arose in the land so that both man and the gods were in danger of perishing from hunger; the gods, as in Mesopotamia, depending upon mankind for their sustenance. Even when the Sun-god arranged a great feast and invited to it thousands of gods, they ate but their hunger was not satisfied; they drank but their thirst was not quenched. Then the Storm- and Weather-god explained that the cause of their disaster was the withdrawal of Telipinu. Thereupon the Sun-god ordered a search for him to be made everywhere by the eagle; in the high mountains, in the deep valleys and the watery depth, but nowhere could he be found. At the request of the "Grandmother" Hannahanna (written with the ideogram of the Sumerian Mother-goddess Nintud) the Weather-god himself next set out to gain access to the city of Telipinu but without success. The Goddess then sent forth the bee, who having found him in his own town (either Lihzina or Hattusa), stung him on his hands and feet. This only made him more furious and determined to destroy all life on the earth. It was not until Kamrusepas, the goddess of healing, exorcised his malice by her magical spells that he was made to return on the wings of the eagle. Then "the sheep went to the fold, the cattle to the pen, the mother tended her child, the ewe her lamb, the cow her calf". The altars were made ready, the embers on the hearth were kindled, and "Telipinu tended the king and queen and provided them with enduring life and vigour". An evergreen was set up in the temple and from it the fleece was suspended in which the fat of sheep was placed, and offerings of corn, wine, oxen and sheep were made to Telipinu.[40]

Kumarbi and the Song of Ullikummi

Although in the text the episode is not connected with a seasonal rite, the theme and its ritual suggest that the myth was associated with the renewal cult drama. The slaying of the dragon is a typical combat story, and although the god neither dies nor descends into the underworld, the disappearing god is in line with the Tammuz and Adonis cycles. The Weather-god and the Mother-goddess, and the king and queen, assume their customary rôles, while in the background are the Sumero-Babylonian cosmic struggles among the gods. This is particularly apparent in the Hurrian song of Ullikummi, the diorite man whom the Hurrian god Kumarbi created in order to regain the kingship from the Storm-god. In the beginning Alalus was king of heaven, attended by Anu, "the first among the gods", until in the ninth year of his reign Anu conspired against him and drove him down to "the dark earth". For the next nine years Anu occupied the throne in heaven and then he in his turn was attacked by Kumarbi, "the father of the gods", equated with the Sumerian Enlil, who bit off his "knees" (i.e. generative organ) and consumed it. Told by Anu that in consequence he had become impregnated with three mighty gods—the Storm-god (?), the river Aranzakh (the Tigris) and Tasmisus, the attendant of the Storm-god, Kumarbi promptly spat them out of his mouth. The subsequent course of events cannot be determined, as the rest of the tablet is largely unintelligible, but when the Storm-god was born eventually Anu with his help plotted to destroy Kumarbi. A battle with the Storm-god ensued, but its outcome is not recorded in that part of the text which is decipherable, though doubtless Kumarbi was defeated and deposed in favour of the victorious Storm-god.[41]

Equally fragmentary are the three tablets containing the main narrative concerning the conspiracy of Kumarbi against his son Teshub, the Storm- and Weather-god who had displaced his father as king of the gods. This Song of Ullikummi opens with Kumarbi seeking the counsel of the Sea, the birth of a son to him named Ullikummi as a result of his union with either the daughter of the Sea or with a "great mountain peak". But his body was made of diorite, and when he was taken down to earth he was placed on the right shoulder of Ubelluris, one of the figures who like Atlas supported the world in the midst of the sea. He grew with such rapidity that in a fortnight he was standing in the sea with the water only up to his knees. The Sun-god seeing his phenomenal growth and vigour went to the Storm-god to inform him of the menace. After the Sun-god's departure the Storm-god and his attendant Tasmisus conferred together, and Teshub with his sister Ishtar then went to Mount Hazzi (i.e. Mount Casius near Ugarit) on the Mediterranean coast to see Ullikummi for themselves. Urged apparently by his wailing sister, Teshub attacked the diorite man, aided by thunder and rain, but without avail. Against Ullikummi the gods were powerless. Increasing in height and girth to 9,000 leagues, he reached up to the house of the gods in the heavens (*kuntarra*) and stood over the gate of the Storm-god's city, Kummiya, compelling Teshub to abdicate. Thereupon Teshub appealed to Ea, who summoned the gods in Apsu to see what could be done to meet the desperate situation. When the council failed to find a solution Ea consulted Enlil and then went to Ubelluris, who was not even aware that Ullikummi had grown on his shoulder, any more than he had been when heaven and earth were built upon him and subsequently were severed with a very ancient copper knife. This, however, suggested to Ea a possible course of action. He sent for this knife, and the gods then cut through the feet of Ullikummi and so destroyed his power. The final section of the text is unintelligible, except for a few boastings on the part of Ullikummi, but in all probability the story ended with Teshub's victory over Kumarbi.[42]

All these ritual myths show clear signs of their purpose having been the enactment of a sacred combat in a seasonal drama which may have been an integral part of the spring festival. Thus, we are told quite explicitly that the myth of Illuyankas was recited at the Purulli Festival, which in all probability was held at the New Year. Both here and in the story of the vanishing god the theme is centred in a blight that descended upon the land as a result of the malice of a dragon-like supernatural being in conflict with the Weather-god of fertility; or of the disappearance of the vegetation divinity causing the paralysis of all life. Not until victory had been achieved in the great struggle against the forces of evil, or the absent deity brought back and his wrath and chagrin appeased, could beneficence be restored on the earth. It was this sequence of events which it would appear was celebrated in the mimetic rites and by the recitation of the cult legends, either at the critical junctures at the turn of the year, or whenever occasion required, for the purpose of restoring and maintaining the right ordering of the cosmic forces and the processes of vegetation.

SYRIA, PALESTINE AND IRAN

Aleyan-Baal and his Adversaries

In the Ugaritic texts the theme recurs in the conflict between Aleyan-Baal and his adversaries in their respective capacities symbolizing the perennial struggle in the seasonal sequence. It is true, as Gordon has contended, that in Canaan no part of the year is as sterile as in Mesopotamia,[43] figs and grapes ripening in the drought of summer. Nevertheless, the fact remains that rain was essential for the fertility of the crops, and Baal was the lord of the earth and of the springs who rode on the clouds.[44] Moreover, when he was in the underworld, having taken the clouds with him, rain and fertility disappeared until his adversary Mot, the ruler of the nether regions, had been overcome by Anat—threshed, winnowed and ground in a mill like the reaped grain. Then fecundity was restored.[45]

As Baal was the Storm- and Rain-god manifest in the clouds, the primary source of fertility, so Mot would seem to have been equated with death, the negation of vitality, "wandering over every mount to the heart of the earth, every hill to the earth's very bowels", turning them into desolation by robbing all living things of the breath of life.[46] But he was treated by Anat as though he were identified with the ripe corn (i.e. the harvested Grain-god). As his name suggests, however, his connexions primarily were with sterility, the desert, death and the underworld,[47] and even as the grain it was as the slain corn-spirit dying at the ingathering of harvest[48] that he was represented.[49] In any case, he was *par excellence* the adversary of Baal, and, therefore, the personification of the forces of barrenness, aridity, of life in decline and death. Consequently, his struggle with Baal was both fundamental and perennial because in the seasonal sequence in the natural order summer with its drought and sterility was followed by the revival in the wet season when "the heavens rain oil and the wadies run with honey".[50] And this was an annual, and not a septennial, phenomenon.

Consequently, in the myth neither of the antagonists was ultimately destroyed. Notwithstanding Anat's drastic treat-ment of Mot, he survived to continue the struggle with his adversary after Baal had been released from the underworld. At their first encounter Baal was completely paralysed with fear and returned to his house, weeping at the approach of his enemy[51] and ready to become his slave without resistance.[52] This loss of vigour was typical of the decline in vitality and the dying vegetation in the dry season even though the fruits ripened. With the return of the rains the renewal of the urge of life in all its power found expression in the mighty battle between Mot and Baal in which, with the aid of the Sun-goddess, Shapash, Baal attacked with all his might and resources. Both were equally strong and, engaging in deadly combat, they bit like serpents, gored each other like wild bulls, and kicked like chargers. They fell to the ground but neither yielded. Then the Sun-goddess intervened, urging Mot to give up the fight and return to the underworld[53] because the season of his reign had come to an end, and it was now the turn of Baal to bring life out of death.

Mot, however, was not the only adversary which Baal had to encounter. In the first place, as has been considered,[54] he was the younger Weather-god, and before he became estab-lished as the son of Dagon, lord of the earth and the controller of vegetation, he had to wrest the pre-eminence from El, the father of the gods, very much as in Anatolia, Kumarbi usurped the leadership of the pantheon formerly held by Anu after he had fought and defeated him. But as when Kumarbi had acquired the throne he in his turn was replaced by Teshub the Weather-god, so El was always conspiring against Baal to undermine his authority and regain the supremacy for himself.

Thus, he lent aid not only to Mot[55] but also to Prince Sea, the monster with whom Baal had to contend to obtain the "kingdom eternal",[56] like Marduk with Tiamat. Already Prince Sea had claimed to be lord and master of the gods,[57] and secured the support of El, who had declared, "Baal is your slave, O Sea!"[58] Moreover, El had ordered a house to be built for Prince Sea on Mount Sapon in the domain of Baal by a master-builder from Egypt, Hayin, whom, as Dr Obermann argues, Baal had always intended should erect him a palace.[59] Therefore, in view of all the provocative circumstances Baal was compelled to take up the challenge and the fight ensued as described in Text No. 68, which gave Baal his assured position as the leading god of the pantheon. Whether or not he actually fought against Lotan, the serpent, is not clear, but Baal's ally Anat said she had "crushed the writhing serpent, the accursed one of seven heads",[60] and Mot vowed that he would be avenged on his adversary (Baal) because he had smitten and destroyed Lotan,[61] who seems to have been equated with the dragonish forces of death and desolation with which Baal was in perpetual conflict. Therefore, taken collec-tively the evidence reveals the Storm-god in the familiar rôle of the divine warrior in the seasonal combat in the cult drama.

Hebrew Dragon Myths

In Hebrew mythology, where the idea of a dying and reviving god was incompatible with the nature of Yahweh, when he was represented as engaging in battle with other gods it was for the purpose of deposing them and asserting his absolute sovereignty as a result of his victory, seizing their power and occupying the throne in unchallenged might.[62] Sometimes he was thought to have fought against demons and dragons like Baal and Marduk, but in so doing he assumed his sovereignty as the sole and supreme creator,[63] conquering chaos and creating an orderly cosmos, endowing it with light and life, and setting in their places the sun, the moon and the constellations.[64] Nevertheless, in the poetical books of the Old Testament there are unmistakable references to a creation story in which Yahweh was in conflict with mythical primeval monsters, such as Leviathan and Rahab, indistinguishable from those we have already encountered elsewhere in the Ancient Near East.[65]

Thus, at the end of the Exile the Deutero-Isaiah called upon the god of Israel to awake and put on the strength of his arm "as in the ancient days" when he clave Rahab in pieces and pierced the crocodile (*tannin*), drying up the waters of the abyss, and later when he delivered his people from bondage in Egypt, making a way for the ransomed to pass over the Red Sea,[66] identified with the vanquishing of the dragon of chaos.[67] Here the reference is to the creation of the universe from the body of Rahab after Yahweh had contended with the hostile monster of the deep, following in the wake of Marduk who utilized the body of Kingu for the same purpose after his contest with Tiamat. Similarly in the book of Job, Yahweh is said to have smitten Rahab and bowed down his helpers, and to have pierced "the fleeing serpent",[68] a dragon perhaps associated with eclipses and the sky, driven away by the breath of Yahweh, as Rahab appears to have been synonymous with the serpent, the crocodile and sea monsters in general.[69]

Leviathan, again, is another name for the Ugaritic Prince Sea (Lotan), the "coiled serpent", who in Isaiah (xxvii. 1) is said to have been punished by Yahweh with his great and strong sword, when he slew the crocodile (*tannin*) that was in the sea. As he is described in Job (xl. 25–41), he is made to appear as a dragon breathing out fire and smoke, impervious to attack by sword, spear or arrow. The club and sling stones were regarded by him as stubble, he laughed at the lance, and treated iron as chaff, and brass as rotting timber. Behind him he left a gleam in the sea, and on earth there was none like him, reigning as lord of the beasts, feared alike by gods and all creatures. By swallowing the sun or the moon he was believed to have produced eclipses,[70] and he was also equated with the tortuous serpent[71] whom Yahweh would punish, and with the crocodile and a many-headed monster,[72] like Lotan in the Ugaritic Baal epic.[73]

The seven-headed serpent is a recurrent figure in the Near Eastern mythology and symbolism as a cult object, though by no means always associated with evil. On the contrary, as a magical emblem it was sometimes an instrument of healing like the Hebrew Nehushtan.[74] But in the Leviathan context it was a demonic being connected with the primeval waters of the abyss with whom Yahweh was in conflict. In later Israelite tradition the primeval victory was interpreted as a foreshadow-ing of the deliverance of the nation from the bondage of Egypt, but in the earlier mythology, of which these few traces remain, there can be little doubt that the theme was that of the conquest of the dragon variously described as Rahab, Leviathan, *Tehôm*, *tannin* and the Serpent (*Nakhash*), identified with the waters of the abyss. When the monster was broken in pieces and the enemies scattered, chaos became an ordered cosmos. Then the sea was divided by the Creator, the mighty rivers were dried up and the destructive waters were transformed into life-giving rains, wells and springs when the dry land appeared, and was made ready for vegetation to emerge and the seasonal sequence to be established.[75]

The Fall of Man

When this was accomplished and the garden had been planted to the east in Eden, according to the Yahwistic creation story, the plans of the beneficent Creator were upset by the interven-tion again of the serpent, but this time in a more subtle guise. Instead of entering into mortal combat with Yahweh, it was the innocent and credulous Eve, "the mother of all living", who was attacked by the soft insinuation, "hath God said that in the day thou eatest of the fruit of the tree in the midst of the

garden thou shalt surely die?" But the ruse succeeded; the fatal
fruit was eaten, the eyes of both Eve and Adam were opened,
and the age of primordial innocence came speedily to an end.
Paradise was lost; the serpent was cursed and condemned to go
on his belly for all time and eat the dust as the arch-enemy of
mankind; children were to be born in pain and sorrow; the
wife was to be in subjection to her husband, and man must
labour for his subsistence in the sweat of his brow, returning at
the last to the dust out of which he had been made.[76] Thus,
starting with such high hopes and bright prospects did the
human race fall from its estate and begin the long trail of
misery and woe which filled the earth with so much violence
and corruption, with death in its train, that the Creator
regretted having made man. So he resolved to blot out the race
altogether, including "beasts and the creeping things, and the
fowls of the air". Only Noah found favour in his eyes, and to
him was revealed, after the ark had been constructed, the
intention to destroy by the approaching deluge the existing
order with its Nephilim strain.[77]

The Yahwist used a number of incidents in the ancient
creation myths and dragon stories in the development of his
Paradise theme and its aftermath, but unlike the Priestly narrative and the account of the Flood and the struggle with
Leviathan, there is no comparable Babylonian or Sumerian
version of either Eden or the Fall of Man. The setting of the
garden, as we have seen, was Palestinian rather than Mesopotamian,[78] and the events leading up to the expulsion are only
very remotely connected with the myth of Adapa and the
Gilgamesh epic, confined for the most part to the loss of
immortality through the guile of the serpent. But whereas the
sin of Adam and Eve was represented as an act of disobedience,
Adapa erred in following the advice he had been given by Ea,
and as a result forfeited immortal life. In the Babylonian
literature the primeval struggle was between the gods, and as
Heidel says, "if it is permissible to speak of a 'fall' at all it was
a fall of the gods, not of man".[79] It was they who disturbed
the peace by their continual conflicts between themselves, and

the strife on earth among mortals was only a repetition of their battles in the heavens. That a similar state of affairs lies in the background of the later Judaeo-Christian eschatology, with its references to a war in heaven, will be considered in the next chapter. But so far as the Genesis narratives are concerned, that aspect of the mythology has been eliminated.

The Deluge

The Hebrew Deluge stories, on the other hand, quite clearly were based on the accounts of the Mesopotamian flood in the Akkadian version of the Gilgamesh epic and its Sumerian counterpart. While there are differences in detail in the two traditions and in the J and P Hebrew versions, suggesting that a number of recensions existed to which the respective redactors had access, they all agree that the purpose was the destruction of mankind by divine decree and the saving of a remnant by the hero of the episode constructing a vessel of given but variable dimensions in which representatives of the animal creation were included. The duration differed in all the accounts, ranging from a week in the Sumero-Babylonian versions to 150 days in the Priestly narrative. At the end when the waters had abated (tested by a dove or a raven) the ship grounded on a mountain, and the hero offered sacrifice for a safe deliverance from the catastrophe. In the case of Utnapishtim and Ziusudra divine rank and immortality were bestowed upon them; in that of Noah a covenant was established with Yahweh in which it was declared that the earth would not again be destroyed by a flood.

In place of the "assembly of the gods", the Genesis narratives naturally made Yahweh solely responsible for the cataclysm, and the cause was the moral depravity of mankind. This went far deeper apparently than the trivial noisy behaviour referred to in the Atrahasis epic, analogous to that which gave rise to the struggle of Apsu against the younger gods. "The whole imagination of the thoughts of the heart" of the people was incorrigibly wicked, according to the Yahwistic tradition, and, therefore, merited destruction, with the exception of Noah, who was represented as righteous and in consequence a worthy progenitor of the new creation with the covenant that was to be made with his descendant Abraham at the beginning of Hebrew traditional history. In all the variants every living creature was supposed to have been exterminated so that virtually a completely new start had to be made and a new world-order established with the rainbow as the covenant sign. Yahweh then became the god of his chosen people Israel by virtue of his covenant with the founder of the theocracy.

Dualism in Israel

While, as we have seen, in the popular cultus before the Exile, Yahweh in practice tended to become indistinguishable from a local Baal, there was no suggestion of two rival dualistic causes at the base of the universe, bisecting creation into two halves, good and evil. Belief in evil spirits, such as the *seraphim* or winged serpents, *se'irim* (satyrs), *lilith* (a night monster), and the *'aluqah* (ghoul), was widespread among the Hebrews as among other Semitic tribes. But there is no indication in the pre-exilic literature, or in the archaeological evidence, that any of these demons was a serious rival in power to Yahweh, challenging his sovereign rule in Israel or endeavouring to pervert his moral government. Their domain was confined for the most part to the desert, or the waste places they haunted, although the serpent, who was regarded as a "demon of the waste" before he was transformed into an angelic being, was venerated in the temple, and apparently in the cultus of the wilderness.[80] Although he was assigned superior knowledge in the Eden story,[81] he was not represented as in any sense comparable with the Satan of later tradition.[82]

The absolute transcendence of Yahweh in prophetic and post-exilic Judaism militated against attributing to any independent supernatural being the origin of evil.[83] God may have implanted the evil imagination (*yetser-ha-ra*) in the heart of man,[84] but it was not until the post-Biblical period that speculation concerning the dual nature of man and the world became rife. In the Wisdom and Rabbinical literature God was said to have created two mutually antagonistic powers; the evil within the soul and the Law (Torah) in the holy nation. Between these two man was free to make his choice.[85] Ben Sirach maintained that the grain of evil seed was sown in the heart of Eve and brought death in its trail,[86] while the author of the Wisdom of Solomon went further, declaring that this evil seed was sown by the Devil who was in open antagonism with Yahweh.[87]

In the canonical literature the Satan is a subordinate figure acting under the control of God[88] as a member of the heavenly court permitted to act as "the adversary" to test the integrity of Job. In this rôle he was a divine agent. Nevertheless, he was the accuser of Israel and responsible for leading David astray.[89] Therefore, once a dualistic conception of good and evil was established, he readily became the Jewish counterpart of the Iranian Ahriman with a host of demons under his command. In the book of Enoch the demonic creation was portrayed as an organized army led by the Prince of Darkness intent on seducing mankind and filling the world with corruption.[90] Thus, from being the adversary of Israel the Satan became the arch-enemy of Yahweh from whom he wrested the control of the whole earth, which henceforth was his domain. His reign was destined to be destroyed ultimately when God became all in all, but in the meantime Satan was virtually the lord of creation.

This reversal of divine omnipotence can hardly be regarded as a natural development of the prophetic movement and of post-exilic monotheism. A latent dualism it is true occurs in the pre-exilic doctrine of Yahweh's choice of Israel, but so far from "the world lying in the Evil One", in the Genesis story (P) the creation was pronounced "very good".[91] The Chosen People, in fact, were represented as the instrument for the establishment of the divine purpose for mankind and the gathering together of all things to their Creator. This conviction survived the severe test of the Exile in the sixth century B.C., and was strengthened by the restoration and settlement of the small Jewish community in and around Jerusalem after the Persian conquest of Babylon in 538 B.C.

From then until Alexander the Great incorporated Palestine in his Macedonian Empire after his victory in 331 B.C., the Jews who returned to Jerusalem and those who remained in Mesopotamia lived under Persian rule at a time when Zoroastrianism was making its influence felt in the Iranian Empire. To what extent, if at all, they were responsible for the development of Jewish Messianic and eschatological thought in Judaism in the fourth and third centuries B.C. will be considered in the next chapter,[92] but it is clear, in any case, that the apocalyptic literature arose very largely as a result of the secular tyranny initiated by Antiochus Epiphanes in 175 B.C., prior to the Maccabaean revolt, and gave expression to a more fundamental dualism. In the book of Daniel, a product of this period, Greece, Persia and Israel were represented as having a "prince", or guardian angel, as its supernatural protector,[93] comparable to the tutelary gods of the Babylonian cities. Therefore, the stage was set for a gigantic struggle between members of two spiritual hierarchies, with Michael, "one of the chief of the princes", contending on behalf of Israel as a divine agent[94] when, as it seemed, demonic supramundane powers were at work in the world trying to frustrate the teleological purposes of Yahweh.

Mazdaean Dualism

It is hardly surprising, therefore, that the stirring events at the beginning of the second century B.C. opened the way for the introduction of Iranian dualistic speculation in the Jewish apocalyptic literature of this period. The eternal polarity of good and evil as a characteristic of Iranian thought found expression in the Avestan dualistic struggle between the two opposed forces led respectively by Spenta Mainyu, the beneficent spirit, and Angra Mainyu, the evil spirit, until when the cycle of the world was completed every trace of evil would be removed and Ahura Mazda would become all in all. Since in the Gathas, Ahura Mazda alone is represented as existing as the all-wise, good and beneficent Creator, the King of righteousness, and the primeval twin spirits of good and evil meet in a higher unity in him, it is arguable that no absolute dualism was involved. How they came into being is not explained, but they appear to have been regarded as pre-mundane, though their opposition only found expression when the world had been created and the ceaseless conflict began between the two opposed forces.[95] But this eternal polarism did not imply a cosmic or ultimate dualism because the Angra Mainyu and Spenta Mainyu had no independent existence apart from Ahura Mazda, and in the end his righteous will must prevail. Spenta Mainyu, the good spirit, as the son of Ahura, occupied the first place in the celestial hierarchy and in creation. His antagonist, Angra Mainyu, and his offspring the daevas, stood at the opposite pole, and are said to have "rushed forth from the regions of the North to lure away the Prophet (Zarathush-tra) from the path of righteousness". They were met, however, by Spenta Mainyu, who repelled his enemy by chanting the ancient text known as the *Ahunavar*, which henceforth became the most potent weapon against the evil spirit.[96]

The struggle between good and evil, however, was too deeply laid to escape developing into a thorough-going dualism, and in the later Avesta the twin-spirits became two opposed gods independent of each other. As Ahura Mazda (later known as Ormuzd) created the good, so Angra Mainyu (or Ahriman) was the author of all evil, including the daevas under his control, and all noxious creatures—serpents, wolves, ants and locusts. In the priestly *Vendidad* Ahura is represented as explain-ing to Zarathushtra how Angra Mainyu had upset all his plans for making Persia a terrestrial paradise by introducing a bitter frost in winter, excessive heat in summer, and all the ills that had to be endured, including in addition to death the 99,999 diseases he had maliciously created.[97]

This conception of a double creation was further developed during the post-Avestan period. The planets were then con-sidered to have been the creation of the evil forces while the stars were made by Ahura Mazda. In the *Bundahish* the animals were divided into two hostile groups with the falcon, magpie, crow and fox set in opposition to the serpent, wolf and locust.

In the third of the four ages into which the history of the universe was divided, going back in idea probably to the fifth century B.C., the forces of evil became predominant, and it was then that the progenitors of mankind were created, from whom the founders of the Iranians were represented as having been descended. To mitigate this dualism the Zervanists derived the twin-spirits from a single pre-existing primeval being, Zervan Akarana, "unlimited time", who generated both Ormuzd and Ahriman. The Gayomarthians, on the other hand, attributed the evil spirit to a thought in the mind of Ahura Mazda, who was the sole Creator of all existence, good and evil alike; a view that has been generally adopted by Parsis, and has some support in the Gathas. [98] But the Lie is there represented as the essence of evil personified in Angra Mainyu, the Druj, who readily became Ahriman in the perpetual conflict between good and evil, so fundamental in Near Eastern myth and ritual from the beginning.

It was not until a break was made with the polytheistic cosmology of the Ancient East by the Jewish and Zoroastrian monotheists and the Ionian and Eleatic pre-Socratic philo-sophers, that the problem became acute of reconciling two radically different kinds of being or substance in a universe grounded in a single divine unity. Behind these monotheistic and monistic systems lay the mythological cosmological back-ground against which the later re-interpretations of the ancient myth and ritual was set. Thus, as the Hebrew and Iranian theologians endeavoured to adapt the current cosmogonies to their own doctrinal requirements, and in transcending them created new myths, so the Greek philosophers in their search for a universal unity in terms of the One and the Many, and the underlying dualisms of form and matter, of order and disorder, of good and evil, transmuted rather than destroyed the mythological tradition they inherited.

GREECE

Zeus and the Titans

To what extent Greek myth and ritual were derived from the Ancient Middle East has long been a matter of debate. So far as the dualistic struggle is concerned, the strife that raged among the various members of the family of primeval gods and monsters descended from Ouranus corresponds to that which ensued in the heavenly battles in the Mesopotamian, Anatolian and Syrian texts. After a spate of concealing and swallowing offspring lest they should dethrone their respective fathers, only Zeus remained as a result of a ruse of his mother Rhea. When he grew to maturity he caused his father to disgorge the older children and set free others he had imprisoned in Tartaros, including the mighty Cyclopes, who in gratitude forged for him his thunderbolts and armed him with lightning.[99] Gathering together his forces, he began his war against the Titans, who as the elder brothers of Kronos represented an older generation of the gods like Anu, Alalu or El. For ten years the struggle went on, but at last Zeus and his Olympian allies prevailed with the powerful aid of his thunderbolts. But first he had to go to the nether regions to secure the help of the Hekatoncheiroi, who hurled stones on them. When the Titans eventually were subdued they were imprisoned in Tartaros under the guard of the Hekatoncheiroi, while Atlas, like Ubelluris in the Hurrian "Song of Ullikummi", was assigned the task of holding up the sky.

The defeat of this older generation of gods seems to reflect the struggle between the invading Indo-Europeans and their pantheon, and that of the indigenous population, and the subsequent union of the two traditions in a composite culture in which Zeus reigned supreme as a syncretistic sky-god. Nevertheless, while this historical situation may have been inherent in the myth of the Titanic contest, its theme assumed the form of the Anatolian and Mesopotamian epics recited in the cult drama in connexion with the sacred combat. Whatever may have been the channels by which they reached the Aegean from Asia Minor, probably in the Late Bronze Age, by way of Phoenicia and Phrygia, Syria and Crete, that they provided the basis for Hesiod's *Theogony* has now become increasingly clear in the light of all the available evidence concerning Near Eastern myth and ritual. That Zeus was as powerless to overcome the Titans until he obtained the help of the Hekatoncheiroi in Tartaros as was the Anatolian Storm, and Weather-god to contend with Ullikummi and Kumarbi without the aid of Ea, whose abode was in the subterranean ocean, can hardly be an accidental coincidence in the two stories.

Zeus and Typhoeus

In its Greek form, however, the Ullikummi episode recurs in Apollodorus' version of the struggle of Zeus with Typhoeus (Typhon), the monstrous offspring of Ge and Tartaros with a hundred snakes' heads.[100] According to Apollodorus this half-human, half-animal, untamable dragon, bellowing as a bull yet speaking the speech of the gods, stood so high that he reached to the sky like the Hittite diorite stone Ullikummi. Against him Zeus arose in all his formidable might after he had conquered the Titans, hurling his thunderbolts and flashing his lightning until the very universe rocked and swayed under the fury of the onslaught. But although Typhoeus was rendered helpless and cast into Tartaros as a result of this violent attack, according to an ancient version of the tale he was not so easily disposed of. On the borders of Syria Typhoeus is said to have wrested from Zeus his sacred *harpé* on Mount Kasion, and cut the sinews of his adversary's hands and feet. Then carrying Zeus across the sea to Cilicia he deposited him in the Corycian cave there, with the sinews wrapped in the skin of a bear and kept under the custody of a serpent-like monster named Delphyna. Hermes and Aegipan, however, succeeded in securing Typhoeus, and restoring the sinews to Zeus enabled him to fly up to the sky on a winged chariot. From his celestial realms he pelted Typhoeus with thunderbolts, and pursued him to Mount Nysa. There he was beguiled into eating human food, but although this reduced his strength he continued his resistance until finally he was chased to Sicily and buried under Mount Etna.[101] Thus, the end of the stormy career of this Anatolian dragon was located in the Western Mediterranean, suggesting the course of the diffusion of the myth from its cradleland in

Asia Minor, where its original form is preserved in the Song of Ullikummi and the closely associated Illuyankas dragon tale with their Mesopotamian and Ugaritic counterparts. In its passage through the Aegean, carried perhaps to some extent by Mycenaean and Hurrian merchants and Phoenician traders,[102] it was adapted to local circumstances and traditions. But it was not the Greeks nor the Phoenicians nor the Syrians or Hurrians who were the inventors of the myth, the ultimate origins of which must be sought in Mesopotamian sources yet to be revealed in oral tradition if not in literary composition.

The endless struggle between good and evil, life and death, light and darkness, prosperity and adversity, the older and the younger generations, personified in a variety of divine figures and forces, and enacted in a sacred combat in a cult drama, has been a recurrent feature in the myth and ritual throughout the region in which civilization arose and spread from its original centre in the Fertile Crescent to its eastern and western outposts. In a changing environment it was continually under-going modifications in its personnel, its mythological form and content, and its ritual modes of expression. But everywhere the fundamental theme remained essentially unchanged because the conflict in its several guises was a constant factor, reflected in the historical circumstances, or climatic conditions, opposed forces in nature, the rival claims of an indigenous and extra-neous culture arising out of conquest and culture contact, or from the contrast between the religion of the soil and that of the sky. Nowhere was this more conspicuous than in the dual personality, character, attributes and functions of Zeus and his conflicts.

CHAPTER VII

Eschatological Mythology

IN the primeval and perennial struggle between the opposed forces in the transition from chaos to cosmos, re-enacted annually at the New Year in the cult drama and at other critical junctures, the maintenance of order was never assured, and always was liable to relapse into chaos. Hence the periodic ritual repetition of the establishment of the order of the world under the rule of the creator god and the renewal of the cycle of vegetation centred in the sacral kingship. It was this precarious situation that led to the eschatological hope of a restoration of order at the end of time which would never require renewal; a projection of the cosmological problem into an indeterminate future. Closely associated with these conceptions of "the last things" was the idea of judgment, the catastrophic end of the world and its renewal, and the state of the dead.

EGYPT

Death and Eschatology

Thus, in Egypt, while no records occur of a cosmological consummation of the universe, the preoccupation with death caused eschatology to be concentrated upon the fate of the soul in the hereafter rather than upon cosmic events. In the natural order equilibrium was the normal and proper course finding expression in the primeval emergence of cosmos out of chaos, and subsequently in the regular sequence of the seasons. Therefore, death, constituting as it did a break in the succession of this established rhythmic scheme, raised a problem that called for serious attention and an adequate solution. At first Pharaoh being a cosmic figure sharing permanence with the divinely ordered universe, it was his immortality that had to be made secure to prevent any interruption in the natural order and its forces. Hence the labour expended upon the royal tombs and the mummification of their occupants, with the attendant rites, to enable them to enter the realms of the gods as gods themselves, and to take their place in the barque of Re, sitting on his throne and accompanying him in his passage across the horizon.

The extension of the prerogative of the Pharaoh to ordinary mortals introduced a more complex eschatological situation inasmuch as, unlike the occupant of the throne, no claim to divinity could be maintained to ensure a transition from this life to a celestial hereafter. Nevertheless, belief in human survival beyond the grave is well attested to in the prehistoric cemeteries on the edge of the desert in the Nile valley long before the royal cult was established,[1] and it only required a development of the mortuary ritual to bring it into line with that reserved for the Pharaoh. That it was centred in the tomb is shown by the increasing care bestowed upon the construction and furnishing of the tomb, and the provision made for the comfort and well-being of the deceased in a prescribed ritual in the predynastic period.

The Body and the Soul

It was these ideas and customs that eventually were collected and recorded in the Pyramid texts during the Fifth and Sixth Dynasties. Inconsistencies abound in the texts so that the soul may be represented as having its abode in the tomb and in the celestial realms at the same time, but logical thought and empirical accuracy are not to be expected in the sphere of mythopoeic speculation and ritual efficacy. From very early times each individual was believed to have an invisible immortal "soul", or a "ghost", which often assumed the form of a bird with a human head that either survived death or came into existence at the time of the dissolution. To this conception of the *ba* that of the *ka* was added in due course. Originally the *ka* was exclusively a royal attribute of divine creative power conceived as a beneficent and protective genius, or spiritual double, who guided the fortunes of the Pharaoh primarily in the after-life when he went to his *ka* at death; though being a god he was also able to have communion with his *ka* during his lifetime. In the Middle and New Kingdoms, when the *ka* became the possession of commoners as well as of the Pharaohs, it acquired a more impersonal character as a vital principle in this life, born with the individual, sustained through his life, and preceding him to the next world. Symbolized by two raised arms with outspread hands, it was distinct from the bird-shaped *ba* with its ghostly attributes and functions in the grave and in relation to the mummy or portrait statue.

This psychology of the dead seems to have arisen from the practice of natural desiccation and mummification as a result of which attempts were made at an early period to recondition the corpse after the dissolution by processes external to him, and thereby to overcome the disturbance in the continuity of life caused by death. Burial in the hot dry sand of the desert, which often was impregnated with natronous compounds, arrested decomposition and produced natural mummies, as in the case of modern burial in the saltpetre caves in New Mexico. This doubtless concentrated attention upon the survival of the physical integument and led to the construction of more elaborate brick-lined tombs at the beginning of the dynastic period. But this at once destroyed natural desiccation and made it essential to devise artificial methods of embalmment and mummification,[2] early attempts at which go back to the Second Dynasty.[3] Effigies of the dead were also regarded as permanent substitutes for the corpse and accorded the same ritual treatment as the actual mummy. Thus, "The Opening of the Mouth" ceremony was performed on the statue in the workshop, and the sculptor was called *s'nh*, "he who makes to live", the reanimation rite being a creative act.[4]

Although "The Book of the Opening of the Mouth" was not compiled until the Nineteenth Dynasty, it contains ancient formulae recited during the performance of the rite to reconsti- tute the body (or statue) of the deceased and restore to it its *ba* and *ka*.[5] The earliest mention of the observance is in the Fourth Dynasty tomb of Methen when the cult of Osiris was coming into prominence, although some of the rites may have been in use in predynastic times.[6] At first apparently the ceremony was performed on a statue, and consisted of lustrations with holy water, censings and the presentation of balls of natron. The eye, nose and ears were touched with a copper chisel and various magical instruments, including a ramheaded rod called "Great Magician" with which the actual "opening of the mouth" was performed.

With the development of the worship of Osiris the rite became practically a repetition of the things said and done by Horus on behalf of his father in the Osiris myth. The revivification of Osiris by the bestowal of the Eye which Horus lost in his fight with Seth to avenge his death was enacted on behalf of the deceased, each of the faculties being restored to reconstitute and reanimate the living person. In the Eighteenth Dynasty the "opening of the mouth" of the statue was transferred to the actual mummy to enable the dead man to take part in the funerary ritual in the chapel at his tomb.[7] Everything had to be done in strict accord with that which was done by Anubis, the funerary physician, to the dismembered body of Osiris to restore it to life and to render it immortal. Moreover, to enable the *ba* to leave the tomb and enjoy the delights of the next life, depicted on the walls of the necropolis, he was equipped with the Book of the Dead, which was a product of the cult of Osiris in the Eighteenth Dynasty, but also containing some earlier references to the barque of Re in the solar tradition. Similarly, in the Coffin texts souls were provided with a guide by land and water to the subterranean *Duat*, where Osiris lived and ruled over the dead. In the Book of Gates on the sarcophagus of Seti I from Thebes (now in the Soane Museum in London) the nightly journey through the nether regions is described from the Osirian standpoint brought into conjunction with the Re eschatological doctrine. Here the judgment is represented as taking place in the Hall of Osiris, the sixth domain through which the sun passed every night, whereas in the socalled Book of the Dead it was preparatory to gaining entrance to the Elysian Fields of Aalu. This, however, is characteristic of the confusion in the Egyptian texts about the hereafter and of the relation of the *ba* to the *ka* and the mummy.

The Judgment

When the Osirian faith had replaced that of Re by the Middle Kingdom (*c.* 2000–1780 B.C.), it was believed that the souls of all were judged before Osiris as the god of the dead when they appeared before him in the Hall of the Double Truth to have their hearts weighed by Anubis against a feather symbolizing truth. The trials of both Horus and Osiris before the Heliopolitan Ennead involved the idea of truth and justice as a moral concept, and in the papyrus of Ani[8] this is emphasized by the setting of the judicial procedure. Symbols of truth are conspicuous in the representation of the hall in which Osiris is shown sitting enthroned with Anubis and the four sons of Horus, Isis and Nephthys behind him. Along one side the remaining eight gods of Heliopolis are ranged headed by Re, while Anubis is supported by Thoth to record the sentence, with the dreaded "Devouress" having the head of a crocodile and the forequarters of a hippopotamus, alert and waiting to consume the soul should it be pronounced unjust. In the case of Ani and his wife in the papyrus of the Nineteenth Dynasty the heart is said to have been addressed as the *ka* of Ani and besought not to witness against him in the council of justice; "not to be hostile to him before the master of the balances". This appeal proved to be effective in this instance, for Thoth at once declared him to be "just by the great balances" and without sin. The nine gods gave their assent, and Ani was then led forward by Horus, who presented him to Osiris to be received into his kingdom.

Although no extant representations of the Judgment are older than the Eighteenth Dynasty, the underlying conception goes back to the beginning of the dynastic period. In tomb inscriptions before the end of the Sixth Dynasty the hope of immortality was made to depend upon just rule, fair dealing, giving bread to the hungry, clothing the naked, and similar charitable and benevolent works.[9] Osiris was the champion of righteousness, justice and truth, qualities personified in the Goddess Maat, the daughter of Re, as early as the Second Dynasty. But Re was no less concerned himself with upholding these ideals, and it was he who originally justified the dead king when his soul was weighed in his balances,[10] and side by side with Osiris was the judge of moral worthiness in the hereafter as the creator of truth. Therefore, the supreme judge, whether he was Osiris or Re, was regarded as righteous, almighty and just, whose every action was directed by Maat.[11]

At first his function was to vindicate the moral worth of the deceased Pharaohs at the assize in his celestial court. With the democratization of the cult of Osiris at the end of the Old Kingdom its moral obligations were extended to all who identified themselves with Osiris, and so secured justification when they appeared before him as their judge, enumerating their own virtues, affirming the fulfilment of the ritual require-ments in respect of ceremonial ablutions, and repudiating a long list of shortcomings in a negative confession, which in Chapter 125 of the Book of the Dead was raised to forty-two denials. These utterances were in the nature of spells with which the deceased fortified himself to secure eternal felicity, however latent in the judgment and its theological setting may have been a genuinely ethical conception of right conduct. Therefore, once they had been recited and the ritual ablutions performed the result of the weighing of the heart was reasonably assured. Without any further delay the gods, who acted as the guardians of the moral code and the judges of virtue, pronounced the soul to be "true of voice" and so justified. It then only remained to make the final declaration of innocence and righteousness in the august presence of Osiris himself. This accomplished, the *ba* became Osiris with all this involved in the life beyond the grave.

The After-life

Raised to what was virtually a divine status, it acquired a heavenly *ka*, though it was in the capacity of the *ba* that it might return to the earth to hunt, fish and visit the tomb in a bird-like form as the living immortal "external soul" of the individual. The material body remained in the grave, and there is no mention in the texts of its resurrection. Nevertheless, closely associated with it a spiritualized entity, the *Akhu*, came into being at death and with the *ka* and *ba* lived on in heaven.[12] Similarly, the mortuary offerings, grave-goods and ushabti figures, representing the servants who would work for him in the celestial realms, all had their spiritual counterparts.[13]

In short, however contradictory, the life hereafter was regarded as a combination of spiritual and material attributes and qualities in which sustenance was still required but under heavenly conditions, and magical spells were transmuted into a form adapted to the requirements of the spirit-world. In the Pyramid texts the deceased king was represented as ascending in a variety of ways and having been received in triumph and enjoying all the delights of eternal blessedness as the son of Re:[14] eating divine food, suckled by a goddess, drinking living waters, feeding on the tree of life and enjoying sexual pleasures.[15] But unless he was provided with adequate supplies of human food there was always the danger of his being compelled to devour his own excreta and urine.[16] Hence the importance of the efficacy of sacrifices and offerings, especially in the Book of the Dead and the Book of Gates, when the celestial hereafter had ceased to be a royal prerogative and its delights were shared by all and sundry who hoped for reunion with their friends and relatives beyond the grave. The magical element persisted, and even the gods were threatened with potent spells if they refused to grant what was requested of them on behalf of the departed, whose principal occupations seem to have been hunting and fishing.

In the Theban recension of the Book of the Dead detailed rubrics occur concerning the use of spells, amulets and rituals, some of which were designed to enable the deceased to deter- mine where the after-life was to be spent. The vignettes show the nature of the heavenly country and its occupations which are clearly a reproduction of those on earth under idealized conditions—sailing on canals, reaping, ploughing with oxen.

Requests are made for an abundant supply of offerings that the *ba* might "eat and drink therein, plough, and reap therein", that his "words might be mighty therein", and that he might "never serve as a slave therein, but be ever in authority".

The eschatology of the Book of the Two Ways, the Book of the Dead, the Book of Gates and the Book of Am Duat is predominantly Osirian, just as that of the Pyramid texts is solar and Heliopolitan, though, as has been considered, both theologies recur in all the texts. Thus, the Osirian way to the underworld (*Duat*) with its streams and canals, blazing fire and boiling water and magic isles is comparable to the solar perilous passage to the celestial realms, while in the Book of Gates and its solarized version, the Book of Two Ways, it is the Sun-god who makes his nightly journey through the *Duat* from west to east to give light and air and sustenance to the denizens of the abode of Osiris, though he was an interloper in the domain of the Lord of the underworld in the west, where at Abydos the original home of Osiris was placed.

When the worship of Osiris was first established at Abydos it was believed that those who were buried there would come under his protection in the next life, rising from death to immortality and sharing in his offerings on festivals. There the ancient mortuary god, Khanti-Amentiu, "First of the Westerners", became completely Osirianized at a very early period when the faith of Osiris made its way up the Nile from the Delta in prehistoric times, and his kingdom was conceived as situated in the west, or below the western horizon, where it merged into the nether regions. Therefore, he was Lord of the dead (i.e. of the *Duat*) before his cult was celestialized, and when everybody became Osiris at death eternal blessedness was attained in his abode, wherever it might be located.

MESOPOTAMIA

The Land of No-Return

In Mesopotamia the eschatological approach was very different from that which prevailed in Egypt. Here the sustained pre-occupation with the hereafter was conspicuously absent. The inevitability of death was accepted as an indisputable and irremedial fact of everyday occurrence, and what lay beyond the grave was so obscure as to be hardly a matter of very serious conjecture. For a time the dead might continue a shadowy existence in a sombre "land of no-return" beneath the earth, ruled by the Goddess Ereshkigal and her husband Nergal—a "house of dust" and darkness, to which all descended when the span of life was ended, irrespective of status, class, age or ethical behaviour. Frequently it was conceived as a great house or an immense city surrounded with walls and having gates strongly guarded and secured by bolts and bars. Sometimes it was represented as a hollow mountain difficult to approach, into which the Apsu flowed; or the entrance might lie in the west across the sea reached by a ferry. It was to this dreary abode of Irkalla that Eridu led Gilgamesh:

> To the house which none leave who have entered it,
> On the road from which there is no way back,
> To the house wherein the dwellers are bereft of light,
> Where dust is the fare and clay their food.
> They are clothed like birds, with wings for garments,
> And see no light, residing in darkness.[17]

The gods had decreed when they created man that death should be the portion of the human race, they having reserved immortality solely for themselves.[18] But although the gods could visit Ereshkigal on ceremonial and other specific occa- sions, it was a perilous undertaking, and those who lived in the nether regions were never allowed to ascend to the heavenly realms.[19] These restrictions, however, and the sinister character of the after-life no doubt were later developments in the Meso- potamian cult of the dead, since in Sumer the mortuary equipment was not very different from that in predynastic Egypt. The normal practice was for the body to be clad in its ordinary clothes and wrapped in a mat or winding-sheet in the flexed position, together with a few personal belongings (e.g. razor and dagger, or necklace and bracelets). It was then enclosed in a wicker or pottery coffin (*larnake*), or in two large pottery jars with their open ends placed together in the form of a *pithos*. Interment was in a simple earth grave, or in a small brick vault, but, apart from the royal tomb at Ur, no attempt was made to erect vast funerary monuments with elaborate equipment as in Ancient Egypt. Neither mummification nor cremation (except possibly sporadically) was adopted. Cemeteries were not very extensive and in towns not infre-quently the grave was dug beneath the house of the deceased under the pavement in one of the rooms, or in a family vault, the door of which was bricked up after each interment.

The Royal Tombs of Ur and the After-life

The royal tombs at Ur (*c.* 2900–2700 B.C.) were very much more elaborate chambered structures with an amazing wealth of furniture and a cultus that involved human sacrifice on a grand scale. The bodies were richly clad and ornamented while the very considerable retinue who accompanied them to the spirit-world were also dressed in their finery, and arranged in an orderly manner, suggestive of the complete absence of a violent death; perhaps having been drugged with hashish or opium.[20] But these stone and brick-vaulted chambers contained the mortal remains of the kings of Ur and their courtiers, attend-ants and guards, who were regarded as divine rulers. Therefore, they "did not die as men die, but were translated", while those who accompanied them to the grave did so in the hope of con-tinuing their service in the royal household in the next life.

The Kingship in Sumer having "descended from heaven" after the Flood in the third millennium B.C., presumably as a gift of the gods, the prehistoric rulers of Ur had acquired a divine status[21] which would seem to have enabled them to gather around them a select band of devoted members of their court and bodyguard who were ready to become willing victims on the occasion of the royal obsequies. If this interpretation of the Ur ritual is substantially correct, the Babylonian conception of the "Land of No-Return", where rulers and commoners alike dwelt in darkness and dust, must have been a later development when any distinctions that were recognized were due merely to the disposal of the body. Those who had been honourably buried and had libations poured out on their graves were thought to drink clean water in the after-life, while the unburied and neglected had to scavenge in the streets for their means of subsistence. Otherwise all shared the same common fate, the only two instances of any one escaping death and being translated to the abode of the gods like Enoch, were, as we have seen, Utnapishtim and his wife, who were given divine status. It is possible, however, that this exception to the general rule is a survival of an earlier tradition in which sacral kings and culture heroes occupied much the same position in relation to eternal blessedness as that of the Pharaohs in Egypt, until for some reason or another the conception of life after death underwent a fundamental change in the Euphrates valley, represented mythologically by Adapa's forfeiture of immortality as a result of his refusing the bread and water of life.

Cosmic Divine Intervention

That climatic and environmental conditions were responsible largely for the production of the mood which found expression in this divergence can hardly be doubted. Both civilizations started from much the same conception of the universe, its processes and destinies, but in Mesopotamia the cosmic order was more dynamic and catastrophic than in Egypt. Cataclysmic events, therefore, were interpreted as divine interventions, the vengeance of the gods descending upon the world and mankind. Thus, the fall of Ur before the invading Elamites was attributed to the disastrous winds Enlil had caused to rage as "a hurricane of heaven howling across the sky"—a shattering storm and tempest, relentless as a flood wave, beat down upon and devoured the city's ships.[22] But although the universe functioned dynamically in a series of apocalyptic happenings under divine direction, no attempt was made to portray the ultimate course of world history. As in the attitude towards death and the hereafter, the future state caused little or no concern. It was life on earth, in the past and the present, which was related to the decree of the gods, but the regularity of the annual decline and revival in nature, later associated with the revolution of the sun and the other celestial bodies determining the annual cycle of death and revival and its cult drama, suggested a periodicity in the order of the cosmos on a larger scale, of a periodic victory of order over chaos and relapse into chaos. Hence the idea of cosmic aeons and revolutions following the pattern of the renewal of life in the present.

The Eschatology of the New Year

It was, in fact, out of the relationship between the New Year rites and the recital of the victory of the Creator over chaos at the beginning of time, and all that lay behind this cosmological myth and ritual, that the later eschatological cosmogony arose. Eschatology, in fact, as Wensinck says, is in reality "cosmology applied to the future".[23] In Mesopotamia the cosmic revolutions found expression in the New Year celebrations when in addition to the renewal of the soil and of the forces in nature on which this depended, the transition from chaos to cosmos was ritually enacted, restored and made secure. A "new age" was begun in the cosmic rhythm of society, and so in the cult drama on the 12th day of Nisan the gods assembled again in the Chamber of Destinies to determine the course of events during the forthcoming year. This was the nearest approach to any conception of "judgment" that was reached in Babylonian eschatology. It lacked, however, any personal application, although latent in it there was a realization of human inadequacy and even of guilt. Mesopotamian man was always conscious of having missed the mark; wittingly or unwittingly of having sinned and come short of that which was required of him, and, therefore, of having incurred the wrath of the gods and merited their vengeance. Consequently, the New Year Festival was not only the occasion of the annual renewal of society; it also constituted a new start for its members rather like the Day of Atonement in post-exilic Israel when the nation underwent a general expiation. As the victory over chaos and the establishment of cosmic order were perpetuated by the recitation and re-enactment of the creation story and all that this involved, so every New Year was a day of judgment determining the destinies of mankind.[24] But it was confined to life on earth and to the fortunes of the ensuing year under the passing conditions of time. No attempt was made to pronounce the individual "true of heart and voice" in a judgment after death leading to a blessed immortality in an idealized spirit-world.

Astral Phenomena

The sense of uncertainty and frustration in the presence of forces unpredictable in their behaviour and beyond human control in their operations led to the elaboration at an early period of a technique for the purpose of ascertaining the will of the gods and the prediction of future fortunes of the community and its members. Thus, omen texts and astrological inscriptions (e.g. the *Enuma Anu-enlil* series) can now be traced back to the Sumerian period since they contain references to the division of the country into Akkad, Elam, Subartu and Amurru, and to such early kings as Rimush and Ibin-sin, who reigned in the middle of the third millennium B.C. It was not until very much later, however, that the movements of the heavenly bodies and the identification of the planets and fixed stars with certain gods were made the basis of a complex astrology under the direction of professional experts.

In course of time every celestial phenomenon was held to have its counterpart in human events in relation to calendars of favourable and unfavourable days, and every individual was brought under the influence of a planet or a fixed star which determined his fate from the cradle to the grave. If an eclipse of the moon occurred in the first watch in the month of Nisan, for example, there would be destruction and violence on the earth. If it happened in the month of Iyyar, the king would die and his son would not succeed to the throne. If it took place in that of Tammuz, agriculture would prosper, but if it happened in Ab, then the Storm-god Adad would send a flood upon the land. The weather being under his control, it varied accord- ing to the month in which his voice was heard in the thunder, and the timbre of its sound. The stars acquired a more personal significance, and together with the planets determined human destinies in an elaborate astral lore which in the wake of the conquests of Alexander the Great in the fourth century B.C. passed from Mesopotamia to Greece and the Eastern Mediterranean. In the Hellenistic world Alexandria became the centre of astrological learning under the direction of Chaldaean experts, and the birthplace of an occult mystical literature and of the hermetic sciences.

Zodiacal Symbolism

The periodic repetition of the movements of the heavenly bodies having been tabulated and calculated with considerable care and precision, each astrologer had at his disposal collections of these observations which he could consult in arriving at his prognostications. The year was divided into months in which the occult character of each day was noted. Thus, the stars in the zodiacal band in the heavens through which the sun, moon and planets appeared to pursue their course, bounded by two circles each about nine degrees distant from the ecliptic, were distinguished and named by the Chaldaean astrologers as a series of constellations which from the fifth century B.C. were reduced from sixteen to twelve. The course of the sun's ecliptic and the five planets were identified with the corresponding Babylonian deities—Ishtar, Nabu, Nergal, Marduk and Ninib —whose movements were thought to be related to the fortunes of mankind.

The influence of the zodiacal symbolism on Babylonian myth and ritual and eschatology was considerable, illustrated, for example, by the division of the Gilgamesh epic into twelve episodes from the time of Asurbanipal in the seventh century B.C., each related to the constellations and their divine figures. The zodiac being regarded as the archetype of the earthly universe in which the will and purposes of the gods were revealed and the course of the cycle of nature determined and consummated in the struggle between light and darkness, the upper and the nether worlds, personified in Ishtar endeavouring to become queen of heaven.

Similarly, the changes of the arc of day and the arc of night, the summer and winter courses of the stars, the sequence of the seasons, all reflect the same principle of aeonic cycles and celestial revolutions in which the evolution of the world ulti-mately is consummated. Beginning with the antediluvian period as a heroic age with its sages, divine kings and magic plants, it passed into the historic epoch when the world was brought by the Flood through the dominion of Ea to that of Marduk, as the transition from chaos to cosmos was repeated. Then came the "procession of the equinoxes", the gradual displacement of the middle line of the zodiac marked out by the track of the sun, with Nebo corresponding to the moon (the upper world) and Marduk with the sun (the nether world), until the position was reversed when Marduk gained the supremacy after Babylon became the capital. Preceding the rise of Babylon, the "Age of the Twins" witnessed the Semitic settlement in Mesopotamia, followed in the zodiac by that of the Bull, corresponding to the reform in the calendar about 2800 B.C. when Babylon became the metropolis, Marduk the head of the pantheon, and Hammurabi the founder of the Empire. This opened a new epoch in Babylonian history, inaugurated by the emperor "taking the hand of Marduk" in the *Akitu* Festival. In fact, in this Age of the Bull all rulers had to be able to claim a mythological relationship with Marduk and Ishtar, until, with the coming of the "Age of the Ram" at the vernal equinox, Nabonasser (797–734 B.C.) initiated a new era. In Babylon the new reckoning was never fully recog-nized, but in Egypt the god Jupiter-Amon adopted the head of a ram, notwithstanding his connexions with Marduk. The Signs of the Zodiac, however, reached the Nile valley by way of the Aegean in the first instance having been adopted by the Greeks from the Babylonians.

IRAN

Avestan World-ages

With the coming of Persian sovereignty in the Euphrates valley in the sixth century B.C., Iranian eschatology with its Zoroastrian and Mazdaean background introduced a new approach to the theory of world-ages. In the Avestan cosmology the earth was divided into either three or seven zones (*keshvars*). In the tripartite division the intermediate *keshvar* was the cradleland of the ancient Iranians, with the northern and southern zones, each separated into two halves, to which were added those in the seven *keshvars* making up the entire world, with the sun, moon and the stars and the whole creation as the work of Ahura Mazda and subject to his laws. According to the Pahlavi *Bundahish*[25] (which, though in its present form belonging to the ninth century A.D., contains much earlier material, going back to the fifth century B.C.) it was divinely decreed that "time was for twelve thousand years", divided into four periods each of three thousand years. The first was "the duration of the spiritual state, where the creatures were unthinking, unmoving, and intangible". It was then apparently that the *fravashi* or spiritual prototypes of later creatures came into existence as angelic beings or genii and guardians and guiding spirits in nature and in man distinct from the *urvan* or the soul located in a living body as its physical integument (*tanu*), human or occasionally animal.[26] Although the relation between the *urvan* and the *fravashi* is very obscure, it seems that from the *fravashi* the spiritual faculties in man were derived so that in the second period of three thousand years, when Gayomard, the primeval man, and the primeval ox, existed undisturbed, the spiritual body of Zarathushtra was framed by the archangels.[27]

At the end of this age the evil spirit rushed in and disturbed creation in this the third trimillennium (i.e. the seventh millennium) and attacked Gayomard and the ox. At the end of thirty years they both fell before the adversary with his thousand demons, but from them sprang respectively mankind and the animals and plants. The first human pair, Mashya and Mashyoi, grew up as a plant for forty years, and then became a man and a woman.[28] Among their descendants were the founder of the first Iranian dynasty, Hoshyang, and his successors, occupying the first thousand years of this third trimillennium. Then followed the millennium of Dahak, the Avestan dragon with three heads,[29] and was assigned to Scorpio, while its successor (Sagittarius) contains the names of the heroic legends of ancient Iran. The fourth millennium, ruled by Capricorn in the zodiac constellation, witnessed the "coming of the religion" of Zara᷄ thushtra, destined, it was maintained, to endure for the next three thousand years. The opening millennium of this division included the reign of the Archaemonians, Alexander the Great, the Ashkanians (Arsacides) and the Sasanians. It was probably during the sixth century of this era (*c.* 540–493 B.C.) that Zarathushtra lived and launched his reforming move᷄ ment.

While according to the ancient cosmological mythology the world periodically renewed the youth of its golden age, Zarathushtra declared the coming of the golden age as defini᷄ tive. It constituted the establishment of the kingdom of order to transform the universe according to the will and purposes of Ahura Mazda, which ultimately would find its consummation in the renovation of the world in all its pristine perfection as it left the hands of the Creator in the beginning. This was the basic conception of the Zoroastrian eschatology and found expression in the doctrine of reward and punishment in this life stretching forward into that which was to come beyond the grave, and in the appointed end towards which all things were moving. The scheme of world᷄ages systematized in the later Avestan literature is of a composite character, derived from a variety of sources in Iranian tradition. The paradise myth of the first man Yima (Yamas of the Hindu Vedas) in the *Vendidad*,[30] for example, in which a tripartite division of the past, present and future sequence of cosmic events was main᷄ tained, was an independent system of pre᷄Zoroastrian tradition in its earliest form, and was never satisfactorily incorporated in Avestan cosmology.[31] Similarly, the four ages of Gold, Silver, Steel and Iron of the present millennium was a combination of two systems introduced at a later period and developing under Manichaean influences.

The State of the Dead

In the Gathas, mythology was not systematized at all. Ahura Mazda was represented as determining the future destiny of mankind and the world, and the ultimate triumph of his righteous rule and reign over all things. When this was accomplished then the balance would be redressed. Those who had chosen the side of Good Thought, Good Deed and Good Word would be rewarded in the abode of light, while the followers of Angra Mainyu would be assigned to Drujo⁄ demana, "the house of the Druj" (Angra Mainyu), a dwelling of darkness which in later Avestan tradition was expanded from a single hell to four abodes—those of Dushmata (evil thought), Dushukhta (evil word), Dushvarshta (evil deed), and finally below all the rest a nameless state of "endless darkness".

Heaven was similarly extended. In the Gathas it was called "the house of song" (Garonmana) where Ahura Mazda dwelt with the celestial beings, or "shining ones", who included the six immortal benefactors (Vohu Monah ("good mind"), Asha Vahishta ("righteousness"), Khshathra Vairya ("domi⁄ nion"), Spenta Aramaiti ("holy thought and piety"), Haurvatat ("perfection and welfare") and Ameretat ("immortality")). Next in rank to them were the more numerous Yazata, or "adorable ones", though only three of them are mentioned by name in the Gathas; viz., Sraosha, the spirit of obedience and the guardian of mankind, his sister Ashi personifying sanctity and spiritual blessings, and Atar, the sacred fire, the son of Ahura Mazda. When in the Avestan period it became a fourfold realm Garonmana remained the highest heaven, "the best existence" (Garonmana) of ineffable bliss and dazzling brightness, which was attained by passing through the three lower inferior heavens —Humata ("good thought"), Hukhta ("good word") and Hvarshta ("good deed"). Thus, heaven and hell were repre⁄ sented like good and evil as a duality in which eternal light, joy, climate and sustenance were opposed by darkness, misery, cold, foul food and all the privations of winter on the Iranian steppes.

The Vision of Arta-i Viraf

The perilous passage over the Chinvat Bridge and the world on the other side has been described in a Pahlavi tractate as a vision of Arta-i Viraf in the Sasanian period in the fifth or sixth century A.D., but probably based on older traditions. In it is recorded the journey of the seer under the guidance of Sraosha and Atar across the "Bridge of the Separator", his angelic attendants taking his hand and conducting him onwards un-hurt. He was then taken to hell and shown its cold and heat, the drought and stench, "the jaws of which like the most frightful pit, descending into a very narrow and fearful place; in darkness so gloomy that it was necessary to hold by the hand and in such stench that everyone into whose nostrils that air ascends will struggle and stagger and fall; and on account of such close confinement no man's existence is endurable".[32] On reaching a river as dreadful as hell, souls and *fravashi* were seen endeavouring to cross it, some easily, others with great difficulty or quite unable to make the passage at all. This river was swollen with the many tears shed unlawfully for the departed. Those who were unable to cross over were those for whom after their demise much lamentation and weeping had been made. Therefore, the seer was told to exhort men in the world to refrain from such displays of grief for the departed.[33]

The greater part of the vision is devoted to a disorderly account of the infernal regions, the crimes committed by its denizens and their grim punishments. The arch-enemy, Angra Mainyu (Ahriman), is placed in the lowest and darkest of the four divisions, located, it seems, in the centre of the earth, like Lucifer in Dante's Inferno. Heaven is treated in much less detail, though in a more orderly manner. It is represented as a celestial abode in four divisions; those of the stars, the moon and the sun, with Garōtsman, "the house of sons", as the climax in which stands the throne of Ahura Mazda bathed in the eternal light of his all-glorious presence. Reference is made to a kind of limbo called Hamistagon in which are those whose good deeds and sins are equal, and who are allowed to remain there in a passive state until the Resurrection, suffering only cold and heat from the atmosphere, but apparently not involving any idea of purification and progressive purgation.[34]

The Judgment

Hamistagon, however, was regarded as the place between heaven and earth, where good and evil deeds were weighed in the balance and the fate of the soul was settled. For three days and three nights both the righteous and the wicked were said to hover over the body, after which they passed to the place of judgment, and thence to their final reward or punishment.[35] Originally, however, *fravashi* were thought to remain near their old homes with their relatives, and to attend the feast held on their behalf, bestowing benefits on the living, before the corpse was taken to the towers of silence to be devoured by vultures. In the later literature the just are represented as being conducted by a fair maiden across the Chinvat Bridge, and the wicked as confronted by their conscience in the form of an ugly old woman. At the bridge the soul is judged in the presence of Ahura Mazda, and Zarathushtra, who pleads for his followers as their advocate and guide. With them are the three spirits, Rashnu, the Yazata presiding over justice, Mithra the pro´ tector of truth, and Sraosha, personifying obedience to the divine law.

In the Gathas the ancient belief in the Bridge of Separation is retained,[36] and further developed in the Later Avesta. There it is given an ethical significance by bringing it into relation with the judgment. Instead of its negotiation being made to depend on magical devices and agility, the fate of those who approach it is determined by "spiritual bookkeeping" assessed by the court with the All´wise Lord, Ahura Mazda, as the supreme Judge. A preponderance of good deeds, words and thoughts over evil in this life is the essential requirement for safe conduct across it and entrance into "the House of Song" on the other side. When the reverse is the case and the evil in the record predominates, the bridge becomes as thin as the edge of a razor and turns at the moment the wicked step upon it, hurling them into the molten lake beneath. The intermediate state (Hamistagon), which, as we have seen, was a prominent feature in the Later Pahlavi period, is perhaps hinted at in the Gathas for those whose good and bad actions are equal,[37] though, at any rate in its more developed form, it was a post- Avestan doctrine arising out of the earlier conception of salvation based on the weighing of merits and demerits in earthly behaviour attendant upon the endowment of free will and divine aid in the choice between good and evil. The mythological bridge-test is not very easily brought into con- junction with the Egyptian precedent of judgment by the weighing of the soul. Nevertheless, behind all the symbolism lay the fundamental Mazdaean doctrine that every man must work out his own salvation and be judged at the last by his works, whether they be good or whether they be evil. Material- istic and anthropomorphic as may have been the eschatology, and grim to a degree as may have been the portrayal of the tortures of the wicked, it was essentially ethical in its evaluations and devoid of the more sensual features of the after-life so prominent in some of the closely related imagery and estimates of the delight of heavenly bliss.[38] Throughout, the underlying principle was that of "evil for evil, good reward for the good, affliction to the wicked, happiness to the righteous. Woe to the wicked, salvation to him who upholds righteousness." The fate of all was decided in strict justice by their deeds in a clear-cut manner of calculation and compensation at the Judgment when the works, thoughts and intentions were to be duly assessed and their merits and demerits determined once and for all.

The Consummation of Creation

As regards the ultimate end of all things the consummation of the process of creation in the Gathas is associated with the appearance of the Saoshyant as the last of the saviours whose function will be that of removing every trace of the evil wrought in the world by Angra Mainyu, the Lie, and ushering in the glorious new world order. The souls in hell will be brought forth and purified, while the righteous in heaven will rise to share in the triumph of the general resurrection and the renovation of the earth. This is in line with the ancient Iranian myth of the golden age, of Yama's heaven, of a land of Cockaigne where death was unknown, and the end of the world by a great conflagration. Zarathushtra transformed these conceptions into the Zoroastrian final dispensation when the universe will reach its destined goal according to the divine plan for creation ordained by Ahura Mazda at its dawn. Then the world will enter upon its new cycle of ineffable bliss, never again to grow old, die, decay and perish.

That Zarathushtra himself was to be the Saoshyant who would bring about this eschatological restoration in his lifetime is suggested in the Gathas.[39] In the Later Avesta and in the Pahlavi literature, however, he was to be succeeded by three Saviours, each appearing at intervals of a thousand years in the fourth and last age, supernaturally born of three maidens while bathing in a lake in which the seed of Zarathushtra had been preserved for the purpose.[40] Then the dead would be raised, and the righteous would be separated from the wicked at the final Judgment, as a prelude to the pouring forth of molten metal on the earth and in hell. To the righteous it would be soothing like "warm milk", but to the wicked it would be agonizing torment burning away all the evil they had contracted. The ultimate fate of Ahriman and his demons is obscure in the Pahlavi eschatology, and no mention is made of it in the Avesta. But since the prevailing belief seems to have been that even hell itself would be consumed by fire at the last when all evil had been destroyed and the entire creation joined together in everlasting praise of Ahura Mazda, it may be inferred that the Druj was expected to be annihilated, or rendered completely innocuous, when the total victory of the All-wise Lord and his archangels had been attained, and all creation restored to its pristine condition. Then the world drama would be over for ever; the curtain would have fallen on the conflict between good and evil; the kingdom of righteousness would have been established in a renovated world, and all things would return in perfect bliss and peace to their origin.

ISRAEL

The Eschatology of the Hebrew Prophets

This Zoroastrian doctrine of "the last things" constitutes the first systematized eschatology in the history of religion, and it had far-reaching effects on the apocalyptic speculations of Judaism, Christianity and Islam. Thus, in Israel the prophetic conception of the "last things" centred in "the Day of Yahweh" as a veritable Day of Judgment when the external forces of the chosen nation would be vanquished by its god and peace and prosperity would be established for ever was quite distinct from the apocalyptic eschatology of the post-Persian period. The pre-exilic Hebrew prophets concentrated upon Israel and its destiny in this world. They were not concerned with what lay beyond the grave or at the end of time. For them Sheol, the subterranean abode of dust, darkness and corruption, was the ultimate habitation of the shades of all men, good and bad alike, whether of Israel or of the Gentiles, analogous to the Babylonian *Aralu*. There kings and commoners alike "slept with their fathers", servants were freed from the service of their masters, and Yahweh was neither remembered, praised nor worshipped,[41] until after the Exile as his omnipotence and omniscience were developed, even Sheol was brought under his jurisdiction.[42] But for the prophets Yahweh was essentially the god of the living, not of the dead, and his "Day of Judgment would be darkness not light" for Israel because of its backslidings and shortcomings;[43] a Day of Wrath[44] when the earth would be "waste and void; and the heavens, and they had no light".[45]

Gradually a more hopeful and optimistic conception emerged, both in respect of the nation and of the departed. Thus, in the epilogue appended to the book of Amos (ix. 11–15), eventually it was declared the Davidic dynasty would be restored and reinstated in its former splendour and power, and the blessings of peace and prosperity would be enjoyed by Israel; the waste cities would be rebuilt and inhabited, and "they shall plant vineyards and drink the wine thereof. They shall no more be plucked up out of their land which I have given them, saith Yahweh."[46] Similarly, Jeremiah looked forward to the time when a new covenant would be made with the house of Israel and with the house of Judah when Yahweh would put his law in their inward parts and write it in their heart. Then, as never before, he would be their god and they would be his people.[47] Likewise Ezekiel prophesied the return of the exiles from their captivity in Mesopotamia, bringing them again to a restored Jerusalem as in former times when their ancestors were delivered from the Egyptians by the mighty hand and stretched out arm of their god. In his holy mountain all the house of Israel would serve him in its own land.[48]

When this was accomplished and the post-exilic community was established as a priestly state under Persian sovereignty after the decree of Cyrus the Great in 538 B.C., Yahweh was depicted in the book of Malachi as visiting his restored temple in the capacity of a judge after he had sent his messenger (Elijah) to prepare the way before him. But who might abide the day of his coming, and who should stand when he appeared? The visitation was to be a drastic expiation—a cleansing fire burning away the dross in the nation, beginning with the priests, the sons of Levi, and extending to the people as a whole, separating the righteous from the wicked.[49] No attempt was made to equate the Day of Yahweh with a Messianic reign, or with the creation of a new heaven and a new earth. God himself was represented as the King, and the bond between him and his chosen people was the covenant (i.e. *běríth*, the cultus), the first condition of which was absolute loyalty to Yahweh and obedience to his commands.[50]

Apocalyptic Eschatology

As prophecy gradually gave way to apocalypse after the Exile, a different type of eschatology arose in which a catastrophic end of the present cosmic order was predicted as a supra-historical event associated eventually with the resurrection of the dead and the hope of a blessed hereafter in a spiritual kingdom wherein dwelt angels and archangels and the whole company of heaven, as against the opposed realm of Satan and his hierarchy of demonic principalities and powers. The covenant with Yahweh now ceased to be confined to Israel as a national entity in this world. Sheol came under his juris' diction and with it the conviction that the ultimate goal of union with God was to be received by him in glory.[51] This belief first found expression in the canonical scriptures of the Old Testament in the apocalyptic book of Daniel at the beginning of the Seleucid period in 198 B.C. when the Hellenizing movement of Antiochus Epiphanes and its reper' cussions on Jewish faith and culture led to the Maccabaean revolt and a clearer perception of the resurrection. In an age of internal strife and intense bitterness rewards and punishments, it was felt, must transcend existing conditions and their in' justices in time and space. Therefore, it was declared, "many of them that sleep in the dust of the earth shall awake, some to everlasting life, and some to shame and everlasting contempt".[52] The fall of the tyrant Antiochus and the overthrow of the Seleucid world-power would be accompanied by a period of trial and tribulation, but from it the faithful Israelites would rise triumphant, and the age of bliss for the righteous would begin.

It was out of this situation that Jewish apocalyptic emerged and while it developed along its own lines in conformity with its own antecedents it was unquestionably strongly influenced by its Iranian counterpart. Thus, eschatology in the book of Daniel is quite distinct from that in the later prophetic writings, as is shown, for instance, in its angelology which was either derived from or influenced by Gathic sources.[53] While Judg' ment and the Day of Yahweh were deeply rooted beliefs in Hebrew religion, the detailed delineation of the later eschato' logy and the doctrines of resurrection seem to require the same explanation in the Maccabaean period. Similarly, the dualistic tendency which found expression in a personal source of evil and an organized demonology opposed to an angelic host is an indication of a common pattern of ideas, each doubtless with its own traditional background and history but converging more and more until at length the Iranian eschatology prevailed. But during the last two centuries before the beginning of the Christian era so many influences were interacting on one another in the Graeco-Roman world and the Middle East that the determination of their several sources and contacts frequently can only be conjectural. This applies particularly to eschatological mythology.

The Messianic Age

Closely associated with speculation about "the last things" during this period was the idea of a Messianic Age. Here, again, Iranian influences were apparent, but in Judaism the concept pursued its own course, having arisen within the context of the Davidic King and developed in relation to its own princes and governors, like Cyrus, Zerubbabel and Simon Maccabaeus, who were regarded as sacred persons anointed and set apart as divine agents to bring "salvation" (i.e. victory) to the holy nation.[54] It was distinct from the figure of the dying and reviving hero in the seasonal cult drama as it stood outside the annual renewal of the forces of nature, having a more definitely eschatological significance. At first it was a nationalistic Kingdom that was expected to be in process of establishment in which material prosperity would prevail and all enemies would be destroyed, notwithstanding the repeated disappointments and the shattering of high hopes of its fulfilment.

As the sovereignty of Yahweh came to be regarded as extending beyond the borders of Israel to the Gentile world and even to Sheol, the Kingdom was thought to embrace all nations and indeed all mankind. This led eventually in the post-exilic community to the conception of a transformed heaven and earth in which the wicked would be eliminated and the righteous would enjoy everlasting life and perpetual bliss. In the Ethiopic book of Enoch, Jerusalem is represented as the centre of the Messianic Kingdom, and there the Gentiles will worship the one and only true God.[55] The righteous will rise with their bodies and be transplanted to the temple of the

Lord, and on the purified earth they will eat of the tree of life and know neither sorrow, plague nor torment.[56] But in the Psalms of Solomon (*c.* 80–70 B.C.) the Messianic Kingdom appears as being only of temporary duration, conterminous with the reign of its single ruler who would destroy his enemies by the word of his mouth,[57] whereas in the post-Christian Jewish apocalyptic literature the Messianic Age sometimes is said to last for ever.[58] Everywhere, however, the emphasis was on the Kingdom, the Messianic Age, rather than on the figure of a personal Messiah after the Davidic King had fallen into the background in the Persian period. The real king would be God himself, the Messiah being merely a figure-head and divine instrument.[59]

The conception of the Son of Man, which is first mentioned in the book of Daniel,[60] has been and still is a matter of endless discussion in its possible Messianic and mythological interpretations. It is very doubtful, in fact, whether the term was equated with the Messiah before it was adopted by the Founder of Christianity.[61] In any case, the Danielic celestial figure was not represented as the leader of the Kingdom in a Messianic guise. He was rather the personification of the "saints of the Most High" who were to possess for ever and ever the fifth Kingdom when its four predecessors had passed away.[62] Nevertheless, in the Messianic tradition the three figures, the King, the Son of Man and the Servant, not only had a common pattern of thought but also retained a common theme very deeply laid in the Kingship myth and ritual of the Ancient Near East.

The Heavenly Man

It is by no means improbable that behind the Danielic and Enochian transcendent figure, whether or not in an individual capacity, lay the idea of a Heavenly Man in the widespread oriental Redemption myth in a number of documents emanating from Gnostic and Manichaean sources, the origin of which, however, in all probability is to be found in the Iranian Gayomard doctrine.[63] Although this, as we have seen, occurs in the post-Christian Pahlavi Parsi literature, it may belong to the much earlier material preserved in these texts and represent the background of the subsequent apocalyptic and Gnostic eschatological interpretations of the Persian cosmic myth. Nevertheless, there are essential differences between the Zoroastrian and the later Jewish and Graeco-oriental syncretistic and composite products. Thus, as Bousset contends, the Vedic conception of the Purusha as the Primal Man who was sacrificed by the gods to form the Brahman, Agni and Indra, and the phenomenal order from his dismembered body,[64] lay behind the Gayomard myth, and the specifically Iranian features in the subsequent Heavenly Man or Son of Man concept represent only one strand of a complex pattern in which Egyptian, Greek and Jewish elements predominate.

It cannot be denied, however, that very largely under Persian and Babylonian influence a cosmic eschatology was worked out in Judaism which appears in the apocalyptic literature and in the New Testament, particularly in relation to the figure of the Son of Man as the head of a new humanity. The same conception may underlie the Davidic transcendent being pictured as coming on the clouds of heaven, though here it is transformed into the embodiment of the nation. As the agent of redemption he acquired the status of the judge of mankind and the world, and in that capacity he was combined with the figure of the Messiah in Christian tradition when that of the Davidic King virtually was eliminated, or at any rate made redundant in the new age. Some of the antecedents certainly must have come from Iranian sources, as did those of the apocalyptic doctrine of angels and the resurrection, and the belief in a personal devil. An early version of the myth of Gayomard is a very likely substratum of the Heavenly Man conception, but if this was its original source it has undergone a marked transformation in Judaeo-Christian eschatology.

In its Danielic, Enochian and Christian form it has lost its cosmological characteristics, and like the Avestan Saoshyant, it belongs essentially to the age to come at the end of the course of world history, rather than to the beginning of the cosmic process. The appearance of the Son of Man, as of the Saoshyant, marked the ushering in of the new order after the resurrection of the new humanity. He was not the source from which the human race was derived, though in a sense he was the first-fruit of the general resurrection, and as such he was at once the redeemer and the judge of mankind. Therefore, in its diffusion westwards from the Ancient Near East the concept of the archetypal man underwent a fundamental change until eventually it emerged in the Gospels and in the Fourth Eclogue of Virgil in a very different guise from that in which it first appeared in its Indo-Iranian original form.

GREECE

Everywhere the division of time into periods provides a congenial soil for the growth of an eschatology. This, we have seen, occurred in Egypt, Mesopotamia and Persia, and it recurred in Judaeo-Christian apocalyptic and in the Graeco-Roman world. Thus, in the Empire the reign of Augustus after the turmoil of the closing days of the Republic was hailed as the dawn of a new era of redemption, marked by the appearance of a star indicating the birth of the Saviour of the world whom Virgil identified with Apollo. The earliest classical authority, however, on the sequence of world ages was Hesiod, who, as has been considered, in his *Works and Days*[65] laid the foundations of the theme which later acquired an eschatological significance. The Hesiodic *Theogony* with its succession of races equated with ages of Gold, Silver, Bronze and Iron assigned to their respective gods by the Orphics— Night, Ouranos, Kronos and Zeus—was a replica of the cosmic constitution beginning with Heaven as the abode of the gods and the immortals (i.e. the Golden Age) with their superior status and powers, to which in the former times human beings were thought to have been nearer. The Golden Age, deeply rooted in folk tradition, became the prototype of the Elysium, the garden of the gods, which eventually was regarded as a future state of bliss and perpetual youth beyond the grave enjoyed by the sons of the gods in the Isles of the Blest.[66]

Hesiodic and Orphic Eschatology

In the earlier Greek popular belief and in the Hesiodic *Theogony* nothing is said, however, of judgment. The gods had their enemies, but they were kept out of harm's way in Tartaros.[67] It was not until Orphic influences introduced an ethical element into the myth and ritual in the sixth century B.C. that ideas of judgment and a lost paradise became prevalent and serious efforts were made to recover the primordial state in an eternity of youth, vigour and happiness, of peace and tranquillity. Then a genuine eschatology began to emerge with a conception of a future life with rewards and punishments, very different from the shadowy existence of the witless wraiths in Hades of the Homeric tradition.

On the Orphic gold tablets discovered in ancient graves in Southern Italy and Crete are extracts from poems, which cannot be later than the fifth century B.C.,[68] used like the Book of the Dead in Egypt to provide the deceased with a guide to the course to be pursued on the road to the spirit-world. The words he was to utter and the claims he had to make on the benevolence of the gods are recorded. A warning is given against approaching a spring to the left of the House of Hades near a white cypress, but on reaching another by the Lake of Memory its guardians were to be asked for cold water flowing from it. They would then give "the child of Earth and starry Heaven", as the soul is designated, a drink from the holy well, just as in the Platonic myth of Er those destined for reincarnation were caused to drink of the well of Lethe, forgetfulness, to make them forget the wearisome journey in the stifling heat of the plain of Lethe. But in the Orphic tablets the "child of Earth and starry Heaven", having been initiated into the saving Mysteries, had got beyond the fear of further rebirth and, therefore, had to avoid altogether the water in the first spring on the left near the cypress. His "real lineage is of heaven" by virtue of his having cultivated in the prescribed ritual manner the Dionysian side of his nature, and "paid the penalty for deeds unrighteous" arising from the Titanic taint.

On a series of vases of the fourth and third centuries B.C.,

recovered from Southern Italy and now in the museum at
Naples, a number of mythological figures occur connected
with the underworld, among whom are Orpheus with Pluto,
and Persephone enthroned in the centre, in a palace, together
with Aiakos, Triptolemos and Rhadamanthus as the judges,
and Hermes as the conductor of the souls.[69] Near Orpheus is
a group consisting of father, mother and child, who may
represent initiates seeking entrance to eternal blessedness. While
it is by no means certain that these scenes are necessarily
"Orphic", as Jane Harrison believed them to be,[70] the fact
remains that the ultimate aim of initiation in all the contemporary Mysteries was the attainment of a virtual apotheosis
through rebirth to a blissful hereafter when "the happy and
blessed one" was declared to have become "a god instead of a
mortal". This applied alike to Orphic, Pythagorean or
Eleusinian initiates, notwithstanding their respective origins,
methods, myth and ritual.

The Eschatology of Pindar and Plato

In the attempt to bridge the gulf which the Olympian religion
had created between gods and men the mystery ritual sought
to devise ways and means of identifying the votary with the
divinity with whom he was brought into communion. The
wave of Dionysiac fervour that passed over Greece in the sixth
century B.C. introduced a new conception of the soul and the
hereafter in which the idea of pre-existence and reincarnation
was implicit, involving a series of purifications in an intermediate state and a number of rebirths until complete union
with the divine was attained and the purpose of the ritual
observances was fulfilled in deliverance from the cycle of births
and deaths. The influence of these Orphic conceptions of the
destiny of the soul appears in the poems of Pindar in the first
half of the fifth century B.C., as, for example, in the Ode to
Theron of Syracuse where a triple incarnation—three generations on earth and three in paradise—is attributed to Pythagoras
by the Scholiasts, represented as an Orphic source.[71] Similarly,
Plato's quotation in the *Phaedrus*,[72] based on Pindar, is

penetrated with these Orphic ideas far removed from the shadowy hereafter of the Homeric tradition.

This Pindaric poem is a landmark inasmuch as it represents a definite break with contemporary Greek thought and practice concerning immortality and the cult of the dead, introducing for the first time (*c.* 476 B.C.) an eschatology of Judgment based on ethical considerations, notwithstanding the archaic moraliz/ing and the traditional legends of the gods and heroes, and the conception of paradise in which games, music and pleasant odours are the rewards of the blessed, described with all the matchless charm and beauty of the poetic art. Not infrequently, in fact, Pindar spoke with a double/voice about existence beyond the grave.[73] But if sometimes his notion of the after/life was as shadowy as that of Homer,[74] his doctrine of metem/psychosis and expiation in the underworld was related to the moral government of the world.

It remained, however, for Plato to bring into the full light of philosophical discussion the conception of the origin and nature of the psyche and of judgment and retribution as integral aspects of the doctrine of reincarnation. Starting from an animistic dualism of body and soul not very different from the Mystery mythological imagery, in the Socratic dialogues the concepts were drawn very largely from Orphic sources and described in Orphic terms with the important distinction that in the cultivation of the spiritual life rational thinking and conduct rather than ritual purification were represented as the primary duties. In the development of his eschatology, however, he concentrated attention on the destiny of the soul more than on its unity and simplicity in structure, and the doctrine of reminiscences, derived in all probability from the Pytha/goreans.[75] The heavenly bodies were accredited with souls, and in consequence of their motions were eternal and not like inanimate nature set in motion from without. From the eternal source of all becoming, all things that contain *nous* proceeded towards, and ultimately returned to, their origin in a circular movement involving pre/existence and rebirth.[76] In assuming a body each individual soul became hampered by its "fall into birth" in spite of its rational and immortal nature inherited from the World-soul. This involved, on the Platonic hypo-thesis, judgment after death, an intermediate state of rewards and purificatory punishments, and rebirth in human or animal form determined by conduct in previous incarnations. For the ordinary man a cycle of ten thousand years was required to secure deliverance, but for a philosopher guileless and true it might be accomplished in three thousand years by living three holy and pure lives in succession. Some souls, however, were incurably evil and remained in Tartaros for ever without any return to earth.[77]

At death the soul was led by its daemon, or guardian spirit, to the place of judgment, and then sent either to bliss or to purgatorial punishments followed by rewards, unless its sins were regarded as incurable, when it was consigned eternally to Tartaros. Of the three classes mentioned in the myths only those who had succeeded in emancipating themselves from earthly desires and interests by philosophic insight were not born again. These having rendered themselves immortal and godlike, they entered into their eternal inheritance in the Isles of the Blest.[78] At the other end of the scale the incurably guilty —the rapacious, unjust and lustful—were condemned to lamen-tation, weeping and woe in Tartaros for ever without any hope of amelioration.[79] Between these two ends the majority of man-kind, "those who have practised the popular and social virtues which come from habit and practice without philosophy or reason", were destined to be transmigrated "in a mild and social nature like their own, such as that of bees or wasps or ants, or, it may be, into bodies of men, and that from them are made worthy citizens". If they then pursued a life of philosophic inquiry during three subsequent reincarnations, each of a thousand years, they might hope to recover their "wings" from the place from which they fell when they first assumed their earthly career.[80]

A great deal of this eschatology, presented in mythical form, was borrowed from Orphic and Pythagorean poetry and legend, and various oriental sources.[81] It was, in fact, more oriental than occidental in its main trend, but such beliefs were widely diffused among the Greeks as a result of the Dionysian-Orphic movement from Thrace in the sixth century B.C. in post-Homeric times as a foreign intrusion. Whatever may have been the origin of Dionysos he was a composite figure with Asiatic elements and Near Eastern affinities, and these found expression in the new eschatology that directly or indirectly emerged from him. It required the genius and philosophic insight of Plato and Socrates, aided by the Ionian dialectic, to cut the Gordian knot into which the many strands of conflicting ideas and cult-practices had become tangled.

The Eleusinian Way of Salvation

Less alien and almost as influential was the Eleusinian way of salvation as a pan-Hellenic mystery open to all who could speak or understand Greek. Through its indigenous rites, which in origin may go back to Mycenaean times, the initiates appear to have been admitted to a paradise in the delectable meadows of Persephone modelled on the Elysian Fields, reserved in the Homeric tradition for the favourites of the gods and now open to all the votaries of Demeter and her daughter who were admitted to her esoteric myth and ritual. Although they were both chthonian deities they secured for their devotees a blissful state very different from the shadowy existence in the Homeric nether regions of Pluto, and yet less undefined than the mystical unity of the Orphic beatific vision. Moreover, in its ritual and mythology it was as syncretistic as it was all-embracing in its appeal, having incorporated the Olympian gods and found a place for the more boisterous revels of the Dionysian rites.

Whatever may have been the profound emotional experiences that the *mystae* underwent in the *telesterion* at the time of their initiation,[82] they emerged reborn, having attained a status that was believed to endure beyond the grave. The situation is summed up in a fragment from the *De Anima* of Plutarch in these words: "Death and initiation clearly closely correspond, word for word, and thing for thing. At first there are wanderings and laborious circuits, and journeyings through the dark, full of misgivings where there is no consummation; then, before the very end, come terrors of every kind, shivers and trembling, and sweat and amazement. After this, a wonderful light meets the wanderer; he is admitted into pure meadow lands, where are voices and dances, and the majesty of holy sounds and sacred visions. Here the newly initiated, all rites completed, is at large."[83] Although in the text Eleusis is not mentioned, in this passage the general purpose and intention of the Hellenic Mystery rites are adequately described, and it was the cult of Demeter that held pride of place in this myth and ritual. Thus, the goddess of fertility was also the bestower of a new quality of life which raised those who received it to a divine estate that endured beyond the grave, and so initiation carried with it the assurance of a better and higher life after death.

It was, however, essentially a magico-religious way of salvation for those who duly performed the prescribed ritual and underwent the resulting mystical experience, rather than a cosmic eschatology with an ethical content like Orphism and its derivatives. Having seen the sacred sights, heard the divine utterances and made the correct confession of faith, the Eleusinian *mystae* were "saved" once and for all through a personal experience of new birth and regeneration which was quite independent of subsequent moral behaviour, asceticisms, philosophic insight or spiritual development. "Thrice happy are those mortals", declared Sophocles, "who see these rites before they depart for Hades; for to them alone is it granted to have true life on the other side. To the rest all there is evil"—an assertion which called forth the retort of the cynic Diogenes: "What! is Pataikion the thief to have a better lot after death than Epaminondas, just because he has been initiated?"[84]

The emphasis on ritual and the lack of a genuine eschatology prevented the Eleusinian Mysteries making an independent contribution to a clearer understanding of either the future destiny of the soul or of the "last things" which loomed so large on the apocalyptic Hebrew horizon and were inherent in the Egyptian Judgment scenes. Nevertheless, this decorous Hellenic sacramental drama, devoid of the orgiastic enthusiasm and ecstatic violence of the Bacchic cults, gained the reverent respect of Plato,[85] and while Orphics may have been initiated at Eleusis there are no indications of their conception of the hereafter and its eschatology having been introduced into the chthonian worship of Demeter. This remained fundamentally Hellenic in its approach to the after-life, extending to its votaries a place in an Elysium which Homer had restricted for the most part to the relatives of Zeus, and which the Orphics and Virgil regarded as a merely temporary resting place in the cycle of reincarnation.

CHAPTER VIII

The Aetiological Myth and the Saga

EGYPT AND MESOPOTAMIA

Aetiology in Myth and Ritual

THE basic myths of the Ancient Near Eastern religions examined in the foregoing pages normally exercised their functions in a cultic ritual setting. It is true, of course, that the story of creation, the origin of death, the destruction of mankind by disastrous floods, or similar catastrophes, the seasonal cycle and its hazards, and speculations about the nature and destiny of man and the universe, have formed the subject-matter of cosmogonic myths everywhere and at all times. But while they frequently have contained an aetiological element they cannot be regarded as fictitious stories invented merely to explain how phenomena, beliefs and customs came into existence in order to satisfy curiosity, as Andrew Lang and his contemporaries imagined.[1] They had a far more serious and practical purpose and aim than this, fulfilling a specific religious, sociological or ethical function, justifying by ancient precedents invested with supernatural primeval reality and significance the existing order of society and its established régime, laws, traditions and way of life, traced back to initial events.

Nevertheless, the aetiological myth cannot be dismissed as a fabrication of an earlier generation of theorists who were led astray by classical authors, such as Ovid, Virgil and Horace, Homer, Sophocles, Aeschylus and Plato, writing at a time when myth was "nothing but the creation of fancy, a kind of Midsummer Night's Dream".[2] Homer unquestionably extracted from the current mythological data all the best tales he could find and wove them into immortal poems concerning the Trojan war and the adventures of its heroes, human and divine. The *Odyssey* and the *Iliad* are excellent literary narratives, giving doubtless a more or less correct picture of the life and manners that prevailed in Mycenaean Greece at the transition from the Bronze Age to the Iron Age, but composed to provide entertainment for princes and nobles in Ionian banqueting halls. Or, again, the Platonic cosmological and eschatological speculations were presented in mythical form in the first instance as stories for their own sake and then to convey fundamental ethical or religious truths or convictions clothed in traditional imagery. Thus, in the *Phaedo* at the end of his story about "the soul and her habitations" it is asserted "either this or something like it is true".[3] The tale in every case was told as a literary narrative with poetic licence to explain some profound philosophic interpretation of ultimate reality or of moral order.

This stage in the development of the aetiological myth represents a relatively late departure from the earlier myth that was essentially and inseparably connected with ritual. To claim, however, with Hocart that myth is simply a description of ritual and cannot be aetiological at all[4] is as unjustifiable as to derive all myths from abstract philosophizings and a "mytho-poeic faculty". It is to ignore the fact that an aetiological element is to be found in many genuine ritual myths and that by no means all myths have a ritual origin and significance either in the past or in their present form. It is, therefore, not true to say that "myth is merely a description of ritual", however frequently this may have been the case. Apart from the many myths which have no more to do with ritual or cultus than has the *Iliad*, not a few are aetiological in the sense of having been devised to explain the sacred action performed, while others may have become predominantly aetiological when the earlier ritual association has been forgotten and ceased to be operative. Therefore, while it cannot be denied that ritual has been a determining element, aetiology in its various aspects has also been an important and recurrent feature.

The Myth of Horus of Edfu

Thus, in Ancient Egypt myths were of common occurrence which in modern parlance could be described as either ritual or aetiological, while others on such a classification would occupy a border-line position. Of those which belong essentially to the ritual category a detailed analysis has already been made and their place and function in the cultus determined. Among others which may properly be called aetiological are those in which the episodes connected with Horus of Edfu are related in a series of incidents in rapid succession. In his long and checkered career the Falcon-god Horus, after his followers had conquered Upper Egypt, assumed the symbol of the sun-disk, which he combined with the outstretched arms of a falcon. In this solar capacity he became the god of Edfu, Horus the Behdetite, the god of heaven, hovering over the earth with his spreading wings, who at the same time was regarded as a manifestation of Re. Thus, in the hieroglyphic text of the legend of the Great Winged Disk, parts of the narrative of which are depicted in the reliefs on the inner face of the west enclosure wall of the Ptolemaic temple of Horus of Edfu in Upper Egypt,[5] the story of the victories of the Behdetite are recounted at length from the standpoint of his priesthood for their own purposes.

The narrative opens with the three hundred and sixty-third year of the reign of the king of Upper Egypt, Re-Harakhte, the Sun-god, when he landed in his boat accompanied by Horus the Behdetite, in the name of Uthes-her (the modern of Edfu). There Horus discovered enemies plotting against Re, and flew up to heaven in the form of the Great Winged Sun-disk in pursuit of them. On reaching them he attacked with such terrific force that his adversaries could neither see with their eyes nor hear with their ears, so that "each slew his fellow in the twinkling of an eye, and not a soul lived". Then as a hawk-god of many colours, as the Great Winged Disk, Horus returned to the barque of Re-Harakhte, and Thoth said to Re, "the god of Behdet is come in the form of the Great Winged Sun-disk who destroys (? or is victorious over) the rebels and foes. Therefore, he is called House of Behdet to this day". Moreover, Re declared that Edfu should be designated the city of the House of Behdet. Then follows a long list of places and

objects called by their respective names because of their associations with the subsequent victories of Horus and of the
mighty deeds he had performed against the enemies of Re
which earned him the name of the "Winged Sun-Disk, great
god, smiter of the enemy, Prince of the city of Heben from this
day". After further triumphs against Seth and the rest of the
foes and fiends he encountered, at the end of the conflict
Re-Harakhte commanded Thoth to cause an image of the
winged disk to be made in every temple in which he (Re-
Harakhte) had rested in the places of the gods in Upper and
Lower Egypt.

It is clear, therefore, that the purpose of this myth was to
explain how and why Edfu became the cult centre of Horus
the Behdetite and his priesthood, and the way in which the
various emblems of the cultus, notably the winged disk,
acquired their names and significance in terms of the Horus
legend, and why its sign (the winged disk) was to be seen over
the doorway of every temple in the land. But while the motif
was primarily aetiological it was, nevertheless, framed in a
cultic setting, the text and reliefs occurring in the temple of
Edfu, and ending with an interpretation of the emblem as a cult
symbol. The myth, in fact, represents a series of explanatory
comments on sacred objects and actions, and it is by no means
improbable that it was recited during a procession in the
temple celebrating the victorious progress of Horus, with
stations at the various points *en route* at which appropriate rites
were performed, as along the sacred way from Athens to
Eleusis. Be this as it may, it was essentially in the nature of a
magico-religious series of utterances in dialogue form repeated
and enacted apparently by the priests of Edfu impersonating
the gods whose words they recited. Therefore, it is hardly
possible to draw any sharp distinction in a case of this kind
between an aetiological and a ritual myth; the narrative beginning as an explanation of the name and dedication of the
sanctuary, and ending in a protective ritual incantation. "Let
this utterance be recited when trouble occurs, and the king
shall not be afraid, but his foes will be slain before him, and

his heart will rejoice over them immediately, as befell the enemies of Re-Harakhte when Horus of Behdet flew against them as the Great Winged Disk. This image shall be made with the face of the king to this day."

This text is significant as an instance of mythological syncre-tism in which the two traditions have been skilfully combined in a composite story in which the Osirian and solar elements have been fused to form a narrative that is at once aetiological and connected with ritual. A story that has its roots in the predynastic and protodynastic history of the Two Lands, and as a popular tale outlived the fall of paganism and was incor-porated in the apocryphal account of the flight into Egypt of the infant Christ to escape the evil intents of Herod. So the age-long conflict of Re and his adversaries went on fusing first with one cult and then with another; each in its turn enacting the conquering of the enemies of the Sun and warding off evil from the king of the gods. Always it was hoped and believed he would everywhere and at all times exercise the same benefi-cent power. Therefore, the image of the winged disk became a permanent symbol of divine protection against destruction wherever it was erected.

The Mesopotamian Deluge Myth

In the Sumero-Babylonian Deluge story and its Hebrew counterpart, although the epics are cast in the form of poems relating to the creation of man, the origin of kingship and the building of antediluvian cities with the catastrophic destruction of "the seed of mankind" in order to explain the course of events and their sequel, yet the literary narrative in the form of an aetiological myth seems to have been embedded in an incantation recited as a spell to invoke the aid of the gods whose part in the primordial drama has been recorded.[6] Thus, although, as we have seen,[7] only the lower portion of one tablet of the Sumerian version has been published, its contents suggest that the cosmological background was briefly depicted, together with the foundation of the antediluvian cities and the dynasty, in order to explain the purposes of the creation of mankind and why Ziusudra and the animals were saved from destruction, and when the wrath of Anu and Enlil had been appeased the hero of the story was deified. It was at this point that the incantational motif element was introduced into the narrative.

As by his offering, prostrations and invocations of the breath of heaven and earth Ziusudra had placated the gods who originally were bent on his destruction, and escaped the impending fate of mankind, so the recital of the myth could bring deliverance in times of distress to those who correctly performed the magical rite and uttered the spell. Similarly, as the prostration of the hero before Anu and Enlil was followed by the bestowal of immortality upon him—the gift of "breath eternal like that of a god"—and a safe passage across the waters of death to the land of Dilmun where the sun rises, the text also may have been regarded as efficacious in ameliorating the destructive power of death which loomed so large in the Babylonian negative conception of the hereafter, even though in the late Gilgamesh epic the magic plant was lost as soon as it was found. Therefore, there may have been an attempt, if not to escape death altogether, at least to obtain a supernatural prolongation of life, just as Sargon of Assyria prostrated himself "for the gift of health, for length of days and the stability of his reign",[8] and Ashurdan I is said to have "attained to gray hair and a ripe old age" by the gifts he offered to the gods.[9]

Consequently, in the precarious conditions that prevailed in Mesopotamia with the fear of disaster and death always in the offing, a ritual element was introduced into the current aetiological mythology. It did not suffice to explain how these misfortunes arose in the beginning, though this was not neglected in the Deluge stories. Ways and means had to be found to bring the destructive forces under control by ritual devices in which the recital of myths as an incantation was regarded as an effectual spell. Moreover, this was not confined to periodic floods or the fear of death. It was applied to such everyday occurrences as toothache believed to have been caused by a worm created by Anu gnawing in the gum of the

sufferer. This is related in an Akkadian cosmological incantation derived from an ancient text of Hurrian origin in which
the descent of the worm is traced back from the marshes in
which it lived, through the canals and rivers to the creation of
heaven and earth by Anu. Weeping before Shamash the Sun-
god and Ea, the controller of magic, the worm asked to be
given food, but refused the offer of ripe figs and apricots,
requesting instead to be caused to dwell on the gums in order
that it might suck the blood of the teeth and gnaw at the gums
to destroy their strength. The incantation closes by invoking
the curse of Ea resulting from the misguided choice of the
worm. "Because thou hast said this, O worm, may Ea smite
thee with the might of his hand." Then follows the direction
for the use of this spell by the dentist who is directed to recite
it three times over a potion of beer and a magic plant and oil
which is to be replaced on the tooth.[10] Thus, the text is at
once a cosmological aetiological myth explaining the origin
and significance of the worm and then the ritual procedure to
be adopted to render the incantation efficacious in curing the
toothache by the power of Ea, assisted perhaps by Anu and
Shamash since they are also mentioned in the text.

While myths of origin are primarily aetiological in character,
inasmuch as their purpose is to place current events and practical affairs in a supposedly historical perspective, this is not, as
has been commonly supposed, to satisfy curiosity and to explain
why things exist or happen as they do. It is rather to validate
and justify what is done, and to give a supernatural sanction
for the established régime and its ways and works. In so doing,
as, for example, in the creation stories, very often an elaborate
and picturesque account is given of how the universe came
into being, and the various gods and divine agencies involved
in the process. It can hardly be denied, therefore, that such
myths contain an aetiological element. Nevertheless, that was
not their original function.

Thus, while in the Babylonian Creation epic the primeval
struggle between cosmic order and chaos was recorded in considerable detail,[11] it was presented as a ritual drama renewed

annually at the turn of each new year. In other words, it was at once aetiological and ritual in its presentation and purpose. Cast in metric form, the poem was twice recited with mimetic actions at the *Akitu* Festival in Babylon in the manner and for the reasons that have been described and considered. In the last analysis, therefore, it must be regarded as a ritual myth since its real function was not to tell the story of creation but to enact it as an ever-present event which every year was in jeopardy in an unstable and fluctuating environment that desperately needed bringing under ritual control.

The Myth of Enlil and Ninlil

On the other hand, the myth of Enlil and Ninlil does set out to explain purely aetiologically how the moon and its three brothers originated. Thus, as recorded on a Sumerian tablet in the Nippur collection in the University Museum at Pennsylvania, Enlil is represented as seducing Ninlil, the Air-goddess, while on the advice of her mother (Nunbarshegunu) she was bathing alone in the canal at Nippur. When she became pregnant and conceived Nanna, the Moon-god, Ninlil was driven to the nether regions, and was followed thither by Enlil, who, taking the form of "the man of the gate", again had intercourse with her. This time she conceived Meslamtaea, or Nergal, king of the underworld. Pursuing his way, Enlil begot two more gods of the nether regions—Ninazu and an unidentified deity. He was then exalted as the king of the underworld in a hymn of praise with which the story ends.[12] Its purpose was to explain the origin and respective characteristics of the Moon-god, Nanna, and his three divine brothers, engendered after the Storm-god of the air and his consort had become transferred to the rule of the underworld, which, according to Jacobsen's rendering, was a punishment for the seduction of Ninlil.[13]

Enki and Ninhursaga

In the intricate story of Enki and Ninhursaga, one of the best preserved of the Sumerian myths, after a eulogy of Dilmun as an island and city devoid of sickness and death and full of sweet water and abundance of crops in fields and farms, the union of "the mother of the land", the Goddess Ninhursaga, with Enki, the Water-god of Wisdom, is described, he having first provided it with fresh water. Thereupon their daughter Ninmu, the plants, was born without pain or effort after nine days of pregnancy, who in the same manner as her mother, herself gave birth to another goddess, Ninkurra, when Enki had impregnated her (i.e. Ninmu). Not content with these incestuous liaisons, Enki cohabited with his granddaughter, Ninkurra, and begot the Goddess Uttu. In spite of the warnings of Ninhursaga, she too succumbed to the advances of Enki after he had brought her gifts of cucumbers, apples and grapes, perhaps as a marriage-offering. No new goddess is said to have been born of this alliance, but Ninhursaga caused eight plants to sprout forth which Enki promptly ate. This so enraged the goddess that she cursed him and disappeared. Thereupon the wells and rivers dried up and Enki began to pine away. The fox then intervened and succeeded in bringing back Ninhursaga to Dilmun, and finally she restored Enki by helping him to give birth to eight deities, one for each ailing part of his body. He then decreed the fate of these gods, the last of whom was Enshag, "lord of Dilmun".[14]

The motifs of this myth are so varied that no single purpose can be assigned to it. Nevertheless, its primary object was to trace the origin of the sons of Enlil and determine their different natures and characteristics, in the familiar agricultural setting of the soil rendered fertile by the fresh water brought up from the earth at the behest of Enki, who personified the salt sea-water as well as the fresh river-water. Thus, it made an attempt to explain the fertility of the soil of Dilmun as the terrestrial paradise where the action of the story took place, wherever this may have been situated, whether in South-western Iran on the eastern shore of the Persian Gulf or on the island of Bahrein in the Gulf.[15] There in what seem to have been marshlands in the neighbourhood of the delta of the Tigris and Euphrates, watered as it is alleged by the Sun-god, different plants were brought into existence apparently by Ninhursaga, symbolizing perhaps the union of the soil and the fertilizing waters. This seems to have been the main motif of the myth, but while, therefore, it was essentially aetiological, the theme became so involved in the subsequent births and the relations of Enki and Ninhursaga that the aims and intentions of the various episodes cannot be determined. But they do not appear to have had a ritual significance.

Enki and Sumer; Eridu and Erech

Similarly, in the account of Enki's activities in the organization of the universe and in particular the equipment of Sumer with flowing streams, fish, vegetation, cattle and sheep, and of its capital Ur as "the shrine of abundance of the land, knees opened, green like the 'mountain'", attention is concentrated upon the way in which the existing order in Mesopotamia was established by a beneficent culture hero.[16] At Nippur he is represented as having built his "sea house" on the shore of the Persian Gulf before the Flood, and then proceeded to raise the city of Eridu from the abyss and make it float over the water like a mountain, filling its gardens with fruit-trees, birds, and its waters with fish. Having erected the temple therein he sought and obtained the blessing of Enlil upon his work.

In a third myth, published by Poebel in 1914 and subsequently enlarged by Kramer in 1937,[17] the transfer of the arts of civilization from Eridu to Erech is described as a result of Inanna, queen of heaven and the goddess of Erech, going to Eridu to consult Enki about her project of making her city the centre of Sumerian culture. Receiving her at a banquet in a drunken condition, he gave her more than a hundred divine decrees which constituted the complex pattern of the civilization, and she returned to Erech in her "boat of heaven" laden with the priceless gifts. When, however, on becoming sober he realized what he had done, Enki sent his servant and a group of sea-monsters to seize Inanna's boat and bring it back with the decrees. At each attempt to circumvent the vessel, the messenger of Inanna, Ninshubur, intervened on her behalf until at length it arrived safely at its destination (Erech), where amid feasting and rejoicing it was unloaded of its contents by the jubilant citizens.

Enki and Ninmah

Finally among these aetiological myths of origins, in the account of the creation of man inscribed on the two Sumerian tablets, one in the Louvre and the other in the University Museum at Philadelphia, it was Enki again who instructed his mother, Nammu, the primeval sea, who gave birth to "the clay that is above the *apsu*", how to fashion human beings to be the servants of the gods and provide them with their sustenance. It proved, however, to be a joint effort of the goddesses Nammu and Ninmah, "the exalted lady" (the epithet of Ninhursaga, the goddess of the earth), and Enki, the god of the sweet waters, and by no means a conspicuous success. Now the purpose of this curious version of the several Babylonian accounts of the creation of man, resulting in the production of a series of oddities, would appear to have been an attempt to explain and pass judgment upon the very abnormal types of humanity, including those suffering from senility, as an apparently un-necessary evil. They were represented as excrescences arising from the irresponsible actions of the gods at a feast when wine had flowed all too freely. In this exuberant mood they indulged in unedifying displays of creative powers with disastrous results alike for the freaks they produced among mankind, and for Enki, who was driven out of heaven and earth by the curse pronounced upon him by Ninmah.[18]

PALESTINE
Ugaritic Aetiological Interpretations

In the Ugaritic texts El was represented as dwelling in a cosmic paradise "a thousand plains, ten thousand fields" from Palestine at "the sources of the two rivers in the midst of the fountains of the two deeps"[19] like the Sumerian Ziusudra in Dilmun. Behind these epics there may lie the story related by Lucian of a mighty chasm under the temple of Atargatis, the Syrian goddess, near the Euphrates, through which the waters of the Flood were drained off.[20] Twice in every year, it was alleged, the water from the sea was taken to the temple by the priests and poured into the chasm in commemoration of the deliverance from the Deluge. It is not improbable, as Albright suggests,[21] that the myth and ritual were based on an aetiological interpretation of the name of the sacred Syrian city identified with the modern Mumbidj, between Aleppo and the junction of the Sajur river with the Euphrates, to explain the chasm left after the fountain had run dry, and to connect it with the traditional source of the fresh water in the primeval abyss.

Another instance of tales of this kind growing up around place-names occurs in the legend of Aqhat where the town of 'Abiluma (the "city of mourners") is associated aetiologically with the expression of grief for the murder of Aqhat, the son of Danel, after he had refused to give Anat his bow.[22] Transforming Yatpan, her accomplice, into a vulture, she caused him to strike Aqhat dead, while he was dining by a well in the precincts of the city of 'Abiluma. Stricken with grief, Danel set out to recover the body of his son, which had been devoured by the mother of the vulture, Samal, and cursed the well and the city of 'Abiluma where the tragedy occurred. For seven years he mourned for Aqhat with the wailing-women of his court, and in the capacity of the "Man of Harnamiyy" (*mt hrnmy*) he offered to the gods and to the stars the clan-sacrifice called by this epithet (Harnamiyy) to assist Paghat in her mission when she set forth to avenge the murder of her brother.[23] Thus, the origin of the tribal offering, Harnamiyy was referred back to the hero Danel and interpreted in terms of this later aetiological myth, the sequel of which has not yet been discovered.[24]

Hebrew Sanctuaries and their Aetiological Myths

Holy places and their associated cultus always have tended to become subject to an aetiological interpretation to explain their name and its religious significance, and to give the sanctuary and its ritual a particular status in relation to the god, ancestor or quasi-divine being with whom it was associated. Thus, in Hebrew tradition the patriarchal stories had an essentially aetiological character designed to explain how the principal national sanctuaries—Bethel, Shechem, Hebron, Beersheba, Penuel or Mahanaim—had acquired their sanctity. Generally this was attributed to one of the ancestors of Israel having been the recipient of a divine visitation at a sacred tree, stone, well or spring. Thus, it was to "the terebinth of Moreh" (the turpentine-tree of oracle) at Shechem to which Abraham is said to have resorted on his arrival in Palestine to seek supernatural guidance through a theogony concerning his possession of the land,[25] and then for oracular reasons to have proceeded to move his tent to the terebinth at Mamre,[26] and erect there an altar to Yahweh. Near by at the local sanctuary in Hebron there was another terebinth of Abraham, while the tamarisk alleged to have been planted by the patriarch in Beersheba[27] probably represents a later interpretation of an ancient sacred grove.

In every case the sanctuaries of course were much older than the Hebrew occupation of Palestine, and the patriarchal stories are merely attempts to give them a place in the cultus of Israel by attaching to them an aetiological myth and a ritual attributed in the first instance to the patriarch who was supposed to have founded the shrine. This is brought out very clearly in the account of the foundation of Bethel by Jacob attributed to his accidental incubation there, resulting in the discovery of the divine occupant of the sacred place in a dream.[28] The setting of this story was a megalithic monument which from time immemorial must have been a Canaanite sanctuary with an established cultus. To transform it into a legitimate place of Hebrew worship it had to be assigned to one of the ancestors of Israel. Therefore, around it grew up the Jacob myth in which the son of Isaac was represented as having fled from the vengeance of his twin brother Esau after he had falsely secured his father's blessing, and to have halted on his way to Haran at this sacred place. He lay down to sleep there, and its divinity is said to have inspired the dream which in its later form was interpreted in terms of a "ladder" or "stair" connecting the earthly sanctuary with its heavenly counterpart like the Meso/potamian ziggurat, thereby calling forth a numinous response on the part of Jacob. Awaking in the morning, he solemnly took the menhir on which he had slept and erected it as a *mazzebāh*, or sacred pillar, and poured oil on the top of it as an offering to the indwelling divine being, who by the com/piler of the narrative was equated with Yahweh. The emphasis, however, was on the naming of the sanctuary[29] because the main purpose of the myth was to explain the origin of Bethel as a patriarchal shrine and the reason why it had been adopted as a holy place in Israel.

Moreover, this is not the only indication of a megalithic cult in Hebrew myth and ritual. Thus, again in the Jacob story, Laban and his son/in/law (Jacob) are said to have erected a sacred pillar (E), or cairn (J), as a witness of their treaty; the covenant having been ratified, according to the J narrative, by a ritual meal on the heap of stones personified as a boundary cairn. Therefore, it and the menhir were interpreted aetiologi/cally as having been a witness of the transaction sealed by a sacrifice and the common meal, marking the boundary which neither party should pass for the purpose of harming the other. Furthermore, in connecting the incident with Mizpah (the "watch/post") of the Jephthah story,[30] the narrator inter/preted the cairn as a symbol of Yahweh watching between Laban and Jacob when they returned to their respective abodes.[31]

Similarly, in the account of the covenant between Israel and Yahweh after the conquest of Palestine by the Hebrew tribes, as recorded in the book of Joshua, Joshua is alleged to have assembled a convocation at Shechem and erected a great stone "under the oak that was in the sanctuary of Yahweh. And he said unto all the people, Behold, this stone shall be a witness unto us; for it hath heard the words of Yahweh which he spake unto us; it shall be therefore a witness against you, lest ye deny your god."[32] Here, again, a local sanctuary was given a Yah/wistic origin by interpreting it in relation to the establishment of Israel in its promised land, and making it a witness of the vows of the people which the menhir is supposed to have heard them pronounce. Thus, it may have been regarded as in some measure a sequel to the circle, or *gilgal*, of twelve stones which Joshua is said to have constructed when he and the people first crossed the Jordan. This pre-Israelite cromlech no doubt was taken over and subsequently dedicated to Yahweh, the Elohist connecting it with the introduction of the rite of circumcision as an initiation ceremony at the threshold of their entry of Canaan "to roll away the reproach of Egypt from the people",[33] just as the Yahwist associated the institution of the ancient rite with the period immediately preceding the Exodus.[34] The circle being represented as a witness of the miraculous passage through the waters of Jordan,[35] it seems fitting that the ultimate triumph of the invasion should be celebrated also at a neighbouring megalithic sanctuary; i.e. at Shechem.

Thus, inauguration-aetiological myths and their cultus developed around most of the more important ancient Canaanite sanctuaries, and in many cases doubtless the original legend was transferred to and re-interpreted in terms of the Hebrew Yahwistic cult. Nevertheless, although the Deuteronomist redactors retained the patriarchal sources of the Yahwist and Elohist narrators when they had recast the narratives to bring them into line with the pre-exilic prophetic reforms in faith and practice, the ancient sanctuaries with their sacred pillars, groves and images were not looked upon with favour. On the contrary, injunctions were issued to hew down the menhirs, destroy the altars and burn the groves[36] rather than to rehabilitate them because it had proved to be impossible to dissociate them from their original purposes and significance. Therefore, the enactments against them were referred back to the days of the conquest of Palestine to give them a venerable sanction in spite of the fact that actually the myth and ritual had been incorporated in Hebrew cultus and given a place in its own ancestral history with the aid of an aetiological story to afford an answer to the question, "what mean these stones?"[37]

It was not, however, until the only legitimate worship of Yahweh was centred in the temple at Jerusalem after the Josiah reformation in the sixth century B.C. that the Deuteronomist injunction became operative. And as soon as this reforming movement had run its course, Manasseh, the reactionary successor of Josiah, promptly re-erected the asherah, or sacred pole, in the temple,[38] encouraged perhaps by the fact that this particular sacred object was not part of the ancient heritage of the patriarchs. But notwithstanding the professed legitimacy of the *mazzebāh*, or menhir, in the Yahweh tradition,[39] ultimately it too suffered the fate of the asherah and was proscribed because of its original Canaanite associations.[40]

The employment of aetiological myths to justify the retention of pre-Israelite or non-Yahwistic pagan cult-practices and beliefs were by no means confined, however, to the patriarchal tradition. Any sacred place, object or name might be explained in relation to a Yahwistic theogony, intervention or motif, and so obtain a new lease of life during the Hebrew occupation of Palestine, even to the extent of surviving the most drastic icono-clastic reforms, and eventually reappearing in a new guise in the post-exilic hierarchic community. Thus, no episode in the history of Israel was quite so deeply laid and indelibly impressed upon the national consciousness as the Exodus. This most significant event was the central feature of the Mosaic tradition in its manifold forms and ramifications from the thorn-bush theogony to the mysterious demise of the hero on the threshold of the invasion of the promised land. Almost at every turn an aetiological myth was invented to account for the more important incidents, culminating in the detailed treatment of the struggle with Pharaoh ending with the mira-culous deliverance from the land of bondage on that fateful night at the vernal equinox when "the destroyer" was abroad wreaking vengeance on the first-born of man and beast outside the privileged territory of Goshen, and the subsequent passage through the Red Sea on dry land to the desert wanderings on the other side of what in fact appears to have been the Gulf of Akaba.

Moses and the Exodus

While, as Frazer says, "there seems to be no sufficient reason to doubt that in its broad outlines the tradition concerning Moses is correct",[41] yet it remains impossible to determine either the date or the precise circumstances of the Exodus, the route followed to the Holy Mount and its location, the duration of the sojourn in the desert, or, indeed, which among the Hebrew tribes were involved in the event and later took part in the entry into Palestine. There has been and are no dearth of theories about all these conjectures, but "there is no feature of this reconstruction which", as Professor Rowley says, "has not been challenged in recent years".[42] The principal sources of the available data are the Biblical records and these for the most part consist of narratives based on aetiological myths drawn up to explain or give a reason for the events they describe, usually in terms of miraculous interventions at certain times and places, such as the thorn-bush, the "Reed" Sea, Horeb or Sinai, Kadesh and so on. And these are all relatively late, belonging to a period separated from the alleged occurrences by not less than 500 years, when the accounts began to acquire their present form and to be written down in the J and E Penta-teuchal documents (c. 850–750 B.C.), though incorporating much earlier tradition. It can hardly be doubted, however, that the interpretations were based on an historical situation in its broad outlines since Moses and the Exodus are common to both the northern and the southern sources, and, therefore, must go back to the time before the kingdoms of Judah and Israel were divided after the death of Solomon. In the early days of the monarchy and in the disturbed period of the judges, there are no indications of outstanding personalities at all likely to have invented a theme of this magnitude and coherence which has every appearance of being history idealized and personified in terms of a series of aetiological myths.

As T. E. Peet has said, "tradition is often incorrect in detail, its chronology is generally poor, it telescopes and duplicates, and its geography is rarely consistent. But in most cases, in which archaeology has permitted a test, the central facts of

tradition are found to contain some kernel of truth."[43] Unquestionably the traditional account of what took place
between the quasi-legendary patriarchal period and the final
Hebrew settlement in Palestine in and after the middle of the
second millennium B.C. is largely mythical, but behind and
within the aetiology there seems to lie a hard core of fact,
however oversimplified and fanciful may have been the account
in the Biblical records, determined by much later religious
beliefs and practices, ethnological situations and the interpretations of place-names and sacred sites.

Nevertheless, when due allowance has been made for all this
aetiological embellishment of the traditions, they do in fact give
indications of the course of events among the Hebrew tribes in
the second millennium B.C. when their ancestors were roving
about with their flocks and herds between Mesopotamia and
Syria, and eventually a section of them settled in Palestine and
Egypt in the Hyksos period (*c.* 1720–1570 B.C.) when the
heterogeneous collection of Asiatics from the East with their
horses dominated the Nile valley until they were expelled at
the end of the Seventeenth Dynasty. Whether or not the
Hebrews are to be equated with a widely dispersed people in
this region at that time designated Habiru in the Amarna
Letters has yet to be settled, but in any case it can hardly be
doubted that some of the composite people who later came to
be known as "Hebrews" went into Egypt in the wake of the
Hyksos infiltrations from the north,[44] while others apparently
remained in Palestine.[45]

The problem, however, is complicated by the absence of an
agreed chronology concerning either the entrance into or the
exodus from the Nile valley of these Hebrew migrations. The
most probable time for the sojourn there would be during the
Hyksos occupation, and for the change in their fortunes to
have occurred when "there arose up a new king over Egypt
which knew not Joseph".[46] But the equation of the Pharaoh
with Ahmose I of Thebes, who expelled the Hyksos, and the
subsequent oppression of the Hebrew slaves with his reign at
the close of the Seventeenth Dynasty and the rise of the New

Kingdom in the great Eighteenth Dynasty under the Thutmoses (*c.* 1546–1440 B.C.)[47] conflicts with the Biblical statement that they were assigned the task of building the store-cities Pithom and Rameses.[48] This would seem to make Rameses II (*c.*1299–1232 B.C.) the oppressor rather than Ahmose and the Thut-moses, and to suggest that the escape was effected at the accession of his successor Merenptah (*c.* 1232–1221 B.C), who we know from a stele discovered in Thebes in 1896 had to quell revolts in Palestine.[49] On this interpretation of the event, which now holds the field,[50] the enslavement coincided with the extensive building operations in the Delta in the second half of the thirteenth century, more than two hundred years after the dating of those who have assigned the Exodus to the accession of Amenhotep II, notwithstanding the fact that this earlier equation seemed to confirm the Biblical chronology of 1 Kings vi. 1, alleging that the building of the temple of Solomon was begun 480 years after the Exodus.

From these conflicting conjectures it is clear that the problem is one of such complexity that no simple solution is possible. Every theory encounters almost insuperable difficulties in trying to reconcile the Biblical traditions with the archaeological data. Similarly, the date and details of the Israelite conquest and occupation of Palestine remain equally very obscure, and we cannot be sure who the Hyksos really were or what exactly was their relation to and with the Hebrews. Some of the complica-tions may have arisen from there having been more than one entry of the tribes into Palestine, and from one section of them —perhaps the Joseph tribes—having migrated to Egypt while the rest remained in Palestine.

The Invasion of Canaan

The account in the book of Joshua of what happened during the final conquest is based mainly on aetiological stories put together by writers and editors in the southern kingdom of Judah who represented the invasion as a single event under the leadership of Joshua after the death of Moses, as ruthless as it was complete in the extermination of the indigenous Canaanite population, and the enslavement of all the other peoples in the land. This certainly is not confirmed either by the subsequent sequence of events as recorded in the book of Judges, or by the extra-Biblical evidence. The compilers of the Joshua narra-tives, however, under the influence of the Deuteronomic contention of the absolute domination of the chosen nation allowing by divine decree no covenant to be made with the inhabitants or mercy shown to them,[51] interpreted what hap-pened in terms of this later law. Therefore, they represented the invasion as a triumphant march to total victory, involving the complete annihilation of the Canaanites and spreading such terror throughout the whole region that the adjacent tribes from far and near hastened across the Jordan to make a covenant with the all-powerful Hebrew bedouins, as, for example, in the story of the Gibeonites.[52] Here a dual narrative attempts to explain why and how they became temple servants, thereby affording a reason both for their subservient position in later days, and for their sanctity, the violation of which justified vengeance on the family of Saul.[53]

Aetiological stories of this nature hardly can be regarded as reliable sources of information about historical events and incidents. When the various traditions were combined in a common narrative in its present form it was for the purpose of presenting Israel as the chosen people and Palestine as the "land of Yahweh" set apart for their occupation. This in theory involved the ruthless extermination or subjection of the original inhabitants, though in practice the penetration of the invading nomadic tribes was in fact a very gradual process, resulting in their intermingling with one another and so producing a composite cult and culture. Precisely how this was achieved is still a matter of debate, but there appears to have been a succession of invasions from the south, beginning with attacks before the time of Joshua.[54] These probably were followed by the conquest of Hebron and Debir by Caleb and the tribe of Judah and their confederates,[55] making due allowance for the editor having inserted a Deuteronomic aetiological version of Caleb's claim to Hebron in accordance with the promise made to him by Moses.[56] But he also included in his narrative an account of Caleb's conquests from an earlier source (Joshua xv. 13–19). In chapter x the subjection of Southern Canaan is attributed to Joshua,[57] whereas in chapter xv. 14 and in Judges i. 10 the capture of Hebron is ascribed to Caleb after the death of Joshua. Similarly, so far from all the local population having been exterminated and the king of Gezer slain by the alleged annihilation under Joshua,[58] it is later maintained that Gezer retained its independence until the time of Solomon.[59] Debir is also said to have been conquered by Othniel, the first of the Judges,[60] and not by Joshua.[61] Therefore, this Deuteronomic section of the narrative in the book of Joshua (x. 28–40) is quite unhistorical.

The part played by Joshua in the conquest of Canaan is difficult to determine in view of the uncertainty about the date of the capture of Jericho and whether or not it can be attributed to his efforts. The composite story of its final sack has so many legendary features, and the archaeological data bearing upon the event are so very uncertain and conjectural,[62] that it is not possible to discover how and when the assault was made. All that can be safely asserted is that the city was occupied by the Hebrews, probably soon after the crossing of the Jordan, possibly before the fall of Lachish towards the end of the thirteenth century B.C.[63] But it remains to be seen what new light may be thrown upon the problem when the present excavation of this important site by Miss Kenyon has been completed and its setting in Near Eastern history finally deter-mined. In any case, the troubled situation in Palestine described in the Amarna Letters in the first half of the fourteenth century B.C. cannot be regarded as reflecting the conditions portrayed in the books of Joshua and Judges, as was formerly supposed.[64]

No historical connexion can be established between the Hebrew invasion under Joshua and the inroads of the Habiru in the south, and the tribes called Sa-Gaz coming from the north.[65] In the Amarna Age it was a succession of raiders who were marauding sporadically throughout the country in sufficient force, it is true, for the prince of Gezer to appeal to

Pharaoh for help "that the Habiru may not destroy us". "The territory of Gazri, that of Askalon, and the city of Lachish", are said to have "given them food, oil and all necessaries". But for the most part it was only very small forces that were sought to quell the insurrections, the king of Tyre, for instance, asking only for ten or twenty soldiers,[66] others for up to fifty men.[67] This would hardly suffice if battles had occurred at all on the scale of those recorded in the Biblical narratives. Therefore, both the chronology and the conditions in Palestine are against placing the Israelite invasion in the Amarna period in the fourteenth century. Moreover, the names of the kings mentioned in the books of Joshua and Judges—Adonibezek of Jerusalem, Haram of Gezer and Jabin of Hazor—are very different from those in the Amarna texts—Abdi-hiba, Yapahi and Abdi-tirshi.

It would seem, then, that the Amarna Age can be dismissed as the setting of the conquest mythology. So far as the historical exploits of Joshua are concerned they appear to have been confined mainly to the central highlands where his own tribe of Ephraim was located, and whither he may have led the Joseph tribes across the Jordan. Whether or not he attacked and destroyed Jericho, he would appear to have functioned on the ridge north-east of Mizpah on which Bethel and the enigmatical Ai were situated.[68] Since, however, Ai was already a ruin,[69] the story of its capture and the Achan incident may have been transferred to Joshua and interpreted in relation to his campaign as a sequel to the miraculous destruction of Jericho, unless, as has been suggested, Ai was confused with Bethel,[70] the fall of which occurred probably in the first half of the thirteenth century.[71] Lachish was captured later in this century, as recent excavation has revealed,[72] and while there are references to the city giving help to the Habiru in the Amarna Letters, the first mention of its destruction is in the Joshua narrative, where the whole population is said to have been annihilated.[73] Both Meek and Albright refer the settlement of the Joseph tribes in the central region to the Amarna Age,[74] and Meek thinks that the Joshua campaign belongs to this period a century before the Exodus under Moses took place, thereby reversing the Biblical tradition. While these reconstructions are not easy to reconcile with the documentary data and raise more problems than they solve, they show that any attempt to correlate the Biblical and archaeological evidence is beset with almost insuperable difficulties because the narratives in their present form have been so drastically transformed and recast to serve the purposes of aetiological mythology. While behind them lies an historical background of fact, the details can only be explained in relation to the subsequent events which the stories were designed to interpret.

GREECE

The Troy Saga and the Iliad

This also applied to a great deal of the classical mythology which often is more in the nature of aetiological saga or *märchen* than of a description of ritual or of historical fact. Thus, in the case of the episode in the siege of Troy, brilliantly related in the *Iliad* of Homer, gods and heroes and ordinary mortals intermingle as actors in the epic drama, all much on the same plane, actuated by the same passions and desires, having an almost identical nature, eating, sleeping, taking their respective sides in the battles and winning victories or suffering defeats. Whatever differences there are between them is in degree rather than in kind, so completely anthropomorphized have the gods become when they are introduced into the stories to give colour to the poetic records of what actually happened.

The scene is laid in the ancient fortress in the north-west corner of Asia Minor, which from the middle of the third millennium B.C. occupied a key position on the Hellespont (*c.* 2600 B.C.) at the centre of the web of trade-routes by land and sea. It was there at the modern Hissarlik that Heinrich Schliemann in the latter part of the last century brought to light the succession of seven ancient cities of Troy, the latest of which (Troy VIIa) is now known to have been Homer's fortress of the *Iliad*. Until recently it was thought that Troy VI with its massive circular mud-brick walls, towers and gateways was the site of the city of the saga, but from the Mycenaean pottery there, it is now known to have come to an end about 1350 B.C., a century before Agamemnon and the Achaeans captured its successor soon after 1200 B.C. It was there in the city known as VIIa, which flourished about 1300 B.C. until it was sacked in the Late Bronze Age by barbarian invaders from Central Europe in the twelfth century, that the great kingdom of Agamemnon was established, and there as a matter of historical fact the Trojan war was fought.

This is as far as the archaeological evidence goes. Whether or not the Iliadic episode in the tenth year of the war is to be regarded as romance or history, its background is clear enough. It is set against the legend of Troy, but it is confined to one short phase in the war lasting only twenty-eight days and centred around the one theme of the wrath of Achilles. No mention is made of the actual background of the events so vividly described with such consummate literary skill. Attention is concentrated upon the essential figures, human and divine, who play their several rôles in the quarrel and its sequel. Indeed, it is on the heights of Olympus rather than within the massive walls of Troy that the councils assemble, and gods and men engage in battle and in debate without any precise definition of where the divine action is taking place. The *Iliad*, it is true, opens with a graphic account of how Agamemnon and Achilles quarrelled at the siege of Troy and Achilles secured from Zeus a pledge that the wrong he had suffered would be avenged on Agamemnon and the Achaeans. Then follows the preparation for the battle and the marshalling of the forces, leading on to the actual contest in the next five books. But the war itself is not described; only the particular episode in it which the poet has selected to explain the suffering, death and dishonour that was caused by the quarrel between the two outstanding figures in the poem. Moreover, it is represented as fulfilling the universal ordering of things—"the plan of Zeus" —not just a particular isolated event. It was not, therefore, the Trojan war and the historical background that were the centre of interest. The Achilles story was told to explain why things happen as they do by divine decree on a universal plane as a sequence of events based on specific causes. The principal actors in the great drama were human beings, with gods appearing to give a divine sanction and background to "the plan of Zeus" and the moral laws upheld in the epic. But for every blessing they gave two sorrows, as Achilles reminded Priam.[75] This stark realism bordering on a hopeless fatalism was the main theme set against an unalterable framework, for the nature of the gods could never change. Nevertheless, it was presented in a manner that extolled heroic achievements for a worthy cause, and whatever suffering and sorrow were involved they were attributed to the gods who caused them and brought war and tears upon struggling humanity.

Whatever else may lie behind this immortal story, it embodies the memories of the Trojan war as a vague historical fact, and the past glories and triumphs of the nation as these were conceived by the Homeric Greeks, and in very broad outline as they have been confirmed by the archaeological evidence. So vividly was the quarrel described that it was thought by the ancients that Homer must have been almost contemporary with the war and had first-hand knowledge of the episode. It is now known that between the dissolution of the Mycenaean Age and the rise of the classical period some three hundred years of chaos and confusion intervened and that it was at the end of these "Dark Ages" that the enigmatic figure of Homer appeared ushering in the new era. Who he was and how much of the two great poems attributed to him he actually wrote remain the "Homeric Question". But however the *Iliad* may have been composed, the main theme, the wrath of Achilles, was essentially aetiological in character and content. It may have been taken over from some older poem, but as it is only the background that appears to belong to traditional mythology the plot and leading idea may have been invented by the poet to give expression to the underlying psychological conceptions, placed in the setting of an event that had actually happened some two hundred years earlier; namely, the Trojan war, the memory of which doubtless was still green. While the exploits of the Olympian gods were introduced into the background of the episode the traditional myths were related for their own sakes because of their influence on human conduct, either as warnings or examples of correct behaviour and chivalry. Normally the gods were not represented as having direct intercourse with ordinary mortals other than Ethiopians and the Phaeacians. In the process of humanization the ancient stories have lost much of their earlier significance and have been made to serve an aetiological purpose, explaining how men should behave and how unjustifiable it is to blame the gods for the evil human beings have brought upon themselves by their own mistakes, follies and shortcomings.

The Homeric Approach to Mythology

At this stage in its development myth had passed into saga and had shed its ritual and cultic connexions altogether. It had become a story told not only with the literary skill of the first and greatest of the Hellenic poets, but also from the distinctive standpoint of the Homeric approach to the current mythology. While Homer did not hesitate to make light of the old sacred tales of the Olympian gods, and to represent Zeus and his confederates as capricious, vengeful and unethical in their general conduct and in their relations with one another and with mankind, he took the mythology as he found it and retold the tales in his own way. He had no systematic theology to expound, and although he repudiated the popular religion and had scant regard for its gods as such, the Olympians were too deeply imbedded in the saga with which he dealt to ignore them. Therefore, he extracted from it all the best tales he could find and wove them into his immortal poems concerning the Trojan war and the adventures of its heroes, human and divine.

Now it is true that Olympus was very largely the projection of the Hellenic world in the pre-Homeric Age which had been long established when the Homeric poetry was written and had behind it a long tradition in the Aegean and the Ancient Near East. The picture was that of warring states with a central palace surrounded by the domains of lesser kings as retainers

and vassals whom the chief summoned to counsels and ban-
quets. While a similar political régime in these respects
prevailed among the indigenous Mycenaeans and the northern
Achaean invaders, the Homeric poems reflect the struggles and
conquests, triumphs and failures, and the normal behaviour of
the chieftains and princes of whom the mountain-gods were
the divine counterparts. The *Iliad* and the *Odyssey* are neither
theological treatises nor historical records of past events, however much many of the incidents may have been founded on
facts. They are just excellent tales told with all the literary effect
of a great writer giving a more or less correct picture of life and
manners that prevailed in Greece at the transition from the
Bronze Age to the Iron Age, composed in the first instance to
provide entertainment for princes and nobles in Ionian banqueting halls. The charge of Xenophanes that Homer ascribed
to the gods all things that among men are a shame and
reproach—"theft, and adultery and deceiving one another"[76]—
can be justified, but it failed to recognize the purpose and nature
of the literature he criticized. Zeus and Apollo were integral
to the *Iliad* and Poseidon and Athena to the *Odyssey* because
they were in the saga from the beginning, and represented the
predominance of the northern invaders at the time when they
were composed. Therefore, they fulfilled an aetiological function in the poems. But they also preserved the memory of an
earlier constitution going back to the Mycenaean Age when
the palace stood on an acropolis surrounded by the dwellings
of the retainers, reproduced in the description of Olympus as
the mountain city of the gods under the monarchical rule of
Zeus.[77]

Nevertheless, although the Homeric Olympian mythology
had behind it a long anthropomorphic tradition derived
directly from many sources,[78] it was Homer and Hesiod, as
Herodotus asserted, who "created the generations of the gods
for the Greeks; they gave the divinities their names, assigned
to them their prerogatives and functions, and made their forms
known".[79] But grand and imposing as were the figures they
created, for the Olympians of Homer were the Olympians of

Pheidias,[80] the anthropomorphic form in which they were conceived and described imposed on them serious limitations, and eventually led to their becoming so much like men that they failed to fulfil their divine functions altogether. Man had a duty to them as he had to his human superiors, but morality consisted of a set of rules determining the relations between superiors and inferiors rather than an ethical code regulating conduct according to an abstract principle of morality. But however capricious and unjust the gods might be, Homer made them the guardians of such moral ideas as existed in his day, and frequently he recast the stories he retold so as to place the heroes on the side of righteousness. Although traces of ritual holiness survived in the refusal of Hector and Achilles to sacrifice to Zeus with unwashed hands,[81] and in cleansing the hall with fire and sulphur after the slaying by Odysseus,[82] murder brought no pollution either to the murderer or to the land, whereas in the Cyclic epics of the seventh and sixth centuries B.C., and later in Attic law, even the accidental slaying of a slave required expiation.

The Literary Myth

Where the Homeric tradition failed by comparison with the earlier popular myth and ritual and the contemporary Mystery cults was in its being essentially and primarily a literary and artistic creation devoid of any genuine religious significance. Transcendentally the gods had little or nothing to offer to mortals since they differed from men only in having greater power and knowledge, and these they exploited merely for their own ends. In other respects they were subject to all the ethical defects and weaknesses to which mankind was heir, and they were too much involved in their own political intrigues to be concerned with human affairs. At its best Homeric Olympian mythology was a product of literary and artistic aetiological imagination, and a symbol of idealized qualities belonging to an age of chivalry which subsequent thinkers such as Socrates and Plato could retain and re-evaluate. In Homer, however, the higher values and realities enshrined in religion and art did not find expression, in spite of the heights attained in literary achievement. The old gods of the sagas remained romantic figures as the chief actors in a heroic age of chivalry and adventure. Sometimes they were allegorized or made symbols of virtue and justice up to a point if they were not given a fanciful naturalistic interpretation in terms of physical pheno-mena, such as the contests between the elements, and so were dismissed by the Sophists as the creation of human imagina-tion. But even as such they were no more than glorified and idealized men, though they did rise above the snakes, or bulls, or monstrous centaurs and giants of earlier mythology.

The Homeric anthropomorphization had eliminated or modified the crude representations of the pre-Hellenic period and given a clear definition and a new significance to the literary and artistic types it produced. That is what Herodotus meant when he attributed to Homer and Hesiod the creation of the gods and the making known of their forms. The *Iliad* and the *Odyssey* made the impression of a consistent unity on the popular mind and gave a distinct shape to the Olympian religion which was rendered permanent and of exquisite beauty in stone and paint as well as in a literature that has become a classic and a text-book for all generations. Thus, they have acquired an immortal heritage which redounds to their glory in all lands, however much they failed to secure and maintain the religious allegiance of the nation, or to make any permanent contribution to philosophic or theological thought and know-ledge. Nevertheless, as material for literature and art they proved to be capable of interpretation as symbols of something beyond themselves in mythology and allegory. Thus, they were given lip-service by doubtful philosophers, but they were gods in whom no one believed seriously. The humanizing of the myths, in fact, constitutes the first steps towards a rationalistic criticism of religion in which man became the measure and master of things and this world the scene of action. The myths had ceased to be representations of reality, and their heroic figures, however impressive, were hardly more than mortals.

Indeed, Hocart affirmed that "the myth detached from all

reality can only continue to exist in a society which is itself divorced from reality, one which has such a reserve of wealth that it can afford to maintain an intelligentsia exempt from the pursuit of bare life, and free to devote all its energies to intel-lectual play, to poetry and to romance". [83] How far this estimate of the situation can be made to apply to the Homeric poems depends on the view taken of their composition. If they were written between about 950 and 800 B.C. they may have been primarily the creation of the "Heroic" state of society when the wealthier Achaean princes possessed works of art in bronze, silver and gold, and lived luxuriously and in a leisurely manner. These conditions no doubt would be likely to produce a man of genius who conceived the idea of composing a long, con-tinuous poem from traditional tales and ballads concerning a dramatic episode during the siege of Troy, and of the adven-tures of one of the heroes who returned from the campaign; unless, like Gilbert Murray, one supposes that the *Iliad* and the *Odyssey* represent traditional books compiled by poets, rhap-sodists and editors through a number of centuries. [84] In any case, the poems were being altered and edited when Athens had become the centre and leader of Greek life and thought and culture, and it was this environment which gave point and vigour to the latent idea in the poems that the Greeks were the advance-guard of a new civilization assailing the forces of an older world.

It was to Ionia that the Homeric saga was addressed, and it was at Miletus, under the influence of Thales, that the great outburst of Hellenic intellectual genius occurred in the seventh and sixth centuries B.C. There the first serious attempt was made to interpret the universe as an intelligible rational cosmic order reducible to a single principle as the cause of all existence. This was the turning-point of human history, but although water, or air, or fire was regarded as the first principle, all things were said to be "full of gods". Therefore, the break with the old mythical tradition was only just beginning. Nevertheless, the arousing of intellectual "curiosity" (φιλοσοφία) in natural processes detached the cosmological mythology more and more from reality, leaving the aetiological saga to be deployed by poets and romanticists as a literary device.

The Platonic Myth

This, however, for Plato was only an "imitation" of the "real things" which themselves were only a copy of the true reality —the "ideas", or "forms", being the essential element. The majority of people, he contended, lived as it were in a cave with their backs to the fire, looking at the shadows on the wall and mistaking them for realities. When they turned to the sunlight and ascended to the mouth of the cave they saw the real things of the upper world as they truly are.[85] Therefore, although Plato derided the attempts of Aristhenes to defend Homer allegorically,[86] he did not himself hesitate to give a symbolical representation of reality in his myth of the cave. But the Platonic myths were not employed as rhetorical or poetic adornments of a literary tale, nor were they merely allegories to demonstrate abstract truth or inculcate moral behaviour. The story was told in the first instance for its own sake to give a clearer vision of the truth it was intended to convey, and very often to fill a gap in scientific knowledge and philosophical reasoning. Thus, at the end of the myth about "the soul and her habitations" he maintained that "either this or something like it is true".[87] It is not easy, however, to determine how much his speculations about reincarnation and human destiny were intended to be scientific truth and how much were accepted frankly as allegorical myth, borrowed very largely from Pythagorean and Orphic poetry and legend.[88] But into this material he introduced his own ideas and interpretations of the indestructibility of the soul, as he conceived the doctrine, and presented them in mythological form for a purpose which was eminently serious and by no means divorced from reality. The Platonic myth, in fact, was nearer to the ritual myth than to the Homeric saga inasmuch as it was an attempt to describe something which purported to be true rather than to explain fictitiously and poetically alleged events in an historical setting.

CHAPTER IX

Myth and Ritual

THE MEANING OF MYTH

The Analysis of Mythological Tradition

In the light of the evidence examined in this inquiry the conception of myth in popular thought and language cannot be sustained since it is not primarily a fictitious narrative setting forth the exploits of supernatural persons and the unusual and fantastic behaviour of natural phenomena, or of historical occurrences. Under the literary influence of Greece the tales of the Olympian gods and heroes, such as Zeus and Semele, Theseus and the Minotaur, Perseus and the Gorgon Medusa, and the heroes of the Trojan war immortalized by Homer, have been handed down as classical examples of themes told with all the literary skill and genius of the poet and the dramatist. Stories of this kind frequently have a direct reference to the past and are generally regarded either as the product of a hypo-thetical "mythopoeic age" or as romantic records of actual events, while tales professing to explain the origin of customs, institutions, and inexplicable or puzzling phenomena are aetiological.

The other main group is composed of legends and saga supposedly based on fact with an intermixture of traditional material told about a heroic character or a particular object, place, name or incident. The same theme may be repeated in association with similar phenomena through a process of diffu-sion, and historical situations may underlie such stories either in their original or diffused form, though it may be exceedingly difficult, if not impossible, to separate the true from the tradi-tional. The facts which they are supposed to explain and from which they are alleged to have originated are the most unstable elements in them, whereas in the themes they recur over a wide area little changed, suggesting transmission through culture contacts. The genetic relationship of much of the myth and ritual discussed in this volume is hardly open to question, belonging as it does in origin mainly to one culture area extending throughout the Ancient Middle East and the Eastern Mediterranean. To derive the complex of belief and practice from any single centre, however, is to court the disaster that has befallen the pan-Egyptian and the pan-Babylonian schools in recent years.

To these two groups of material may be added the folk-tale motifs which, unlike the aetiological stories, legends and saga, are neither explanatory nor factual in their purpose or content. They are for the most part a product of the unsophisticated section of society—"the folk"—and are recited primarily for the mere delight in telling stories. Nevertheless, they are above all traditional, handed down from one generation to another, repeated as they are received and remembered and retold with, or very frequently without, additions or changes. Eventually they may be written down and so acquire to some extent a literary character and influence notwithstanding their oral sources. Moreover, the themes and techniques employed in their recitation tend to conform to a pattern. They are nearly always fictional in intent like the snake episodes or the Uncle Remus cycle; or they may be fables, having a definitely moral significance as in the collection associated with the name of the Ionian slave Aesop (*c.* 600 B.C.). But folk-tales have a variety of motifs and these may be very loosely strung together without rationalistic background and dominated by wishful thinking, supernatural interventions and mighty deeds and adventures. But, on the other hand, the motifs often are incorporated in literary myths and legends, as, for example, in recording fights with dragons and other fabulous monsters in the struggle between good and evil and the sacred combat, and so acquire a more sophisticated content and significance.

The Myth

True myth, however, cannot be identified with any of these several types of traditional lore. It is not a product of

imagination in the sense of speculative thought or philosophizings about the origins of phenomena in the form of an aetiological tale invented to explain objects and events that arouse
attention. It is not idealized history or allegorized philosophy,
ethics or theology; still less is it an idle story told for intellectual
amusement or for popular entertainment according to prescribed
custom; or a day-dream to be interpreted by the symbols of
psycho-analytical exegesis. All these may retain elements of the
myth, but the myth itself is distinct from the fantasy, poetry,
philosophy and psychology with which it has become associated in its ramifications, developments and degenerations,
and their interpretations.

Similarly, the notion of a "mythopoeic mind", like that of
a "mythopoeic age", must be rejected. This too is the creation
of sophisticated theorists, allied to the contention of Lévy-Bruhl
and his school that primitive people are so completely dominated by a mystical mentality that they are incapable of adopting
a rational attitude to their natural environment. Everything is
supposed to be permeated by forces, influences and actions
which, though imperceptible to sense, are nevertheless real,
because the reality in which the primitive moves is itself
mystical and he is himself in a prelogical stage of mentality.[1]
Consequently, the world of fact, on this hypothesis, becomes
full of fantasy and mysticism which finds expression in mythopoeic imagination and ritual behaviour. In terms of "collective
representations" in which objects are not divided from one
another but united in a bond so intimate that each participates
in the other, making a thing what it is not, one and the same
entity may be simultaneously present in many places and act
upon one another, and generally behave in an irrational
manner, as is taken for granted in many myths and folk-tales.
But however naïve and fantastic some of these beliefs, stories
and practices may appear today to the modern mind, they are
in fact perfectly rational, intelligible and logical once their
premises and presuppositions are granted. It is not lack of
logic that characterizes their outlook but a particular attitude
to the relation between the sacred and the profane, the natural

and the supernatural, mind and matter, cause and effect. Agent and act are not clearly differentiated because logic is at fault, but because of an imperfect understanding of natural laws and processes, and a different conception of the relation of the sacred order to the phenomenal world of everyday affairs, with little or no awareness of universality and continuity of natural causation.

Neither among savages, peasants, nor any other section of mankind has a "mythopoeic mind" existed in any age or state of culture as a distinct entity. It is true that prior to the rise of philosophic and scientific speculative thought and empirical knowledge, natural phenomena were conceived in terms of human experience, and human experience was conceived in terms of cosmic events.[2] Moreover, as Marett says, "the savage has no word for 'nature'. He does not abstractly distinguish between an order of uniform happenings and a higher order of miraculous happenings. He is merely concerned to mark and exploit the difference when presented in the concrete."[3] So long as all goes well and smoothly the attitude of human beings towards the ordinary and commonplace is not very different at any time or under any cultural conditions. It is when mental stress and tension is produced by unpredictable and uncontrollable adversity, circumstances and events beyond human comprehension and control that there is a strong incentive to resort to supernatural agencies and sacred power by the aid of symbolic actions and their oral representations acting as a vent of collective emotion and anxiety.

Since the primitive is more limited in his empirical knowledge and control of natural forces and processes upon which he depends for his daily needs and well-being than peoples in a relatively higher state of culture, he is more inclined to seek supernatural intervention, especially at the critical junctures in his own affairs and in those of the community of which he is an integral part. In primitive society the pressure of events in the external world and in the circle of human relationships— the perpetual struggle for existence and survival, the innumerable daily frustrations and hazardous experiences often completely outside human control and comprehension—creates a tension seldom felt in a modern civilized community to the same extent except in times of intense strain. When such a situation does occur the reaction is not very different. But when subsistence depends entirely on the chase or the hazards of the seasons, with all the attendant dangers and uncertainties of a precarious environment, the emotional stress is endemic. Therefore, under these conditions myth and ritual as the recognized method of dealing with the existing order are fundamental.

Around crucial events such as the creation of the world, the loss of immortality, the destiny of man, the sequence of the seasons and the struggle between good and evil, a sacred narrative has taken shape to bring them into direct relation with the existing physical, cultural, social, ethical and religious conditions and organization. The chief purpose of these myths has been to stabilize the established order both in nature and in society, to confirm belief, to vouch for the efficacy of the cultus, and to maintain traditional behaviour and status by means of supernatural sanctions and precedents. Since the stories told purport to give an authoritative reason for things as they are by explaining what once happened in primeval times, and has ever since shaped the course of events, they have an aetiological significance. But their purpose has not been to supply intelligible explanations of natural phenomena and historical occurrences, or of peculiar features of the landscape, as in many folk-tales recited at special seasons. What happened at the creation of the world and in the brave days of old has a practical importance because it has determined subsequent belief and practice, behaviour and the whole structure of the universe and of society.

To take an example from modern myth-makers: among the native tribes of Australia a number of initiated men are set apart for the purpose of acting as custodians of tribal tradition, ritual and sacred sites. It is their business to safeguard the transmission of this lore and to see that everything that was prescribed by the heroes and ancestors in the Dream Time of long ago is carried out precisely as it was ordained. In describing the paths along which the ancestors are supposed to have travelled, and locating the places at which they halted to perform ceremonies, the sacredness of the existing totemic centres is affirmed and established for all time.[4] Moreover, not only does this mythological topography confirm the faith respecting the things done at the cult-centres, but it links the group with its tribal territory and provides inter-tribal common routes leading to the water-holes and the various sacred sites which have to be visited from time to time. As long as the course followed corresponds to that taken by the ancestors the same protection and hospitality are afforded as they were to the medieval pilgrims in Europe on their journey along the very ancient ways that led to Santiago de Compostela, a sacred site which, incidentally, goes back in its megalithic associations behind the adventures of the body of the son of Zebedee to the Bronze Age.

In this way myth and ritual function to promote social intercourse and security and to maintain the established tradition as a living reality within the milieu of primeval tradition as a consolidating dynamic. The things done at the threshold of creation live on as the unifying influence in the present by the continual repetition of the mystical events in the duly authorized ritual. Thus, the creative period is an ever-present reality, and the things done therein are re-enacted in the traditional ceremonial and retold in the sacred lore. By grounding the established order in a mythological primeval reality, stability is given to the social structure and religious organization, and an adequate reason is provided for the things done and believed. The interest in the past is centred in its bearing on the existing régime and the infallible precedents it affords for present practice and procedure. The inconsistencies and irrationalities in the stories are of no consequence because they are irrelevant to their function in placing on an unassailable foundation the general rules of conduct, the tribal institutions, and the sentiments that control social behaviour and religious belief.

The Folk-tale

It is against this background that the folk-tale and popular stories with which myth is so closely associated and interwoven have to be placed. Here, again a good deal of light may be thrown on the archaeological material in the ancient documents and texts concerning the myth and ritual of early man by an examination of the data in relation to the thought and practice of living peoples in a primitive or peasant state of culture. Like their remote predecessors in the Ancient Near East and the Aegean, the "folk" have been born into a mythological tradition which has coloured the whole of their life. It has given assurance in the hazards and unpredictable occurrences of everyday experience, and stability to the normal routine. The seasonal sequence of ploughing, seed-time and harvest, of lambing and shearing, and the crises in the human cycle of birth, marriage and death, have their appropriate and essential place in popular tradition.

Arising as an integral part of the cultus, the tales as well as the rites have their function in producing "phatic communion", or *rapport*, between members of the community; a sense of "togetherness" stimulated by common sacred utterances and actions transmitted from one generation to another in a prescribed pattern, giving order and consistency to a collective effort at specified times of festivity or lamentation. As the spoken word is thought to exercise supernatural power in its utterance and repetition, it gives efficacy to the actions performed and the episodes recounted as an "uttered rite". Emotional situations of continual recurrence require perpetual satisfaction, and the stories told and repeated with regular precision as a seasonal performance usually relate to certain events of outstanding importance which have a permanent significance in the moral, social and religious organization of society.

But the folk-tale in the proper sense of the term, unlike the genuine myth, may be related merely as an act of sociability for entertainment to wile away the evening hours when the day's work is over, and a good reciter of the traditional stories is always in demand in a primitive community. Even so, that originally they had a more serious purpose, such as the promotion of the growth of the crops and similar vital concerns, is suggested by the fact that particular types of tales with specific motifs are invariably told on these occasions at different times in the year by a member of the community who has an exclu/ sive right to recite them. The ancient custom has survived, though its purpose may be only very vaguely understood and remembered, sacred actions always tending to outlive the underlying beliefs. Moreover, although the stories are learnt by heart from the previous "owners" of them and are accurately repeated by an experienced raconteur, they may be retold with certain variations, as well as with carefully rehearsed dramatic effect. Having now no definite end in view beyond entertain/ ment, and being related merely for the pleasure of telling and hearing good stories well told, the raconteur is at liberty to improvise and improve upon his technique, provided that the actual tale is faithfully recorded. But at this stage the myth is well on its way to degenerating into an idle tale devoid of any serious significance because it is in the process of ceasing to be a vital element in a living culture.

As a seasonal occupation and diversion it retains the vestiges of its earlier function as an integral part of the religious, social and economic structure of the community, a direct expression of its subject/matter. When, however, they cease to have a functional value, unorganized and detached folk/tales are at best picturesque survivals destined to extinction like other "bygones"; or they may become a source of embarrassment to the body politic, as in the case of the vestigial organs in the physical organism. Having simply "remained over", they have degenerated into *superstitio*, which may be defined perhaps as "survival" rather than as "superstition". But in any case they have ceased to exercise their proper purpose as a living reality through detachment from the vital issues of the community in which they occur. They are no longer the reiterated presentation of an event replete with sacred power, and their study may become merely a palaeontology of fossils in human culture, or be exploited for the nefarious ends of some leech or wizard or astrologer. But when the folk/tale has acquired a fixed form and by continual repetition and diffusion has lived on as a permanent element in society with its roots deeply laid in the oral tradition, it may become a communal possession and eventually be committed to writing. Being the product of a single culture with themes easily adapted to local variation in detail, plot and literary convention, and always told in a stereotyped manner, these stories have a remarkable uniformity in type and content everywhere. Therefore, usually they remain singularly stable.

The Märchen *or Fairy-tale*

The *märchen* or fairy-tale is a story on a limited number of basic themes, such as those collected by Grimm from a variety of sources, and familiar today in the Cinderella cycle or in Cupid and Psyche. Its principal figures make no pretence of being historical characters. They are content to be the hero or heroine who after a bad start in life attains high rank by the aid of supernatural intervention, or of magic sleep obliterating time (e.g. Sleeping Beauty), and after marrying the prince or princess lives happily ever after. Tales of this "once upon a time" nature have been recorded from Ancient Egypt in the thirteenth century B.C., in Asia and in many parts of Europe, as well as among primitive peoples on the fringes of civilization and in peasant lore, though "fairies" by no means always occur in them. In origin they were essentially religious, belonging for the most part to the ritual combat cycle, and although they have generally now lost their magico-religious significance, the struggle between good and evil has survived as the dominant theme—personified by the "good fairy" and a Lucifer type of supernatural opponent playing their respective rôles in relation to a prince and a peasant bride, bringing good out of evil in Cinderella fashion.

The origin of the fairy concept is still in doubt. Belief in an enchanted land inhabited by a "race" or organized society of supernatural beings who usually are invisible, generally benevolent, often mischievous, whimsical, and sometimes of diminutive stature, belong to a relatively advanced state of culture. It has been suggested, however, that it arose from an earlier dwarfish race coming into contact with a taller people and lingering in mountains and caves, preying upon their conquerors.[5] Others have seen in fairies semi-divine beings like the medieval *fées* and the German "white ladies", reduced in stature and importance from their former estate as the gods of a dominant people,[6] either as a survival of animistic spirits associated with natural phenomena, or of people who have refused to accept Christianity.[7] The contest theme would suggest that somewhere in the background lies the Horus-Seth, Marduk-Tiamat, Yahweh-Leviathan struggle between two opposed forces with the good fairy and his or her opponent in these respective rôles.

There is probably some truth in all these possible solutions of the problem, as the fairy concept hardly can be reduced to a single source, though wherever it occurs in its typical form it has much the same characteristics, and the stories follow more or less identical motifs in their common tale-types. The number of motifs are considerable, but the types of which they are the variants conform to a particular pattern originating in oral tradition. Long before printed versions appeared in chap-books in the seventeenth and eighteenth centuries, fairy-lore played its part in medieval romance, the Arthurian cycle and Chaucer, Spenser and Shakespeare. But it was not until Perrault's *Histoires ou Contes du Temps Passé* was introduced from France in the days of Louis XV that the tales in their present form became established in England, where they represent a blending of the Germanic dwarf-elf type and the Celtic *side* (fairy) lore.[8]

But whatever may be their relation to modern European fairy-tales, stories of the *märchen* type are neither myth nor saga in the true sense of the terms. Unlike the myth, they make no pretence to being "a narrative resurrection of a primeval reality", or an interpretation of natural phenomena, established custom, or of ritual situations and cult practices. Similarly, they are not concerned with historical events adorned with a romantic halo and other additions, as in the case of the saga or legend. The *märchen* aims at nothing more than entertainment, and makes no claim for its episodes having a factual basis. It is enough that it is a good story capable of being well told for the amusement rather than for the edification or instruction of its hearers.

The Legend and Saga

The legend of the saga type, on the other hand, is attached to some specific place or to an historical or pseudo-historical event or incident, such as an ancient sanctuary like Bethel, a city like Troy, a disastrous flood or lost lands (e.g. Lyonesse or Atlantis). Therefore, it is concerned essentially with the past, and is narrated as a record of what is thought to have taken place in time and space. Legends of this nature are founded on the fortunes and exploits of what are believed or represented to have been real people and actual occurrences. Indeed, the Deluge legends in Sumerian, Babylonian and Hebrew tradition in the first instance almost certainly were based upon a local inundation in Mesopotamia in the fourth millennium B.C., traces of which have now been found at Ur and Kish. Similarly, the great cycles of the sagas concerning the siege of Troy and other events in the Heroic Age in Greece and the Troad appear to be associated with the chief centres of the Mycenaean period and their rulers,[9] the traditions having become crystallized under Athenian influence some three or four centuries later. But while in the Homeric poems the political geography and some of the historical occurrences of the Mycenaean Age are accurately reproduced, there are discrepancies and errors of fact in the *Iliad*; for example, such as the disposal of the dead by cremation, the use of the round shield of classical times,[10] and the absence of any reference to the cult of the Mother-goddess so prominent in the Minoan-Mycenaean tradition.

Nevertheless, the actual conflict and siege of Troy, the campaign of the Argive kings against Thebes, and the Minoan domination of the Aegean as the ruling sea-power, provide a historical background to the stories with remarkable fidelity, though the mortal remains of Agamemnon and his household were not interred in the "Treasury of Atreus" at Mycenae as Schliemann imagined, or at Amyclai in Sparta as Pausanias contended.[11] Even the story of Lyonesse, the lost land between Cornwall and the Scilly Isles, has not been without its sup/ porters in South/west Britain, and it is within the bounds of possibility that it arose as a reminiscence of a time when the existing coastline stood farther out than at present.[12] In short, legend is deficient or distorted history containing generally a nucleus of fact with an admixture of later traditional accretions, embellishments and ethnological and other aetiological inter/ pretations, often derived from mythological or romantic and courtly sources, so that gods and national heroes frequently occur side by side in the incidents and adventures narrated.

In the ancient world, as in primitive states of culture at all times, history as the term is understood today had little or no significance because intellectually the human mind was not aware of being in the historical process. It was not until the organic structure and vital rhythm of society began to collapse that an historical perspective developed, as the individual became conscious not only of himself and the community of which he was an integral part, but also of the passage of events in a determinable sequence as a process of becoming. Objec/ tively regarded, history is the sum/total of events, but a mere catalogue of happenings is not history. As the authors of a recent brilliant satire affirmed, "history is what you can remember". But it is manifestly impossible for the historian under any circumstances, ancient or modern, to remember and record all the events in a given series of occurrences, partly because everything that happens cannot be ascertained, and also because it is only events that have some purpose, signifi/ cance and permanent interest that are remembered at all. In other words, history subjectively regarded is the apprehension and interpretation of the things that occur in a series of events that have sufficient interest and importance to remain im/ printed on the corporate memory of the community. This corporate memory may take the form of legend and saga as oral tradition, or as written records and narratives recorded on clay tablets, papyrus, vellum, paper, or any other material suitable for the purpose. But while magical texts or jottings as an aid to memory may have been preserved by accident, or for practical purposes in a ritual context as "words of power", to become part of a permanent tradition in an "historical" sense, events must have an interest and meaning distinct from isolated experiences devoid of any social or corporate content at all, or wider reference in any department of human affairs and natural occurrences.

In myth, legend and saga history is to be found in connexion with the most striking facts of life embodying events of profound significance and of recurrent concern. The sources of written history, in fact, often appear to lie in certain ritual situations of this kind intimately associated with the pressing problems of daily life, together with the military activities and heroic adventures of outstanding personages, the importance of which has been recognized and given permanent record. Such legends frequently have become attached to the cultus and acquired a sociological significance, handed on by carefully prescribed rules from one generation to another. Inasmuch as it has incorporated and perpetuated a corpus of significant events referred back to a remote past, it has acquired what is virtually an historical content, whether recognized as such or not. As the body of tradition has grown in extent and complexity it has embraced a great variety of legendary and mythological lore in which actual happenings are represented in terms of the exploits, adventures and wanderings of gods and heroes, ancestors and fabulous creatures, humans and animals. When stories of this character have been handed on to more sophisticated ages they have become a mixture of legendary history, romance, fantasy and allegory, employed sometimes as the subject-matter of the themes of poets and dramatists; or even as the reflections of philosophers.

THE FUNCTION OF RITUAL
The Cult Legend and the Sacred Drama

As has been considered in some detail in this volume, it was around the figure of the sacral king that a great collection of myths, legends and liturgies took shape in the cult drama in the ancient civilizations of the third and fourth millennia B.C. in the Fertile Crescent, Mesopotamia and Asia Minor, and thence were diffused through the Eastern Mediterranean and the Aegean to the Graeco-Roman world, associated with the names of a variety of divine beings such as Osiris, Tammuz, Aleyan-Baal, Teshub, Dionysos and so on. The persistence and widespread transmission of this cultus is to be explained as the result of culture contact upon a situation calling forth a perpetual tension in the life of agricultural communities dependent upon the weather and the seasons for their means of subsistence. Therefore, under different designations of the divine hero the same sacred drama was re-enacted to regenerate nature at its most vital centre symbolized by the death and revival of the god and his earthly embodiment or servant the king, often accompanied by the queen.

Whether or not the claim to divine descent was based on the alleged fact that certain outstanding men actually were called or regarded as gods during their lifetime, or were deified by posterity after their death, the seasonal drama reflects historical situations and events—i.e. the food-supply, rain, the sun, propagation and stability—around which ritual and its myth developed to secure health, wealth and prosperity in perpetuity. The methods by which these good things were procured in the beginning were reproduced in the sacred actions performed and in the recitation of the creation story as the predominant theme in the cult legend. The myth gave the ritual its intention, and the ritual liberated the life when nature was in urgent need of renewal in the spring, or when its forces were in a state of decline in the autumn.

By setting forth the beginning of things in narrative form as a cult legend the primeval reality was affirmed and translated into action in a set of dramatic performances in order to make supernatural power accessible here and now. The purpose, however, was not to explain the cosmic processes, but to maintain a right relationship with, and to secure the release of, the spiritual forces that controlled them and regulated human affairs. Therefore, in the cult drama the veritably present and effective divine power vouched for in the legend was re-enacted and made accessible in the ritual for the good of the community as a collective experience. To this end the sacred had to possess a form, visibly and audibly, so that ritual and myth were, as they have always been, two facets of the same sacramental activity.

Ritual and Belief

Regarded in this way as the means whereby the secular is brought into a vital relationship with the sacred through the medium of the "uttered rite" in the prescribed cultus, it is difficult in this setting to separate the one from the other, since the actions performed and the story reiterated in confirmation of them are virtually one and the same localization of the sacred in time and space under human conditions. While, as has been considered, there are other types of myth, legend, *märchen* and folk-tale which are independent of any ritual expression or interpretation, especially in the more specialized later developments of mythology, so far as the participation of the sacred in symbolic form is concerned, the ritual myth would seem to be the fundamental mode of its expression. Moreover, for the reasons which have been given,[13] the *dromenon*, "the thing done", rather than the *muthos*, "the words spoken", has constituted the essential and permanent element in this traffic with the supernatural. Beliefs being in a constant state of flux, it has been the more stable rite that has gone on acquiring first this meaning and then that, but always fulfilling its proper function, releasing supra-mundane power and efficacy.

Our modern habit is to look at religion from the side of beliefs rather than from that of rites largely because until comparatively recently almost the only forms of religion studied seriously in Christendom have been those of Christianity and Judaism where ritual has been regarded as important only in connexion with its interpretation.[14] Even among anthropologists the tendency has been for attention to be concentrated on belief as the ultimate source of ritual on the assumption that the latter is but the former put into practice, with the idea of the soul as the basic concept.[15] But, as Robertson Smith pointed out, "the antique religions had for the most part no creed; they consisted entirely of institutions and practices". These were rigidly fixed while the meaning attached to them was extremely vague, the same rite being explained by different people in different ways.[16]

Moreover, rites were connected with myths rather than with dogmas, and invariably were related to ritual and established traditional practices. When, however, a myth became attached to a sanctuary it in its turn frequently produced appropriate rites, as, for example, in the offering of sacrificial oblations to the in-dwelling deity. Nevertheless, generally such secondary myths have constituted a re-interpretation of earlier practices in relation to a particular divine being, as, for instance, when the shrine at Bethel was given a Yahwistic significance and connected with the Jacob tradition. Throughout these adaptations to changing "ownerships" the ritual remained the constant feature while the beliefs were in a state of flux, shifting from one cult legend to another as circumstances required.

Everywhere, it seems, ritual as a product of unreflected habit normally has preceded the development of specific ideas concerning the how and why of what was done. When the activity has been of a purely practical nature the ritual enjoined by custom in process of time has required justification and explanation in terms of a supernatural sanction. Some sacred authority has been needed to account for and consolidate the time-honoured conventions and rigidly observed ritual practices, around which a story has collected and become the key to the dramatic representations of the desires and emotions and social necessities which it has embodied. In this way deities have been assigned special functions, the hierarchy of heaven has been regulated and sometimes divided into two warring camps of opposed factions, and the gods have been represented as the rewarders of virtue and the punishers of vice, however these qualities may have been conceived as the stories have become moralized and systematized.

Whatever the hidden reality of their unrecorded past may

have been, myth and ritual serve to cover certain inconsistencies created by historical events rather than to record and re-enact them exactly. The persons and beings we find in them are what they appear to be on the surface and not symbols of hidden realities. As to any explanatory function of these myths and their associated rites, as Malinowski has pointed out, there is no problem which they cover, no curiosity which they satisfy, no theory which they contain.[17] Thus, the many stories about the manner in which the present order of events came into being, which recur all over the world, are certainly not the result of an innate inquisitiveness regarding the way in which the natural order has arisen any more than they are a poetic creation of fancy, romantic story-telling, or imaginative episodes called into play when abstract ratiocination could go no further. All these are products of a long process of literary development and transformation, and of philosophic specula-tion. While an aetiological element often can be discerned in the genuine myth, the ritual efficacy and sociological function constitute the essential feature of the things done and said in a cultic setting which represents their normal context.

The Ritual Myth

In the great collection of myths and liturgies that recur in the texts belonging especially to the third and second millennia B.C. in the Near East—in Mesopotamia, Egypt, Palestine and Anatolia—and in the Eastern Mediterranean and the Aegean, which have been examined in this volume, the events alleged to have taken place in primeval times are recalled in a myth and re-enacted in a ritual to renew the processes of fertility and to stabilize society in relation to the transcendental sacred powers believed to be ultimately responsible for the right ordering of life on earth in its various phases and aspects. The same methods are employed and often the same words are repeated as those supposed to have been used by the original divine creators or transformers in the formative period of the world's history to release their potency by recapitulation. The victory of the beneficent forces at the threshold of creation is set forth and enacted in terms of a primordial struggle between the gods involving not infrequently the death of the divine hero at the hands of a supernatural adversary, the suffering god finding a counterpart in the mourning goddess. Both were known by many names and epithets, but they fulfilled the same essential rôles in the ritual and myth, giving expression to the anxiety inherent in an uncertain physical environment and human situation, and at the same time to the latent power of revival as evidenced by the renewal of nature in the spring interpreted in terms of the marriage of the Mother-goddess to the liberated god.

In the dramatization of the myth and ritual at the Annual Festival, lamentation, a sacred combat, the humiliation and restoration of the king and his ceremonial intercourse with the queen amid general rejoicing, frequently recurred symbolizing the yearly decay and revival of vegetation. In the Babylonian version of the Sumerian observance the *Enuma elish* in the cuneiform texts of the eighth century B.C. had undergone a good deal of revision by the Babylonian priests to bring it into line with the story and significance of Marduk. Its main theme and ritual presentation, however, remained essentially unchanged as an integral part of the seasonal drama the ceremonial of which went back at least to the time of Sargon (*c.* 2500 B.C.). At the Babylonian Festival the renewal was effected by the recital of the victory of Marduk over the powers of chaos at the beginning of time, and the accompanying rites, in the same manner as the earlier rebirth of Tammuz or Dumuzi, revived natural life. Similarly, Ashur replaced Marduk and Zu Tiamat, the leader of the forces of evil, when Assyria dominated Babylon; unless Zu was introduced into the story at an earlier stage in its development, since he was also the opponent of Ninurta, the son of Enlil, before Marduk was assigned the principal rôle.[18]

The variations in personnel, however, did not alter the purpose and significance of the observance which arose out of the seasonal situation before the myth was given any definite form, and was adapted to the particular needs and conditions of its specific environment. In Egypt the New Year celebrations were co-ordinated with the orderly fructifying waters of the Nile, whereas in Mesopotamia they gave expression to the dubious and hazardous behaviour of the rains and the rivers at the end of winter and in late autumn when the waters had seceded from the fields in the devastating heat and drought of summer. It was at these two critical turning-points in Nisan and Tishri that the great *rite de passage* was held to secure the deliverance of "the faithful son of the waters" (Dumuzi) from his captivity in the mountain of the nether regions, and by his liberation effecting the transition from death to life, transforming lamentation into jubilation.

Under the unstable conditions that prevailed in Mesopotamia the powers and functions of particular deities waxed and waned with local circumstances and political events so that the pantheon was in a constant state of flux. Marduk rose to pre-eminence at the expense of Enlil when the centre of jurisdiction passed from Nippur to Babylon, until with the rise of Assyrian domination he was in great measure overshadowed by Ashur. Each and every god was at the mercy of the fortunes of his cult-centre and lacked the stabilizing influence of a throne securely occupied by a single Pharaoh of heavenly birth reigning as a living Horus. Moreover, the sun from being the source of life and beneficence, the celestial father of the reigning monarch, was as devastating as the Tigris and Euphrates when they were in full flood. Therefore, the Mesopotamian cult-legend was subject to continual variation, and its principal god was a complex figure with peculiarities of his own which differentiated him from other comparable divinities elsewhere in the Fertile Crescent and in the Aegean.

The relation of Tammuz to Ishtar, for instance, was quite different from that of Osiris to Isis. While the Babylonian suffering god was a virile figure and never a dead god like Osiris, he was, nevertheless, inseparable from and dependent upon the sorrowing Goddess who embodied the permanent element in nature, whereas Tammuz represented the impermanent succession of the seasons and the reproductive power of nature. Osiris, on the other hand, although he was the progenitor *par excellence* and after his death begot Horus, yet he himself remained the dead god, ruling the *Duat* and judging its denizens. So firmly established was this aspect of the Osirian faith that even after his kingdom had been solarized under Heliopolitan influence its chthonian characteristics survived. As the son of Geb, the Earth-god, and Nut, the Sky-goddess, Osiris was brought into relation with the annual rebirth of nature, and it was his resurrection effected by Thoth rather than his death on which the ritual emphasis was laid.

As the generative force in the soil[19] he was the god of resurrection manifest in the sprouting vegetation, especially the barley, spelt, wheat and grain. Therefore, though he was essentially a dead king he personified the annual ebb and flow of vegetation, and his death was so transfigured that it became the vitalizing force in nature reflected in the seasonal sequence and the vicissitudes of the Nile. It was this perpetual dying to come to life again that was celebrated and enacted in the two great festivals of autumn and spring when the inundation receded after the harvest and in due course reappeared renewing the face of the earth with verdure. In all the symbolism, ritual and drama that adorned these celebrations the death and resurrection of Osiris was the central theme regarded as two aspects of a single event, represented realistically with the lamentation and exultation appropriate to the occasion. Eventually it was embodied in the Mysteries of the Ptolemaic and Graeco-Roman periods when Isis became the Saviour-goddess, and the rites were then calculated to confer immortality on those who were initiated into them.

If the Osiris cult originally came from Western Asia, the vegetation tradition persisted in a ritual which was little changed in its essential purpose and mythological guise in its adaptation to the environmental conditions of the Nile valley and its Delta, notwithstanding the contrast between Osiris and his Asiatic counterparts. In each region the local characteristics of the ritual myth were preserved, but the fundamental theme remained intact in spite of the climatic vagaries and the differing physical features because behind it lay the same recurrent rhythm in nature. In Western Asia and the Aegean, where the Great Mother was regarded as the source of all life, the annual decline was attributed to the loss of her son (Tammuz, Adonis, Attis) or daughter (Persephone), while in Egypt Osiris being the progenitor, it was his death that was bewailed by his sister-spouse Isis when the Nile was at its lowest.

Similarly, the revival of vegetation was equated with the restoration of the young god, or the resurrection of the dead king, throughout the ancient world. In Mesopotamia and Egypt he was the husband of the Goddess and their nuptials were celebrated annually by their earthly counterparts, the king and the queen, to revive and renew the processes of fertility everywhere. In the Levant, on the other hand, the maiden daughter of the sorrowing mother, abducted while gathering flowers in the Eleusinian meadows, was the personification of the transience of spring, withering in the heat of summer before it came to full fruition. In Syria and Asia Minor Adonis "died ere his prime", and Attis was emasculated, leaving the Goddess the sole source of life and generation like Osiris in the Egyptian ritual myth. But in spite of all these variations in the office and function of the principal figures in the cult drama, the mourning and search of the Goddess remained a constant feature reflecting the withering of vegetation.

Liturgies and Ritual Texts

This found its clearest expression in the Mesopotamian Tammuz liturgies and its Annual Festival because in the Euphrates valley the suffering Shepherd-god was essentially a virile generative force—the "resurrected child" of the Goddess—restoring fecundity as the new life springs forth after the rains, and defeating the powers of Chaos in the perennial struggle between life and death, growth and decline. Therefore, the incarceration of Tammuz or Dumuzi was celebrated with bitter lamentation and wailing and the singing of dirges over the effigy of the dead god when the scorched earth seemed to threaten a return of the desolation that befell nature, the people, the city and its temple, when Ishtar wandered in barren fields and empty sheepfolds during her sorrowful search for Tammuz in the underworld. In the laments of the priests and people the cry of the suffering Shepherd-god echoed until he was released by the Goddess and restored to the upper world. Then sorrow was turned into joy and defeat into victory, celebrated by a royal banquet furnished with gifts from deified kings (e.g. Ur-Nammu, Pur-Sin) offered to Ishtar to rejoice her heart, ending with a doxology addressed to the reunited gods in the bridal chamber for their bestowal of renewed life, vigour and prosperity.

In the Ras Shamra ritual texts, as we have seen, the same central theme of a struggle between life and death in nature and the measures taken to secure the renewal of the beneficent forces of fertility at their ultimate source recurs in the Anat-Baal cycle. Here, again, as Pedersen says, "we have to do with a cult drama which offers at once a myth and ritual, what happens in the cult being identical with what happened in the divine primeval times or eternity".[20] Thus, although the myths were composed in poetical form as epics, as Virolleaud has contended,[21] their nature and function can hardly have been other than that of liturgical rituals to ensure the renewal and continuance of the fructifying forces in nature, celebrated by priests and priestesses in their official capacities.[22] Since the mythological interlude in the Nikkal-Kotarot text in the Ugaritic series describing the wooing of the Moon-goddess Nikkal by the Moon-god Y-r-h was recited at sunset it may have been a wedding-song, as Gaster suggests,[23] leading up to the nuptial rite which was performed in the presence of the Moon-god, who like the k-s-r-t, the daughters of the New Moon, was propitious at weddings and childbirth, as is shown in the myth of Aqhat.[24]

Therefore, although the Ras Shamra texts are very difficult to interpret in their present condition, it would seem that they contain a Canaanite version of the Tammuz ritual myth in which the hero Aleyan-Baal was lord of the rain and verdure whose descent into the underworld symbolized the decline in the processes of vegetation. As in Mesopotamia, their revival was associated with his subsequent liberation and a sacred marriage ritual to promote fertility in nature and mankind recorded in the form of liturgical texts recited or sung in the temples in Ugarit dedicated to Baal and his father, Dagon. There amid stone phalli, female figurines and plaques, representations of animal masks worn by priests, and bulls' horns,[25] the cult drama was celebrated in the prescribed manner, the texts explaining the actions performed.

In a liturgy the spoken words and the "manual acts" are dependent one upon the other and indissolubly bound together. When the text acquires a theological and literary character of its own in process of interpretation of the rite it then develops into a cult legend, the narrative often becoming divorced from its original ritual setting. Thus, in the Anatolian Telipinu myth,[26] while the succession of ceremonial acts to be performed during its liturgical recitation are included in the text more or less in the form of rubrics, the story of the vanished young vegetation god and the attempt to make him return by ritual and persuasive methods is set forth in narrative form with a break for the cultic performances and incantations. Having accomplished their purpose in making Telipinu abandon his anger and return to his temple, the myth continues relating how he thereupon again took thought for the land, released it from blight, restored fertility and provided the king and queen with enduring life and vigour.

In this combination of ritual and narrative we have an instructive example of a liturgical text exercising its dual function in the cult drama and in mythology. Arising within the context of a particular ritual for specific purposes, the story takes its shape first as the cult legend and then expanded into a confused narrative it loses much of its original meaning and significance. Thus, within the general theme there are several versions which cannot be easily related to one another, and yet they belong to the same group of texts centred in the missing god. They are all concerned with a state of blight that descended upon the earth when the god of agriculture vanished in a temper, and with the efforts made to induce him to resume his beneficent offices. As literature the stories have little merit because they were compiled in the first instance as seasonal rituals and invocations for liturgical purposes to restore and renew vitality at the turn of the year. Therefore, it was the dramatization of the prescribed ritual that mattered, since it was the performance of the sacred actions which determined the course of events. But around this situation the literary texts took their form and content which often assumed a character of their own, bearing little or no relation to the cult drama in which they arose.

Greek drama?

The Literary Legends and the Ritual Myth

This becomes most apparent in Greek mythology where the literary myth and legends very frequently ceased to be cultic in any real sense at all, as they were recorded by the classical writers in their poems, dramas, histories and orations of the glories and activities of the cities and heroes of Hellas; of Agamemnon, the legendary founder of Mycenae, of Perseus, the son of Danae who reigned over Tiryns, of Minos who ruled the waves from Crete, and of Zeus, the father of gods and men exercising his universal sway as the head of the Olympian pantheon. All the great heroic cycles of Greek saga, in fact, were connected with the Minoan-Mycenaean sites, while the Homeric circle of the twelve gods was centred in the sacred mountain, as was Yahweh in Horeb or Sinai in Hebrew tradition. The invading Hellenes brought with them a complex mythology in which Zeus, the Sky- and Weather-god, was purely Hellenic, while other aspects (e.g. the Hesiodic theogony of Ouranus and Kronos) reveal Anatolian influences (e.g. the Hittite myth of Kumarbi[27]). The Gilgamesh epic, again, was translated into Hurrian and Hittite and fragments of it may have been rendered into Greek.

The literary myth, however, at this stage of its development frequently had little or no connexion with any specific rite, either as a direct expression of the ritual itself or as an explanation of the actions performed. Outstanding events like the

Trojan war were made the basis of the Homeric immortal stories that have been discussed to extol the achievements of the heroes of the Peloponnesian expedition. Many of these literary traditions have now been confirmed by archaeological research, notably at Mycenae,[28] and placed in an historical setting which goes back to the Early Helladic period (c. 2500–2100 B.C.) at the beginning of the Bronze Age, long before the traditional founding of the city by Perseus in the first half of the fourteenth century (c. 1340 B.C.). But it is manifestly impossible to determine by excavation the accuracy of the traditions concerning the legendary kings and heroes of Mycenae and Argos, and the various episodes in the Trojan War in the *Iliad* and the *Odyssey*, or the chronology of the *Marmor Parium*.

The mass of literary material current in the Homeric Age was transformed into remarkable tales in which gods and men freely intermingled and behaved very much as people did behave in those days long after the events narrated could have occurred. The heroic deeds of former times served the purposes of the stories and delighted the audiences who listened to them. They were accepted and enjoyed as Shakespeare is accepted and appreciated today as a literary genius. They were not, however, ritual myths any more than they were true history, being devoid of any serious practical significance in the economy of daily life and in the vital concerns of the community. Essentially they were artistic creations like the representations of the Olympian gods by the Greek sculptors. In so far as an historical situation lay behind them, the reality of the literary narratives was confined to what was alleged to have happened in the legendary past, in which fact and romance were intermingled, rather than to a recurrent ritual situation in the rhythm of nature.

Myth, Ritual and Reality

Much the same applies to the patriarchal narratives in the book of Genesis in Hebrew tradition. This collection of short stories grouped round sacred places and characters having particular names and pursuing a way of life which remained essentially unchanged for generations gives an accurate description of the manners and customs of cattle-rearers and breeders of sheep and goats in the pastoral region of and adjoining Palestine. More-over, the narratives seem to contain a few references to historical personages and events going back to the third millennium B.C. But the principal motif was to explain the rivalries between the settled Israelites and their nomadic neighbours (e.g. the stories of Isaac and Ishmael, of Jacob and Esau), the causes and extent of tribal migrations (e.g. Abraham's migration from Ur to Palestine), and the way in which local sanctuaries and their cultus were established (Bethel, Shechem, Hebron, Beersheba, etc.). In all this doubtless reminiscences of actual events and historical conditions and situations were incorporated and handed on from one generation to another by oral tradition until they were recorded in narratives which, if they do not reach the literary heights of the Homeric poems, afford a singularly vivid and accurate picture of the general conditions they purport to describe, notwithstanding an ever-present halo of romance, documentary inconsistencies and defective chrono-logy. The same story is told of different persons and different accounts are given of the same event. If Abraham may have been an historical character, in the Jacob narratives unquestion-ably an ethnological motif predominates, tribal relationships and rivalries having been represented in terms of individual adventures of the eponymous ancestor of Israel. Similarly, the amalgamation of clans has been described in terms of matri-monial alliances. But that the patriarchs originally were gods who were transformed in course of time into the ancestors of clans by their worshippers is as improbable as the fantastic suggestion that Abraham was a manifestation of the Moon-god in an astral mythology.

Nevertheless, while the narratives would appear to contain an historical element in relation to tribal conditions and possibly occasionally to actual persons, they are historical only in the sense of being the record of certain significant episodes in the life of the nation long before the period in which they are alleged to have taken place. So far from being contemporary records, an interval of a thousand or fifteen hundred years separates them from the actual events described. Each story has its own independent existence and was drawn up for its particular purpose, ethnological or religious. Therefore, to discover the point of interest and its significance in the composite narratives as a whole, each story has to be examined and evaluated as a separate entity in detachment from the general tradition in its final form.

The function of myth and ritual, however, is not to chronicle past events so much as to enable a community to deal effectively with the practical issues which press upon it daily in the serious business of living, often in a precarious and unpredictable environment. The origin of the stories and of the sacred actions with which frequently they are intimately associated, often can be traced back to historical situations and perplexing and critical occurrences; the aim being to give stability to the social structure and to establish a state of equilibrium between man and nature and the sacred order upon which human welfare is believed to depend. Therefore, myth and ritual express the most deeply rooted hopes, fears and emotions of a community concerning the practical and urgent problems of daily life, physical and spiritual. In primitive society, both ancient and modern, attention is concentrated upon ways and means of maintaining the food-supply by ensuring the continuance of the processes of nature in their regular succession, and of all things upon which life depends (i.e. rain, the sun, the seasons and human effort and ingenuity) and which make for health, wealth and prosperity in perpetuity, and for harmony, security and solidarity in society. The methods by which these ends were procured in the beginning are reproduced in the sacred actions performed and the tales told to confer the object of universal desire, namely, life in ever-increasing fullness and abundance. The myth gives the ritual its intention, and the ritual liberates the life when nature requires renewal. In this way an historical situation is as it were brought up to date as an ever-recurrent reality, the essential truth and significance of which is made efficacious through the repetition of the ritual in relation to concrete events. Not only is the emotional tension relieved but a new hope is engendeied in respect of vital human needs extending from the periodic crises in the earthly career of the individual from the cradle to the grave, and their counterparts in nature, to the assurance of eternal bliss when the final transition has been effected.

Since these are universal requirements and reactions of every-day occurrence and experience, that they have tended to assume a common pattern in their varying modes of myth and ritual expression is what is to be expected. This has been particularly apparent in the Ancient Near East, where from the middle of the fourth to the middle of the first millennium B.C. they took shape under similar conditions with certain determining and differentiating features, and where culture contact was inevitable. While in recent years these similarities doubtless have been over-emphasized sometimes to the neglect of their differences,[29] yet the fact remains, as the foregoing inquiry has demonstrated, that a clearly defined body of beliefs and practices became associated with the Annual Festival as an integral part of the seasonal cult drama with the same under-lying purpose and significance, notwithstanding diversities in the presentation of the theme.

Thus, although the status and office of the Pharaoh in Egypt were very different from those of the Mesopotamian kings with their restricted sovereignty and mortal nature, and dependence upon the Goddess in the exercise of their regenerative functions in the rôle of her bridegroom, the sacral kingship, nevertheless, occupied a central position in the myth and ritual. If in Asia Minor monarchs were not divine in their own right by virtue of their direct descent from the gods as in the Nile valley, they were cult figures, and the persistence and widespread develop-ment and diffusion of the cultus is to be explained as a result of adaptation to the physical environment coupled with culture contact upon a situation calling forth a perpetual emotional tension in the life of communities dependent upon water, the weather and the seasons for their means of subsistence.

Myth, in short, gave expression to the fundamental experi‑
ence of a divinely ordered world in which a conflict of
supernatural powers and forces was immanent, the one hostile
and the other beneficial to their well‑being. To fulfil its proper
functions it must always be a symbolic representation of the
Ultimate Reality, however this may be conceived and inter‑
preted, concerning the essential meaning and facts of existence
and of human destinies. Its imagery is "nothing less than a
carefully chosen cloak for abstract thought", representing the
form in which the experience has become conscious.[30] En‑
shrined in it are the deepest realities, the things by which men
live. These are at once material, dealing with the food‑supply,
the cycle of birth and death in nature and man; spiritual,
relating to the divine ordering of the universe and its processes;
and ethical, formulating compelling reasons for human
conduct and the regulation of society. It is a reality lived.
Consequently, every vital religion must have its mythology
because myth is the natural language of religion just as ritual
is its dramatization in worship.

It is true that in the more advanced religions the fantastic
elements and frivolous imagination, such as characterize fable
and fairy‑tale and sometimes saga and legend, usually have
been eliminated in their myths, or transformed into symbolical
allegories or fantasies. With the development of rational thought
and empirical knowledge the control of nature by magico‑
religious ritual techniques has been abandoned and has lost its
former significance. Nevertheless, mythological thinking re‑
mains applicable to certain aspects of reality, or of human
experience; as, for example, in the determination of man's
spiritual relation to the universe and the apprehension of a
fundamental divine order as its ultimate ground, which can
be formulated, presented and expressed only in the language
of myth. Myth, then, reveals an aspect of reality about the
whole of which human experience is a part. Moreover, once
such transcendental apprehensions become a conviction they
acquire a sense of finality which gives them an absolute
authority. Therefore, in the last analysis myth and ritual derive

their validity from their own order of reality, and it is in this sphere that they have to justify their claims, verifiable at the threefold bar of history, reason and spiritual experience.

Behind all genuine religious experience and symbolization there must be transcendental reality, but since representation is necessarily selective in character, the underlying truth is conditioned by its medium and mode of expression. Myth does not embody historical truth in the sense of being an accurate description of a particular course of events in the precise manner in which they actually occurred in time and space, though it may be doubtful whether events which are expressed mythologically have any meaning unless they have a background in the historical process. For instance, unless the universe has a beginning in time any interpretation or explanation of its temporal origins must be devoid of meaning. But once this initial fact is granted its precise mode of occurrence can be described mythologically for specific purposes in accordance with current ideas, however erroneous these may be in respect of what actually happened in history.

This kind of discrepancy may discredit the myth as an historical statement of fact, but as Bultmann says, the real purpose of myth "is not to present an objective picture of the world as it is, but to express man's understanding of himself—the world in which he lives".[31] It is the application of human values to non-human phenomena. At a deeper level of experience there are recurrent situations of profound emotional and spiritual significance which can only find expression in symbolical representation. For this purpose myth and ritual often are the most adequate and efficacious ways of setting forth fundamental realities and values, since it is their primary function to communicate transcendental beliefs and concepts in their own particular mode of presentation.

Mythology may also take the form of imaginative and aetiological stories as told by Plato to elucidate abstract metaphysical problems, or by the ancient Hebrew narrators to explain the origin and significance of places, events and spiritual realities in their sacred tradition. But since the ritual control of the primary needs of the human race appears to be in fact older and more fundamental than curiosity, speculative thought and aetiological interpretation, the original function of myth would seem to have been to afford a reason for or assign a purpose to the performance of a rite as a living reality rather than to impart knowledge or explanation. As Aldous Huxley says, "whether we like it or not, we are amphibians, living simultaneously in the world of experience and in the world of notions, God and ourselves, and the world of abstract, verbalized knowledge about these primary facts. Our business as human beings is to make the best of both these worlds."[32]

Myth and ritual belong to the same order of reality as poetry, art and music. Each according to its own technique externalizes and expresses a feeling, a mood, an inner quality of life, an emotional impulse and interpretation of reality. Art is not an attempt to reproduce or imitate nature, to tell a story, to explain phenomena, or to convey and present knowledge in the scientific and philosophic manner in concepts and logical propositions. It is the objectification of invisible qualities and values—an interpretation of Reality as a personal impression or experience in relation to a particular object or abstract rhythm, dictated by inspiration and controlled by expert craftsmanship. So myth and ritual give verbal and symbolic form and meaning to the emotional urge and rhythmic relations of life as a living reality, recounting and enacting events on which the very existence of mankind has been believed to depend, and proclaiming and making efficacious an aspect and an apprehension of truth and reality transcending historical occurrences and empirical reasoning and cosmological and eschatological speculations.

NOTES

CHAPTER I

1. *Lectures on the Science of Religion,* 1873, pp. 118ff., 353ff.; *Contributions to the Science of Mythology,* 1897, vol. i, pp. 68f.
2. *An Essay on Man,* 1945, p. 110.
3. *Primitive Culture,* 1903, vol. i, p. 35.
4. *Custom and Myth,* 1904, pp. 25f.
5. Tylor, *Researches into the Early History of Mankind,* 1865, pp. 3, 5, 325.
6. *G.B.,* pt. i, pp. 220ff.; Hegel, *The Philosophy of Religion,* 1895, vol. i, pp. 290ff.
7. *G.B.,* pt. ix., pp. 374, 385.
8. *G.B.,* pt. x, p. 105.
9. *Myth in Primitive Psychology,* 1926, pp. 21ff.
10. *Faith, Hope and Charity in Primitive Religion,* 1932, p. 106.
11. Tylor, *J.R.A.I.,* xviii, 1889, p. 245.
12. *Man,* vol. l, 1950, p. 121.
13. *Op. cit.,* p. 121.
14. *Myth in Primitive Psychology,* 1926, p. 21.
15. *The Formation of the Alphabet,* British School of Archaeology in Egypt, 1912, vol. iii, p. 7.
16. Breuil, Obermaier and Alcalde del Rio, *La Pasiega a Puente Viesgo,* Monaco, 1913.
17. *Quatre cents siècles d'art pariétal,* 1954, pp. 131, 134f.
18. Windels, *The Lascaux Cave Paintings,* 1949; Brodrick, *Lascaux: A Commentary,* 1948.
19. Cartailhac and Breuil, *L'Anthrop.,* xix, 1908, pp. 15ff.; Breuil, *Bull. de la soc. préhist. de l'Ariège,* 1950, pp. 26, fig. 22.
20. Bégouen, *C.R. Acad. Inscrip.,* 1923, p. 14; Breuil, *Quatre cents siècles d'art pariétal,* 1954, pp. 236ff.
21. *La Grotte-Temple du Peche-Merle,* Paris, 1929, p. 183.
22. *L'Anthrop.,* xxxiii, 1912, pp. 657ff.; *C.R. Acad. Inscrip.,* 1912, pp. 532ff.
23. Bégouen, *Antiquity,* iii, 1929, p. 17.
24. *Quatre cents siècles d'art pariétal,* 1954, p. 176.
25. *La Caverne d'Altamira,* Monaco, 1909, p. 139.
26. *Elementary Forms of the Religious Life,* 1913, pp. 47, 206.
27. G. Lalanne, *L'Anthrop.,* xxii, 1911, pp. 257ff.; xxiii, 1912, pp. 129ff., 143; Burkitt, *Eurasia Septentrionalis Antique,* ix, Helsinki, 1934, pp. 113ff.; L. Passemard, *Les statuettes féminines dites Vénus stéatopyges,* Nîmes, 1938, pl. ii, fig. 8, pl. iii; Luquet, *Art and Religion of Fossil Man,* 1930, pp. 16, 85, 110.

28. Capitan, *Les Combarelles aux Eyzies*, 1924, pl. vi.

29. Saint-Périer, *L'Anthrop.*, xxxii, 1922, p. 356; xxxiv, 1924, pp. 346ff.; Salmony, *I.P.E.K.*, vii, 1931.

30. Cf. Didon, *Bull. de la soc. hist. et archéol. du Périgord, 1911*, pl. vi, no. 28; Boule, *Les Hommes Fossiles,* 2nd ed., 1923, p. 266.

31. *Dating the Past,* 1953, pp. 274ff.

32. For a further discussion of the evidence cf. James, *Prehistoric Religion*, 1957, chap. i.

33. Obermaier, *Fossil Man in Spain*, 1925, pp. 136ff.

34. Blanc, *Accad. Naz. dei Lincei*, 1939, p. 205.

35. R. R. Schmidt, *Die diluviale Vorzeit Deutschlands*, Stuttgart, 1912.

36. Hauser and Klaatsch, *Archiv. für Anthropol.*, vii, 1909, p. 290.

37. A. and J. Bouyssonie and L. Bardon, *L'Anthrop.*, xix, 1908, p. 513; xxiv, 1913, pp. 616ff.

38. Breuil, *L'Anthrop.*, xxxi, 1913, pp. 343ff.; Capitan and Peyrony, *Revue anthrop.*, xxii, 1912, p. 29.

39. Verneau, *Les Grottes de Grimaldi*, 1906, vol. i, pp. 64ff.; vol. ii, pp. 23, 260, 277ff.

40. *Op. cit.,* vol. ii, pp. 298ff.

41. *Op. cit.,* vol. ii, pp. 33, 298.

42. *Comptes-Rendus de l'Acad. des Sciences*, lxxiv, 1872, pp. 1060f.

43. James, *Prehistoric Religion*, 1957, pp. 153ff.

44. Cf. chap. iii, pp. 84f.

45. Sethe, *Die altaegyptischen Pyramidentexte*, Leipzig, 1908–22; Mercer, *P.T.*, 1952, vols. i–iv.

46. *De Iside et Osiride.*

47. *P.T.*, 721.

48. *P.T., 2092.*

49. Cf. *G.B.*, pt. iv (vol. ii), pp. 160f.

50. *P.T.*, 699, 1019, 1524.

51. Blackman, *Analecta Orientalia*, xvii, 1938, p. 2; Davies and Gardiner, *The Tomb of Amenemhet*, 1915, p. 115.

52. Frankfort, *Kingship and the Gods*, 1948, pp. 123ff.

53. Blackman, *op. cit.*, p. 2.

54. Brugsch, *Religion und Mythologie der alten Aegypter*, Leipzig, 1885, p. 621.

55. Breasted, *Development of Religion and Thought in Ancient Egypt*, 1914, p. 23.

56. *P.T.*, 25, 589, 767, 848, 1553, 2111.

57. Brit. Mus. Stelae, nos. 797, 19, 62.

58. *P.T., 589.*

59. *P.T., 507f.*, 388.

60. Cf. Falkenstein, *Antiquity*, x, 1936, p. 137.

61. Heidel, *The Gilgamesh Epic and Old Testament Parallels,* 1949; R. Campbell Thompson, *The Epic of Gilgamesh*, 1928; Speiser, *Ancient Near Eastern Texts*, Princeton, 1950; S. N. Kramer, *Sumerian Mythology*, Philadelphia, 1944.

62. Tablet XI.

63. Chap. ii, p. 56.

64. Heidel, *op. cit.*, pp. 207 ff.

65. Woolley, *Excavations at Ur*, 1954, pp. 57 ff.

66. T. Jacobsen, *The Intellectual Adventure of Ancient Man*, Chicago, 1946, pp. 126 ff.

67. Gordon, *Ugaritic Handbook*, 1947; *Ugaritic Literature*, 1949; R. de Laughe, *Les Textes de Ras Shamra-Ugarit*, Paris, 1945; T. H. Gaster, *Thespis*, 1950; G. R. Driver, *Canaanite Myths and Legends*, 1956.

68. *Scripta Minoa*, 1909, vol. i, pp. 68 ff.; cf. vol. ii, ed. by Myres, 1952, pp. 8 ff.; Myres, *Antiquity*, xxvii, June 1953, pp. 105 f.; Dikaios, *Antiquity*, xxvii, 1953, pp. 233 ff.

69. *Scripta Minoa*, 1909, vol. ii, p. 40; Emmett and Bennett, *The Pylos Tablets*, Princeton, 1951.

70. *J.H.S.*, lxxiii, 1953, pp. 84 ff.; *Antiquity*, xxvii, 1953, pp. 196 ff.; *Documents in Mycenaean Greek*, Cambridge, 1956, pp. 21 ff., for a detailed description of the script and the contents of the tablets. For Linear A, see C. H. Gordon, *Antiquity*, 1957, pp. 124 ff.

71. Dikaios, *Antiquity*, xxvii, 1953, pp. 233 ff.; Myres, *Antiquity*, xxvii, 1953, p. 105; Ventris and Chadwick, *Documents in Mycenaean Greek*, pp. 60 ff.

72. The premature death of Dr Ventris in September 1956 as the result of a motor accident is a tragedy at the beginning of this important decipherment.

73. Ventris and Chadwick, *op. cit.,* p. 110.

74. Ventris and Chadwick, *op. cit.,* pp. 125 ff.; Chadwick, *Antiquity*, xxxi, 1953, pp. 198 f.

75. Nilsson, *The Minoan-Mycenaean Religion*, 1927, pp. 368 ff.; Evans, *Palace of Minos*, 1921, vol. i, pp. 368 ff.

76. Ventris and Chadwick, *op. cit.,* pp. 284 ff.

77. Meriggi, *Glotta*, xxxiv, 1954, pp. 22 ff.; Furumark, *Eranos*, li, 1954, pp. 103 ff.

CHAPTER II

1. Cf. chap. i, pp. 41 f.

2. Spencer and Gillen, *Native Tribes of Central Australia*, 1938, pp. 171 ff., 614 ff.; *Northern Tribes of Central Australia*, 1904, pp. 436 ff.

3. Brugsch, *Zeitschrift für aegypt. Sprache und Altertumskunde*, xix, 1881, pp. 71–111; Loret, *Recueil de travaux relatifs à la philologie et archéologie égyptiennes et assyriennes*, iii, 1882, pp. 43 ff.; iv, 1883, pp. 21 ff.; v, 1884, pp. 85 ff.; Gardiner, *J.E.A.*, ii, 1915, p. 123.

4. Brugsch, *Thesaurus*, 1891, p. 1190; Blackman, *Myth and Ritual*, Oxford, 1933, p. 22, fig. 4.

5. M. A. Murray, *The Osireion at Abydos*, 1904, p. 28.

6. *J.E.A.*, ii, 1915, p. 124.

7. Sethe, *Urkunden des aegyptischen Altertums*, Leipzig, 1908, vol. iv, p. 134.

8. Brugsch, *Religion und Mythologie der alten Aegypter,* Leipzig, 1885–8, p. 621; Loret, *Recueil de travaux . . .,* iii, 1882, pp. 43 ff.; iv, pp. 21 ff.; v, pp. 85 ff.

9. Gardiner and Davies, *The Tomb of Amenembet,* 1915, p. 115; G.B., pt. iv, vol. ii, pp. 90 f.

10. Frankfort, *Kingship and the Gods,* 1948, pp. 123 ff.

11. Blackman, "Studia Aegyptica", *Analecta Orientalia,* xvii, 1938, p. 2.

12. Gauthier, *Les fêtes du dieu Min,* 1931, pp. 194, 235.

13. Quibell and Petrie, *Hierakonpolis,* pt. i, 1900, p. 9, pl. xxvi C.4.

14. G. A. Wainwright, *The Sky-Religion in Egypt,* 1938, p. 18, n. 3.

15. Petrie, *The Making of Egypt,* 1939, p. 46.

16. Frankfort, *Kingship and the Gods,* 1948, p. 188.

17. Erman and Blackman, *The Literature of the Ancient Egyptians,* 1927, p. 137.

18. *J.E.A.,* ii, 1915, p. 125.

19. Moret, *Du caractère religieux de la royauté pharaonique,* Paris, 1902, pp. 104 f.

20. Frankfort, *op. cit.,* p. 190.

21. Frankfort, *The Intellectual Adventure of Ancient Man,* 1946, p. 23.

22. Cf. chap. iii, pp. 88 f.

23. Ezek. viii, 14; Langdon, *Tammuz and Ishtar,* 1914, pp. 11, 14 f.; *Analecta Orientalia,* x, 1935, pp. vi f.; Moorgate, *Tammuz,* 1949, pp. 81 ff.

24. Cf. chap. iv, pp. 115 f.

25. Frankfort, *Cylinder Seals,* 1939, p. 117, pl. xix a–d; xx g; xxi a.

26. Langdon, *Tammuz and Ishtar,* 1914, pp. 10 f., 20.

27. Zimmern, *Der alte Orient,* xxv, 1926, p. 18.

28. Pallis, *The Babylonian Akitu Festival,* 1926, pp. 124 ff., 173; Delitzsch, *Mitteilungen der deutschen Orient Gesellschaft,* no. 33, 1907, p. 34; cf. no. 38, 1908, p. 19.

29. Pallis, *op. cit.,* p. 198.

30. Pallis, *op. cit.,* p. 109; S. Smith, *J.R.A.S.,* 1928, pp. 849 ff.; Tallqvist, *Sumerisch-akkadische Namen der Totenwelt,* Helsinfors, 1914, p. 26, n. 4.

31. Gaster, *Thespis,* 1950, pp. 57 ff.; Driver, *Canaanite Myths and Legends,* 1956, pp. 11 ff.; Virolleaud, *Syria,* xiii, 1932, pp. 113 ff.

32. Virolleaud, *Syria,* xv, 1935, pp. 29–45; xvii, 1936, pp. 150–73; Driver, *op. cit.,* pp. 73 ff.

33. Chap. iv, pp. 123 f.

34. Figs and grapes, for instance, ripened at the height of summer.

35. Gordon, *Ugaritic Literature,* 1949, pp. 3 ff.; *Antiquity,* xxviii, 1954, pp. 186 ff.; *Baal-Anat Cycle,* 67, II. 5–6.

36. Kapelrud, *Baal in the Ras Shamra Texts,* 1952, pp. 120 ff.

37. *Legend of Aqht,* 1, 44–6.

38. Gen. xli. 27 ff.

39. 1 Kings xviii. 19 ff.

40. Judges xviii.

41. Judges xvii–xviii; 1 Sam. xix. 13 ff., xxi, 9 f.

42. Jer. vii. 18; xliv. 15–25; Ezek. viii. 14.
43. Hos. ix. 10; Amos v. 21, 25; Jer. vii. 22f.
44. K. Marti, *Jahwe und seine Auffassung in der altesten Zeit*, Gotha, 1908, p. 322; Albright, *Archaeology and the Religion of Israel*, 1946, p. 64; Albright, *Journal of Biblical Literature*, lxvii, 1948, p. 380.
45. Luckenbill, *American Journal of Theology*, xxii, 1918, pp. 24ff.; Driver, *Zeitschrift für die alttestamentliche Wissenschaft*, xlvi, 1928, pp. 7ff.
46. Exod. iii. 13–15; vi. 2f.; cf. Meek, *Hebrew Origins*, 1950, pp. 93ff.
47. Gen. ii. 4–25, iv. 26.
48. *From Joseph to Joshua*, 1950, p. 144.
49. Hos. ii. 5, 8.
50. Isa. xxviii. 23ff.
51. 2 Kings xviii. 4; cf. Num. xxi. 8; Deut. viii. 15; 1 Kings i. 9; Isa. vi. 2, xiv. 29; Albright, *Archaeology and the Religion of Israel*, 3rd ed., 1953, p. 189, n. 51.
52. Joshua xxiv. 2.
53. Gen. xxvi. 5.
54. Albright, *Archaeology and the Religion of Israel*, 3rd ed., 1953, p. 114; J. B. Pritchard, *Palestinian Figurines*, 1943.
55. Judges v.
56. Meek, *Hebrew Origins*, 1950, pp. 143ff.
57. Gen. xxviii.
58. 1 Kings xii. 33.
59. J. Hoschander, *The Priests and Prophets*, 1938, pp. 31ff.
60. Meek, *op. cit.*, p. 217.
61. Hos. ii. 16f.
62. 2 Sam. vi; 1 Kings v. 15; 2 Kings xii. 5–17; 1 Chron. xxii. 2–19; xxv; cf. Johnson, *Sacral Kingship in Ancient Israel*, 1955, pp. 12ff.
63. 1 Kings xii. 12, 16.
64. 1 Kings xii. 26ff.; 2 Chron. xi. 15, xiii. 8.
65. Albright, *From the Stone Age to Christianity*, 1940, pp. 203, 229f.
66. 1 Kings xii. 26–33.
67. 1 Kings viii. 2.
68. Exod. xxiii. 16, xxxiv. 22.
69. Exod. xii.
70. Num. xxix. 1; Lev. xxiii. 24.
71. Exod. xii. 2ff.
72. Cf. Snaith, *The Jewish New Year Festival*, 1947, p. 588.
73. Cf. Jer. viii. 20.
74. Zech. xiv. 16f.
75. 1 Kings xviii; cf. Mowinckel, "Das Thronbesteigungsfest Jahwas und der Ursprung der Eschatologie", *Psalmenstudien*, ii, Kristiania, 1922, pp. 102ff.
76. Mowinckel, *op. cit.*, p. 230; P. Volz, *Das Neujahrsfest Jahwas*, Tübingen, 1912, p. 15.

77. Ps. xlvii, lxviii.

78. Ps. lxviii. 9.

79. Mowinckel, *op. cit.*; Volz, *op. cit.*; Johnson, *Sacral Kingship in Ancient Israel*, 1955; Snaith, *The Jewish New Year Festival*, 1947, pp. 195 ff.; Oesterley, *Myth and Ritual*, 1933, pp. 125 ff.

80. Ps. xxiv, xlvii, xlviii; cf. Johnson, *op. cit.*, pp. 63 ff.

81. Johnson, *The Old Testament and Modern Study*, ed. by H. H. Rowley, Oxford, 1951, p. 195.

82. Cf. A. S. Kapelrud, *Norsk Teologisk Tidsskrift,* xli, 1940, p. 57.

83. Chap. iii.

84. Ezra vi. 19 ff.; 2 Chron. xxx; Jubilees xlix. 16.

85. Nilsson, *A History of Greek Religion*, 1925, pp. 108 ff.; *Greek Popular Religion*, 1940, p. 51.

86. Farnell, *C.G.S.*, vol. iii, 1907, pp. 32 ff.

87. *Greek Popular Religion*, pp. 51 ff.

88. T. W. Allen, E. E. Sikes and T. W. Halliday, *The Homeric Hymn*, 3rd ed., 1936, pp. 10 ff.

89. *Refutatio omnium haeresium*, v. 8; cf. Farnell, *C.G.S.*, vol. iii, 1907, pp. 177, 183.

90. Cf. John xii. 24; 1 Cor. xv. 36.

91. Chap. iii, pp. 102 f.

92. Proclus, ad Plato, *Timaeus* (Lobeck), p. 293.

93. *C.G.S.*, vol. iii, 1907, p. 185.

94. *Orpheus and Greek Religion*, 1935, pp. 41, 107.

95. Diodorus Siculus, iii, 62, 8 ff.; *Frag.* 301.

96. Nonnus, *Dionysus,* vi, pp. 155 ff.; Lobeck, *Aglaophamus*, 1829, p. 561; *Orphica,* ed. E. Abel, 1885, p. 235.

97. Julian, *Adv. Christianos*, i, pp. 167 f.; Origen, *Contra Celsum*, iv, 17; Clement of Alex., *Protrepticus*, ii, 18, 2; Pindar, *Frag.* i, 35 (Bergk, p. 127); Plato, *Laws*, 70C; *Phaedo* 70C.

98. Pausanias, X, iv, 1, 2; Aristophanes, *Frags.* 353 ff.

99. Livy, 8–19.

100. Lucretius, *De rerum natura*, ii, 600–43; Lucian, *De Dea Syria*, c, 51.

101. Arnobius, *Adversus Gentes*, v, 5 ff.; Firmicus Maternus, *De errore profanarum religionum*, 3, 22; Diodorus Siculus, iii, 59; Julian, *Orat.*, v, 159; Livy, 10–14.

102. Cumont, *The Oriental Religions in Roman Paganism*, 1911, p. 56; Showerman, *Classical Journal*, ii, 1906, p. 29.

103. Julian, *Orat.*, v, 163C.

104. Cumont, *op. cit.*, pp. 56 ff.; Wissowa, *Religion und Kultus der Römer*, Munich, 1912, pp. 321 ff.; Hepding, *Attis, seine Mythen und sein Kult*, Giessen, 1903, pp. 160 ff.; Bailey, *Phases in the Religion of Ancient Rome*, 1932, vol. ii, pp. 198 ff.

105. Cf. C. B. Lewis, *Folk-Lore*, xlvi, 1935, p. 63.

106. R. Chambers, *Book of Days*, 1886, vol. i, p. 577, col. 1; J. F. Thiselton Dyer, *British Calendar Customs*, 1876, pp. 251 f.; W. Hone, *Every Day Book*, 1820, vol. ii, pp. 615 ff.; Brand, *Popular Antiquities*, 1777, vol. i, pp. 212 ff.

107. Stubbes, *The Anatomie of Abuses*, 1877–82, p. 149.

108. A. R. Wright, *British Calendar Customs*, 1938, pp. 224 ff.

109. Mannhardt, *Der Baumkultus der Germanen und ihrer Nachbarstämme*, Berlin, 1875, pp. 342 ff.

CHAPTER III

1. Frankfort, *Kingship and the Gods*, 1948; *The Problem of Similarity in Ancient Near Eastern Religions*, 1951; Hooke, *The Siege Perilous*, 1956, pp. 173 ff.; Evans-Pritchard, *The Divine Kingship of the Shilluk of the Nilotic Sudan*, 1948; Engnell, *Studies in Divine Kingship in the Ancient Near East*, Uppsala, 1943.

2. *Early History of Kingship*, 1905, pp. 127 ff.

3. *The Pagan Tribes of the Nilotic Sudan*, 1932, p. 90.

4. *G.B.*, pt. iv, pp. 16 ff.

5. Evans-Pritchard, *op. cit.*, pp. 21, 34 f.

6. Seligman, *Egypt and Negro Africa*, 1934, pp. 28 ff.; Meek, *The Northern Tribes of Nigeria*, 1925, vol. i, pp. 255 ff.; vol. ii, pp. 58 ff.; *A Sudanese Kingdom*, 1931, pp. 164 ff.

7. Hofmayr, *Die Shilluk, Geschichte, Religion und Leben eines Niloten Stammes*, 1925, pp. 152 f.; Pumphrey, *Sudan Notes and Records*, 1941, pp. 19 ff.; Oyler, *Sudan Notes*, 1920, pp. 296 ff.

8. Frankfort, *Studies presented to F. L. Griffiths*, 1932, pp. 445 ff.

9. Chap. ii, pp. 51 f.

10. Sethe, *Die altaegyptischen Pyramidentexte*, Leipzig, 1908–22, Ut. 587.

11. Frankfort, *Kingship and the Gods*, 1948, pp. 151 ff.

12. Breasted, *Ancient Records of Egypt*, Chicago, 1907, vol. iii, p. 400.

13. Sethe, *Urkunden des aegyptischen Altertums*, Leipzig, 1903, vol. iv, pp. 219–21.

14. Moret, *Du caractère religieux de la royauté pharaonique*, Paris, 1902, pp. 49, 72.

15. Sethe, *Urgeschichte und aelteste Religion der Aegypter*, 1930, p. 180, sect. 222.

16. Erman, "Hymnen an das Diadem der Pharaonen", *Abhandlungen der Preussischen Akademie, Phil. hist. Klasse*, no. 11.

17. *P.T.*, 220–2.

18. Sethe, *Urgeschichte und aelteste Religion der Aegypter*, 1930, pp. 67 ff.; *P.T.*, 194 f.

19. *P.T.*, 196–203.

20. Sethe, *Urkunden des aegyptischen Altertums*, Leipzig, 1903, vol. iv, p. 227; cf. Naville, *Deir el-Bahari*, 1894, pp. 15 ff.

21. Moret, *Du caractère religieux de la royauté pharaonique*, pp. 53 ff.; Sethe, *op. cit.*, vol. iv, pp. 244 f.

22. Naville, *Deir el-Bahari*, 1894, iii, pl. lx, 1, 3–11; Moret, *op. cit.,* pp. 79 ff.

23. Sethe, *Dramatische Texte zu altaegyptischen Mysterienspielen*, 1928, i–ii; cf. Frankfort, *Kingship and the Gods*, pp. 123 ff.

24. Erman, *Life in Ancient Egypt*, 1894, p. 57; Blackman, *Luxor and its Temples*, 1923, p. 167.

25. Breasted, *Ancient Records of Egypt*, Chicago, 1905–8, vol. ii, p. 99; D. R. MacIver, *Buhen*, Philadelphia, 1911, p. 34; Blackman, *Proceedings of the Society for Biblical Archaeology*, vol. xl, 1918, p. 90.

26. Sethe, *Urkunden des aegyptischen Altertums*, Leipzig, 1903, vol. iv, p. 262, n.b.

27. Blackman, *Journal of Manchester Egyptian and Oriental Society*, 1918–19, p. 30; Loret, *Recueil de travaux*, xxxix, pp. 44 ff.; *E.R.E.*, xii, pp. 798 ff.; Moret, *The Nile and Egyptian Civilization*, 1927, pp. 392 ff.

28. Moret, *Du caractère religieux de la royauté pharaonique*, p. 256 ff.; Breasted, *Zeitschrift für aegyptische Sprache und Altertumskunde*, xxxix, pp. 55 ff.

29. Breasted, *Development of Religion and Thought in Ancient Egypt*, 1914, p. 39; M. A. Murray, *Ancient Egypt*, ii, 1926, pp. 33 ff.

30. Gardiner, *J.E.A.,* xxx, pp. 28 f.

31. Frankfort, *Kingship and the Gods*, 1948, p. 86.

32. Moret, *op. cit.,* p. 105, fig. 21; Seligman, *Egypt and Negro Africa*, pp. 15 ff.

33. Griffiths, *J.E.A.,* xxviii, 1942, p. 71; Gardiner, *op. cit.,* p. 123; Frankfort, *op. cit.,* p. 79.

34. Seligman, *op. cit.,* p. 2; Frazer, *G.B.*, pt. iv, pp. 153 ff.; Mercer, *Religion of Ancient Egypt*, 1954, pp. 122, 362 f.; Breasted, *Development of Religion and Thought in Ancient Egypt*, 1914, p. 39.

35. Moret, *op. cit.,* p. 256.

36. Langdon, *The Legend of Etana and the Eagle*, Paris, 1932, pp. 11 f.; Jacobsen, *The Sumerian King-List,* Chicago, 1939; *Assy. Studies,* no. 11, p. 58.

37. Heidel, *The Babylonian Genesis*, 1951, 2nd ed., p. 37.

38. Harper, *The Code of Hammurabi*, 1904, p. 3.

39. Langdon, *op. cit.,* p. 9.

40. Jacobsen, *op. cit.,* pp. 169 ff.

41. Thureau-Dangin, *Sumerische und Akkadische Königinschriften*, Leipzig, 1907, pp. 156 ff.; Jacobsen, *J.A.O.S.,* lix, 1939, pp. 486 ff.; Labat, *Caractère religieux de la royauté assyro-babylonienne*, 1939, pp. 63 ff.

42. Thureau-Dangin, *op. cit.,* p. 219.

43. Barton, *The Royal Inscriptions of Sumer and Akkad*, New Haven, 1929, p. 275.

44. Wetzel, *Analecta Orientalia*, x, 1935, p. 17.

45. Gadd, *Ideas of Divine Rule in the Ancient East,* 1948, pp. 45 f.

46. Frankfort, *op. cit.,* p. 221.

47. Thureau-Dangin, *Les Inscriptions de Sumer et d'Akkad*, 1905, pp. 47, 49.

48. Harper, *The Code of Hammurabi*, 1904, p. 3.

49. S. Smith, *J.E.A.,* viii, 1922, pp. 41 ff.

50. T. Bauer, *Zeitschrift für Assyriologie und verwandte Gebiete,* xlii, Leipzig, 1934, pp. 170 ff.

51. A. Poebel, *Historical and Grammatical Texts*, Philadelphia, 1914, p. 76.

52. K. F. Müller, *Mitteilungen der vorderasiatisch-aegyptischen Gesellschaft*, Heft 3, 1937, pp. 8f.

53. Frankfort, *op. cit.*, p. 297; cf. chap. iv, p. 117.

54. Thureau-Dangin, *op. cit.*, p. 139; Labat, *op. cit.*, pp. 55 ff., 63 ff.; Jacobsen, *J.N.E.S.*, 1943, pp. 120f.

55. *Oxford Edition of Cuneiform Texts*, vol. vi, no. 73, col. ii, 15 ff.

56. Chap. ii, p. 56.

57. Virolleaud, *La légende phénicienne de Danel*, 1930, p. 145; *Les Poèmes de Ras Shamra*, 1939, pp. 10f.

58. 1 *A.B.*, ii. 1–6.

59. 2 *A.B.*, iv. 68.

60. 3 *A.B.*

61. Gaster, *Thespis*, 1950, pp. 115 ff.; Driver, *Canaanite Myths and Legends*, 1956, pp. 73 ff.; Gordon, *Ugaritic Literature*, 1949, pp. 9 ff.

62. *Krt*, 65 ff., 160 ff.; 2 *Aqht*, 1, 17.

63. Cf. chap. ii, pp. 60 ff.

64. Amos iv. 25, ix, 10; Jer. xxxv. 6–10; 2 Kings x. 15f.

65. Judges viii. 27.

66. Chap. ii, p. 65.

67. Ps. lxxxix; cf. 1 Kings viii. 66–xi. 36, xii. 16.

68. 2 Sam. vi. 14.

69. Ps. cxxxii. 1–10.

70. 1 Kings ix. 25.

71. Hos. iii. 3–5, x. 9, xiii. 9–11.

72. 1 Sam. viii. 7, x. 17, 19; cf. xii, xv.

73. 2 Sam. vii. 12f.

74. Ps. cx. 4; Gen. xiv. 18 ff.; Heb. vii. 13.

75. Johnson, *Sacral Kingship in Ancient Israel*, 1956, pp. 32f., 46f.

76. Ezek. xvi. 3.

77. *The Jewish New Year Festival*, 1947, p. 218.

78. Widengren, *Sakrales Koenigtum in Alten Testament und in Judentum*, 1955, pp. 44 ff.

79. Ezra iii. 10; Neh. xii. 45f.; 1 Chron. xxiv–xxv; 2 Chron. vii. 6, xxxv, 15.

80. Ezek. xxxiv. 24, xxxvii. 25; cf. 2 Sam. vii. 12 ff.; Mic. v. 2; Zech. vi. 9 ff.; Hag. ii. 23.

81. Zech. i, ii. 4 f., vi. 9 ff.; Ezra iii. 1–6; Hag. i–ii.

82. Evans, *The Palace of Minos*, vol. i, 1921, p. 5; vol. iv, 1935, pp. 907 ff.

83. Nilsson, *The Minoan-Mycenaean Religion*, 2nd ed., 1950, pp. 473 ff.

84. These reliefs were noted by the author in the Museum at Eleusis. Other examples are now in the National Museum at Athens.

85. *Theog.*, p. 453 ff.

86. Aristotle, *Polit.*, vii (vi), 8, p. 1322B; cf. Nilsson, *op. cit.*, p. 485, no. 1.

87. Cook, *Zeus*, 1940, vol. iii, pp. 269, 733.

88. *Iliad*, ii, 100 ff.

89. A. J. B. Wace, "Chamber Tombs at Mycenae", *Archaeologia*, lxxxii, 1932.

90. Evans, *op. cit.,* vol. iv, pp. 964 ff.

91. Evans, *The Prehistoric Tombs of Knossos*, 1906, pp. 165, 170.

92. Evans, *op. cit.,* p. 171.

93. Evans, *The Shaft-graves and the Bee-hive Tombs of Mycenae*, 1929, pp. 66 ff.; G. E. Mylonas, *Ancient Mycenae*, 1957, pp. 85 ff.

94. H. J. Kantor, *Journal of American Archaeology*, li, no. 1, 1947, pp. 50 ff.; Blagen and Wace, *Klio*, 1939, pp. 131 ff.

95. G. Kato, *Die Schachtgräber von Mykenai*, pp. 342 ff.

96. Wace, *B.S.A.*, 1921–3, pp. 186 ff.

97. Rodenwaldt, *Tiryns*, Athens, 1912, vol. ii, p. 225.

98. Wace, *op. cit.,* pp. 223 ff.

99. *Inscriptiones Graecae*, iv, 492.

100. *Mycenae*, 1949, p. 86.

101. R. E. M. Wheeler, *Ancient India*, no. 3, 1947, pp. 76 ff.; *The Indus Civilization*, 1954, pp. 14 ff.

102. Mackay, *Further Excavations at Mohenjo-Daro*, 1938, vol. i, p. 20.

103. Chap. iv, p. 133.

104. *Aitareya Brahmana*, i. 1. 14; viii. 4. 12; *Taittiriya Brahmana*, ii. 2. 10. 1–2.

105. *Rig-veda*, iv. 42.

106. *Satapatha Brahmana*, v. 3. 3. 12.

107. *Manu*, vii. 3–7.

108. *Rig-veda*, i. 164. 46.

109. *Satapatha Brahmana*, v. 4. 2. 1; *Aitareya Brahmana*, viii. 5 ff.; *Rajaturangini*, iii. 239 ff.

110. Cf. Piggott, *Prehistoric India*, 1950, pp. 286 ff.; Wheeler, *op. cit.,* pp. 59 ff.

111. R. Ghirshman, *Fouilles de Sialk*, Paris, 1938, vol. i, pp. 72 ff.

112. Contenau, *Syria*, viii, 1927, p. 198, figs. 2–3; *Délégation en Perse, Mémoires,* i, p. 125, fig. 276; p. 130, pl. vii. 14, viii. 19.

113. E. E. Herzfeld, *Archaeological History of Iran*, 1935, p. 8.

114. F. Spiegel, *Eranische Altertumskunde*, Leipzig, 1871–8, vol. iii, pp. 596 ff.

115. Dhorme, *La religion assyro-babylonienne*, Paris, 1910, p. 157.

116. Isa. xliv. 28–xlv. 4.

117. iv. 5. 14; vi. 5. 57; viii. 1. 23.

118. *Behistun*, i. 5.

119. King and Thompson, *The Sculptures and Inscriptions of Darius the Great on the Rock of Behistun in Persia*, 1907, p. 71.

120. *Behistun*, iv, p. 62.

121. E. F. Schmidt, "The Treasury of Persepolis and other Discoveries in the Homeland of the Achaemenians", *Oriental Institute Communications,* xxi, 1939, pp. 14 f.; R. G. Kent, *J.N.E.S.,* iv, 1945, p. 230; F. H. Weissbach, *Die Keilinschriften der Achämeniden*, 1911, pp. 107, 123 ff.

CHAPTER IV

1. Chap. i, pp. 29f.
2. *Tammuz and Ishtar*, 1914, p. 5.
3. Chiera, *Sumerian Religious Texts*, 1924, I, v, 14ff.; IV, 55ff.
4. Thureau-Dangin, *Revue d'assyriologie et d'archéologie orientale*, xix, Paris, 1884, pp. 175ff.; Jacobsen, *J.N.E.S.*, iv, 1946, p. 150.
5. Jacobsen, *The Intellectual Adventure of Ancient Man*, Chicago, 1946, p. 166; Kramer, *A.N.E.T.*, pp. 41f.
6. E. D. van Buren, *Analecta Orientalia*, xiii, 1944, pp. 2f.
7. Langdon, *J.R.A.S.*, 1926, pp. 35ff., col. vi, 6ff.
8. *Oxford Edition of Cuneiform Texts*, vol. i, no. 15, col. v, 11, 17–21; Langdon, *Sumerian Liturgical Texts* (Pennsylvanian Bab. Sect. 1917), vol. x, no. 2, pp. 148ff.; line 77, 4f.
9. *Kingship and the Gods*, 1948, p. 297.
10. Cf. Zimmern, *Berichte über die Verhandlungen der kgl. Sächsischen Gesellschaft der Wissenschaften, Phil. hist. Klasse*, Band 68, 1916.
11. Chap. ii, p. 57; iii, p. 97.
12. *P.T.*, 466a.
13. *P.T.*, 1125.
14. Wiedemann, *Religion of the Ancient Egyptians*, 1897, p. 143.
15. *Der sehende und blinde Gott*, Munich, 1942, pp. 40f.
16. Murray, *J.R.A.I.*, xlv, 1915, pp. 308ff.; Sethe, *Urgeschichte und aelteste Religion der Aegypter*, 1931, p. 85.
17. Wiedemann, *op. cit.*, pp. 138, 140.
18. *P.T.*, 729, 809, 910ff.
19. Erman, *A Handbook of Egyptian Religion*, 1907, pp. 215ff.
20. Junker, *Die Onurislegende*, Vienna, 1917, pp. 116ff.
21. Blackman, *Myth and Ritual*, Oxford, 1933, p. 34.
22. Blackman, *Luxor and its Temples*, 1923, pp. 70ff.; W. Wolf, *Das schöne Fest von Opet*, Leipzig, 1931, pp. 73ff.
23. Sethe, *Urkunden*, iv, pp. 219ff.; Blackman, *J.E.A.*, vii, 1921, p. 17.
24. Blackman, *J.E.A.*, xi, 1925, p. 250.
25. Gayet, *Le temple de Louxor*, 1894, pl. lxiiiff.
26. Cf. chap. iii, p. 85.
27. Sethe, *Urkunden*, iv, p. 29; Breasted, *Ancient Records of Egypt*, Chicago, 1906, ii, 33, p. 14.
28. Breasted, *op. cit.*, iv, 943, p. 482.
29. Erman, *A Handbook of Egyptian Religion*, 1907, p. 73.
30. J. B. Pritchard, *Palestinian Figurines*, New Haven, 1943, pp. 38ff., 55ff.; Albright, *A.A.S.O.R.*, xxi, 1941, pp. 25ff., 69.
31. Gordon, *Ugaritic Handbook*, 1947, no. 2010, p. 275.
32. *A.B.* III, 10ff., IV, 50ff.; Gordon, *Ugaritic Literature*, 1949, p. 25, 32f.
33. *A.B.* VI; IV, 6ff.
34. 67: VI, 25ff.

35. 49: II, 5 ff.
36. 4 *A.B.*, ii, 28.
37. Dussaud, *Revue de l'histoire des religions,* iii, 1935, pp. 15, 44 ff.
38. Montet, *Les nouvelles fouilles de Tanis, 1929–32,* Paris, 1933, pl. 54, pp. 107 f.
39. Petrie, *Tanis,* vol. i, pl. 7, no. 44.
40. Pritchard, *op. cit.,* p. 79 ff.
41. Mariette, *Denderah,* 1870–80, vol. i, p. 25 f.
42. *A.B.* II, 5 ff.
43. *A.B.* VI, 132.
44. Chap. ii, p. 59.
45. *Syria,* xiv, 1933, fasc. 2, pp. 128 ff.
46. Gaster, *J.A.O.S.,* lxvi, 1946, p. 54.
47. Gaster, *op. cit.,* p. 55.
48. Virolleaud, *Syria,* xiv, 1933, p. 148; Dussaud, *Revue de l'histoire des religions,* 1933, p. 12; Hooke, *The Origins of Early Semitic Ritual,* 1938, p. 41.
49. Text 76.
50. 76, ii, 25–111, 20; 67, v, 18 ff.
51. 67, v, 17–22.
52. 52; 45; 51, iv, 47 f.; 51, v, 66 f.
53. *Baal in the Ras Shamra Texts,* 1952, p. 73.
54. 51, ii, 21 ff.
55. 51, i, 22 f.; iii, 25 f.
56. 2 Kings xxiii. 4.
57. Judges ii. 13, x. 6; 1 Sam. vii. 4, xii. 10.
58. Judges vi. 25, 28, 30; Deut. vii. 5, xvi. 21; 1 Kings xv. 13, xvi. 33; 2 Kings xiii. 6, xvii. 10, xviii. 4, xxiii. 4, 6, 14; Jer. xvii. 2.
59. Alt, *Festschrift Georg. Beer,* 1935, pp. 1–18.
60. 1 Kings xviii. 19.
61. i, 197–206.
62. Albright, *B.A.S.O.R.,* no. 94, 1944, pp. 30 f.; J. Gray, *The Krt Text in the Literature of Ras Shamra,* Leiden, 1955, pp. 12, 43 f.; Gordon, *Ugaritic Literature,* 1949, p. 72.
63. 1 Kings xix. 14.
64. Jer. vii. 17 f.
65. Jer. xliv. 15 ff.
66. Gustav Holscher, *Die Profeten, Untersuchung zur Religionsgeschichte Israels,* Leipzig, 1914, p. 140; Vincent, *La religion des Judéax-Araméens d'Elephantine,* Paris, 1937.
67. 1 Sam. ii. 22.
68. Amos ii. 7 ff.
69. Jer. v. 7, iv. 30.
70. Isa. lvii. 8; Ezek. xxiii. 17; Canticles iii.
71. Ps. xlv. 9 ff.
72. Isa. viii. 3.

73. J. M. P. Smith, *Zeitschrift für die Alttestamentliche Wissenschaft*, xxiv, p. 222.

74. 1 Kings xv. 12.

75. Hos. iv. 14f.

76. Deut. xxiii. 17f; 2 Kings xxiii. 7.

77. Hos. ii. 8ff, 14, iv. 10, 14; Ezek. xvi. 20; cf. May, *A.J.S.L.*, xlviii, 1932, pp. 86ff.; cf. *A.J.S.L.*, xxxix, 1922, pp. 1ff.; Schoff, *The Song of Songs: A Symposium*, 1924, pp. 49ff.

78. Hos. ii. 2ff.

79. Hos. ii. 9.

80. Hos. ii. 14–20; Jer. ii. 2; Ezek. xvi. 8.

81. R. S. Hardy, *A.J.S.L.*, lviii, 1941, pp. 185ff.

82. R. Dussaud, *Religion des Hittites et des Hourrites*, Paris, 1945, pp. 338ff.; E. Laroche, *Journal of Cuneiform Studies*, vi, 1952, pp. 115ff.; *Recherches sur les noms des dieux hittites*, 1947, pp. 47f., 106; *K.U.B.*, xxi, 27; Gurney, *Annals of Archaeology and Anthropology*, xxvii, 1940, pp. 10, 22ff.

83. B. Bittel, R. Naumann and H. Otto, *Yazilikaya*, 1941, pp. 27ff.; E. Laroche, *Recherches sur les noms des dieux hittites*, pp. 38, 47, 58.

84. That they represent "weapons", as Bittel suggests (*op. cit.*, p. 113), is most unlikely.

85. *The Hittite Empire*, 1929, pp. 116ff.

86. W. M. Müller, *Mitteilungen der Vorderasiatischen Gesellschaft*, vii, no. 5, 1902, pp. 193ff.; J. B. Pritchard, *Ancient Near Eastern Texts*, 1905, pp. 199ff.

87. *K.U.B.*, xxi. 27; Garstang, "The Sun Goddess of Arinna", *Annals of Archaeology and Anthropology*, vol. vi, no 3, 1914, pp. 112ff.; Garstang and Strong, *The Syrian Goddess*, 1913, p. 7, no. 20.

88. Gurney, *The Hittites*, 1952, pp. 139ff.

89. G. R. Levy, *The Sword from the Rock*, 1954, p. 34.

90. Cf. chap. iii, p. 106.

91. Pezard and Pottier, *Les Antiquités de la Susiane*, Paris, 1913, p. 129; Contenau, *Syria*, viii, 1927, p. 198, figs. 2–3; *Délégation en Perse, Mémoires*, i, p. 125, fig. 276; p. 130, pl. vii, 14.

92. *Sacred Books of the East*, XXIII, pp. 52ff.

93. Herodotus, i, 131.

94. Strabo, xi, 532; xii, 559.

95. *Prehistoric India*, 1950, pp. 127, (cf.) 105; Stein, *Memoirs of the Archaeological Survey of India*, no. 37, 1925, pp. 38, 42, 60, 75; pl. ix, P, W, 9, P, 262; pl. xii, K, 14; pl. xvi, D, N, d, 9, S, J, 68.

96. Stein, *op. cit.*, pl. ix, P, C, 17.

97. Chap. iii, p. 107.

98. Cf. Brunton and Caton-Thompson, *Bedarian Civilization*, p. 29; Woolley, *Antiq. Journ.*, xi, 1931, p. 368; Zammit, *Archaeologia*, lxx, 1919, p. 197.

99. Marshall, *Mohenjo-daro and the Indus Civilisation*, 1931, vol. i, pp. 338ff.,

Vats, *Excavations at Harappa*, 1940, vol. i, pp. 292; Piggott, *Ancient India*; no. 3, 1947, pp. 126 ff.

100. Marshall, *op. cit.*, vol. i, pp. 50 f., 339.

101. *Further Excavations at Mohenjo-daro*, 1938, vol. i, p. 259; *The Indus Civilization*, 1948, pp. 53 f.

102. Marshall, *op. cit.*, vol. iii, pl. xc, iv, 11; Mackay, *Further Excavations at Mohenjo-daro*, vol. ii, pl. lxxii, 7; lxxvi, 5; Vats, *op. cit.*, pls. lxxvi, lxxvii.

103. Marshall, *op. cit.*, vol. i, pl. xii, 17.

104. Mackay, *op. cit.*, vol. i, pp. 335 f., 407; Vats, *op. cit.*, vol. i, pp. 51, 53, 55 ff., 116, 369 ff.

105. Marshall, *op. cit.*, vol. i, pp. 111, 355; Mackay, *op. cit.*, vol. i, p. 671.

106. Gadd, in Hall and Woolley, *Ur Excavations, Al 'Ubaid*, 1927, vol. i, pp. 142 f.

107. Evans, *The Palace of Minos*, 1928, vol. ii, p. 842; Nilsson, *The Minoan-Mycenaean Religion*, 2nd ed., 1950, pp. 342 f.

108. Persson, *The Religion of Greece in Prehistoric Times*, 1942, p. 34.

109. *The Palace of Minos*, vol. i, pp. 161 f.

110. *Op. cit.*, vol. ii, pp. 383 ff.

111. Nilsson, *op. cit.*, p. 267.

112. Evans, *The Mycenaean Tree and Pillar Cult*, 1901, p. 19.

113. Evans, *Palace of Minos*, 1928, vol. i, pp. 463 ff., 500 f.

114. *Op. cit.*, pp. 221 f.

115. Evans, *B.S.A.*, ix, 1902–3, p. 149.

116. *B.S.A.*, vi, 1899–1900, pp. 76 f.

117. B. E. Williams, in *Gournia*, ed. by H. B. Hawkes, Philadelphia, 1908, p. 47.

118. Evans, *B.S.A.*, viii, 1901–2, pp. 95 ff.

119. Paribeni, *Monumenti Antichi*, xix, pp. 5–86; Evans, *Palace of Minos*, 1928, vol. i, pp. 438 ff.; Nilsson, *The Minoan-Mycenaean Religion*, 2nd. ed., 1950, pp. 428 ff.

120. *Themis*, 1912, p. 178.

121. Nilsson, *op. cit.*, p. 433.

122. Cf. Homer, *Odyssey*, 125–7; Hesiod, *Theog.*, 869; Diodorus, v, 25 ff.; Harrison, *Themis*, 1912, p. 54, n. 7; Harrison, *Prolegomena to the Study of Greek Religion*, Cambridge, 1903, pp. 456 ff.

123. Hawkes, *Prehistoric Foundations of Europe*, 1940, pp. 153 ff.; J. B. Ward-Perkins, *Antiquity*, xvi, 1942, pp. 26 f.

124. Cf. M. A. Murray, *Excavations in Malta*, 1929, pp. 11, 29.

125. Zammit and Singer, *J.R.A.I.*, liv, 1924, pp. 79 ff.; pl. v, 6; pl. xix, 10; pl. xv, 49; pl. xviii, 53, 54.

126. Zammit, *Prehistoric Malta*, Oxford, 1930, p. 80, pl. xxii.

127. *J.R.A.I.*, *op. cit.*, pl. xviii, 54.

128. *Op. cit.*, pl. xi, 29; pl. xx, 30.

129. *The Hal-Saflieni Hypogeum*, 1910, p. 40; *J.R.A.I.*, *op. cit.*, pl. ix, 22.

130. Zammit, *Prehistoric Malta,* 1930, pp. 13, 15, 84, 95.

131. Childe, *Dawn of European Civilization,* 5th ed., 1950, pp. 261 f., 267.

132. Siret, *Revue préhistorique,* 1908, pp. 10 ff., 21; Correia, *Comisión de investi-gaciones paleontológicas y prehistóricas,* Madrid, 1921, 27, pp. 63, 75, figs. 50, 56.[1]

133. Le Rouzic, *Carnac, Menhir-statues avec Signes Figuratifs et Amulettes ou Idoles des Dolmens du Morbihan,* Nantes, 1934, pp. 13 ff.; Kendrick, *The Archaeology of the Channel Islands,* 1928, vol. i, p. 32; *Antiq. Journ.,* v, 1925, pp. 429f.

134. Piggott, *The Neolithic Cultures of the British Isles,* 1954, p. 88, figs. 14, 1–4, 10.

135. Curwen, *Sussex Archaeological Collections,* vol. lxx, 1929, p. 56, fig. 175.

136. Drew and Piggott, *P.P.S.* (N.S.), vol. ii, 1936, pp. 86 ff.

137. Piggott, *The Neolithic Cultures of the British Isles,* 1954, p. 42, pl. iv; J. and C. Hawkes, *Prehistoric Britain,* 1947, p. 39.

CHAPTER V

1. Sethe, *Dramatische Texte zu altaegyptischen Mysterienspielen,* 1928, pp. 47 ff.

2. *P.T.,* 1479, 1521.

3. *P.T.,* 1248, 1479; cf. Budge, *The Gods of the Egyptians,* 1904, vol. i, pp. 322 ff.

4. *P.T.,* 1652.

5. *P.T.,* 466b.

6. Cf. chap. i, p. 40.

7. Sethe, *op. cit.,* vol. i, pp. 53 ff.; *Zeitschrift für aegyptische Sprache und Alter-tumskunde,* xxxix, Leipzig, 1901, pp. 39 ff.

8. Jacobsen, *The Intellectual Adventure of Ancient Man,* 1946, pp. 57 ff.

9. Badawi, *Der Gott Chnum,* Glückstadt, 1937, pp. 56 ff.; Budge, *From Fetish to God in Ancient Egypt,* 1934, pp. 173, 256.

10. R. V. Lanzone, *Dizionario di mitologia egiziana,* Turin, 1881–6, pl. 336, 4.

11. *P.T.,* 265 b–c.

12. Sethe, *Urgeschichte und aelteste Religion der Aegypter,* 1930, p. 163.

13. G. Roeder, *Urkunden zur Religion des alten Aegypten,* 1915, pp. 13 ff.

14. Cf. Naville, *Book of the Dead,* 151 à bis 9.

15. Frankfort, *Ancient Egyptian Religion,* 1948, pls. 9, 10.

16. Frankfort, *op. cit.,* pp. 19 ff.; Wilson, *The Intellectual Adventure of Ancient Man,* 1946, pp. 44 f.

17. *P.T.,* 819c, 632.

18. Kees, *Totenglauben und Jenseitsvorstellungen der alten Aegypter,* 1926, pp. 209 ff.; Plutarch, *De Iside et Osiride,* pp. 39, 43.

[1] Since the present book was in proof, *The Eye Goddess* by O. G. S. Crawford has appeared, tracing the diffusion of the cult from the Ancient East (Brak) to North-west Europe.

19. Nelson, *Ramses III's Temple*, 1928, pt. i, pl. 54.
20. Jacobsen, *The Intellectual Adventure of Ancient Man*, 1946, pp. 131 f.
21. Tablet I, 1–104.
22. Tablets I, 108–61; II, 1–10, 61–6; IV, 1–33.
23. Tablet IV, 57–146.
24. Tablet V.
25. Tablet VI, 22–40.
26. Tablets VI, 45–80; VII; Speiser, *Near Eastern Texts*, ed. by Pritchard, 2nd ed., 1955, pp. 60 ff.; Heidel, *The Babylonian Genesis*, 2nd ed., 1951, pp. 1–10; Jacobsen, *The Intellectual Adventure of Ancient Man*, 1946, pp. 170 ff.
27. Chap. ii, p. 55.
28. Kramer, *Sumerian Mythology*, 1944, pp. 30 ff.; *J.A.O.S.*, lxiii, 1943, p. 71; lxiv, 1944, pp. 7 ff.
29. *Textes religieux sumériens du Louvre*, Paris, 1930, 10, 36–7; 72.
30. Chiera, *Sumerian Religious Texts*, 1924, pp. 26 ff.
31. Chiera, *Sumerian Epics and Myths*, 1934, p. 116; Langdon, *Sumerian Liturgies and Psalms*, 1919, p. 14; Kramer, *op. cit.*, pp. 53 ff., 69 ff., 72 ff.
32. Cf. chap. vi, pp. 185 ff.
33. Chap. vi, pp. 192 ff.
34. Albright, *Archaeology and the Religion of Israel*, 1946, p. 72; *Journal of Biblical Literature*, 1940, p. 106; Montgomery, *J.A.O.S.*, liii, 1933, pp. 102 ff.
35. Chap. iv, p. 124.
36. *Baal-Anat*, 51: vii, 14 ff.
37. Cf. Gen. vii. 11, viii. 2; 2 Kings vii. 2, 19; Mal. iii. 10.
38. *Thespis*, New York, 1950, p. 181.
39. Schaeffer, *The Cuneiform Texts of Ras Shamra-Ugarit, 1939*, pp. 68.
40. *A.B.*, 49: IV, 27, 29.
41. *A.B.*, 67: V, 14 f.
42. Judges xvi. 23; 1 Sam. v. 1–7.
43. *A.B.*, VII–VIII.
44. Cf. chap. iv, pp. 122 f.
45. Chap. iv, p. 127.
46. Job xxviii. 23 ff., xxxvii, xxxviii; Ps. xxiv, xxxiii. 6 f., lxv, civ.
47. Isa. lx. 1 f.
48. Isa. xl. 22; Ps. civ, 3 ff.
49. Ps. civ. 3, 32 ff.
50. Chap. vi, pp. 200 ff.
51. Cf. Job xxxvi. 27.
52. Pausanias, x, 4. 4.
53. Eusebius, *Chronicon*, ed. by A. Schoene, vol. i, 1875, col. 16.
54. Heidel, *The Babylonian Genesis*, 1951, pp. 67 ff., 118; *The Gilgamesh Epic*, pp. 106 ff.

55. Kramer, *Sumerian Mythology*, 1944, pp. 68 ff.; Jacobsen, *J.N.E.S.*, vol. v, 1946, pp. 143 f.
56. Ezek. xxviii. 1–4.
57. Chap. vi, pp. 201 f.
58. Chap. vi, pp. 199 ff.
59. Chap. vi, pp. 205 ff.
60. Jacobsen, *J.N.E.S.*, vol. v, 1946, pp. 138 ff.
61. Tablet VII. 2.
62. Kramer, *Sumerian Mythology*, 1944, p. 39.
63. King, *The Seven Tablets of Creation*, 1902, p. 123.
64. Exod. xx. 11.
65. Exod. xxiii. 12; Deut. v. 14 f.
66. Cf. chap. ii, p. 67.
67. Ps. lxxiv. 12–14, civ; Isa. li. 9.
68. *Iliad*, xv, 192.
69. *Iliad*, xv, 197 ff.
70. Goetze, *A.N.E.T.*, 1950, pp. 121 ff.
71. *A.J.A.*, lii, 1948, pp. 123 ff.; *Kumarbi, Mythen vom churritischen Kronos*, 1946.
72. Cf. Theocritus, iv, 43.
73. Chap. iv, pp. 136 ff.
74. Evans, *The Palace of Minos*, 1928, vol. ii, p. 48; Pendlebury, *The Archaeology of Crete*, 1939, p. 327.
75. *History of Greek Religion*, Oxford, 1925, p. 31.
76. Cf. *Stob*, i, i, 12; Adams, *The Vitality of Platonism*, Cambridge, 1911, Essay liv, pp. 105 f.
77. Homer, *Iliad*, xvii, 425; *Odyssey*, iii, 2; xi, 315.
78. *Theog.*, 116 ff.
79. Orpheus, *Frags.*, 210 ff. (Kern.)
80. Guthrie, *Orpheus and Greek Religion*, 1952, pp. 107 ff.
81. I. M. Linforth, *The Arts of Orpheus*, 1941, pp. 353 ff.
82. O. Gruppe, *Griechische Kulte und Mythen*, Leipzig, 1887, pp. 612 ff.
83. Guthrie, *op. cit.*, p. 128.
84. Guthrie, *op. cit.*, p. 75; Diog. 1. *prooem.*, 3.

CHAPTER VI

1. J. A. Wilson, *A.N.E.T.*, 1955, pp. 10 f.; Budge, *Legends of the Gods*, 1912, pp. 14 ff.
2. Cols. xxvi, 21–xxvii, 6; xxviii, 20–xxix, 6; Budge, *From Fetish to God in Ancient Egypt*, 1934, pp. 516 ff.
3. Chap. ii, p. 40.
4. *P.T.*, 298, 370, 1150; Sethe, *Zur Altaegyptischen Sage vom Sonnenauge das in der Fremde war*, Leipzig, 1912, p. 38.

5. Kees, *Der Götterglaube im alten Aegypten*, 1941, p. 237.
6. A. de Buck, *The Egyptian Coffin Texts*, Chicago, 1938, II, Spell 160, pp. 373 ff.; *The Book of the Dead*, chap. cviii; Sethe, *Zeitschrift für aegyptische Sprache und Altertumskunde*, lix, 1924, pp. 73 ff.
7. B.M., 10470; cf. Budge, *The Papyrus of Ani*, 1913, iii, sheet 29; *A.N.E.T.*, 1955, pp. 9 f.
8. *P.T.*, 2011.
9. Budge, *The Papyrus of Ani*, pls. 3–4.
10. Bleeker, *De beteekenis van de Egyptische godin Maat*, Leiden, 1929, p. 33; Frankfort, *Ancient Egyptian Religion*, New York, 1948, pp. 54 ff.
11. J. A. Wilson, *A.N.E.T.*, 1955, p. 251.
12. Erman and Blackman, *The Literature of the Ancient Egyptians*, 1927, p. 57.
13. Breasted, *Ancient Records of Egypt*, 1906, vol. iii, pp. 45–67.
14. Erman and Blackman, *op. cit.*, p. 109.
15. *Tod und Leben nach den Vorstellungen der Babylonier*, Leipzig, 1931, 27a.
16. Cf. chap. i, pp. 43 f.
17. Heidel, *The Babylonian Genesis*, 1951, pp. 132 f.
18. Pritchard, *A.N.E.T.*, 1955, p. 103; Meissner, *Babylonien und Assyrien*, vol. ii, Heidelberg, 1925, pp. 188 f.; Heidel, *op. cit.*, pp. 147 ff., cf. pp. 122 ff.
19. Heidel, *op. cit.*, p. 124.
20. Reisner, *Sumerisch-babylonische Hymnen*, Berlin, 1896, vii, rev. 17–24.
21. Poebel, *Historical Texts*, Univ. of Pennsylvania, iv, no. 1, Philadelphia, 1914, pp. 9 ff., cf. v, 1.
22. Poebel, *op. cit.*, pp. 9 ff.; Kramer, *A.N.E.T.*, 1955, pp. 42 ff.; *Sumerian Mythology*, 1944, pp. 97 ff.
23. Kramer, *J.A.O.S.*, lxiv, 1944, pp. 8 ff.
24. Tablet XI, 14 (*A.N.E.T.*, 1957, p. 93).
25. Tablet XI, 18 f.
26. Tablet XI, 119 f.
27. Speiser, *A.N.E.T.*, 1955, p. 104 f.
28. Tablet I, 21 ff., cf. chap. v, p. 154.
29. Tablet XI, 19–31; cf. 170 ff.
30. Cf. chap. i, pp. 43 f.
31. Speiser, *A.N.E.T.*, 1955, pp. 99, cf. 104 f.
32. Kramer, *Sumerian Mythology*, 1944, pp. 78 f., cf. pp. 30 ff.; *J.A.O.S.*, lxiii, 1943, pp. 73 ff.
33. Cf. chap. v, pp. 146 f.
34. Kramer, *op. cit.*, pp. 80 ff. For the text see p. 117, n. 76.
35. Kramer, *op. cit.*, pp. 82 ff.
36. Goetze, *A.N.E.T.*, 1953, pp. 125 ff.
37. Gaster, *Thespis*, 1950, pp. 317 ff.
38. *Op. cit.*, pp. 318 ff.
39. *Op. cit.*, pp. 337, 339, 340, 344 ff.

40. *K.U.B.,* xvii, 10; xxxiii, 1–12; *A.N.E.T.,* 1955, pp. 126 ff.; Gaster, *op. cit.*
pp. 361 ff.; Otten, *Die Uberlieferungen des Telipinu-Mythus* (Mitteilungen
der Vorderasiatisch-Egyptischen Gesellschaft, 46, 1), Leipzig, 1942.
41. Goetze, *A.N.E.T.,* 1955, pp. 120 f.; *A.J.A.,* lii, 1948, pp. 123 ff.; *K.U.B.,*
xxxiii, 120.
42. Goetze, *A.N.E.T.,* 1955, pp. 121 ff.; *J.A.O.S.,* lix, 1949, pp. 178 ff.;
H. G. Güterbock, *Kumarbi Efsanesi,* Ankara, 1945; *The Song of Ullikummi,*
1952; *K.U.B.,* xxxiii, 96, i; Otten, *Mythen vom Gotte Kumarbi, Neue
Fragmente,* 1950, no. 8.
43. *Ugaritic Literature,* 1949, p. 4.
44. 1 *A.B.,* iii, 3, 9, 21; iv, 29, 40; 1 *A.B.,* iv, 27, 38; 1 *A.B.,* ii, 7; 2 *A.B.,* iv,
68; III: ii. 18.
45. 67: *A.B.,* v, 14 ff.; vi, 8 f.; 49: 11. 30–37.
46. 1 *A.B.,* ii, 15–20.
47. 2 *A.B.,* vii, 55–7; viii, 10–14.
48. Frazer, *G.B.,* pt. vii, pp. 216 ff.
49. Jacobs, *Harvard Theological Review,* xxxviii, 1945, pp. 80 f.; Gaster,
op. cit., 1950, p. 124.
50. 49: III. 6 f., 12.
51. 51: VII. 42.
52. 67: 11. 10 ff.
53. 49: 11. 5 ff.
54. Chap. v, pp. 160 f.
55. 49: VI. 27 ff.; VII. 46 f.
56. 129: 8–9; 22: 137.
57. 137: 17, 33.
58. 137: 36.
59. J. Obermann, *J.A.O.S.,* lxvii, 1947, p. 196.
60. *'nt.* III: 38 f.
61. 67: 1. 1 ff.
62. Ps. xcv. 3, xcvi, 4 f., xcvii. 7; cf. lxxiii. 3, 8, lxxxii. 8.
63. Ps. xciii. 1, xcv. 5, xcvi. 10; cf. 1 Sam. ii. 8; Isa. xxxvii. 16.
64. Gen. i. 14–18.
65. Gunkel, *Schöpfung und Chaos in Urzeit und Endzeit,* 1895.
66. Isa. li. 9 f., cf. xxx. 7; Ezra xxix. 3, xxxii. 2 f.
67. Ps. lxxxvii. 4.
68. Job ix. 13 f., xxvi. 12 f.
69. Isa. li. 9; Gen. i. 21; Ps. cxlviii. 7; Job xxvi. 12.
70. Job iii. 8.
71. Isa. xxvii. 1.
72. Prov. i. 9, iv. 9; Ps. lxxiv. 14.
73. *'nt.* III; 39; 67: 1: 30.
74. Num. xxi. 4–9; 2 Kings xviii. 4.
75. Ps. lxxiv. 13 ff.; Gen. i. 9 f.

76. Gen. iii.
77. Gen. vi. 5–8, vii. 1–5.
78. Chap. v, pp. 164f.
79. *The Babylonian Genesis*, 1951, p. 125.
80. 2 Kings xvii. 4; Num. xxi. 4–9; Isa. xiv. 29, xxx, 6, cf. vi.
81. Gen. iii. iff.
82. Wisdom ii. 24; Rev. xii. 9.
83. Amos iii. 6.
84. Gen. vi. 5.
85. Eccles. xv. 11–17.
86. Eccles. xxv. 24; 2 Esdras iii. 21f., iv. 30–2, vii. 118.
87. Wisd. of Sol. ii. 23f.
88. Job i. 6ff.; Zech. iii. 1f.
89. 1 Chron. xxi. 1.
90. 1 Enoch xix. 1f., cf. vi. 5, 7; Jubilees x. 10–13, xi. 4ff., xii. 20; *Testament of the Twelve Patriarchs*, Reuben iii. 3–6; Simeon iv. 8, 9.
91. Gen. i. 31.
92. Chap. vii, pp. 235ff.
93. Dan. viii. 16; ix. 21f.; x. 13, 21; xii. 1.
94. Dan. x. 5ff., 20ff.
95. *Yasna*, 45, 22.
96. *Vendidad*, chap. xix, 1–10.
97. *Vendidad*, chap. i.
98. *Yasna*, xlv, 9.
99. Hesiod, *Theog.*, 501ff.
100. Apollodorus, *Bibliotheca*, i, 40ff.; Hesiod, *Theog.*, 820ff.; Roscher, "Typhoeus, Typhon", art. in *Lexikon der griech. und rom. Mythologie*.
101. Apollodorus, *Bibliotheca*, i, 6, 3.
102. R. D. Barnett, *J.H.S.*, lxv, 1945, p. 101; cf. Güterbock, *A.J.A.*, lii, 1948, p. 133.

CHAPTER VII

1. Cf. James, *Prehistoric Religion*, 1957, pp. 34ff.
2. Elliot Smith and W. R. Dawson, *Egyptian Mummies*, 1924, pp. 23f., 73.
3. Quibell, *Report of the British Association*, 1912, p. 612.
4. Gardiner, *E.R.E.*, viii, p. 23.
5. Budge, *The Book of the Opening of the Mouth*, 1909, 2 vols.
6. Lepsius, *Denkmaler*, ii, p. 4; Mercer, *P.T.*, vol. iv, 1929, pp. 36ff.; Budge, *op. cit.*, vol. i, p. vii.
7. Blackman, *J.E.A.*, xxi, 19, pp. 6f.; Moret, *Le rituel du culte divin journalier en Egypte*, 1902, pp. 147ff.; J. A. Wilson, *J.N.E.S.*, iii, 1944, pp. 210ff.

8. Cf. chap. vi, pp. 181 f.

9. Budge, *Osiris and the Egyptian Resurrection*, 1911, vol. i, pp. 303 ff.

10. Moret, "Le Jugement du Roi Mort", *Annuaire de l'Ecole Prat. des Hautes Etudes*, 1922; Breasted, *Development of Religion and Thought in Ancient Egypt*, 1914, pp. 250 f.

11. Budge, *From Fetish to God in Ancient Egypt*, 1934, p. 280.

12. *P.T.*, 318, 350c, 474, 623 f, 837; Budge, *From Fetish to God in Ancient Egypt*, 1934, pp. 326 ff.

13. *Book of the Dead* (Budge), p. 76, n. 1; (Ani), pp. 88 f.

14. *P.T., Ut.* 467; cf. *P.T.*, 364, 390, 891, 913, 1090.

15. *P.T.*, 382, 484, 1118 f.

16. *P.T.*, 382, 484, 1118 f.

17. *A.N.E.T.*, 1955, p. 87; *Epic of Gilgamesh*, vii, 34–9.

18. *Op. cit.*, X, iii, 1–5; *A.N.E.T.*, 1955, p. 90.

19. A. L. Oppenheim, *Orientalia*, xix, 1950, pp. 147 f.

20. Woolley, *Ur Excavations*, 1934, vol. ii, pp. 16 ff., 33 ff.

21. Jacobsen, *The Sumerian King-List*, 1939, p. 58.

22. Kramer, *Assyriological Studies*, xii, Chicago, 1940, 34, 35 (173–89).

23. Wensinck, *Acta Orientalia*, Leiden, 1923, pp. 158 ff.

24. Wensinck, *op. cit.*, p. 182.

25. Chap. xxxiv.

26. *S.B.E.*, v, p. 5; *Yasna*, xxxix, 2, 4; *Vendidad*, xiii, 15; *Yasht*, xiii, 74.

27. *S.B.E.*, xlvii, pp. 21 f. These three divisions are connected with the zodiacal constellations—Cancer, Leo and Virgo.

28. *Bundahish*, iv; x, 1–3; xiv, 1–3; xv, 1–5; *S.B.E.*, v, pp. 52–9; xviii, p. 105.

29. *Bund.*, xxxi, 6; *Yasht*, xix, 47 f.

30. *Vendidad*, ii; *Yasna*, ix, 4 f.; *Yasht*, ix, 9 ff.

31. Söderblom, *La vie future d'après de Mazdéisme*, 1901, pp. 175 ff.

32. Hoshangji, Haug and West, *The Book of Arta Viraf*, 1872, xviii, 1–9.

33. *Op. cit.*, xvi, 2–12.

34. *Op. cit.*, vi.

35. *Yasht*, xxii, 2 ff.

36. *Yasna*, li, 13; xlvi, 10 f.; Moulton, *Early Zoroastrianism*, 1913, pp. 166 ff.

37. *Yasna*, xxxiii, 1; xlviii, 4.

38. Cf. *Yasht*, xxii, 7–15.

39. *Yasna*, xlv, 10.

40. *S.B.E.*, xxiii, p. 195, n. 2.

41. Isa. xiv. 11, xxxviii. 18; Job iii. 19; Ps. vi. 5, lxxxviii. 4, 5, cv. 17 f.

42. Ps. cxxxix. 8, cf. lxxiii. 23 f.

43. Amos v. 18.

44. Zeph. i. 15.

45. Jer. iv. 23.

46. Amos ix. 15.

47. Jer. xxxi. 31 ff.
48. Ezek. xx. 33 ff.; Exod. vi. 6, xiii. 9.
49. Mal. iii. 1–6, 13–iv. 3.
50. Isa. xxiv–xxvii.
51. Ps. lxxiii. 23 f.
52. Dan. xii. 2.
53. Dan. x. 13, viii. 16; cf. Tobias xii. 15; Enoch xx. 1–7, lxxxi. 5, xc. 21 f.
54. Lam. iv. 20; Ps. ii. 7, xlv. 11, lxxxix. 29; cf. chap. iii, pp. 100 f.
55. Enoch xxv. 5, x. 21.
56. Enoch xxv. 4 ff, cf. x. 7, 17, 20, lxxxiii–xc.
57. Ps. of Sol. xvii. 37 f., 50.
58. Sibylline Oracles iii. 781 f., iv. 187 ff.
59. Ps. of Sol. xvii.
60. Dan. vii. 13; Enoch xlvi. 1 f., lxii. 2 f., xlviii. 2 f.
61. Rowley, *The Relevance of Apocalyptic*, 1947, pp. 30 ff.
62. Dan. vii. 18.
63. Bousset and Gressman, *Die Religion das Judentums im späthellenistischen Zeitalter*, 1926, pp. 469 ff.; Reitzenstein, *Poimandres*, 1906, sect. 11–26; J. M. Creed, *Journal Theol. Stud.*, xxvi, 1925, pp. 113 ff.
64. *Rig Veda*, x, 90; cf. Bousset, *Hauptprobleme der Gnosis*, 1907, pp. 211 ff.
65. 109–201; cf. chap. vi, pp. 174 f.
66. *Iliad*, xii, 5; *Odyssey*, iv, 85, 563; vii, 201.
67. *Theog.*, 713 ff.; *Iliad*, xiv, 279.
68. Harrison, *Prolegomena to the Study of Greek Religion*, 1903, pp. 573 ff., 660 ff.; Guthrie, *Orpheus and Greek Religion*, 1935, pp. 171 ff.
69. Cf. Harrison, *op. cit.*, pp. 601 ff.; Guthrie, *op. cit.*, pp. 187 ff.
70. Harrison, *op. cit.*, pp. 601 ff
71. *Olympia*, ii, 55 f., 62 ff.; *Frag.*, 133 (Bergk); Farnell, *The Works of Pindar*, 1932, vol. ii (Commentary), p. 19.
72. *Phaedrus*, 249A.
73. Cf. *Frags.*, 129, 131, 133, 137, 104C (Schroeder ed.).
74. *Frag.*, 131.
75. *Phaedo*, 72E–77D, 78–81; *Meno*, 81 ff.; cf. Burnet, *The Socratic Doctrine of the Soul*, 1916, p. 256.
76. *Phaedrus*, 245 ff.
77. *Phaedrus*, 248 f.; *Republic*, x, 614 f.; *Gorgias*, 253.
78. *Republic*, 500D, 519B, 631A; *Phaedrus*, 248C–249.
79. *Republic*, 615B; *Gorgias*, 525 B, C.
80. *Phaedrus*, 248 ff., 249B; *Republic*, 618A, 620 ff.
81. Taylor, *Plato and his Works*, 1928, p. 308, n. 1.
82. Cf. chap. ii, pp. 73 f.
83. *Frags.*, vol. vii, p. 23; *Stobaeus*, ed. Meineke, vol. iv, p. 107.
84. Plutarch, *De audiendis poetis*, 21F.
85. *Republic*, 363 ff.; *Laws*, 815C; *Phaedo*, 69C.

CHAPTER VIII

1. Lang, *Myth, Ritual and Religion*, 1899, vol. i, p. 162.
2. Hocart, *The Labyrinth*, 1935, pp. 263 ff.
3. 114D.
4. *Man*, xxxvi, 1936, 230, p. 167.
5. Naville, *Textes relatifs au Mythe d'Horus*, Geneva, 1870, pls. 12–19; E. A. W. Budge, *Legends of the Gods*, 1912, pp. 52 ff.; *From Fetish to God in Ancient Egypt*, 1934, pp. 47 ff., 468 ff.; Wiedemann, *Religion of the Ancient Egyptians*, 1897, pp. 69 ff.; Fairman, *J.E.A.*, xxi, 1935, pp. 26 ff.
6. King, *Legends of Babylon and Egypt in relation to Hebrew Tradition* (Schweich Lectures, 1916), 1918, pp. 49 ff.
7. Chap. vi, pp. 187f.
8. H. Winckler, *Die Keilschrifttexte Sargons*, Leipzig, 1889, vol. ii, pl. 36, pp. 173 f.
9. Budge and King, *Annals of the Kings of Assyria*, 1902, pp. 94, ll. 49–54.
10. R. Campbell Thompson, *The Devils and Evil Spirits of Babylonia*, 1904, vol. ii, pp. 161 ff.; Thureau-Dangin, *Revue d'Assyriologie et d'archéologie orientale*, xxxvi, 1939, pp. 1 ff.; Speiser, *A.N.E.T.*, 1955, pp. 100 f.
11. Chap. v, pp. 154f.
12. Kramer, *Sumerian Mythology*, 1944, pp. 43 ff.; G. Barton, *Miscellaneous Babylonian Inscriptions*, 1918, pp. 34 ff.
13. Jacobsen, *The Intellectual Adventure of Ancient Man*, 1946, pp. 153 f.; Kramer, *Journal of Cuneiform Studies*, ii, 1948, p. 57.
14. Kramer, *Sumerian Mythology*, 1944, pp. 54 ff.; *B.A.S.O.R.*, Supplementary Studies no. 1, 1945, pp. 3 ff.; Kramer, *A.N.E.T.*, 1955, pp. 37 ff.
15. Kramer, *B.A.S.O.R.*, no. 96, 1944, pp. 18 ff.
16. Kramer, *Sumerian Mythology*, 1944, pp. 59 ff.
17. Poebel, *Historical and Grammatical Texts*, publication of the Bab. Section V, 25, Philadelphia, 1914; Kramer, *Sumerian Mythology*, pp. 56 ff.
18. Kramer, *Sumerian Mythology*, 1944, pp. 70 ff.
19. Albright, *Archaeology and the Religion of Israel*, 1946, p. 72; *Journal of Biblical Literature*, 1940, p. 106.
20. Strong and Garstang, *The Syrian Goddess*, 1913, pp. 51 ff.
21. Albright, *op. cit.*, p. 195.
22. 3 *Aqhat*, 8; Gordon, *Ugaritic Literature*, 1949, p. 92.
23. 1 *Aqhat*, 160 ff.
24. Gordon, *op. cit.*, pp. 85 ff.; J. Obermann, *J.A.O.S.*, Supplement no. 6, 1946; Ginsberg, *A.N.E.T.*, 1955, pp. 149 f.
25. Gen. xii. 6 f.
26. Gen. xiii. 18, xviii. 1.
27. Gen. xxi. 33.
28. Gen. xxviii. 10–22.
29. Gen. xxviii. 18.

30. Judges x. 17 xi. 11, 34. Mizpah seems to be the designation of megalithic sites on eminences in various localities, perhaps as a play on the term *mazzebāh*.
31. Gen. xxxi. 44–54.
32. Joshua xxiv. 26 ff.
33. Joshua iv, v. 2 f., 8 f.
34. Exod. iv. 24–6.
35. Joshua iv. 6 f.
36. Deut. vii. 5, xii. 3, xvi. 21 f.
37. Joshua iv. 21.
38. 2 Kings xxi. 7, cf. xxiii. 6, 7.
39. Gen. xxviii. 18, 22, xxxi. 45–51; Exod. xxiv. 4; Isa. xix. 19.
40. Mic. v. 13 f.
41. *Folk-lore in the Old Testament*, 1918, vol. ii, p. 437.
42. *From Joseph to Joshua* (Schweich Lectures, 1948), 1950, p. 4.
43. *Egypt and the Old Testament*, 1923, p. 64.
44. Gen. xii. 10 ff., xxvi. 1 ff.
45. Cf. Albright, *B.A.S.O.R.*, no. 38, 1935, pp. 10 ff., no. 74, 1939, pp. 11 f.; Meek, *B.A.S.O.R.*, no. 61, 1936, pp. 17 ff.; *Hebrew Origins*, 1950, pp. 7 ff.; Rowley, *From Joseph to Joshua*, 1948, pp. 140 ff.
46. Exod. i. 8.
47. Garstang, *Joshua-Judges*, 1931, pp. 146 ff.; Jacks, *The Date of the Exodus*, 1925; Robinson, *History of Israel*, 1932, vol. i, p. 80.
48. Exod. i. 11.
49. Griffiths, *The Exodus in the Light of Archaeology*, 1923, p. 49; Barton, *Archaeology and the Bible*, 6th. ed., 1933, p. 375.
50. Rowley, *op. cit.*, pp. 108 ff.
51. Deut. vii. 12, xx. 10–17; cf. 2 Sam. vii. 9.
52. Joshua ix.
53. 2 Sam. xxi. 1–11.
54. Num. xv. 44 f., xxi. 1–3; Burney, *Israel's Settlement in Canaan*, 1918, pp. 28 ff.
55. Joshua xv. 13–19; Judges i. 10–15.
56. Joshua xiv. 6–15.
57. Joshua x. 40 ff.
58. Joshua x. 28–39.
59. Joshua xvi. 10; 1 Kings ix. 16.
60. Joshua xv. 17; Judges i. 11–13.
61. Joshua x. 38 f.
62. Garstang, *Joshua-Judges*, 1931, pp. 145 ff.
63. Burrows, *What Mean These Stones?*, 1941, pp. 76 f.
64. Garstang, *op. cit.*; Jacks, *The Date of the Exodus*.
65. Garstang, *op. cit.*, p. 255; S. A. Cook, *Cambridge Ancient History*, 1924, vol. ii, pp. 256 f.; Dhorme, *La religion des hébreux nomades*, 1937, p. 80.

66. *Tell el Amarna Texts*, 148: 14; 149: 19, 16.
67. *Op. cit.*, 238: 11; 295: Rev. 6.
68. Joshua viii.
69. Vincent, *Revue biblique*, xlvi, 1937, pp. 231 ff.
70. Albright, *B.A.S.O.R.*, no. 56, 1934, p. 11.
71. *Op. cit.*, no. 57, 1935, p. 30; no. 58, 1935, p. 13.
72. Tufnell, Inge and Harding, *Lachish*, ii, 1940, pp. 22 f.; Albright, *From the Stone Age to Christianity*, 1946, p. 194; Vincent, *Revue biblique*, xlviii, 1939, p. 419 n.
73. Joshua x.
74. Albright, *B.A.S.O.R.*, no. 58, 1935, pp. 10 ff.; Meek, *Hebrew Origins*, 1950, p. 20.
75. *Iliad*, xxiv, 508–42; Lang, Leaf and Myers, *The Iliad of Homer*, 1909, p. 494.
76. *Frags.* 11, 15, 16 (Diels).
77. Nilsson, *The Mycenaean Origin of Greek Mythology*, 1932, p. 237.
78. Harrison, *Themis*, 1912, pp. 445 ff.
79. Herodotus, ii, 53.
80. A. Lang, *World of Homer*, 1910, p. 117.
81. *Iliad*, vi, 267 f.
82. *Odyssey*, xii, 481 f.; cf. *Iliad*, ii, 661–6.
83. *The Labyrinth*, 1935, p. 278.
84. *Rise of the Greek Epic*, 1924, pp. 232 ff., 256.
85. *Republic*, 514 f.
86. *Phaedrus*, 229C.; *Republic*, 378D.
87. *Phaedo*, 114D.
88. Cf. A. E. Taylor, *Plato and his Work*, 1929, p. 308, n. 1.

CHAPTER IX

1. *La mentalité primitive*, Paris, 1921; *L'expérience mystique et les symboles chez les primitifs*, Paris, 1935.
2. Frankfort, *The Intellectual Adventure of Ancient Man*, 1946, p. 4.
3. *The Threshold of Religion*, 1914, p. 109.
4. A. P. Elkin, *Australian Aborigines*, Sydney and London, 1938, pp. 26 ff.
5. MacCulloch, *Folk-lore*, 1932, pp. 362 ff.
6. F. Curtin, *Tales of the Fairies*, 1895, p. 42.
7. J. Keightley, *Fairy Mythology*, 1900, p. 432.
8. J. Rhys, *Celtic Folklore*, 1901; cf. A. G. Krapp, *The Science of Folklore*, 1930: for bibliography of literary sources, pp. 41 ff.
9. H. M. Chadwick, *The Heroic Age*, Cambridge, 1912, pp. 186 ff., 194 ff.
10. *Iliad*, vi, 416 ff.; ix, 546; xxiii, 69 ff; xviii, 464 ff.
11. iii, 19, 5.

12. G. E. Daniel, *Myth or Legend*, 1955, pp. 11 ff., 105.

13. Chap. i, pp. 28f., 37.

14. Robertson Smith, *The Religion of the Semites*, 1927, pp. 16f.

15. W. Wundt, *Völkerpsychologie*, 1912, vol. ii, pt. ii, pp. 171 ff.; Tylor, *Primitive Culture*, 4th ed., 1903, vol. i, pp. 427 ff.

16. Robertson Smith, *op. cit.*, p. 20.

17. *Frazer Lectures*, ed. W. R. Dawson, 1932, p. 98.

18. Ebeling, *Tod und Leben nach den Vorstellungen der Babylonier*, 1931, p. 33, ll. 24–6; Labat, *Le caractère religieux de la royauté assyro-babylonienne*, Paris, 1939, p. 167; Frankfort, *Kingship and the Gods*, p. 317.

19. *P.T.*, 1976–82; *Ut.* 482.

20. *Acta Orientalia*, 18, 1939, p. 3.

21. *Syria*, XII, 1931, pp. 193 ff.; *Eranos-Jahrbuch*, 1939, pp. 21 ff.

22. Hooke, *Origins of Early Semitic Ritual*, 1938, p. 32; W. C. Graham-May, *Culture and Conscience*, Chicago, 1936, pp. 122 ff.; Egnell, *Studies in Divine Kingship*, Uppsala, 1945, pp. 97 ff.; Hvidberg, *Gradog Latter i det Gamle Testamenta*, Kavanharm, 1938, pp. 37 ff.; Gaster, *Thespis*, 1950, pp. 57 ff., 232.

23. *J.R.A.S.*, 1938, pp. 38 ff.

24. II, ii, 25–43; cf. Gordon, *B.A.S.O.R.*, no. 65, 1937, pp. 29 ff.; Ginsberg, *Orientalia*, viii, 1939, pp. 317 ff.

25. Cf. Schaeffer, *The Cuneiform Texts of Ras Shamra*, 1939, pp. 47 ff., 64, pl. xi, fig. 2; pl. xxxii, fig. 2.

26. *Telipinu Myth*, iv, 6ff., 26f.; cf. chap. vi, pp. 193 ff.

27. Chap. vi, pp. 195f.

28. G. E. Mylonas, *Ancient Mycenae*, 1957.

29. Cf. Frankfort, *The Problem of Similarity in Ancient Near Eastern Religions*, Oxford, 1951.

30. Frankfort, *The Intellectual Adventure of Ancient Man*, p. 7.

31. *Kerygma and Myth*, 1933, p. 10.

32. *Adonis and the Alphabet*, 1956, p. 15.

ABBREVIATIONS

A.A.S.O.R.   *Annual of the American Schools of Oriental Research*, New Haven.

A.B.   *Aleyan-Baal Texts.*

A.B.S.A.   *Annual of the British School of Athens*, Athens.

A.J.A.   *American Journal of Archaeology*, Bryn Mawr.

A.J.S.L.   *American Journal of Semitic Languages and Literatures*, Chicago.

A.N.E.T.   *Ancient Near Eastern Texts relating to the Old Testament*, edited by J. B. Pritchard, Princeton, 2nd ed., 1955.

Antiq. Journ.   *The Antiquaries Journal* (Society of Antiquaries, London).

B.A.S.O.R.   *Bulletin of the American Schools of Oriental Research*, New Haven.

C.G.S.   *Cult of the Greek States*, by L. R. Farnell, Oxford, 1896–1909.

C.R. Acad. Inscrip.   *Comptes rendus des Séances: Académie des Inscriptions et Belles-Lettres*, Paris.

E.R.E.   *Encyclopaedia of Religion and Ethics*, edited by Hastings, Edinburgh, 1908–26.

G.B.   *The Golden Bough*, by J. G. Frazer, 3rd ed., 1911–17.

I.P.E.K.   *Jahrbuch für Prähistorische und Ethnographische Kunst*, Cologne.

J.A.O.S.   *Journal of the American Oriental Society*, New Haven.

J.E.A.   *Journal of Egyptian Archaeology*, London.

J.H.S.   *Journal of Hellenic Studies*, London.

J.N.E.S.   *Journal of Near Eastern Studies*, Chicago.

J.R.A.I.   *Journal of the Royal Anthropological Institute*, London.

J.R.A.S.   *Journal of the Royal Asiatic Society*, London.

K.U.B.   *Keilschrifturkunden aus Boghazhöi*, Berlin, 1921–38.

L'Anthrop.   *L'Anthropologie*, Paris.

P.P.S.   *Proceedings of the Prehistoric Society*, London.

P.T.   *The Pyramid Texts*, by S. A. B. Mercer, vols. i–iv, 1953.

S.B.E.   *Sacred Books of the East*, Oxford, 1879–1910.

BIBLIOGRAPHY

CHAPTER I

Boule, M., and Vallois, H., *Fossil Men*, London, 1957.

Breasted, J. H., *Development of Religion and Thought in Ancient Egypt*, 1914.

Breuil, H., *Quatre cents siècles d'art pariétal*, Montignac, 1954.

Burkitt, M. C., *Prehistory*, Cambridge, 1925.

Cassirer, E., *An Essay on Man*, New Haven, Yale Press, 1945.

Driver, G. R., *Canaanite Myths and Legends*, Edinburgh, 1956.

Durkheim, E., *Elementary Forms of the Religious Life*, E. T. by Swain, 1915.

Evans, Sir Arthur, *Scripta Minoa*, vol. i, Oxford, 1909; vol. ii edited by J. L. Myres, 1952.

Frankfort, H., *Kingship and the Gods*, Chicago, 1948; *The Intellectual Adventure of Ancient Man*, Chicago, 1946.

Frazer, Sir J. G., *The Golden Bough*, 3rd ed., 1917.

Gaster, T. H., *Thespis*, New York, 1950.

Gordon, C. H., *Ugaritic Handbook*, Rome, 1947; *Ugaritic Literature*, 1949.

Heidel, A., *The Gilgamesh Epic and Old Testament Parallels*, Chicago, 1949.

James, E. O., *Prehistoric Religion*, 1957.

Lang, A., *Custom and Myth*, new ed., 1904.

Malinowski, B., *Myth in Primitive Psychology*, 1926.

Marett, R. R., *Faith, Hope and Charity in Primitive Religion*, Oxford, 1932.

Max Müller, F., *Contributions to the Science of Mythology*, 1897.

Mercer, S. A. B., *The Pyramid Texts*, vols. i–iv, 1952.

Obermaier, H., *Fossil Man in Spain*, New Haven, 1925.

Tylor, E. B., *Primitive Culture*, 4th ed., 2 vols., 1903; *Researches into the Early History of Mankind*, 1865.

Ventris, M., and Chadwick, J., *Documents in Mycenaean Greek*, Cambridge, 1956.

Verneau, R., *Les Grottes de Grimaldi*, Monaco, 1906.

Windels, F., *The Lascaux Cave Paintings*, 1949.

CHAPTER II

Albright, W. F., *Archaeology and the Religion of Israel*, Baltimore, 1946.

Allen, T. W., Sikes, E. E., and Halliday, T. W., *The Homeric Hymn*, 3rd ed., Oxford, 1936.

Bailey, C., *Phases in the Religion of Ancient Rome,* Oxford, 1932.

Brugsch, H., *Religion und Mythologie der alten Aegypter,* Leipzig, 1885–8.

Cumont, F., *The Oriental Religions in Roman Paganism,* Chicago, 1911.

Driver, G. R., *Canaanite Myths and Legends,* Edinburgh, 1955.

Erman, A., and Blackman, A. M., *The Literature of the Ancient Egyptians,* 1927.

Farnell, L. R., *Cult of the Greek States,* vol. iii, Oxford, 1907.

Frankfort, H., *Kingship and the Gods,* Chicago, 1948; *The Intellectual Adventure of Ancient Man,* Chicago, 1946; *Cylinder Seals,* 1939.

Frazer, Sir J. G., *Golden Bough,* 3rd ed., part iv (Adonis), 1914.

Gardiner, A. H., and Davies, N. de G., *The Tomb of Amenemhet,* 1915.

Gaster, T. H., *Thespis,* New York, 1950.

Gauthier, H., *Les fêtes du dieu Min,* Cairo, 1931.

Gordon, C. H., *Ugaritic Literature,* Rome, 1949.

Guthrie, W. K. C., *Orpheus and Greek Religion,* 1935.

Johnson, A. R., *Sacral Kingship in Ancient Israel,* Cardiff, 1955; in *The Old Testament and Modern Study,* edited by H. H. Rowley, Oxford, 1951.

Kapelrud, A. S., *Baal in the Ras Shamra Texts,* Copenhagen, 1952.

Langdon, S., *Tammuz and Ishtar,* Oxford, 1914.

Meek, J. T., *Hebrew Origins,* New York, 2nd ed., 1950.

Moorgate, A., *Tammuz,* Berlin, 1949.

Nilsson, M. P., *A History of Greek Religion,* Oxford, 1925; *Popular Greek Religion,* New York, 1940.

Pallis, S. A., *The Babylonian Akitu Festival,* Copenhagen, 1926.

Rowley, H. H., *From Joseph to Joshua* (Schweich Lectures, 1948), 1950.

Snaith, N. H., *The Jewish New Year Festival,* 1947.

Wainwright, G. A., *The Sky-Religion in Egypt,* Cambridge, 1938.

CHAPTER III

Blackman, A. M., *Luxor and its Temples,* 1923.

Breasted, J. H., *Ancient Records of Egypt,* vols. ii, iii, Chicago, 1905–6.

Cook, A. B., *Zeus,* vol. iii, Cambridge, 1940.

Driver, G. R., *Canaanite Myths and Legends,* 1956.

Evans, Sir Arthur, *The Palace of Minos,* vol. i, 1921, vol. iv, 1935; *The Shaft-graves and Bee-hive Tombs of Mycenae,* 1929; *The Prehistoric Tombs of Knossos,* 1906.

Evans-Pritchard, E. E., *The Divine Kingship of the Shilluk of the Nilotic Sudan,* Cambridge, 1948.

Frankfort, H., *The Problem of Similarity in Ancient Near Eastern Religions,* Oxford, 1951; *Kingship and the Gods,* Chicago, 1948.

Frazer, Sir J. G., *The Early History of Kingship,* 1905.

Gadd, C. J., *Ideas of Divine Rule in the Ancient East,* Oxford, 1948.

Gaster, T. H., *Thespis,* New York, 1950.

Gordon, C. H., *Ugaritic Literature,* Rome, 1949.

Harper, R. F., *The Code of Hammurabi,* Chicago, 1904.

Heidel, A., *The Babylonian Genesis,* 2nd ed., Chicago, 1951.

Hooke, S. H., *The Siege Perilous,* 1956; *Myth and Ritual,* Oxford, 1933.

Jacobsen, T., *The Sumerian King-List,* Chicago, 1939.

Johnson, A. R., *Sacral Kingship in Ancient Israel,* Cardiff, 1956.

Kapelrud, A., *Baal in the Ras Shamra Texts,* Copenhagen, 1952.

Labat, R., *Caractère religieux de la royauté assyro-babylonienne,* Paris, 1939.

Mackay, E. J., *Further Excavations at Mohenjo-daro,* Delhi, 1938.

Meek, C. K., *The Northern Tribes of Nigeria,* 1925; *A Sudanese Kingdom,* 1931.

Mercer, S. A. B., *Religion of Ancient Egypt,* 1949.

Mylonas, G. E., *Ancient Mycenae,* 1927.

Naville, E. H., *The Temple of Deir el-Bahari,* 1894.

Nilsson, M. P., *The Minoan-Mycenaean Religion,* 2nd ed., Lund, 1950.

Obermann, J., *Ugaritic Mythology,* New Haven, 1948.

Piggott, S., *Prehistoric India,* 1950.

Seligman, C. G., *The Pagan Tribes of the Nilotic Sudan,* 1932; *Egypt and Negro Africa,* 1934.

Sethe, K., *Urgeschichte und aelteste Religion der Aegypter,* Leipzig, 1930; *Dramatische Texte zu altaegyptischen Mysterienspielen,* Leipzig, 1928.

Snaith, N. H., *The Jewish New Year Festival,* 1947.

Thureau-Dangin, F., *Les inscriptions de Sumer et d'Akkad,* Paris, 1905.

Virolleaud, C., *La légende phénicienne de Danel,* Paris, 1930.

Wace, A. J. B., *Mycenae,* Princeton, 1949.

Wheeler, Sir R. E. M., *The Indus Civilization,* Cambridge, 1950.

Widengren, G., *Sakrales Koenigtum im Alten Testament und im Judentum,* Stuttgart, 1955.

CHAPTER IV

Bittel, B., Naumann, R., and Otto, H., *Yazilikaya,* Leipzig, 1941.

Blackman, A. M., *Luxor and its Temples,* 1923.

Chiera, E., *Sumerian Religious Texts,* Upland, 1924.

Childe, V. G., *Dawn of European Civilization,* 5th ed., 1950.

Erman, A., *A Handbook of Egyptian Religion,* 1907.

Evans, Sir Arthur, *The Palace of Minos*, vols. i, ii, 1921, 1928; *The Mycenaean Tree and Pillar Cult*, 1901.

Frankfort, H., *Kingship and the Gods*, Chicago, 1948.

Garstang, J., *The Hittite Empire*, 1929.

Gordon, C. H., *Ugaritic Handbook*, Rome, 1947; *Ugaritic Literature*, Rome, 1949.

Gurney, O. R., *The Hittites*, 1952; *Annals of Archaeology and Anthropology*, 27, Liverpool, 1940.

Harrison, J. E., *Themis*, Cambridge, 1912.

Hawkes, C. F. C., *The Prehistoric Foundations of Europe*, 1940.

Hooke, S. H., *The Origins of Early Semitic Ritual*, 1938.

James, E. O., *Prehistoric Religion*, 1957.

Kapelrud, A. S., *Baal in the Ras Shamra Texts*, Copenhagen, 1952.

Langdon, S., *Tammuz and Ishtar*, Oxford, 1914.

Laroche, E., *Recherches sur les noms des dieux hittites*, Paris, 1947.

Mackay, E. J. H., *Further Excavations at Mohenjo-daro*, Delhi, 1938.

Mariette, A., *Denderah*, Paris, 1870–80.

Marshall, Sir J., *Mohenjo-daro and the Indus Civilization*, 1931.

Nilsson, M. P., *The Minoan-Mycenaean Religion*, 2nd ed., Lund, 1950.

Persson, A. W., *The Religion of Greece in Prehistoric Times*, California, 1942.

Piggott, S., *Prehistoric India*, 1950; *The Neolithic Cultures of the British Isles*, 1954.

Stein, Sir Aurel, *Memoirs of the Archaeological Survey of India*, No. 37, 1925; *An Archaeological Tour in Waziristan and North Baluchistan*, 1929; *An Archaeological Tour in Gedrosia*, 1931.

Strong, H. A., and Garstang, J., *The Syrian Goddess*, 1913.

Vats, M. S., *Excavations at Harappa*, 2 vols., Delhi, 1940.

Wiedemann, A., *Religion of the Ancient Egyptians*, 1897.

Zammit, T., *Prehistoric Malta*, Oxford, 1930; *The Hal-Saflieni Prehistoric Hypogeum, Malta*, 1910.

CHAPTER V

Albright, W. F., *Archaeology and the Religion of Israel*, Baltimore, 1946.

Budge, E. A. W., *The Gods of the Egyptians*, 2 vols., 1904; *From Fetish to God in Ancient Egypt*, Oxford, 1934.

Chiera, E., *Sumerian Religious Texts*, Upland, 1924; *Sumerian Epics and Myths*, Chicago, 1934.

Cook, A. B., *Zeus*, vol. i, Cambridge, 1914.

Frankfort, H., *Ancient Egyptian Religion*, New York, 1948.

Güterbock, H. G., *Kumarbi, Mythen vom churritischen Kronos,* Zurich–New York, 1946.

Ginsberg, H. L., *Ancient Near Eastern Texts,* edited by J. B. Pritchard, 2nd ed., Princeton, 1955.

Guthrie, W. K. C., *Orpheus and Greek Religion,* 1952; *The Greeks and their Gods,* 1950.

Heidel, A., *The Babylonian Genesis,* 2nd ed., Chicago, 1951.

Jacobsen, T., *The Intellectual Adventure of Ancient Man,* Chicago, 1946.

Kees, H., *Totenglauben und Jenseitsvorstellungen der alten Aegypter,* Leipzig, 1926.

King, L. W., *The Seven Tablets of Creation,* 1902.

Kramer, S. N., *Sumerian Mythology,* Philadelphia, 1944.

Langdon, S., *Sumerian Liturgies and Psalms,* 1919.

Linforth, L. M., *The Arts of Orpheus,* Berkeley, 1941.

Mercer, S. A. B., *Pyramid Texts,* vols. i–iv, 1952.

Pedersen, Johs, *Israel, its Life and Culture,* 4 vols., Copenhagen, 1947.

Roeder, G., *Urkunden zur Religion des alten Aegypten,* 1915.

Rose, H. J., *Handbook of Greek Mythology,* 2nd ed., 1933.

Schaeffer, C. F. A., *The Cuneiform Texts of Ras Shamra-Ugarit* (Schweich Lectures, 1936), 1939.

Sethe, K., *Dramatische Texte zu altaegyptischen Mysterienspielen,* vols. i–ii, Leipzig, 1928; *Urgeschichte und aelteste Religion der Aegypter,* Leipzig, 1930.

Speiser, E. A., in *Near Eastern Texts,* edited by J. B. Pritchard, 2nd ed., Princeton, 1955.

Wilson, J. A., *The Intellectual Adventure of Ancient Man,* Chicago, 1946.

CHAPTER VI

Breasted, J. H., *Ancient Records of Egypt,* vols. i–iv, Chicago, 1906.

Budge, E. A. W., *Legends of the Gods,* 1912; *From Fetish to God in Ancient Egypt,* Oxford, 1934.

Dhalla, M. N., *Zoroastrian Theology,* New York, 1914.

Erman, A., and Blackman, A. M., *The Literature of the Ancient Egyptians,* 1927.

Gaster, T. H., *Thespis,* New York, 1950.

Goetze, A., in *Ancient Near Eastern Texts,* edited by J. B. Pritchard, 2nd ed., Princeton, 1955.

Gordon, C. H., *Ugaritic Literature,* Rome, 1949.

Gunkel, H., *Schöpfung und Chaos in Urzeit und Endzeit,* Göttingen, 1895.

Güterbock, H. G., *The Song of Ullikummi,* New Haven, 1952.

Heidel, A., *The Babylonian Genesis,* 1951.

Hesiod, *Theogony,* edited by F. A. Paley, 2nd ed., 1883.

Kees, H., *Der Gotterglaube im alten Aegypten,* Leipzig, 1941.

Kramer, S. N., *Sumerian Mythology,* Philadelphia, 1944.

Moulton, J. H., *Early Zoroastrianism,* 1913.

Obermann, J., *Ugaritic Mythology,* New Haven, 1948.

Otten, H., *Mythen vom Gotte Kumarbi, Neue Fragmente,* No. 8, Berlin, 1950.

Wilson, J. A., in *Ancient Near Eastern Texts,* edited by J. B. Pritchard, 2nd ed., 1955.

CHAPTER VII

Bousset, W., and Gressmann, H., *Die Religion des Judenstums im spät-hellenistische Zeitalter,* 3rd ed., 1926; *Hauptprobleme der Gnosis,* Leipzig, 1907.

Breasted, J. H., *Development of Religion and Thought in Ancient Egypt,* 1914.

Budge, E. A. W., *The Book of the Opening of the Mouth,* 1909; *Osiris and the Egyptian Resurrection,* 2 vols., 1911; *From Fetish to God in Ancient Egypt,* Oxford, 1934; *The Book of the Dead,* 2nd ed., 1923.

The Bundahish, edited and translated by D. Justi, Leipzig, 1868; E. W. West in *The Sacred Books of the East,* V, 1880.

Charles, R. H., *A Critical History of the Doctrine of a Future Life,* 1913.

Darmesteter, J., and Mills, L. H., *Sacred Books of the East,* IV, XXIII, XXXI.

Eisler, R., *The Royal Art of Astrology,* 1947.

Guthrie, W. K. C., *Orpheus and Greek Religion,* 1935.

Harrison, J. E., *Prolegomena to the Study of Greek Religion,* Cambridge, 1903.

Hoshangji, T. A., Haug, M., and West, E. W., *The Book of Arda Viraf,* Bombay, 1872.

Jacobsen, T., *The Sumerian King-List,* Chicago, 1939.

James, E. O., *Prehistoric Religion,* 1957.

Mercer, S. A. B., *The Pyramid Texts,* vols. i–iv, 1952.

Moret, A., *Le rituel du culte divin-journalier en Egypte,* Paris, 1902.

Moulton, J. H., *Early Zoroastrianism,* 1913.

Rowley, H. H., *The Relevance of Apocalyptic,* 1947 (with full bibliography of the Biblical literature).

Smith, Sir G. Elliot, and Dawson, W. R., *Egyptian Mummies,* 1924.

Söderblom, N., *La vie future d'après de Mazdéisme,* Paris, 1901.

Speiser, E. A., in *Ancient Near Eastern Texts,* edited by J. B. Pritchard, 2nd ed., 1955.

344 *Bibliography*

Taylor, A. E., *Plato and his Works*, 1928.

West, E. W., *Sacred Books of the East*, V, XVIII, XXIV, XXXVII, XLVII.

Woolley, Sir Leonard, *Ur Excavations*, vol. ii, 1934.

CHAPTER VIII

Albright, W. F., *Archaeology and the Religion of Israel*, Baltimore, 1946; *From the Stone Age to Christianity*, new edition, 1957.

Barton, G., *Miscellaneous Babylonian Inscriptions*, 1918; *Archaeology and the Bible*, 6th ed., 1933.

Budge, E. A. W., *Legends of the Gods*, 1912; *From Fetish to God in Ancient Egypt*, Oxford, 1934; and King, L. W., *Annals of the Kings of Assyria*, 1902.

Burney, C. F., *Israel's Settlement in Canaan*, 1918.

Burrows, M., *What Mean These Stones?* New Haven, 1941.

Dhorme, P. E., *La religion des hébreux nomades*, Paris, 1937.

Frazer, Sir J. G., *Folk-lore in the Old Testament*, vol. ii, 1918.

Garstang, J., *Joshua-Judges*, 1931.

Ginsberg, H. L., in *Ancient Near Eastern Texts*, edited by J. B. Pritchard, 2nd ed., 1955.

Gordon, C. H., *Ugaritic Literature*, Rome, 1949.

Griffiths, F. Ll., *The Exodus in the Light of Archaeology*, 1923.

Harrison, J. E., *Themis*, Cambridge, 1912.

Hocart, A. M., in *The Labyrinth*, edited by S. H. Hooke, 1935.

Jack, J. W., *The Date of the Exodus*, 1925.

Jacobsen, T., *The Intellectual Adventure of Ancient Man*, Chicago, 1946.

King, W. L., *Legends of Babylon and Egypt in relation to Hebrew Tradition* (Schweich Lectures), 1918.

Kramer, S. N., *Sumerian Mythology*, Philadelphia, 1944; in *Near Eastern Texts*, edited by J. B. Pritchard, 2nd ed., 1955.

Lang, A., Leaf, W., and Myres, E., *The Iliad of Homer*, 1909.

Lang, A., *The World of Homer*, 1910.

Meek, J. T., *Hebrew Origins*, 2nd ed., New York, 1950.

Murray, G., *Rise of the Greek Epic*, 1924.

Naville, E., *Textes relatifs au mythe d'Horus*, Geneva, 1870.

Nilsson, M. P., *The Mycenaean Origin of Greek Mythology*, Cambridge, 1932.

Obermann, J., *Ugaritic Mythology*, New Haven, 1948.

Peet, T. E., *Egypt and the Old Testament*, Liverpool, 1923.

Robinson, T. H., *History of Israel*, 2 vols., 1932.

Rose, H. J., *Handbook of Greek Mythology*, 4th ed., London, 1946.

Rowley, H. H., *From Joseph to Joshua* (Schweich Lectures, 1948), 1950.

Speiser, E. A., in *Ancient Near Eastern Texts*, edited by J. B. Pritchard, 2nd ed., 1955.

Thompson, R. Campbell, *The Devils and Evil Spirits of Babylonia*, 2 vols., 1904.

Thureau-Dangin, F., *Revue d'Assyriologie et d'archéologie orientale*, XXXVI, 1939.

Wiedemann, A., *Religion of the Ancient Egyptians*, 1897.

CHAPTER IX

Chadwick, H. M., *The Heroic Age*, Cambridge, 1912.

Curtin, F., *Tales of the Fairies*, 1895.

Daniel, G. E., *Myth and Legend*, 1955.

Elkin, A. P., *Australian Aborigines*, Sydney and London, 1938.

Frankfort, H., *The Intellectual Adventure of Ancient Man*, Chicago, 1946.

Gaster, T. H., *Thespis*, New York, 1950.

Gomme, G. L., *Folklore as an Historical Science*, 1908.

Hooke, S. H., *Origins of Early Semitic Ritual*, 1938; *Myth and Ritual*, Oxford, 1933.

Hartland, E. S., *Science of Fairy Tales*, 1891.

Keightley, J., *Fairy Mythology*, 1900.

Krapp, A. G., *The Science of Folklore*, 1930.

Lévy-Bruhl, L., *La centralité primitive*, Paris, 1921; *L'expérience mystique et les symboles chez les primitifs*, Paris, 1935.

Marett, R. R., *The Threshold of Religion*, 1914.

Mylonas, G. E., *Ancient Mycenae*, 1957.

Preller, L., *Griechische Mythologie*, Carl Robert, Berlin, 1894.

Raglan, Lord, *The Hero: a Study in Tradition, Myth and Drama*, 1936.

Rhys, J., *Celtic Folklore*, 1901.

Roscher, W. H., *Ausführliches Lexikon der griechischen und römischen Mythologie*, Leipzig, 1884–1937.

Rose, H. J., *Handbook of Greek Mythology*, 4th ed., 1946. (A popular abridgement has now been published under the title, *Gods and Heroes of the Greeks*, 1957.)

Smith, W. Robertson, *Lectures on the Religion of the Semites*, new edition by S. A. Cook, 1927.

Thompson, Stith, *The Folktale*, New York, 1945.

Tylor, E. B., *Primitive Culture*, 4th ed., 1903.

INDEX